# HARRAP'S
# MODERN GERMAN GRAMMAR

D. Cherry.

Transitive — object.
intransitive — no object.

June

# Harrap's Modern Language Series

General Editor: J. E. MANSION

# HARRAP'S MODERN
# GERMAN GRAMMAR

## WITH EXERCISES AND VOCABULARIES

BY

### W. H. VAN DER SMISSEN

AND

### W. H. FRASER

JOINT AUTHOR OF
HEATH'S "PRACTICAL FRENCH GRAMMAR"

## GEORGE G. HARRAP & CO. LTD.

LONDON      BOMBAY      SYDNEY

*First published July* 1911
*by* GEORGE G. HARRAP & CO.
182 *High Holborn, London, W.C.*1

*Reprinted : July* 1913 ; *November* 1919 ; *January* 1925 ;
*April* 1927 ; *January* 1929 ; *April* 1930 ; *June* 1931 ;
*July* 1932 ; *July* 1933 ; *May* 1935 ; *November* 1936

*Made in Great Britain.   Printed by The Riverside Press, Edinburgh*

# PREFACE

THIS book is intended to serve as a guide to the use of the spoken and written German of the present day, and makes no claim to be a compendium of all forms and usages in either speech or literature.

The grammatical material has been arranged with a view to its convenient use in the exercises, and with the object of facilitating the rapid acquisition of a reading knowledge of the language. The elementary statements of grammatical theory in the earlier part of the book have been supplemented and summarized in the more advanced lessons, thus enabling the learner to review and amplify the knowledge previously acquired in detail. Thus, for instance, in the treatment of the verb, each mood and tense of both weak and strong verbs is taken up successively, and afterwards the whole theory of conjugation is stated in methodical form.

The exercises have been made continuous, wherever it was found practicable to do so, and are constructed on the same general plan as those in the elementary part of Fraser and Squair's *French Grammar*. It is hoped that this form of exercise will not only render the learner's task less dreary than exercises made up of detached sentences, but will also encourage him to acquire phrases rather than words, which so often change their signification with the context.

In the use of the exercises teachers will naturally be guided by their own judgment and the character of their classes, but, in the opinion of the authors, it will be found advantageous first of all to practise very thoroughly the German and oral portions, and afterwards pass on to the translation of the English and to elementary composition. The oral exercises are not intended to be exhaustive, but rather suggestive for further drill along the same line, as the authors attach the very greatest importance to this method of teaching.

The reading extracts are not intended to replace a Reader, but to add variety, with perhaps a spice of entertainment, to the acquisition and practice of grammar. The extracts in verse are designed primarily for memorizing; the prose extracts may be used as exercises in translation, and may serve also for practice in conversation and composition.

The Appendix contains reference lists and paradigms, which it is hoped will prove useful, particularly B, 4 and 5, which are intended as a guide to the correct use of prepositions.

The principal authorities consulted in the preparation of the work were: on orthography, the decisions of the Orthographic Conference of Berlin, 1901, and Duden's *Orthographisches Wörterverzeichnis;* on grammatical points, Blatz' *Grammar* and Muret-Sanders' larger dictionary; on pronunciation, the various manuals of Professor Viëtor of Marburg, whose *German Pronunciation* (3d ed., Reisland) and *Deutsches Lesebuch in Lautschrift* (I. und II. Teil) are especially commended to the attention of teachers.

# CONTENTS

# CONTENTS

# CONTENTS

# INTRODUCTION

## The German Alphabet.

| German form. | Roman form. | German name. | German form. | Roman form. | German name. |
|---|---|---|---|---|---|
| 𝔄, 𝔞 | A, a | *ah* | 𝔑, 𝔫 | N, n | *enn* |
| 𝔅, 𝔟 | B, b | *bay* | 𝔒, 𝔬 | O, o | *oh* |
| ℭ, 𝔠 | C, c | *tsay* | 𝔓, 𝔭 | P, p | *pay* |
| 𝔇, 𝔡 | D, d | *day* | 𝔔, 𝔮 | Q, q | *koo* |
| 𝔈, 𝔢 | E, e | *eh* | 𝔕, 𝔯 | R, r | *err* |
| 𝔉, 𝔣 | F, f | *eff* | 𝔖, ſ, 𝔰 | S, s | *ess* |
| 𝔊, 𝔤 | G, g | *gay* | 𝔗, 𝔱 | T, t | *tay* |
| 𝔥, 𝔥 | H, h | *hah* | 𝔘, 𝔲 | U, u | *oo* |
| 𝔌, 𝔦 | I, i | *ee* | 𝔙, 𝔳 | V, v | *fow* |
| 𝔍, 𝔧 | J, j | *yot* | 𝔚, 𝔴 | W, w | *vay* |
| 𝔎, 𝔨 | K, k | *kah* | 𝔛, 𝔵 | X, x | *iks* |
| 𝔏, 𝔩 | L, l | *ell* | 𝔜, 𝔶 | Y, y | *ipsilon* |
| 𝔐, 𝔪 | M, m | *emm* | ℨ, 𝔷 | Z, z | *tset* |

### REMARKS ON THE ALPHABET.

1. The approximate pronunciation of the German names of the letters is given above in English characters; these names should be learned, and used in spelling words.

2. Three of the vowels may be modified by the sign ̎ (called 'umlaut'): Ä ä, Ö ö, Ü ü; as capitals, in the older spelling, these are: Ae, Oe, Ue.

3. Diphthongs are: Ai ai, Au au, Ei ei, Eu eu, Äu äu, and the rarer forms ay, ey, ui.

4. The following change their form slightly when printed as one character : ch=ch ; ck=ck ; ſſ, ſʒ=ß ; tʒ=tz.

5. The character ß always replaces ſſ when final : Fuß, Haß, Fluß ; within a word, it stands after long vowels, after diphthongs, and before another consonant (elsewhere ſſ) : Füße, heißen, häßlich, mußte; *but* Flüſſe, müſſen, ꝛc. ; hence all vowels are to be pronounced short before ſſ.

6. The form ß occurs only as final in words or stems ; elsewhere ſ : Haus, das, häuslich ; Häuſer, leſen, haſt.

7. Since the sounds of German depend to a considerable extent upon syllabication, stress, and quantity, these subjects will be treated in the following paragraphs, before rules are given for the pronunciation of the alphabet.

## Syllabication.

1. In German the syllable ends in a vowel wherever possible, which is frequently not the case in English : Mi-li-tär, 'mil-i-ta-ry' ; the neglect of this principle is a serious defect in pronunciation.

2. Hence single consonants within a word, and also such consonant groups as can be pronounced undivided, belong to the following syllable, both in speaking and writing : ha-be, ge-brau-chen, ge-ſchenkt ; other consonant groups are divided : wer-den, Tin-te.

3. In writing, however, doubled consonants are divided at the end of a line : müſ-ſen ; so also dt, pf, ng, ck, the latter becoming k-k : Städ-te, Emp-fang, ſin-gen, Stük-ke (for Stücke) ; compounds are divided according to their parts : Huf-eiſen, hin-ab, Donners-tag.

4. 'Open' syllables are those ending in a vowel or h : da, lo-ben, brau-che, be-ſteh-en.

5. 'Closed' syllables are those ending in a consonant, or coming before a doubled consonant : war-ten, Tin-te, kalt, das, hat-ten.

NOTE. — This distinction is important for the rules of quantity.

## Stress.

The relative force with which a syllable in a group is uttered is called 'stress' (less properly 'accent') : Freu'ndſchaft, 'frie'ndship'; mein Ba'ter iſt ſchon a'lt. Several degrees of force may be distinguished in longer words and in phrases, but for practical purposes it is sufficient to consider only the syllable of strongest or chief stress. In words of two or more syllables the chief stress is as follows : —

1. In simple German words, on the stem : Freu'ndſchaft, Freu'ndlichkeit, le'ſen, gele'ſen, rei'nlich.

2. In compounds, usually on the part most distinctive for the meaning : Au'genblick, me'rkwürdig, u'nangenehm.

3. But in compounded particles, usually on the second component : dahe'r, herbei', obglei'ch.

4. In loan-words, usually on the syllable stressed in the language from which the word has been taken : Stude'nt, Phyſi'k, Philoſo'ph, elega'nt, Natio'n, Solda't.

5. Always on the suffixes –ei, –ieren, –ur (of foreign origin) : Arzenei', ſtudie'ren, Glaſu'r.

6. Never on the prefixes be–, emp–, ent–, er–, ge–, ver–, zer–.

7. No special rules are required for German sentence-stress (emphasis), as it corresponds closely to that of English.

## Quantity.

1. Vowels in German may be distinguished as 'long,' 'half long,' and 'short' : loben (long), Militär (half long), kalt (short).

2. Long vowels become half long, or even short, when unstressed, usually without change in the quality of the sound : die'ſer (long), dieſer Ma'nn (half long).

NOTE. — In practice it is sufficient to distinguish long and short (the latter including half long and short).

3. Vowels are regularly long : —

(*a*) In open stressed syllables; and a long stem vowel usually retains its length in inflection : da, loben; lobte.

(*b*) When doubled, or followed by silent һ or e (the latter only after i) : Staat, Lehrer, Sohn, Kuh, dieser.

(*c*) As diphthongs : glauben, heißen, Leute.

(*d*) In final stressed syllable ending in a single consonant (including monosyllables capable of inflection, or ending in r) : Gebot, genug, dem, Rat, bot, gut, war, wir; so also vowel before ß persisting in inflection : saß (saßen), Fuß (Füße).

4. Vowels are regularly short :—

(*a*) In unstressed syllables : haben, gehabt, u'nartig.

(*b*) In closed syllables (including monosyllables ending in more than one consonant) : Sommer, Winter, alt, fest; so also before –ß not persisting in inflection : Fluß (Flüsse).

(*c*) In uninflected monosyllables ending in a single consonant (not –r) : mit, ob, in, im, von, vom ; *but* für, her (long).

5. Before ch, some are long, some short : Sprache (long), lachen (short).

## General Remarks on Pronunciation.

Every language has certain characteristics peculiar to the utterance of its sounds, which taken together may be called its 'basis of articulation.' The principal distinctions between German and English, in this respect, are the following :—

1. The action of the organs of speech, in general, is more energetic and precise in German than in English. The pronunciation of English strikes the German ear as slovenly. The energy and precision referred to are especially obvious in vowels requiring lip rounding (as observed, for example, in 'who,' 'no,' 'saw,' etc.). Moreover, great care should be taken not to obscure German vowels in unstressed syllables, which is the rule in English.

2. The tongue, both for vowels and consonants, is generally either further advanced or retracted than in the articulation of corresponding English sounds.

3. English long vowels (as a in 'fate,' oo in 'poor') are usually diphthongal, particularly before liquids, whereas German long vowels are uniform in quality throughout.

4. The utterance of every German initial vowel, unless wholly unstressed, begins with the 'glottal stop,' which consists in suddenly closing the glottis and forcing it open by an explosion of breath, as in slight coughing : aus, hinaus, essen, ohne, über, überall.

NOTE. — Corresponding English vowels begin with gradual closure of the glottis, and strike the German ear as indistinct, since the German sound is fully resonant throughout. The learner may be enabled to realize the nature of this sound by the experiment of placing the hands to the sides and exerting a sudden, forcible pressure, the mouth being open as if to form a vowel. When this is done, the glottis (*i.e.* the space between the vocal chords) closes automatically, and is at once forced open.

5. It must never be forgotten that the sounds of any two languages hardly ever correspond exactly, and hence that comparisons between German and English are only approximate. In describing the sounds below, brief cautions have been added in parenthesis, in order to obviate this difficulty in part.

### Pronunciation of the Alphabet.

#### VOWELS.

1. Vowels are either 'front' or 'back,' according to their place of articulation in the mouth, and are so grouped below.

2. They are pronounced long or short according to the rules given above (pp. xi–xii), the commonest exceptions only being noted.

3. All vowels must be distinctly uttered.

4. Do not drawl or diphthongize the long vowels.

5. Doubled vowels and those followed by e or h, as a sign of length, are omitted from the conspectus, but included in the examples.

## 1. *Front Vowels.*

**i** 1. When long, like i in 'marine' (slightly closer; avoid diphthong, especially before l and r; avoid i as in 'bit,' when unstressed): Mine, mir, wir; dieſer, Lied, ſtudieren, ihn, ſtiehlſt.

EXCEPTION. — (Short, see 2 below): April'l, vielleiʹcht, Viertel, vierzehn, vierzig.

2. When short, like i in 'bit' (avoid i as in 'mirth' before r): Kind, ſingen, wird, biſt, gebiſſen, gelitten; mit, im.

3. Like y in 'yes,' when unstressed before e in loan-words: Famiʹlie, Patieʹnt.

**ü** 1. When long, has no English counterpart; same tongue position as for i, 1, with tense lip rounding: Blüte, müde, grün, ſüß, Füße; Mühe, früher.

2. When short has no English counterpart; same tongue position as for i, 2, with slight lip rounding: hübſch, Glück, fünf, fürchten, Küſte, Müller, müſſen.

**y** Like i or ü (see above): Aſyl (long), Myrte (short).

**e** 1. When long, like a in 'stated' (avoid diphthong, especially before l and r): leſen, leben, reden, ſchwer, dem, den (but see 4 below); Beet, Schnee, ſtehen, fehlen, lehren.

EXCEPTION. — (Short, see 2 below): des, es, wes.

2. When short, like e in 'let' (avoid e as in 'her,' before r): ſchenken, ſenden, geſtern, beſſer, Betten, Herr, gern.

EXCEPTION.—(Long, see 1, above): Dresden, Erde, erſt, Pferd.

3. In unstressed final syllables and in be–, ge–, like a in 'soda' (tongue slightly advanced): habe, Gabe, loben, lobet, Bruder, dieſer, dieſem, Vogel; beſtellen, gelobt.

4. The e of der, dem, den, des, es, when unstressed, varies between 3 and 2, above, according as the stress is more or less completely removed: der kalte Wiʹnter.

**ä** 1. When long, like **a** in 'care' (avoid diphthong, especially before **l** and **r**): ſäen, wären, Schläge; Ähre, mähen.

2. When short, identical with **e** short (**e**, 2, above): Hände, Bäcker, Äpfel, hätte, längſt.

EXCEPTION. — (Long): nächſt, Städte.

**ö** 1. When long, has no English counterpart; same tongue position as for **e**, 1, with tense lip rounding and protrusion: hören, böſe, Böte, ſchön, größer; Söhne.

2. When short, has no English counterpart; same tongue position as for **e**, 2, with slight lip rounding: Köpfe, Glöcklein, können, Götter.

EXCEPTION. — (Long): öſtlich, Öſterreich.

## 2. *Back Vowels.*

**a** Like **a** in 'ah!' 'father' (tongue flat and mouth well open; lips neither rounded nor retracted; avoid **a** as in 'all' and **a** as in 'at').

1. Long: ſagen, da, Anna, Papa', bat, war, ſaß; Staat, nah, Bahn; Sprache, ſtach.

EXCEPTION. — (Short): das, was.

2. Short: warten, hacken, lachen, niemand, Ball, hatte; als, ab, am.

EXCEPTION. — (Long): Arzt, Bart, Magd, Papſt.

**o** 1. When long, like **o** in 'omen' (tense lip rounding and protrusion; avoid diphthong, especially before **l** and **r**): loben, Roſe, groß, rot, hoch; Boot, Kohl, Ohr.

2. When short, like **o** in 'not' (always definitely rounded; never lengthened, even before **r**): klopfen, Gott, wol= len, Sonne, morgen, Wort; ob, von.

EXCEPTION. — (Long): Lotſe, Obſt, Oſten, Oſtern.

NOTE. — The Eng. short **o** has often very feeble rounding, especially in American Eng., approaching the sound of **a** in 'hat.'

B

**u** 1. When long, like **oo** in 'too' (tense lip rounding and protrusion; avoid diphthong, especially before **l** and **r**):
bu, rufen, Blume, Fuß, guten, nur; Kuh, Stuhl.

   2. When short, like **u** in 'put' (definitely rounded; never
lengthened, even before **r**): und, wurde, Mutter,
Fluß; um, zum, zur.

## Diphthongs.

**ai** ⎫ Like **i** in 'mile' (first element more deliberately uttered;
**ay** ⎭ equals German a, 2 + i, 2): Kaiser, Bayern.

**au** Like **ou** in 'house' (first element more deliberately uttered;
equals German a, 2 + u, 2): Frau, Baum, Bauer.

**äu** Like **oi** in 'boil' (first element more deliberately uttered;
equals German o, 2 + i, 2): Räuber, Mäuse, Bäume.

NOTE. — The second element is sometimes slightly rounded.

**ei** ⎫ The same sound as **ai**, above; mein, Meile, seiner, klei=
**ey** ⎭ ner, einst, Meyer.

**eu** The same sound as **äu**, above: neu, heute, Feuer, euer,
seufzen.

**ui** Equals German u, 2 + i, 2: hui! pfui!

## CONSONANTS.

1. It is very important to remember that all final consonants
are short in German, although not always so in English; compare man and 'man,' sang and 'sang.'

2. Double consonants have only a single sound, as also in
English: gefallen, 'fallen'; but when two consonants come
together through compounding the sound is lengthened in
careful diction, but not fully doubled: mitteilen; similarly
also contiguous final and initial consonant, when necessary for
distinctness: not tun.

3. When alternative pronunciations are given below the
preferable one is put first.

## *Alphabetical List of Consonants.*

**b** 1. When initial in word or syllable, or doubled, like b in
'ball': bald, lieben, verbleiben, Ebbe.

2. When final, in word or syllable, like p in 'tap': ab, Weib,
lieb, abgehen, Schreibtisch, liebte, lieblich, liebster.

**c** 1. Before front vowel, like ts in 'sets': Cicero, Cäsar.

2. Before back vowel, like c in 'call': Canto, Cassel.

NOTE. — c alone is now found only in loan-words and proper nouns.

**ch** 1. After back vowel, has no English counterpart; compare
Scotch ch in 'loch' (formed by slight contact of the
back of the tongue with the soft palate; voiceless):
Bach, machen, noch, suchen, rauchen.

NOTE. — 'Voiceless' means without vibration of the vocal chords; compare 'fine' (voiceless) with 'vine' (voiced).

2. After front vowel, after consonant, and in –chen, like h
in 'hue' very forcibly pronounced (avoid k as in 'kill'
and sh as in 'ship'; it is best obtained by unvoicing the
y in yes): ich, schlecht, weich, Bücher, solches, Mädchen;
so also in Chemie', before a front vowel.

3. Before s in a stem syllable, like k (which see): Lachs,
Ochsen, wachsen; also some loan-words, Christ, Chor, 2c.

**ck** Like k (which see): dick, schicken.

**d** 1. When initial in a word or syllable, or doubled, like d in
'day' (tongue advanced to the gums): du, drei, Feder,
Hände, würde, addieren.

2. When final in a word or syllable, like t in 'take' (tongue
advanced to the gums): Lied, Hand, und, Händchen,
endlich, Gesundheit.

**f** Like f in 'fall': kaufen, Frau, fünf, hoffen.

**g** 1. When initial in a word or stressed syllable, or doubled,
like g in 'began,' 'gain,' 'begin': gab, Aufgabe,
gehen, gegeben, Gitter, grün, Egge.

NOTE. — The place of contact between tongue and palate varies along with the vowel or consonant of the syllable, as in English; similarly also for the sounds of **ť, ng, nť.**

2. After a back vowel within a word (when followed by a vowel), either like **g, ı**, or voiced **dj, ı** : Tage, fagen, zogen, Zuge.

NOTE. — This second sound is foreign to English; it may be formed by making the sound usually heard in gargling, without, however, drawing the tongue far enough back to cause the uvula to trill.

3. After a back vowel when final or before a consonant, like **dj, ı** : Tag, lag, zog, Zug, fagte, wogte.

4. After a front vowel or a consonant within a word (and followed by a vowel), either like **g, ı**, or **j** (which see): legen, Berge, Bürger, Schläge, Wiege, Könige.

NOTE. — Like **j** almost universally in the combination **ig.**

5. After a front vowel, (*a*) when final, (*b*) final after a consonant, (*c*) before a consonant, like **dj, 2** : Teig, Sieg, König; Berg, Talg; legte, liegt.

6. Like **z** in 'azure' (tongue advanced, lips protruded) in many French loan-words : E≈ta'≈ge, Cou≈ra'≈ge.

**ȟ** 1. Like **h** in 'have' (strongly and briefly uttered) : haben, gehabt, heißen, geholfen, A'horn.

2. It is silent before the vowel of an ending and as a sign of length : gehen, gesehen ; Kuh, Reh, weh ; see also **dj, th, fdj.**

**j** 1. Regularly, like **y** in 'yes' (tongue closer to the palate ; strongly buzzed): ja, jeder, Juni, Joch, juchzen.

2. In French loan-words, like **g, 6**, above : Journa'l, Jalousie'.

**ť** Like **c** in 'can' or **k** in 'ken,' 'keen' (comp. note to **g, ı**): ťam, ťennen, Kind, ťlein, fanť.

**ĺ** Like **1** in 'lip' (tongue advanced to gums): loben, lieben, als, glücklich, wollen, voll.

m      Like m in 'make': mit, Baum, kommen, Lamm.

n      Like n in 'name' (tongue advanced to gums) : nennen,
       und, Hände, an, Mann, Männer.

ng     Like ng in 'sang,' 'length' 'sing' (abruptly uitered ;
       comp. note to g, 1 ; never as in English 'finger'):
       sangen, lang, längst, sing, Finger.

nk     Like nk in 'thank,' 'think' (abruptly uttered ; comp.
       note to g, 1) : Dank, danken, lenken, sinken.

p      Like p in 'pit' (pronounce fully before f): Puppe,
       Sirup, pflanzen, Pferd.

ph     Like f (which see): Philoso'ph, Philosophie'.

qu     Like k + w (which see): Quelle, quer.

r      Has no English counterpart; it is formed either (1) by
       trilling the point of the tongue against the upper gums
       ('lingual' r), or (2) by drawing the root of the tongue
       backward so as to cause the uvula to vibrate ('uvular' r) :
       Rat, rot, rund, rein, war, wir, Herz, werden.

   NOTE. — Either sound is correct in conversation.   The lingual r, however, is more readily acquired by English-speaking students.

f   1. When initial in a word or syllable before a vowel, like z in
       'zeal' (tongue advanced towards gums): sehen, so, sich,
       süß, Rose, Zinsen, gelesen.
    2. When final in a word or syllable, and before most con-
       sonants, like s in 'seal' (tongue advanced, as above) ;
       so also ß, ss, always : Gras, weshalb, fast, Maske,
       essen, Fuß, Füße, Flüsse.
    3. When initial before p or t, like sh in 'ship' (tongue ad-
       vanced ; lips protruded) : stehen, gestanden, spielen,
       gespielt, Kinderspiel.

sch    Like sh in 'ship' (see f, 3): Schiff, schreiben, Tisch.

**t**  1. Like t in 'tame' (tongue advanced to gums): Tag, teilen, Tisch, Tinte, Mutter, ritt.

2. In loan-words before i = tʒ : Natio'n, Patie'nt.

**th**  Same as t, 1 : Theater.

**tz**  Same as z (which see): Satz, sitzen.

**v**  1. Same as f (which see): Vater, viel, von, brav.

2. In most Latin or Romance loan-words = w (which see) Vase, Provia'nt, Revo'lver, Vera'nda.

**w**  Like v in 'vine' (less strongly buzzed): war, wo, wir, weshalb, Schwester, zwei.

**x**  Same as ks : Axt, Nixe.

**z**  Same as tʒ : zu, Herz, Skizze.

### Pronunciation of Loan-words.

The German pronunciation of loan-words is usually an approximation to the original sound, the original stress of the foreign word being in most cases retained. A full treatment of the subject is beyond the limits of this work, but the pronunciation of the more common consonants of foreign origin has been indicated above.

### Exercises on Pronunciation.

NOTE.—The words in *A, B, C, D*, have been taken, with few exceptions, from the first five exercises of the Grammar. The numerals after the letters correspond to those used in explaining the pronunciation (pp. xiv–xx).

*A.* Simple vowels.—a (1): Vater, Marie', Tafel, aber, da; a (2): alt, Mann, Ball, Garten, Tante; e (1): Feder, erst, Lehrer, sehr; e (2): Geld, Herr, Messer, Fenster; e (3): Rose, viele, loben, aber; i (1): wir, die, viele; i (2): Tinte, ist, immer, artig; i (3): Li'lie; o (1): wo, rot, oder, groß, wohl; o (2): Onkel, Stock, oft, Sommer; u (1): Buch, Bruder, Blume, Stuhl; u (2): Hund, jung, Mutter, Puppe.

*B.* Vowels with umlaut. — ä (1): Mädchen, erzählen, Märchen; ä (2): Bäcker; ö (1): böse, schön; ö (2): Götter, können, Hörner; ü (1): grün, gütig, Schüler, Tür; ü (2): hübsch, fünfzig.

*C.* Diphthongs. — ai: Kaiser; au: auch, Frau, aufmerksam, Aufgabe; ei: klein, Bleistift, Fleisch, rein; eu: neu, Deutsch.

*D.* Consonants. — b (1): aber, Ball, Bruder, Brief; b (2): hübsch, Schreibtisch; c: Cäsar, Cicero; ch (1): Buch, auch, machen; ch (2): ich, nicht, Mädchen, weich; ch (3): wachsen, Chor; ck: Bäcker, Stock; d (1): da, Feder, oder, drei, addieren; d (2): lud, und, gründlich; g (1): gut, gern, Garten, groß; g (2): Tage, sage; g (3): Tag, klug; g (4): Berge, Könige; g (5): artig, gütig, regnen; g (6): Etage, Courage; h (1): hart, Hut, Herr, hier; h (2): sah, sehen, weh; j: (1) ja, jung; j (2): Journal; k: kalt, klein; l: alt, klug, Ball; m: Mann, immer; n: nein, Tante, Mann; ng: jung, Spaziergang, Ring, singen; nk: Onkel; p: Puppe; ph: Philosoʼph; qu: Quelle, quer; r: rot, Rose, rund, wer, Garten, Herr; s (1): Rose, böse, sehr; s (2): als, Haus, groß, Messer, wessen; s (3) Stuhl, Bleistift, Stock, spielen; sch: schwarz, schön, Schwester, Deutsch; t (1): rot, Tinte, Mutter; t (2): Natioʼn, Patieʼnt; th: Theaʼter; tz: Platz; v (1): Vater, viele; v (2): Vase, Verbum; w: wo, wer, Schwester, schwarz; x: Hexe, Axt; z: ganz, Zimmer, fünfzig, erzählen.

*E.* To be repeated several times in succession: 1. Drei breite Bachblätter, drei breite, ꝛc. 2. Fischers Fritz fischt frische Fische, Fischers Fritz, ꝛc. 3. Der Kottbusser Postkutscher putzt den Kottbusser Postkutschkasten, der Kottbusser, ꝛc.

*F.*                    Sehnsucht.

Ach! aus dieses Tales Gründen,
  Die der kalte Nebel drückt,
    Könntʼ ich doch den Ausgang finden,
Ach! wie fühltʼ ich mich beglückt!

Dort erblick' ich schöne Hügel,
Ewig jung und ewig grün;
Hätt' ich Schwingen, hätt' ich Flügel,
Nach den Hügeln zög' ich hin.

— Schiller.

## Use of Capitals.

Capital letters are required in German, contrary to English usage, in the following cases: —

1. As initial of all nouns and all words used as nouns: die Feder, 'the pen'; das Nützliche, 'the useful'; etwas Neues, 'something new'; das Reisen, 'travelling'; nouns used with other functions take a small initial: Abend, 'evening,' but abends, 'in the evening'; Leid, 'sorrow,' but es tut mir leid, 'I am sorry.'

2. As initial of the pronoun Sie = 'you' (in all forms except sich), and of the corresponding possessives: Haben Sie Ihre Feder? 'Have you your pen?'

3. Similarly, but in correspondence only, du, ihr = 'you,' and their possessives: Wir erwarten Dich und Deine Schwester, 'We expect you and your sister.'

4. Proper adjectives are not written with a capital unless formed from names of persons or forming part of a proper name: das deutsche Buch, 'the German book'; but, die Goetheschen Schriften, 'Goethe's writings'; das Deutsche Reich, 'the German Empire.'

## Punctuation.

The rules of punctuation correspond in general to those of English, but the following points should be noted: —

1. A dependent sentence (relative, adverbial, etc.) is introduced by a comma.

2. Infinitive clauses with zu are regularly preceded by a comma.

3. An exclamatory point is used in beginning letters: Sehr geehrter Herr!

## German Script.

Ä ä　　　　Ö ö　　　　Ü ü

Ch ch ck　　St ft ff ß tz

(Transcription of the German letter on page 172.)

Hamburg, 23. Oktober, 1909.
Friedrichstr. 21/III.

Liebe Klara!

Entschuldige, bitte, daß ich Dir
so lange nicht geschrieben habe.
Ich bin sehr beschäftigt gewesen,
wie Du gleich sehen wirst. Erst =
ens sind wir am 11. ds. aus unserer
alten Wohnung, Schillerstraße 155,
nach der obigen Adresse umgezogen;
wobei es natürlich sehr viel zu tun
gab. Zweitens feierten wir am 19.
des lieben Vaters Geburtstag. Er
erhielt viele hübsche Geschenke, dar-

unter einer schönen Ausgabe von
Shakspeares Werken in 10 Bänden,
wovon die ersten drei die Trauerspiele, der vierte, fünfte und sechste
die Lustspiele; und Band 7 bis 9 die his-
torischen Schauspiele enthalten, während sich im 10 Bande die Gedichte befinden. Es war sein 49. Geburtstag,
da er am 19. Oktober 1858 geboren wurde.
Am wievielten November hast Du
eigentlich Geburtstag? Ich habe
leider den Tag vergessen. Heute über
acht Tage, den 30.16., erwarten wir
meinen ältesten Bruder aus England.
Hoffentlich werde ich spätestens am 10.
Dezember zu dir kommen können, um
dir den lange versprochenen Besuch ab-
zustatten. Also auf Wiedersehen! Mit
herzlichen Grüßen an deine lieben
Eltern verbleibe ich stets

     Deine dich innig liebende Freundin
         Elisabeth Meyer

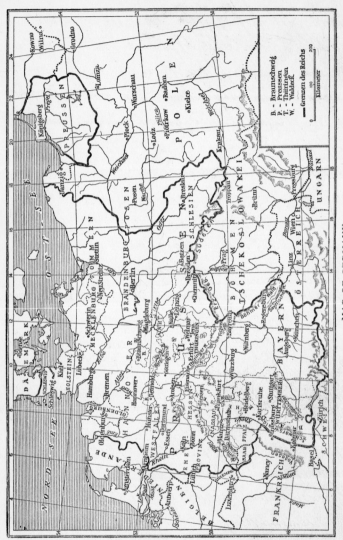

MAP OF GERMANY

*See Lesson XLI*

# LESSON I

**1.** Gender and Agreement.

| | |
|---|---|
| Der Mann ist alt. | The man is old. |
| Die Frau ist klug. | The woman is clever. |
| Das Buch ist neu. | The book is new. |
| Das Mädchen ist hübsch. | The girl is pretty. |
| Der Hund ist groß. | The dog is large. |
| Der Winter ist kalt. | The winter is cold. |
| Die Tinte ist schwarz. | The ink is black. |

OBSERVE: 1. The subject of a sentence is always in the nominative.

2. Predicate adjectives remain undeclined in German.

3. The definite article agrees with its noun in gender, number, and case, and has the following forms in the nominative singular:

*Masc.* der        *Fem.* die        *Neut.* das

4. There are three genders in German: masculine, feminine, and neuter.

5. Names of males are almost always masculine, and names of females feminine, but all nouns in –chen and –lein (diminutives) are neuter, regardless of sex.

6. Names of animals and things may be of any gender — to be learned from the vocabulary or dictionary.

**2.** Nominative Pronouns.

| | |
|---|---|
| Ist der Mann klug? Ja, er ist klug. | Is the man clever? Yes, he is clever. |
| Ist der Winter warm? Nein, er ist kalt. | Is the winter warm? No, it is cold. |

5

| | |
|---|---|
| Die Frau ist nicht alt; sie ist jung. | The woman is not old; she is young. |
| Die Tinte ist nicht rot; sie ist schwarz. | The ink is not red; it is black. |
| Das Buch ist alt; es ist nicht neu. | The book is old; it is not new. |
| Das Mädchen ist nicht klein; es ist groß. | The girl is not small; she is large. |

OBSERVE: The personal pronoun of the third singular agrees in gender with the noun to which it refers, and has the following forms in the nominative:

*Masc.* er        *Fem.* sie        *Neut.* es

## EXERCISE I

*N.B.* The definite article before nouns shows their gender.

| | |
|---|---|
| aber, but. | das Mädchen, the girl. |
| alt, old. | der Mann, the man. |
| das Buch, the book. | nein, no (*adv.*). |
| da, there. | neu, new. |
| die Feder, the pen. | nicht, not. |
| groß, large, tall, big, great. | oder, or. |
| hier, here. | rot, red. |
| der Hund, the dog. | schwarz, black. |
| ist, is. | der Sommer, the summer. |
| ja, yes. | die Tinte, the ink. |
| kalt, cold. | warm, warm. |
| klein, small, little. | wer? who? |
| klug, clever, intelligent. | der Winter, the winter. |
| der Lehrer, the teacher (*m.*). | wo? where? |
| die Lehrerin, the teacher (*f.*). | |

*A.* 1. Das Buch ist neu. 2. Die Tinte ist schwarz. 3. Der Winter ist kalt. 4. Der Sommer ist warm. 5. Das Mädchen ist klein. 6. Das Buch ist nicht alt; es ist neu. 7. Die Tinte ist nicht rot; sie ist schwarz. 8. Das Mädchen ist nicht klein; es ist groß.  9. Ist die Feder hier?  10. Ja, sie ist hier.  11. Wer ist da?  12. Das Mädchen ist da.  13. Wo ist der Lehrer?  14. Er ist nicht hier; er ist da.  15. Der Lehrer ist hier, aber die Lehrerin ist nicht hier.  16. Ist der Sommer kalt?  17. Nein, er ist warm; er ist nicht kalt. 18. Ist der Hund klug?  19. Ja, er ist klug.

*B.* Answer the following questions in German: 1. Ist das Buch groß?  2. Ist das Mädchen klein?  3. Ist die Tinte schwarz?  4. Ist der Sommer kalt?  5. Ist der Winter kalt oder warm?  6. Wo ist die Feder?  7. Wer ist hier?  8. Wer ist nicht hier?  9. Ist der Lehrer nicht da?  10. Wo ist das Mädchen?  11. Ist der Hund nicht klug?  12. Ist das Buch alt oder neu?

*C.* 1. The book is large.  2. The ink is red.  3. Is the man clever?  4. He is clever.  5. Where is the pen?  6. It is not here.  7. The summer is warm; it is not cold.  8. Is the winter warm?  9. No, it is cold.  10. Where is the dog? 11. It is here.  12. Is the ink black?  13. No, it is red. 14. Is the teacher here?  15. Yes, she is here.  16. Is the girl large?  17. No, she is small.  18. Is the book old or is it new?  19. It is old; it is not new.  20. Where is the teacher?

*D.* Lesestück (extract for reading):

| | |
|---|---|
| Eins, zwei, drei, | Warm ist nicht kalt, |
| Alt ist nicht neu, | Kalt ist nicht warm, |
| Neu ist nicht alt, | Reich ist nicht arm. |

NOTE.— For vocabulary of these extracts, see end of the volume.

## LESSON II

**3.**　　　　　Nominative of ein and kein.

| | |
|---|---|
| Ein Stein ist hart. | A stone is hard. |
| Eine Rose ist rot. | A rose is red. |

| | |
|---|---|
| Ein Ei ist rund. | An egg is round. |
| Kein Sommer ist kalt. | No summer is cold. |
| Keine Rose ist grün. | No rose is green. |
| Kein Kind ist alt. | No child is old. |

OBSERVE: The indefinite article ein and its negative kein agree with their nouns, and have the following forms in the nominative singular:

| | | |
|---|---|---|
| *Masc. and Neut.* ein | *Fem.* eine |
| *Masc. and Neut.* kein | *Fem.* keine |

### 4. Nominative of Some Possessives.

| | |
|---|---|
| Mein Vater ist groß. | My father is tall. |
| Deine Mutter ist gut. | Your (thy) mother is good. |
| Sein Kind ist klein. | His child is small. |
| Ist das ihr Buch? | Is that her (their) book? |
| Unsere Mutter ist alt. | Our mother is old. |

OBSERVE: Possessive adjectives have the same endings as the indefinite article in the nominative singular, and agree.

### 5 Nominative of welcher?

| | |
|---|---|
| Welcher Mann ist alt? | Which man is old? |
| Welche Blume ist rot? | Which flower is red? |
| Welches Kind ist hübsch? | Which child is pretty? |

OBSERVE: The interrogative welcher? 'which?' has the following forms in the nominative singular, and agrees:

*Masc.* welcher       *Fem.* welche       *Neut.* welches

### EXERCISE II

| | |
|---|---|
| der Bäcker, the baker. | hart, hard. |
| der Ball, the ball. | hübsch, pretty. |
| der Bruder, the brother. | der Hut, the hat. |
| grün, green. | immer, always. |
| gut, good. | jung, young. |

das Kind, the child.
die Mutter, the mother.
nie, never.
der Ring, the ring.
die Rose, the rose.
rund, round.
schlecht, bad.

die Schwester, the sister.
sehr, very.
der Stuhl, the chair.
der Vater, the father.
was? what?
weich, soft.
weiß, white.

*A.* 1. Ein Ring ist rund.  2. Mein Vater ist nicht jung.
3. Ist mein Ball rund? 4. Ja, er ist rund.  5. Unser Vater
ist alt.  6. Wo ist der Ring?  7. Er ist hier.  8. Ist ein
Mädchen immer jung?  9. Ja, ein Mädchen ist nie alt.
10. Seine Feder ist hier.  11. Unser Bäcker ist groß, aber
sein Bruder ist klein.  12. Meine Mutter ist hübsch.  13. Kein
Kind ist alt.  14. Der Bäcker ist alt.  15. Sein Hut ist weiß.
16. Meine Feder ist gut, aber ihre Feder ist schlecht.  17. Ist
ihr Stuhl weich?  18. Nein, er ist nicht weich, er ist sehr hart.
19. Eine Rose ist rot.  20. Eine Rose ist nicht grün.  21. Kein
Sommer ist kalt.  22. Mein Bruder ist groß, aber ihre
Schwester ist klein.

*B.* Answer in German : 1. Ist eine Rose schwarz? 2. Welche
Rose ist weiß?  3. Wo ist mein Ball?  4. Welche Feder ist
gut?  5. Welcher Stuhl ist weich?  6. Welches Buch ist groß?
7. Wer ist nie alt?  8. Wer ist immer jung?  9. Was ist
immer rund?  10. Ist ihre Schwester groß oder klein?
11. Ist unser Bäcker jung oder alt?  12. Ist sein Hut schwarz
oder weiß?  13. Ist ihre Feder hart?  14. Wo ist unsere
Lehrerin?  15. Ist kein Sommer kalt?

*C.* 1. The summer is warm.  2. No winter is warm.  3. Is
her pen hard or soft?  4. My ink is red; it is not black.
5. Her father is old.  6. No child is old.  7. Our sister is not
tall, but she is pretty.  8. His brother is tall, but her brother
is small.  9. Which chair is hard?  10. Which ink is black?
11. Is her chair hard or soft?  12. His chair is hard, but my

c

chair is soft. 13. Which child is pretty? 14. His pen is not good; it is very soft. 15. Is our dog not here? 16. No rose is green. 17. A rose is red or white.

*D.* Lesestück:

Eins, zwei, drei,       Hart ist nicht weich,
Alt ist nicht neu,      Frisch ist nicht faul,
Arm ist nicht reich,     Ochs' ist kein Gaul.

## LESSON III

**6.** Present Indicative of **sein,** to be.

*Singular.*               *Plural.*

| | | | |
|---|---|---|---|
| ich | bin, I am. | wir sind, | we are. |
| du | bist, thou art, you are. | ihr seid, | ye (you) are. |
| er (sie, es) | ist, he (she, it) is. | sie sind, | they are. |

Formal : Sie sind, you are (*sing.* or *plur.*).
Interrogatively : bin ich? bist du? zc.

**7.** Pronouns of Address.

| | |
|---|---|
| Bist du da, mein Kind? | Are you there, my child? |
| Seid ihr da, Kinder? | Are you there, children? |
| Sind Sie krank, Herr A.? | Are you ill, Mr. A.? |
| Sind Sie hier, meine Herren? | Are you here, gentlemen? |
| Ist das Ihr Buch, Herr B.? | Is that your book, Mr. B.? |

OBSERVE : 1. **Du,** 'thou,' 'you,' is familiar, and its plural is **ihr,** 'ye,' 'you'; the corresponding possessives are **dein, euer,** respectively, declined like **mein.**

2. **Sie,** 'you,' is formal, is always written with a capital, and requires the verb in the third plural, whether one person is addressed or more than one.

3. 'Your' in formal address = **Ihr,** declined like **ihr** = 'her,' and always written with a capital.

**8.**          The Demonstrative **das.**

| | |
|---|---|
| Das ist der Vater. | That is the father. |
| Das ist die Mutter. | That is the mother. |
| Das sind meine Schüler. | Those are my pupils. |

OBSERVE: **Das** remains unchanged here; the verb agrees with the real subject, which follows.

**9. Word Order.** The predicate adjective comes at the end of a principal sentence in simple tenses:

| | |
|---|---|
| Das Wetter ist heute schön. | The weather is fine to-day. |

## EXERCISE III

artig, well-behaved, good.
auch, also, too.
böse, bad, cross, angry.
die Frau, the woman, wife, Mrs.
ganz, quite.
der Garten, the garden.
gütig, kind.
der Herr, the gentleman, Mr.
in, in.
die Kinder, the children.
krank, ill, sick.
die Lehrer, the teachers.
das Messer, the knife.
die Messer, the knives.

der Onkel, the uncle.
scharf, sharp.
schön, beautiful, handsome, fine.
die Schule, the school.
der Schüler, the pupil, scholar.
die Schüler, the pupils, scholars.
die Tante, the aunt.
u'nartig, naughty, bad.
und, and.
wessen? whose?
wohl, well.
2c., etc.

IDIOM: **Herr Lehrer,** teacher (*voc.*); **der Herr Lehrer,** the teacher (forms of respect).

*A.* Continue the following throughout the tense: 1. Ich bin krank, du bist, 2c. 2. Bin ich artig? bist du? 2c. 3. Ich bin nicht klein, du, 2c. 4. Bin ich nicht groß? bist du? 2c.

*B.* 1. Die Schüler sind nicht hier; sie sind nicht wohl. 2. Die Lehrer sind hier und die Schüler sind auch hier.

3. Unsere Schule ist groß und schön. 4. Ich bin klein, aber Sie sind groß. 5. Sind Sie krank, Frau Braun? 6. Nein, ich bin ganz wohl. 7. Sie sind sehr gütig, Herr Schäfer. 8. Ist das Ihre Feder? 9. Du bist unartig, mein Kind. 10. Seid ihr artig, Kinder? 11. Ja, Herr Lehrer, wir sind artig. 12. Unser Garten ist schön und er ist auch groß. 13. Der Hund ist groß, aber er ist nicht böse. 14. Die Messer sind nicht scharf. 15. Wer ist das? 16. Das ist meine Schwester. 17. Das sind die Schüler. 18. Das ist unsere Lehrerin. 19. Unser Onkel ist in New York. 20. Ihre Tante ist in Berlin.

*C.* Answer in German: 1. Ist das Kind artig? 2. Sind die Kinder nicht artig? 3. Bist du wohl, mein Kind? 4. Sind Sie nicht wohl, Herr Schäfer? 5. Wessen Feder ist das? 6. Wessen Ball ist das? 7. Wer ist da? 8. Was ist das? 9. Ist Ihr Hund nicht böse? 10. Ist mein Garten nicht schön? 11. Wo ist Ihre Tante? 12. Ist Ihr Onkel nicht auch in Berlin?

*D.* 1. My aunt is in New York. 2. Where is your uncle? 3. He is also in New York. 4. Are you quite well, Mr. Schäfer? 5. No, I am not very well. 6. Are you ill, my child? 7. No, I am quite well. 8. Are you there, father? 9. Yes, I am here. 10. Is that your school? 11. Yes, that is my school. 12. It is not large, but it is handsome. 13. Children, you are naughty. 14. No, we are quite good. 15. My brother and my sister are in Berlin. 16. Whose knives are those? 17. What is that? 18. Who is that? 19. That is my mother. 20. Who are you? 21. I am Mrs. Braun.

*E.* Lesestück:

> Der Winter ist kalt, der Sommer ist warm;
> Die Eltern sind reich, die Kinder sind arm;
> Die Feder ist leicht, das Eisen ist schwer;
> Die Schüssel ist voll, der Teller ist leer.

# LESSON IV

**10.**    Present Indicative of **haben,** to have.

|  | I have, etc. |  | Have I? etc. |
|---|---|---|---|
| ich habe | wir haben | habe ich? | haben wir? |
| du haft | ihr habt | haft du? | habt ihr? |
| er hat | fie haben | hat er? | haben fie? |
| Formal: Sie haben. | | Formal: haben Sie? | |

**11. Accusative Forms.**    1. The direct object is put in the accusative, which has the same form as the nominative, except in the masculine singular.

2. Observe the following forms of the masculine singular accusative, and of the nominative and accusative plural of all genders:

| *Sing.* | de**n** | ein**en** | fein**en** | mein**en,** ⁊c. | welch**en** |
|---|---|---|---|---|---|
| *Plur.* | di**e** | —— | fein**e** | mein**e,** ⁊c. | welch**e** |

**12.**                    Repetition.

| Der Mann und **die** Frau. | The man and woman. |
|---|---|
| Die Feder und **die** Tinte. | The pen and ink. |
| Mein Vater und **meine** Mutter. | My father and mother. |

OBSERVE : The article, possessive adjective, etc., must be repeated before each noun in the singular.

**13.**                    The Comparative Degree.

| Du bift kleiner **als** ich. | You are smaller than I. |
|---|---|
| Er geht **so** schnell **wie** ich. | He walks as quickly as I. |
| Er ift älter **als** sein Freund. | He is older than his friend. |

OBSERVE: 1. Most adjectives and adverbs form the comparative by adding –**er** to the stem of the positive.

2. 'Than' after comparatives = **als**; 'as' . . . 'as' or 'so' . . . 'as' = **so** . . . **wie.**

3. Many monosyllabic adjectives and adverbs with stem vowel **a, o, u,** have umlaut (ä, ö, ü, respectively) in the comparative.

4. The noun after als has the same case as that which precedes.

NOTE. — Adjectives with umlaut in comparative are marked by ($^{u}$) in the vocabularies; see also vocabularies and Lesson XXXIX for irregular comparison.

## EXERCISE IV

als, than.
au'fmerksam, attentive.
der Bleistift, the pencil.
die Blume, the flower.
die Bücher, the books.
drei, three.
das Fenster, the window.
die Fenster, the windows.
das Fleisch, the meat.
fünfzig, fifty.
das Geld, the money.
der Junge, the boy.
die Kreide, the chalk.
Marie', Mary.
nur, only.
die Puppe, the doll.

die Puppen, the dolls.
rein, clean.
der Schreibtisch, the writing-desk, writing-table.
das Schulhaus, the schoolhouse.
die Schulstube, the schoolroom.
der Stock, the cane, stick.
die Tafel, the blackboard.
die Tür, the door.
viele, many.
wie? how?
das Zimmer, the room.
die Zimmer, the rooms.
zu, too.

*A.* Continue the following (see Exercise III): 1. Welchen Ball habe ich? welchen Ball hast du? 2c. 2. Ich habe keinen Bleistift. 3. Welche Bücher habe ich? 4. Habe ich nicht ihre Bücher? 5. Ich habe keine Messer. 6. Ich habe den Stock.

*B.* Supply the proper form of der, ein, kein, or of a possessive adjective in the following: 1. Hat Marie . . . Blume? 2. Wer hat . . . Messer (*sing.*)? 3. Habe ich . . . Buch? 4. Hast du . . . Feder? 5. Haben wir . . . Garten? 6. Habt ihr . . . Geld? 7. Haben Sie . . . Tinte? 8. . . . Hund hat Fleisch. 9. . . . Junge hat . . . Ball. 10. . . . Mädchen hat . . . Puppe. 11. Hat es . . . Puppe?

*C.* 1. Unſer Schulhaus iſt groß und ſchön. 2. Es hat viele Zimmer und Fenſter. 3. Die Zimmer ſind groß. 4. Sie haben Fenſter. 5. Unſer Zimmer hat nur ein Fenſter. 6. Das Fenſter iſt groß, aber es iſt nicht immer rein. 7. Hier iſt unſer Lehrer. 8. Was hat er? 9. Er hat einen Schreib= tiſch. 10. Er hat auch eine Feder und Tinte. 11. Seine Schüler haben auch Feder und Tinte. 12. Unſere Schulſtube hat eine Tafel. 13. Die Tafel iſt ſchwarz. 14. Wie viele Schüler hat Ihre Schule? 15. Sie hat fünfzig Schüler. 16. Sind die Schüler aufmerkſam? 17. Sie ſind nicht immer aufmerkſam. 18. Unſere Lehrer haben Kreide. 19. Das Fenſter iſt kleiner als die Tür. 20. Der Lehrer iſt älter als ſeine Schüler. 21. Die Schüler ſind nicht ſo klug wie ihr Lehrer.

*D.* Oral exercise on the above.

*E.* 1. Our teacher has a chair and writing-desk. 2. Has he also a cane? 3. No, he has no cane. 4. The pupils have their books. 5. Have you your books? 6. Yes, but I have no pencil. 7. Mary has my pencil and pen. 8. Which doll have the girls? 9. They have no doll. 10. How many teachers has your school? 11. It has three teachers. 12. Have they many pupils? 13. Yes, they have fifty pupils. 14. Are their pupils attentive? 15. No, not always. 16. Has your teacher her pen or pencil? 17. No, but she has her chalk. 18. Has your sister a doll? 19. No, she has no doll; she is too big. 20. She is taller than her brother.

*F.* Leſeſtück:

Ein Kindesherz ſoll ſein:      Wie der Spiegel ſo wahr,
Wie die Lilie ſo rein,      Wie der Quell ſo friſch,
Wie der Tau ſo klar,      Froh wie die Vöglein im Ge=
     büſch.

*G.* Sprichwörter (proverbs): 1. Beſſer ſpät als nie. 2. Et= was iſt beſſer als gar nichts. 3. Zeit iſt Geld. 4. Ende gut, alles gut.

## LESSON V

**14.**      Present Indicative of **machen,** to make.

I make, am making, do make, etc.    Am I making? do I make? etc.

| | | | |
|---|---|---|---|
| ich mache | wir machen | mache ich? | machen wir? |
| du machst | ihr macht | machst du? | macht ihr? |
| er macht | sie machen | macht er? | machen sie? |

Formal: Sie machen.      Formal: machen Sie?

### EXAMPLES.

| | |
|---|---|
| Ich mache eine Puppe. | I am making a doll. |
| Spielen sie Ball? | Do they play ball? |
| Wir lieben unseren Vater. | We love our father. |
| Du arbeitest. | You are working. |
| Regnet es? | Is it raining? |

OBSERVE: 1. There are no auxiliary forms in German corresponding to the English 'I am making,' 'Does he play?' etc.

2. Most verbs form the present indicative like machen, but when the infinitive stem ends in -t or -d, or consonants after which t cannot be pronounced, the second singular ends in -est, and the third singular and the second plural in -et.

**15.**      Imperative of **machen.**

*Singular.*                   *Plural.*

mache (du), make (thou).        macht (ihr), make (ye).

Formal: machen Sie, make.

**16. Adjective as Adverb.** Most adjectives may be used as adverbs without change:

| | |
|---|---|
| gut, good, well. | schön, beautiful(-ly). |
| fleißig, diligent(-ly). | angenehm, agreeable(-ly). |

## EXERCISE V

| | |
|---|---|
| arbeiten, to work. | machen, to make, do. |
| die Aufgabe, the exercise. | das Märchen, the fairy-tale, story. |
| bitte, please. | |
| der Brief, the letter. | die Märchen, the fairy-tales, stories. |
| die Brüder, the brothers. | |
| Deutsch, German. | oft, often. |
| erzählen, to tell (narrate). | regnen, to rain. |
| fleißig, diligent, industrious. | schnell, quick, fast. |
| gern, willingly, gladly. | schreiben, to write. |
| Karl, Charles. | singen, to sing. |
| das Klavier, the piano. | der Spaziergang, the walk. |
| lehren, to teach. | spielen, to play. |
| lernen, to learn, study. | wen? whom? |
| das Lied, the song. | wenig, little (not much). |
| loben, to praise. | |

IDIOMS: 1. **Ich spiele gern,** I am fond of playing, like to play.
2. **Einen Spaziergang machen,** to take (go for) a walk.
3. **Klavier spielen,** to play the piano.

*A.* Continue the following, giving also the imperative : 1. Ich schreibe einen Brief, du, 2c. 2. Ich mache einen Spaziergang. 3. Ich singe ein Lied. 4. Ich spiele nicht Ball. 5. Arbeite ich schnell? 6. Ich lerne schneller als Karl.

*B.* 1. Unsere Lehrer loben ihre Schüler. 2. Die Lehrerin lehrt ihre Schüler. 3. Die Schüler lernen gern. 4. Kinder, lernt ihr gern Deutsch? 5. Ja, wir lernen sehr gern Deutsch. 6. Kinder lernen nicht immer gern. 7. Wir schreiben eine Aufgabe. 8. Karl schreibt einen Brief. 9. Marie, schreibe eine Aufgabe. 10. Arbeitet fleißiger, Kinder. 11. Marie arbeitet sehr fleißig. 12. Kinder spielen immer gern. 13. Karl, spielst du gern Ball? 14. Ja, Herr Lehrer, ich spiele sehr gern Ball. 15. Bitte, erzählen Sie ein Märchen, Herr Lehrer. 16. Unsere Mutter erzählt oft Märchen. 17. Meine

Schwester singt sehr schön; sie singt ein Lied.　18. Spielen Sie Klavier, Frau Schäfer?　19. Ich spiele ein wenig, aber nicht sehr gut.　20. Meine Brüder machen oft einen Spaziergang.　21. Machen Sie gern einen Spaziergang?　22. Ja, ich mache sehr gern einen Spaziergang.

*C.* Answer in German: 1. Wer lobt die Schüler?　2. Lernst du gern, Karl?　3. Arbeitet ihr fleißig, Kinder?　4. Wer schreibt?　5. Was schreibt er?　6. Wer spielt?　7. Was spielen sie?　8. Spielen Sie Klavier?　9. Lernen Sie gern Deutsch?　10. Was erzählt die Lehrerin?　11. Wer singt? 12. Was singt sie?　13. Regnet es, oder regnet es nicht?

*D.* 1. We are learning German.　2. I like to learn German. 3. Do you like to learn German?　4. Charles likes to learn German.　5. Mary works diligently.　6. Her brother learns very quickly.　7. He learns more quickly than I.　8. Our teacher is telling a story.　9. The teacher teaches and the pupils learn.　10. Do pupils always like to learn?　11. Charles is not so clever as Mary.　12. What are you writing, Mary? 13. I am writing a letter.　14. Please sing a song, Mrs. Schäfer. 15. Do not play, my child; write an exercise.　16. My father and mother are taking a walk.　17. Do they often take a walk? 18. Our house is larger than their house.　19. Our garden is smaller than their garden.

# LESSON VI

Review Lessons I–V.

## EXERCISE VI

| | |
|---|---|
| angenehm, pleasant, agreeable. | heiß, hot. |
| brauchen, to use, want, need. | hell, bright. |
| dunkel, dark. | der Himmel, heaven, sky. |
| das Feuer, fire. | hören, to hear. |
| das Gras, grass. | jetzt, now. |
| heftig, violent. | kurz, "er, short. |

lang, "er, long.

legen, to lay.

die Luft, air.

manchmal, frequently.

mehr, more.

die Nacht, night.

naß, "er, wet.

nicht mehr, no longer.

der Ofen, stove.

der Regen, rain.

scheinen, shine.

der Schnee, snow.

die Sonne, sun.

der Staub, dust.

der Tag, day.

trocken, dry. ~TROCKEN~

wieder, again.

*A.* 1. Wir haben jetzt Sommer. 2. Der Tag ist länger und die Nacht ist kürzer. 3. Die Luft ist oft sehr heiß. 4. Wir haben manchmal Regen. 5. Der Regen ist sehr angenehm. 6. Er macht das Gras naß und legt den Staub. 7. Es regnet jetzt heftig; ich höre es. 8. Die Sonne scheint nicht mehr. 9. Der Himmel ist dunkel. 10. Die Sonne scheint jetzt wieder hell und macht das Gras trocken. 11. Wir haben jetzt keinen Schnee. 12. Machen Sie kein Feuer. ~Danb~ 13. Wir brauchen jetzt kein Feuer. 14. Wir brauchen unseren Ofen nicht mehr.

*B.* Oral: 1. Ist es jetzt Winter? 2. Ist der Tag kürzer als die Nacht? 3. Ist die Nacht so lang wie der Tag? 4. Regnet es? 5. Hört ihr nicht den Regen, Kinder? 6. Regnet es hier oft? 7. Haben wir Schnee? 8. Ist das Gras naß? 9. Haben Sie einen Ofen? 10. Brauchen wir jetzt Feuer?

*C.* Continue: 1. Ich habe keinen Ofen, du, 2c. 2. Ich höre nicht den Regen. 3. Ich bin nicht wohl. 4. Brauche ich kein Feuer?

*D.* 1. It is now winter. 2. The day is shorter than the night. 3. The air is colder. 4. We need a stove. 5. We need also a fire. 6. We have no fire. 7. Our room is quite cold. 8. We have snow. 9. The snow is white and clean. 10. The air is often very cold, but it is pleasant and bright.

~Home work~

11. My room has a stove.   12. I use the stove very often.
13. Charles and Mary need a stove.   14. Their room is not very warm.   15. Please make a fire.

*E.* Lesestück:

> Ich liebe die Blumen, ich liebe das Spiel,
> Ich liebe die Vögel, ich liebe gar viel,
> Die Erde, den Himmel, die Sonne, den Stern,
> Ich liebe das alles, ob nah' oder fern.

## LESSON VII

**17.**          Declension of Definite Article.

|  | SINGULAR. | | | PLURAL. |
| --- | --- | --- | --- | --- |
|  | *Masc.* | *Fem.* | *Neut.* | *All Genders.* |
| *Nom.* | der | die | das | die, the |
| *Gen.* | des | der | des | der, of the |
| *Dat.* | dem | der | dem | den, (to, for) the |
| *Acc.* | den | die | das | die, the |

**18.**          Use of the Cases.

| | |
| --- | --- |
| Wer ist da? Der Mann ist da. | Who is there?  The man is there. |
| Wessen Buch hat er? | Whose book has he? |
| Er hat das Buch **des** Schülers. | He has the pupil's book. |
| Wem schickt er das Buch? | To whom does he send the book? |
| Er schickt **dem** Lehrer das Buch. | He sends the teacher the book. |
| Wen lobt sie?  Sie lobt **den** Schüler. | Whom does she praise?  She praises the pupil. |
| Was haben Sie?  Ich habe **die** Feder. | What have you?  I have the pen. |

OBSERVE: 1. The nominative is the subject, and answers the question 'who?' (wer?) or 'what?' (was?).

2. The genitive corresponds to the English possessive or objective with *of*, and answers the question 'whose?' 'of whom?' 'of what?' (weſſen?).

3. The dative is the indirect object, and answers the question 'to whom?' (wem?).

4. The accusative is the direct object, and answers the question 'whom?' (wen?) or 'what?' (was?).

NOTES. — 1. Any of these cases, except the nominative, may be governed by a preposition.

2. It is important to remember that some verbs which are transitive in English govern a dative only in German, as indicated in the vocabularies.

**19. Contraction.** The prepositions an, 'on,' 'at,' in, 'in,' von, 'of,' 'from,' zu, 'to,' are contracted with the unemphasized definite article as follows:

$$\text{an dem} = \text{am} \qquad \text{in dem} = \text{im} \qquad \text{von dem} = \text{vom}$$
$$\text{zu dem} = \text{zum} \qquad \text{zu der} = \text{zur}$$

**20. Case Forms of Nouns.** 1. Most masculine and neuter nouns have the genitive singular in –s or –es; the dative singular is often, and the accusative usually, the same as the nominative; but masculine and neuter monosyllables usually add –e in the dative singular.

2. Feminines remain unchanged in the singular, and most of them have –n or –en throughout the plural.

3. The nominative, genitive, and accusative plural are always alike, and the dative ends in –n.

## EXERCISE VII

auf (*dat.*), on, upon.
der Baum, tree.
bekommen, to get, receive.
die Blumen, flowers.
der Blumenkohl, cauliflower.
bringen, to bring.
danken (*dat.*), to thank.

für (*acc.*), for.
der Gärtner, gardener.
das Gemüse (*sing.* only), vegetables.
gern haben, to be fond of, like.
in (*dat.*), in.
der Kohl, cabbage.

die Küche, kitchen.
mit (*dat.*), with.
der Nachbar, neighbour.
nach Hause, home.
pflanzen, to plant.
pflücken, to pick, pluck.
die Rosen, roses.
schenken, to give (as a present).
schicken, to send.
die Stadt, town, city.
stehen, to stand.

der Tisch, table.
unter (*dat.*), under.
usw. (und so weiter), etc., and so forth.
das Veilchen, the violet.
die Veilchen, the violets.
verkaufen, to sell.
viel, much.
wem? (to, for) whom?
wohnen, to dwell, live.
zu (*dat.*), to.

*zu – to the*

*A.* Continue the following: 1. Ich schenke dem Lehrer das Buch, du, 2c. 2. Ich habe den Bleistift der Lehrerin. 3. Ich bin der Schüler des Lehrers. 4. Ich erzähle den Kindern das Märchen. 5. Ich arbeite im Garten.

*B.* 1. Das ist der Garten des Nachbars. 2. Wir spielen oft *in dem* im Garten des Nachbars. 3. Wir haben auch einen Garten. 4. Mein Vater arbeitet mit dem Gärtner im Garten. 5. Mein Vater pflanzt jetzt Blumen. 6. Der Gärtner pflanzt das Gemüse. 7. Sie pflanzen auch den Kohl und den Blumenkohl. 8. Mein Vater pflanzt viele Blumen: Rosen, Veilchen, usw. 9. Das Kind des Gärtners ist auch im Garten. 10. Es spielt unter dem Baume. 11. Wir pflücken oft Blumen für meine Mutter. 12. Sie hat Blumen sehr gern. 13. Sie braucht die Blumen für den Tisch und das Gemüse für die Küche. 14. Meine Tante wohnt in der Stadt. 15. Sie hat keinen Garten. 16. Mutter schickt meiner (*dat.*) Tante oft Blumen. 17. Vater bringt das Gemüse zur Stadt. 18. Er verkauft viel Gemüse in der Stadt und bringt das Geld nach Hause. 19. Er bekommt viel Geld für sein Gemüse. 20. Wir schenken dem Lehrer und der Lehrerin oft Blumen. 21. Die Blumen stehen auf dem Schreibtisch der Lehrerin. 22. Die Lehrerin dankt den Schülern.

*C.* Answer in German: 1. Wessen Garten ist das? 2. Wer ist im Garten? 3. Mit wem arbeitet er? 4. Welches Gemüse pflanzt der Gärtner? 5. Wer pflanzt die Blumen? 6. Welche Blumen pflanzt er? 7. Wessen Kind ist im Garten? 8. Wo spielt es? 9. Wer pflückt Blumen? 10. Für wen sind sie? 11. Braucht sie Blumen für die Küche? 12. Wo wohnt Ihre Tante? 13. Wem schickt Ihre Mutter die Blumen? 14. Wo verkauft Ihr Vater das Gemüse? 15. Wo stehen die Blumen?

*D.* Supply an article in the blank spaces: 1. . . . Ball . . . Schülers ist hübsch. 2. Haben Sie . . . Buch . . . Frau? 3. Ich habe nicht . . . Puppe . . . Mädchens. 4. Schenken Sie . . . Onkel . . . Buch. 5. Steht . . . Tisch in . . . Zimmer? 6. . . . Feder liegt auf . . . Schreibtisch . . . Lehrers. 7. Wo ist . . . Bleistift . . . Lehrerin?

*E.* 1. That is our garden. 2. We work often in the garden. 3. The children like to play in the garden. 4. They play with the neighbour's children. 5. The gardener is working in the garden. 6. He is planting the flowers. 7. Father is planting the vegetables. 8. Which vegetables is he planting? 9. He is planting the cabbage and cauliflower. 10. Are you fond of flowers? 11. Yes, I am very fond of flowers. 12. To whom does your mother send flowers? 13. She sends flowers to my (meiner) aunt. 14. My aunt lives in the city, but she has no garden. 15. We need the flowers for the table and the vegetables for the kitchen. 16. The flowers on the teacher's table are very pretty. 17. My mother sends the teacher (*f.*) violets. 18. Send the teacher the violets.

*F.* Lesestück:

Es regnet. Gott segnet
Den hohen Baum, den kleinen Strauch
Und all die tausend Blumen auch.
O frischer Regen! Du Gottes Segen!

# LESSON VIII

**21.** **Present Indicative of tun, to do.**

I do, I am doing, etc.

| | |
|---|---|
| ich tue | wir tun |
| du tuſt | ihr tut |
| er tut | ſie tun |

Formal: Sie tun.

**22.** **Infinitive after Verbs.**

Ich wünſche, Ball zu ſpielen. I wish to play ball.

Ich habe Luſt, einen Spazier= I have a mind (want, wish) to
gang zu machen.　　　　　　take a walk.

OBSERVE: 1. Many verbs and nouns take an infinitive with
zu to complete their meaning.

2. This infinitive comes at the end of its clause, which is
preceded by a comma in German.

**23.** **Accusative Personal Pronouns.**

Personal pronouns have the following forms in the accusa·
tive, and agree in gender and number with the antecedent:

|  | *Singular.* | *Plural.* |
|---|---|---|
| *1st Pers.* | mich, me. | uns, us. |
| *2d Pers.* | dich, thee, you. | euch, you. |
| *3d Pers.* | ihn, him, it; ſie, her, it; es, it. | ſie, them. |

Formal: *Sing.* and *Plur.* Sie, you.

### EXAMPLES.

| | |
|---|---|
| Lobt er **mich** (uns)? | Does he praise me (us)? |
| Er lobt **Sie.** | He praises you. |
| Hat ſie den Ball? Sie hat ihn. | Has she the ball? She has it. |
| Hat er die Roſe? Er hat ſie. | Has he the rose? He has it. |

**24.**     **Dative Personal Pronouns.**

Personal pronouns have the following forms in the dative,
and agree :

| *Singular.* | *Plural.* |
|---|---|
| 1*st Pers.* mir, (to, for) me. | uns, (to, for) us. |
| 2*d Pers.* dir, (to, for) thee, you. | euch, (to, for) you. |
| 3*d Pers.* ihm, (to, for) him. ihr, (to, for) her. | ihnen, (to, for) them. |

Formal : *Sing.* and *Plur.* Ihnen, (to, for) you.

NOTE. — The neut. dat. ihm is used only of persons or animals.

### EXAMPLES.

| | |
|---|---|
| Geben Sie mir (uns) Geld. | Give me (us) money. |
| Ich gebe dir (euch) Brot. | I give bread to you. |
| Sie schenkt ihr ein Buch. | She gives her a book. |
| Er baut ihnen ein Haus. | He builds them a house. |
| Er baut Ihnen ein Haus. | He builds a house for you. |

OBSERVE : The German dative forms are rendered into English by a pronoun simply before the direct object, and by a
pronoun with 'to' or 'for' after the direct object.

### EXERCISE VIII

| | |
|---|---|
| besuchen, to visit, call on. | lieben, to love. |
| der Freund, friend. | das Papie'r, paper. |
| die Freunde, friends. | tun, to do. |
| jawohl, yes (indeed), O yes. | warum? why? |
| der Lärm, noise. | wünschen, to wish. |

IDIOMS: **Besuche machen,** to make calls, pay visits.
          **Lust haben** (zu + infin.), to have a mind to, want to.

*A.* 1. Lobt der Lehrer euch oft, Kinder?   2. Ja, er lobt uns
oft.   3. Die Schüler sind aufmerksam und der Lehrer lobt sie.
4. Wir lieben unsere Tante und bringen ihr oft Blumen.
5. Unser Vater ist sehr gütig und wir lieben ihn.   6. Er
erzählt uns oft Märchen und wir hören sie gern.   7. Liebst du
mich, mein Kind?   8. Jawohl, ich liebe dich, Vater.   9. Die

D

Kinder des Nachbars sind artig und wir spielen gern mit ihnen. 10. Wir spielen nicht gern mit dir; du bist unartig. 11. Der Gärtner bringt das Gemüse zur Stadt und verkauft es da. 12. Er verkauft mir viel Gemüse. 13. Verkauft er euch auch Gemüse? 14. Was schenken Sie dem Mädchen? 15. Wir schenken ihm eine Puppe. 16. Ich habe Lust, einen Spaziergang mit Ihnen zu machen. 17. Ich höre einen Lärm; hören Sie ihn auch? 18. Besuchen Sie Ihre Freunde oft? 19. Ja, wir besuchen sie oft. 20. Ich habe keine Lust, Besuche zu machen. 21. Ich wünsche einen Brief zu schreiben; wer hat meine Feder? 22. Karl hat sie. 23. Wo ist mein Papier? 24. Ich habe es hier.

*B.* Answer in German: 1. Wer hat meinen Bleistift? 2. Hat er auch meine Feder? 3. Hören Sie den Lärm? 4. Wen liebst du, mein Kind? 5. Spielt ihr gern mit mir? 6. Wer pflanzt das Gemüse? 7. Wo verkauft er die Blumen? 8. Haben Sie Lust, einen Spaziergang mit uns zu machen? 9. Was schenkst du dem Nachbar? 10. Was schenkst du mir? 11. Schicken Sie der Frau Blumen? 12. Lobt der Lehrer seine Schüler? 13. Was erzählt euch die Lehrerin? 14. Was schenkt die Mutter den Kindern? 15. Was schenkt Ihnen Ihre Mutter? 16. Wem schenkt sie den Ball? 17. Was tut der Gärtner? 18. Was tut ihr, Kinder? 19. Was tun Sie, Herr Braun?

*C.* 1. What do you wish to do? 2. I wish to visit my friend. 3. I like to visit him. 4. The gardener's children wish to play with us. 5. We do not want to play with them. 6. We like to play with you, Charles. 7. Our neighbour gives us flowers. 8. His gardener brings them to us. 9. We thank him for his flowers. 10. Does he bring you also flowers? 11. The gardener sells his vegetables; he sells them in the city. 12. We do not praise you; you are not attentive. 13. Why do you not learn your lesson? 14. I am learning it now. 15. Do you need your book? 16. Yes, I need it; please bring it to me.  17. Do you hear me?  18. Yes, I hear you quite well.

*D.* Lefeftück:

Am Haus ift ein Garten,  Da ruf' ich und fing' ich,
Da bin ich fo gern!  So laut es nur geht:
Da hüpf' ich und fpring' ich  Im Garten, im Garten,
Um Baum und um Beet;  Da bin ich fo gern!

# LESSON IX

**25.**  **Mein Model and Possessive Adjectives.**

|  | SINGULAR. |  |  | PLURAL. |
|---|---|---|---|---|
|  | *Masc.* | *Fem.* | *Neut.* | *All Genders.* |
| *N.* | mein | meine | mein | meine, my |
| *G.* | meines | meiner | meines | meiner, of my |
| *D.* | meinem | meiner | meinem | meinen, (to, for) my |
| *A.* | meinen | meine | mein | meine, my |

REMARKS: 1. Thus are declined the possessive adjectives:

mein, my.  fein, his, its.  unfer, our.  Ihr, your.
dein, thy.  ihr, her, its, their.  euer, your.

Also, ein, a, one (sing. only); fein, no, not any.

NOTE. — **Unfer** usually drops **e** before final –m or –n (unferm, unfern).

2. Observe the correspondence between the pronoun of address and the possessive:

Du lernft deine Aufgabe.  You learn your lesson.
Ihr lernt eure Aufgabe.  You learn your lesson.
Sie lernen Ihre Aufgabe.  You learn your lesson.

3. Observe also the correspondence for the third person, especially for fein and ihr, of inanimate objects:

Die Blume verliert ihre Farbe.  The flower loses its colour.
Das Gras verliert feine Farbe.  The grass loses its colour.
Sie hat ihren Hut.  She has her hat.

4. The termination of the possessive adjective depends on the gender, number, and case of the noun it qualifies (the thing possessed); the stem depends on the gender and number of the noun or pronoun to which it refers (the possessor), as in the examples above.

NOTE.— The neut. diminutive das Mädchen, 'the girl,' takes the pers. pron. and poss. adj. referring to it in the fem., unless a child is meant: Das Mädchen liebt **ihre** Mutter; **sie** liebt sie, 'The girl loves her mother; she loves her.'

## EXERCISE IX

das Badezimmer, bath-room.
das Bett, bed.
brennen, to burn.
der Bücherschrank, book-case.
essen, to eat.
fünf, five.
das Geschenk, gift, present.
gewöhnlich, usually, generally.
das Haus, house.
hinter (*dat.*), behind.
liegen, to lie, be situated, be.
neben (*dat.*), near, beside.
schlafen, to sleep.
das Schlafzimmer, bed-room.
sitzen, to sit.
sonst, else, or else, otherwise.
das Speisezimmer, dining-room.
der Spiegel, mirror.
das Studierzimmer, study (room).
die Stühle, the chairs.
suchen, to look for, seek.
vier, four.
das Wohnzimmer, sitting-room.
zehn, ten.

*A.* Continue the following, including all forms of the third person: 1. Ich suche meinen Bleistift, du ... deinen ... 2c. 2. Ich schicke meinem Bruder ein Geschenk, 2c. 3. Ich schenke meiner Schwester eine Puppe. 4. Ich brauche mein Buch (meine Bücher) nicht. 5. Ich besuche den Freund meines Bruders (meiner Schwester). 6. Ich suche das Haus meiner Freunde. 7. Ich liebe meine Mutter.

*B.* 1. Hier steht unser Haus. 2. Ist es nicht hübsch? 3. Ich wohne im Hause mit meinen Brüdern und meiner

Schwester. 4. Unser Vater und unsere Mutter wohnen auch im Hause. 5. Unser Haus hat nur zehn Zimmer und eine Küche. 6. Wir sitzen gewöhnlich im Wohnzimmer. 7. Wir essen im Speisezimmer und schlafen in unsern Schlafzimmern. 8. Das Studierzimmer meines Vaters ist groß und schön. 9. Er arbeitet jetzt in seinem Studierzimmer. 10. Seine Bücher stehen im Bücherschrank oder liegen auf seinem Schreibtisch. 11. Im Winter brennt immer ein Feuer im Zimmer. 12. Das Haus hat fünf Schlafzimmer. 13. Im Schlafzimmer meiner Mutter stehen ihr Bett und vier Stühle. 14. Die Fenster ihres Zimmers sind groß und machen es hell. 15. Ihr Spiegel steht neben dem Fenster. 16. Das Badezimmer ist neben dem Schlafzimmer meines Vaters. 17. Hinter dem Hause ist ein Garten. 18. Haben Sie auch einen Garten hinter Ihrem Hause?

*C.* Answer in German, introducing possessive forms where possible: 1. Was sucht Karl? 2. Wem schicken Sie ein Geschenk? 3. Wessen Bücher brauchen Sie? 4. Wen besuchen Sie? 5. Ist das Ihr Haus? 6. Wer wohnt in Ihrem Hause? 7. Wie viele Zimmer hat Ihr Haus? 8. Wo arbeitet Ihr Herr Vater? 9. Wo ist sein Studierzimmer? 10. Wo sind seine Bücher gewöhnlich? 11. Was liegt sonst auf seinem Schreibtisch? 12. Was liegt auf Ihrem Tische? 13. Wo steht der Spiegel Ihres Bruders? 14. Welches Zimmer ist groß und hell? 15. Wessen Garten ist das? 16. Wo ist der Garten des Nachbars?

*D.* 1. That is my house. 2. Your house is quite pretty. 3. I live here with my wife and our two children. 4. The sister of my wife lives here also (also here). 5. She is the aunt of my children. 6. My house has only ten rooms. 7. The children sleep in a room beside my wife's bedroom. 8. Our children are small and they sleep in one bed. 9. In their room [there] are also two chairs and a table. 10. Their

table stands near the window.   11. I work usually in my study.
12. My wife likes to sit there beside me.   13. Our children
play in the garden behind the house.   14. My neighbour's
children are playing with them.   15. What is the girl doing?
16. She is playing with her dog.   17. Is the boy playing with
the dog?   18. No, he is playing with his ball.   19. My children like to play with our neighbour's children.

*E.* Leſeſtück:

> Die Sonne geht zur Ruh',
> Vom Felde kommt die Kuh
> Und auch die Schäflein allzumal,
> Sie freu'n ſich ſchon auf ihren Stall.
> Im Baum da ſingt kein Vogel mehr,
> Die dunkle Nacht zieht ſchnell daher,
> Bald wird der Mond am Himmel ſtehn,
> Ich denk, 's iſt Zeit zu Bett zu gehn!
> Gut' Nacht!   Gut' Nacht!   Auf Wiederſehn!

# LESSON X

**26.**     Imperfect Indicative of ſein and haben.

| I was, etc. | | I had, etc. | |
|---|---|---|---|
| ich war | wir waren | ich hatte | wir hatten |
| du warſt | ihr wart | du hatteſt | ihr hattet |
| er war | ſie waren | er hatte | ſie hatten |
| Formal: Sie waren. | | Formal: Sie hatten. | |

**27.**     Imperfect Indicative of machen, to make.

| I made, was making, did make, etc. | | Was I making? did I make? etc. | |
|---|---|---|---|
| ich mach te | wir mach ten | machte ich? | machten wir? |
| du mach teſt | ihr mach tet | machteſt du? | machtet ihr? |
| er mach te | ſie mach ten | machte er? | machten ſie? |
| Formal: Sie machten. | | Formal: machten Sie? | |

Observe: A large number of verbs (called 'weak') form the imperfect indicative like machen, but infinitive stems ending in -t, -d, or consonants after which t cannot be pronounced, insert e between stem and ending (arbeitete, regnete, ⁊c.).

### 28. Strong Imperfects.

| Singen, to sing.<br>I sang, etc. | Bleiben, to remain.<br>I remained, etc. | Tun, to do.<br>I did, etc. |
|---|---|---|
| ich sang | ich blieb | ich tat |
| du sangst | du bliebst | du tatst |
| er sang | er blieb | er tat |
| wir sangen | wir blieben | wir taten |
| ihr sangt | ihr bliebt | ihr tatet |
| sie sangen | sie blieben | sie taten |

Observe: 1. Many verbs (called 'strong') form the imperfect indicative by changing the stem vowel, without adding a tense ending.

2. The person endings are the same as in other verbs.

Note. — The impf. indic. of such strong and irregular verbs as are used in the exercises will be given, for the present, in the vocabularies.

### 29. Adverbial Accusative.

| Er war diesen Sommer hier. | He was here this summer. |
|---|---|
| Er war einen Monat hier. | He was here a month. |
| Das Buch kostete einen Taler. | The book cost three shillings. |

Observe: Time and price are usually expressed by the accusative.

### 30. Word Order.

| Ich habe heute kein Geld. | I have no money to-day. |
|---|---|
| Mein Vetter ist heute hier. | My cousin is here to-day. |
| Heute ist das Wetter schön. | The weather is fine to-day. |
| Im Garten steht ein Baum. | A tree stands in the garden. |

Observe: 1. Adverbial expressions of time precede noun objects and other adverbs.

2. When any member of a principal sentence other than the subject precedes the verb the subject comes after the verb, which is the second idea in a principal assertive sentence.

## EXERCISE X

a'ntworten, to answer, reply.
bald, *comp.* eher, soon.
beginnen, begann, to begin, commence.
bleiben, blieb, to remain, stay.
dann, then.
der Dollar, dollar.
erreichen, to reach.
frisch, fresh, cool.
früher, earlier, formerly.
geben, gab, to give.
gehen, ging, to walk, go.
gestern, yesterday.
der Gott, God.
die Hand, hand.
der Knecht, man-servant, labourer.
die Knechte, labourers.
kosten, to cost.

lange (*adv.*), long, a long time.
die Lieder, songs.
nach (*dat.*), after.
neulich, lately, the other day.
ohne (*acc.*), without.
der Regenschirm, umbrella.
sagen, to say, tell.
sehen, sah, to see.
singen, sang, to sing.
die Stunde, hour.
der Wald, forest, wood(s).
wann? when?
weiter (*adv.*), further, along, on.
das Wetter, weather.
wohin? where (to)? whither?
wunderschön, very beautiful.
zu Hause, at home.

*A.* 1. Neulich machte ich einen Spaziergang mit einem Freunde. 2. Er hatte einen Stock in seiner Hand und ich hatte meinen Regenschirm. 3. Das Wetter war schön und die Luft frisch. 4. „Ist es nicht schön unter Gottes Himmel?" sagte ich. 5. „Jawohl!" antwortete mein Freund, „es ist wunderschön." 6. Wir gingen weiter und sahen bald einen Garten. 7. Im Garten waren Knechte. 8. Sie arbeiteten sehr fleißig. 9. Sie pflanzten Blumen und Gemüse. 10. Wir sahen auch ein Haus neben dem Garten. 11. Hinter dem Hause war ein Wald. 12. In dem Hause wohnte der Gärt-

ner mit seiner Frau und seinen Kindern. 13. Die Frau des
Gärtners schenkte uns Blumen und wir dankten ihr. 14. Wir
blieben eine Stunde im Walde hinter dem Garten und mein
Freund sang ein Lied. 15. Dann gingen wir nach Hause.
16. Es begann zu regnen und wir brauchten den Regenschirm.
17. Nach einer Stunde erreichten wir unser Haus in der
Stadt.

*B.* Continue: 1. Gestern war ich nicht hier, . . . du, rc.
2. Ich hatte meinen Stock, du . . . deinen, rc. 3. Früher
wohnte ich in der Stadt. 4. Ich arbeitete eine Stunde.
5. Ich blieb eine Stunde im Walde. 6. Ich sang viele Lieder.
7. Ich ging gestern zur Stadt. 8. Mein Regenschirm kostete
einen Dollar, dein, rc.

*C.* Answer: 1. Was tat ich neulich? 2. Wer ging mit mir?
3. Wie war das Wetter? 4. Wer arbeitete? 5. Wo?
6. Wessen Haus sahen wir? 7. Wer wohnte mit ihm? 8. Wo
war sein Haus? 9. Was schenkte uns die Frau? 10. Was
war hinter dem Garten? 11. Wie lange waren wir da?
12. Was tat mein Freund? 13. Was taten wir dann?
14. Brauchten wir den Regenschirm? 15. Wohin gingen wir?
16. Wann erreichten wir unser Haus?

*D.* 1. I visited my friend Schäfer yesterday. 2. I said to
him: "Do you want to take a walk with me?" 3. "No," replied he, "I do not want to take a walk to-day, I am not quite
well." 4. Then I went without him. 5. He remained at home.
6. The weather was not very fine, but it was not raining. 7. I
wished to visit a friend. 8. My friend lived in a house near
the wood. 9. His house had a garden. 10. His gardener was
working in the garden with the man-servant. 11. He was
planting cabbage and cauliflower. 12. The gardener's wife
was picking flowers. 13. My friend gave me the flowers.
14. I remained an hour in his house. 15. His wife played
on the (auf dem) piano, and sang me a song. 16. I thanked

her for the song.    17. Then we took a walk in the woods
behind his house.    18. After an hour I went home again.
19. It began to rain, and I needed my umbrella.

## LESSON XI

**31.**                    Dieſer Model.

| | SINGULAR. | | | PLURAL. |
| *Masc.* | *Fem.* | *Neut.* | | *All Genders.* |
| *N.* dieſer | dieſe | dieſes, this | | dieſe, these |
| *G.* dieſes | dieſer | dieſes, of this | | dieſer, of these |
| *D.* dieſem | dieſer | dieſem, (to, for) this | | dieſen, (to, for) these |
| *A.* dieſen | dieſe | dieſes, this | | dieſe, these |

REMARKS : 1. In the same way decline **jener**, 'that' (yonder);
**jeder**, 'each,' 'every'; **welcher?** 'which?'

NOTES.— 1. Dieſer is commonly used for 'that,' as well as for 'this.'

2. The unchanged **dies** (also jenes and welches?) is used, like **das**
(§ 8), before ſein : **Dies** iſt meine Schweſter, 'This is my sister';
**Welches** ſind meine Bücher? 'Which are my books?'

2. Thus also the short forms of the possessive pronouns :

| meiner, mine. | ſeiner, his, its. | unſ(e)rer, ours. |
| deiner, thine. | ihrer, hers, its, theirs. | eurer, yours. |
| | Ihrer, yours. | |

Further, **einer**, one ; **keiner**, none.

NOTE.—The contracted forms meins, deins, ſeins, eins, keins, are
often used in the nom. and acc. neut. sing.

**32.**            Use of Possessive Pronouns.

Ich habe meinen Hut; er hat I have my hat; he has his;
  ſeinen; ſie hat ihren.            she has hers.
Wir haben unſere Bücher und We have our books, and you
  Sie haben Ihre.            have yours.
Dieſer Hut iſt mein(er).            This hat is mine.

Observe: 1. The possessive pronouns correspond with their antecedent like the possessive adjectives (§ 25, 4), but their case depends on their relation in the sentence.

2. When used as predicates, they may also have the uninflected forms mein, dein, sein, ꝛc.

### EXERCISE XI

der Abend, evening.
an (dat.), on, by, at.
auf Besuch, on a visit.
auf dem Lande, in the country.
die Aussicht, view, prospect.
bei (dat.), at, near, by.
bei uns, at our house.
bewundern, to admire.
fahren, fuhr, to go (in a vehicle), drive, etc.
die Fe'rien (pl. only), holidays.
heute, to-day.
die Insel, island.
der Kahn, row-boat, canoe, skiff.

das Landhaus, country-house.
der Mo'nat, month.
das Motorboot, motor-boat.
der See, lake.
sitzen, saß, sit.
so, as, thus.
das Ufer, shore, bank.
die Veranda, veranda.
verbringen, verbrachte, to spend, pass (time).
von (dat.), of, from.
das Wasser, water.
die Zeit, time.

*A.* 1. Wo verbrachten Sie diesen Sommer die Ferien? 2. Wir verbrachten unsere auf dem Lande; wo verbrachten Sie Ihre? 3. Wir verbrachten unsere an einem See. 4. Unser Landhaus steht auf einer Insel in diesem See. 5. Ein Freund meines Vaters, Herr Müller, hat auch eins, aber seins ist nicht auf der Insel, es steht am Ufer des Sees. 6. Wie verbrachten Sie die Zeit? 7. Wir verbrachten sie gewöhnlich auf dem Wasser. 8. Ich hatte ein Motorboot und meine Freunde hatten auch eins. 9. Ihres war größer als meins. 10. Mein Freund Albert war bei uns auf Besuch. 11. Jeder von uns hatte einen Kahn. 12. Seiner war nicht so groß wie meiner. 13. Wir fuhren jeden Tag auf dem Wasser. 14. Er fuhr in seinem Kahne und ich in meinem. 15. Jeden Abend saßen

wir auf unserer Veranda und bewunderten die Aussicht.
16. So verbrachten wir einen Monat sehr angenehm.

*B.* Fill in the blanks with a suitable word or words of the dieser model: 1. Mein Regenschirm kostete einen Dollar; wie viel kostete ..........? 2. Ist Ihre Feder so gut wie ......? 3. Dieses Buch ist ......; welches ist .....? 4. Mein Vater ist älter als ..... 5. Ich habe kein Messer; haben Sie ....? 6. Haben Sie einen Bleistift? Ich habe ....... 7. Mein Bleistift ist kleiner als ..... 8. Ihr Bleistift ist kleiner als ..... 9. Welcher Hut ist größer, ..... oder .....? 10. Wo ist ein Stock? Hier ist ......

*C.* Answer, using pronominal forms: 1. Hat Herr Müller ein Landhaus? 2. Welches Landhaus ist schöner, dieses oder jenes? 3. Wessen Motorboot ist größer? 4. Wessen ist kleiner? 5. Welches Motorboot bewundern Sie? 6. Fuhr sein Kahn schneller als deiner? 7. Wessen Kahn brauchten sie gestern? 8. Welchen Kahn brauchen wir heute, diesen oder jenen? 9. Auf welcher Veranda saßen Sie? 10. Wessen Freund ist Albert? 11. Sind diese Bücher mein? 12. Wessen Bleistift ist dies?

*D.* 1. Has your father a country-house? 2. Yes, he has one. 3. Where is his country-house? 4. It is (stands) on (an) the shore of a lake. 5. My father's friend, Mr. Müller, has also one. 6. His is beside ours. 7. His house is larger than ours, but ours is prettier than his. 8. Here we passed our holidays this summer. 9. Where did you pass yours? 10. I passed mine on an island in the lake. 11. My friend Albert Schäfer visited me there. 12. Each of us had a canoe. 13. Which canoe went (fahren) faster, yours or his? 14. His went faster than mine. 15. We went on the water every day, or took a walk on the shore. 16. The view from our veranda was very fine. 17. We often sat there and admired it. 18. Thus we passed the summer very pleasantly. 19. After a month we went (fahren) to the city with my father and mother.

*E.* Leſeſtück:

> Du biſt wie eine Blume
> So hold und ſchön und rein;
> Ich ſchau' dich an, und Wehmut
> Schleicht mir ins Herz hinein.
>
> Mir iſt, als ob ich die Hände
> Aufs Haupt dir legen ſollt',
> Betend, daß Gott dich erhalte
> So rein und ſchön und hold.
>
> — Heine.

# LESSON XII

Review Lessons VII–XI.

### EXERCISE XII

bitten, bat, to request; ask for (um, *acc.*).

der Durſt, thirst.

durſtig, thirsty.

entſchuldigen, to excuse.

die Fami'lie, family.

das Fräulein, young lady, Miss.

die Gabel, fork.

die Gabeln, forks.

die Kartoffel, potato.

die Kartoffeln, potatoes.

kommen, kam, to come.

leid tun (*dat. of pers.*), to be sorry.

lieber, rather.

der Löffel, spoon.

die Löffel, spoons.

die Magd, maid.

die Milch, milk.

das Mütterchen, mother dear.

oben, at the top, above.

reichen, to pass, hand.

richtig, right, correct.

ſcheinen, ſchien, to seem.

ſchmecken, to taste.

ſchneiden, ſchnitt, to cut.

der Spargel, asparagus.

ſpät, late.

der Teller, plate.

die Teller, plates.

die Uhr, clock, watch.

um (*acc.*), around, for.

unten, at the bottom, below.

Wilhelm, William.

zur Schule, to school.

zwei, two.

zwiſchen (*dat.*), between.

IDIOMS: 1. **Ich habe Durst** (bin durstig), I am thirsty.
2. **Das schmeckt mir,** I like (the taste of) that.
3. **Ich esse lieber,** 2c., I would rather eat, I prefer, etc.
4. **Diese Uhr geht richtig,** This watch is right.
5. **Ich danke,** No, thank you.

*A.* 1. Die Familie sitzt am Tische. 2. Oben sitzt der Vater, unten die Mutter, zwischen ihnen sitzen die Kinder. 3. Unser Vater schneidet uns das Fleisch. 4. Er schneidet es mit einem Messer. 5. Wir essen von unseren Tellern. 6. Jeder von uns hat einen Teller, ein Messer, eine Gabel und einen Löffel. 7. Mein Messer ist scharf. 8. Wilhelm hat auch eins, aber seins ist nicht so scharf wie meins. 9. Meins ist schärfer als seins. 10. Die Magd reicht den Kindern das Gemüse. 11. Wir haben heute Kartoffeln und Spargel. 12. Wünschest du Spargel, mein Junge? 13. Ich danke, Mütterchen; er schmeckt mir nicht. 14. Ich esse lieber Kartoffeln. 15. Was wünschest du, Bertha? 16. Ich bitte um Milch; ich habe Durst. 17. Es ist jetzt Zeit, zur Schule zu gehen. 18. Gestern kamen wir spät. 19. Die Lehrerin schien böse zu sein. 20. Wir sagten: „Es tut uns leid, Fräulein Braun; unsere Uhr geht nicht richtig." 21. Dann entschuldigte sie uns.

*B.* Oral exercise on the above.

*C.* Continue the following: 1. Ich sitze (saß) am Tische, du, 2c. 2. Ich schneide Fleisch mit einem Messer. 3. Ich habe (hatte) keinen Teller. 4. Ich kam spät zur Schule. 5. Ich reiche (reichte) den Kindern die Kartoffeln. 6. Ich habe (hatte) Durst. 7. Ich entschuldige (entschuldigte) die Kinder. 8. Es tut (tat) mir leid, es . . . dir, 2c.

*D.* 1. The children were sitting at the table with their father and mother. 2. Their father cut the meat. 3. He cut it with a knife. 4. Each of them had two knives, two forks, and two spoons. 5. Charles' knife was sharp; it was sharper than William's. 6. William's knife was not so sharp as his. 7. The maid handed each child the vegetables.　8. They had potatoes and asparagus.　9. They like potatoes and asparagus.　10. Mary was thirsty, and her mother gave her milk.　11. Yesterday the children were (came) late to (the) school.　12. Their clock was wrong.　13. Ours is always right.　14. Their father and mother asked the teacher to excuse them.

*E.* Lefeſtück :

Tiſchgebet.

Speiſe, Vater, deine Kinder,
Tröſte die betrübten Sünder,
Sprich den Segen zu den Gaben,
Welche wir jetzt vor uns haben,
Daß ſie uns zu dieſem Leben
Stärke, Kraft und Nahrung geben.
— Johann Heerman.

## LESSON XIII

**33.**　　　　Strong Declension of Nouns.

I. der **Hund,** dog.　　II. der **Sohn,** son.

| *Sing.* | *Plur.* | *Sing.* | *Plur.* |
|---|---|---|---|
| *N.* der Hund | die Hunde | der Sohn | die Söhne |
| *G.* des Hund(e)s | der Hunde | des Sohn(e)s | der Söhne |
| *D.* dem Hund(e) | den Hunden | dem Sohn(e) | den Söhnen |
| *A.* den Hund | die Hunde | den Sohn | die Söhne |

III. die **Hand,** hand.

| *Sing.* | *Plur.* |
|---|---|
| die Hand | die Hände |
| der Hand | der Hände |
| der Hand | den Händen |
| die Hand | die Hände |

NOTE. — For classes of nouns so declined, see Lesson XIX.

REMARKS : 1. These three models are merely variations of the same type of noun declension (called the primary form of the 'strong declension ').

**2.** Feminines are invariable in the singular; masculines and neuters take –es in the genitive and –e in the dative singular.

Notes. — 1. The e of the gen. and dat. sing. is usual in monosyllables, less so in polysyllables, but e of the gen. is always retained after final ⼔ sound.

2. The e of the dat. sing. is omitted when a prep. immediately precedes. aus Holz, 'of wood'; but exceptionally, zu Hauſe, nach Hauſe.

3. Nouns in -nis double the last consonant before an ending: Bedürf= nis, 'need,' gen. sing. Bedürfniſſes, nom. plur. Bedürfniſſe; so also ß = ſſ after short stem vowel: Fluß, 'river,' Fluſſes, Flüſſe. *single ß's*

**3.** All add –e in the plural with additional –n in the dative.

**4.** Many masculines with stem-vowel a, o, u, au, and all femi- nine monosyllables of this model, take umlaut in the plural.

**34. Essential Parts.** By observing the case forms which are identical, the full declension of any noun may be inferred from the nominative singular, genitive singular, and nominative plural, which are given in the dictionary for this purpose.

**35. Compound Nouns.** In compound nouns the last com- ponent only is declined; they usually follow the gender of the last component:

| *Nom. Sing.* | *Gen. Sing.* | *Nom. Plur.* |
|---|---|---|
| der Handſchuh, glove. | des Handſchuh(e)s | die Handſchuhe |
| der Obſtbaum, fruit-tree. | des Obſtbaum(e)s | die Obſtbäume |

Note. — Compounds with –mann have as plur. –männer (individuals or occupations), or –leute (collectively): Staatsmänner, 'statesmen'; Landleute, 'country-people.'

**36. Rule of Gender.** Most nouns in –ich, –ig, –ing, –ling, and foreign nouns in –al, –an, –ar, –ier, –or are masculine.

### EXERCISE XIII

*N.B.* The gen. sing. fem. is not given, being the same as the nom.

der Arm, –(e)s, –e, arm.

der Arzt, –es, ᵘe, physician, doctor.

bekommen, bekam, to get, re- ceive.

bringen, brachte, to bring.

der Fluß, –es, ᵘe, river.

der Fuß, –es, ᵘe, foot.

der Handschuh,–(e)s,–e,glove.

das Heu, –(e)s, hay.

das Jahr, –(e)s, –e, year.

der Kopf, –(e)s, ᵘe, head.

die Kuh, ᵘe, cow.

nützlich, useful.

der Obstbaum,–(e)s, ᵘe, fruit-tree.

der Offizie'r, –(e)s,–e, officer (military).

das Pferd, –es, –e, horse.

prächtig, splendid, magnificent.

das Schaf, –(e)s, –e, sheep.

das Schiff, –(e)s, –e, ship.

sieben, seven.

das Tier, –(e)s, –e, animal, beast.

die Woche, –n, week.

zwölf, twelve.

NOTE. — The sign ᵘ indicates umlaut.

*A.* 1. Decline in full without umlaut: der Brief, mein Arm, welcher Tag, dieses Jahr, kein Knecht. 2. With umlaut: der Hut, mein Stuhl, dieser Baum, welcher Sohn, diese Kuh, der Obstbaum. 3. Supply the remaining cases of the following, explaining how they may be inferred from the forms given: *Nom. Sing.* Geschenk (*n.*), *Gen.* –(e)s, *Plur.* –e ; Tisch (*m.*), –es, –e ; Kopf (*m.*), –(e)s, ᵘe ; Freund (*m.*), –es, –e ; Stadt (*f.*), —, ᵘe ; Schaf (*n.*), –(e)s,–e ; Fuß (*m.*), –es, ᵘe ; Offizier (*m.*), –(e)s, –e ; Monat (*m.*), –(e)s, –e.

*B.* 1. Die Söhne des Arztes besuchen ihre Freunde in der Stadt. 2. Auf diesem Stuhle liegen zwei Hüte : meiner und Ihrer. 3. Meine Handschuhe liegen auf dem Tische. 4. Das Haus meines Freundes steht am Ufer des Flusses. 5. In seinem Garten stehen zwei Obstbäume. 6. Die Schiffe fahren auf den Flüssen. 7. Die Knechte bringen den Pferden Heu. 8. Wir geben den Pferden, den Kühen und den Schafen Heu. 9. Diese Tiere sind uns sehr nützlich. 10. Die Pferde der Offiziere sind prächtig. 11. Wir haben zwei Hände, zwei Füße, zwei Arme, aber nur einen Kopf. 12. In jedem Jahre sind zwölf Monate. 13. Sieben Tage machen eine Woche.

E

14. Ich schickte heute meinem Freunde einen Brief. 15. In diesem Briefe erzählte ich ihm von meinen zwei Hunden. 16. Diese waren ein Geschenk von meinem Vater. 17. Jeden Tag mache ich einen Spaziergang mit meinen Hunden. 18. Ich bekam gestern Geschenke von meinen Freunden. 19. Es ist sehr angenehm, Freunde zu haben und Geschenke zu bekommen.

*C.* Oral exercise on the above.

*D.* 1. I received a present yesterday from my father. 2. He sent me two dogs. 3. These were quite young and very handsome. 4. I am very fond of these animals. 5. They take a walk every day with me. 6. I get presents often from my father and my friends. 7. That is very pleasant for me. 8. I received two letters from my friend Albert to-day. 9. My brother brought them home. 10. In these letters Albert told (erzählen) me about (von) his holidays. 11. He spent them in the country. 12. His uncle has a house there. 13. His uncle has many animals — horses, cows, sheep, etc. 14. He has also many fruit-trees behind his house. 15. They are large and very fine. 16. The house is on (an) the shore of a river. 17. His uncle has also a ship. 18. My friend used to sail (fuhr) every day in this ship. 19. Albert is the son of a physician in this city. 20. His father lives near (neben) us. 21. My father and his are friends.

*E.* Lesestück:

### Wandrers Nachtlied.

Über allen Gipfeln
Ist Ruh',
In allen Wipfeln
Spürest du
Kaum einen Hauch;
Die Vögelein schweigen im Walde.
Warte nur, balde
Ruhest du auch.

—Goethe.

## LESSON XIV

**37.**　　　Perfect Indicative of **haben, spielen.**

I have had (played, been playing), etc.

ich habe gehabt (gespielt)　　　wir haben gehabt (gespielt)
du hast gehabt (gespielt)　　　ihr habt　gehabt (gespielt)
er hat　gehabt (gespielt)　　　sie haben gehabt (gespielt)

Formal: Sie haben gehabt (gespielt).

OBSERVE: 1. Verbs conjugated with **haben** form this tense by adding the past participle to the present of **haben,** as auxiliary.

2. The past participle of weak verbs is usually formed by prefixing **ge–** and adding **–t** (or **–et** after b, t, etc.; see § 27) to the stem, *e.g.* spiel=en, ge=spiel=t; arbeit=en, ge=arbeit=et.

NOTE.— The past part. of all strong verbs will be given for the present in the vocabularies.

**38.**　　　　　Use of Perfect Tense.

The German perfect corresponds to the English perfect, but also often replaces the English past, especially when referring to a period recently completed, or to an independent fact:

　　Ich habe es gehört.　　　　I have heard it.
　　Ich habe es gestern gehört.　I heard it yesterday.

**39.**　　　Pluperfect Indicative of **haben, loben.**

I had had (praised, been praising), etc.

ich hatte　gehabt (gelobt)　　　wir hatten gehabt (gelobt)
du hattest gehabt (gelobt)　　　ihr hattet gehabt (gelobt)
er hatte　gehabt (gelobt)　　　sie hatten gehabt (gelobt)

OBSERVE: Verbs conjugated with **haben** form this tense by adding the past participle to the imperfect of **haben,** as auxiliary.

**40.**    Word Order in Principal Sentences.

Verb.

| Er | ift | heute nicht krank. |
| Der Vater des Schülers | war | hier. |
| Hier | ift | der Vater des Schülers. |
| Im Sommer | find | die Bäume schön. |
| Das Kind | hat | heute nicht viel gespielt. |

OBSERVE: 1. In principal sentences making a statement, the verb is the second idea (not necessarily the second word).

2. Any member, except the verb, may occupy the first place.

3. When any member other than the subject precedes the verb, the subject, with its attributes and enlargements, is thrown after the verb, and occupies the third place.

4. The auxiliary is the verb in compound tenses, and the past participle comes last in the perfect and pluperfect.

NOTES.— 1. The connectives und, aber, oder, denn, do not affect the word order.    2. The rules of word order are often disregarded in verse.

**41.**              Cardinal Numerals.

| | | |
|---|---|---|
| 1. eins | 11. elf | 21. ein und zwanzig |
| 2. zwei | 12. zwölf | 22. zwei und zwanzig |
| 3. drei | 13. dreizehn | 30. dreißig |
| 4. vier | 14. vierzehn | 40. vierzig |
| 5. fünf | 15. fünfzehn | 50. fünfzig |
| 6. sechs | 16. sechzehn | 60. sechzig |
| 7. sieben | 17. sieb(en)zehn | 70. sieb(en)zig |
| 8. acht | 18. achtzehn | 80. achtzig |
| 9. neun | 19. neunzehn | 90. neunzig |
| 10. zehn | 20. zwanzig | 100. hundert |

101. hundert (und) eins    123. hundert (und) drei und zwanzig

200. zweihundert           1001. tausend und eins

1000. tausend              1,000,000. eine Millio'n

1897. achtzehn hundert sieben und neunzig, or
tausend acht hundert sieben und neunzig.

OBSERVE: 1. The form eins is used in counting.

2. In compound numbers from 21 upwards, the units precede the tens, and are joined to them by unb: 25 = fünf unb zwanzig (Eng. 'five and twenty'); 156 = hundert sechs und fünfzig.

3. Hundert and tausend generally omit ein before and may omit und after them.

**42. Multiplicative Adverbs.** They are formed by adding –mal, 'time,' to the cardinals.

Einmal; zweimal; zehnmal. Once; twice; ten times.

### EXERCISE XIV

des Abends, in the evening.
addieren, to add (arith.).
Deutschland, n., –s, Germany.
der Dezember, December.
dividieren, to divide (arith.).
durch (acc.), through, by.
England, n., –s, England.
Englisch, English (language).
fast, almost, nearly.
finden, fand, gefunden, to find.
geben, gab, gegeben, to give.
gestern morgen, yesterday morning.
heute morgen, this morning.
das Vergnügen, –s, pleasure.

lassen, ließ, gelassen, to leave, let.
der Morgen, –s, —, morning.
des Morgens, in the morning.
multiplizieren, to multiply.
das Schaltjahr, –(e)s, –e, leap-year.
die Schlittenfahrt, –en, sleigh-ride (drive).
schreiben, schrieb, geschrieben, to write.
subtrahieren, to subtract.
tanzen, to dance.
tun, tat, getan, to do.

IDIOMS: 1. **Eine Schlittenfahrt machen,** to take (go for) a sleigh-ride (drive).

2. **Ich habe viel Vergnügen gehabt,** I have enjoyed myself very much.

*A.* Continue: 1. Ich habe (hatte) einen Hund gehabt, du hast (hattest), 2c. 2. Ich habe (hatte) meinem Freunde einen Brief geschrieben, du . . . deinem, 2c. 3. Was habe ich gestern morgen getan? 4. Neulich habe (hatte) ich einen Spaziergang gemacht. 5. Heute morgen habe ich meiner Mutter Blumen geschenkt. 6. Ich habe (hatte) diese Woche im Garten gespielt. 7. Eins und eins macht zwei, zwei und eins macht drei (continue up to thirty). 8. Zweimal eins ist zwei, zweimal zwei ist vier (continue up to thirty).

*B.* Read in German: 2 mal 11 ist 22, 3 mal 12 ist 36, 4 mal 8 ist 32, 5 mal 9 ist 45, 6 mal 7 ist 42, 7 × (mal) 10 ist 70, 8 × 11 ist 88, 9 × 12 ist 108, 10 × 10 ist 100, 11 × 11 ist 121, 12 × 12 ist 144. Addieren Sie 2,341, 25,891 und 989,346. Subtrahieren Sie 27,763 von 31,551. Multiplizieren Sie 591 mit 478. Dividieren Sie 2,581,640 durch 61.

*C.* 1. Im Dezember haben wir viel Schnee gehabt. 2. Gestern haben wir viel Vergnügen gehabt. 3. Des Morgens hatten wir eine Schlittenfahrt gemacht und des Abends hatten wir getanzt. 4. Mein Bruder hat Deutsch gelernt. 5. Er hat vier Jahre in Deutschland gewohnt. 6. Früher hatte er in England gewohnt. 7. Er hat in unserer Schule Deutsch gelehrt. 8. Da hatte er 25 Schüler. 9. In Deutschland hatte er Englisch gelehrt. 10. Seine Schüler haben viel von ihm gelernt. 11. Sie sind fast immer fleißig und aufmerksam. 12. Haben Sie meinen Bleistift gehabt? 13. Nein, ich habe ihn heute morgen nicht gehabt. 14. Ich hatte ihn in meinem Studierzimmer gelassen. 15. Er war auf dem Tische, aber jetzt liegt er nicht mehr da. 16. Ich habe ihn da gesucht, aber nicht gefunden.

*D.* 1. We often went for a sleigh-ride in (the) January. 2. Yesterday we enjoyed ourselves very much. 3. In the morning we went for a walk. 4. In the evening we played and danced. 5. I have been looking for my pencil, but I have not found it. 6. Have you had it? 7. No, but it was in your study this morning. 8. It was on your table. 9. Here it is; I have found it now. 10. My sister is living in Germany now. 11. She had lived five years in England. 12. She had been teaching German in a school. 13. She had more than thirty pupils. 14. A year has twelve months. 15. They are called (heißen) January, etc. (see below). 16. Four of (von) these months have thirty days. 17. Seven have thirty-one days.

*it has = es gibt*
*there are = sie*

18. (The) February has usually twenty-eight days, but in a leap-year it has twenty-nine.   19. The days of the week are called Sunday, etc.   20. Each week has seven days.   21. The year has usually three hundred and sixty-five days, but in a leap-year it has three hundred and sixty-six.

*E.* Commit to memory: Die Monate des Jahres sind: Januar, Februar, März, Apri'l, Mai, Ju'ni, Ju'li, Augu'st, September, Oktober, November, Dezember.

Die Tage der Woche sind: Sonntag, Montag, Dienstag, Mittwoch, Donnerstag, Freitag, Sonnabend oder Samstag.

Die vier Jahreszeiten sind: Frühling, Sommer, Herbst, Winter.

NOTE.—All are masc., and usually require art.; names of months are rarely inflected.

## LESSON XV

**43.**     **Strong Declension of Nouns** (*continued*).

### IV. das Dorf, village.

| Singular. | Plural. |
|---|---|
| *N.* das Dorf | die Dörf er |
| *G.* des Dorf(e)s | der Dörf er |
| *D.* dem Dorf(e) | den Dörf ern |
| *A.* das Dorf | die Dörf er |

NOTE.—For classes of nouns so declined, see Lesson XIX.

REMARKS: 1. The singular is after the Hund model (§ 33).

2. The Dorf model differs from the Hund model by adding **-er** in the plural (a, o, u, stems always with umlaut), and is called the 'enlarged form.'

| V. der Maler, painter. | | VI. der Vater, father. | |
|---|---|---|---|
| *Singular.* | *Plural.* | *Singular.* | *Plural.* |
| *N.* der Maler | die Maler | der Vater | die Väter |
| *G.* des Maler s | der Maler | des Vater s | der Väter |
| *D.* dem Maler | den Maler n | dem Vater | den Väter n |
| *A.* den Maler | die Maler | den Vater | die Väter |

Notes. — 1. For classes of nouns so declined, see Lesson XIX.
2. Nouns in –n do not add –n in dat. plur.: Garten, Gärten.

Remark : These models differ from Hund and Sohn only in the omission of e in the various endings, and are further variations of the strong declension — called the ' contracted form.'

**44. Rules of Gender.** 1. Most nouns in –el, –er, are masculine.
2. Collectives beginning with Ge– and ending in –e are generally neuter.

**45.** **Pres. and Impf. Indic. of können, müssen.**

| *Present.* | | *Imperfect.* | |
|---|---|---|---|
| I can, am able to, etc. | I must, have to, etc. | I could, was able to, etc. | I had to, was obliged to, etc. |
| ich kann | ich muß | ich konnte | ich mußte |
| du kannst | du mußt | du konntest | du mußtest |
| er kann | er muß | er konnte | er mußte |
| wir können | wir müssen | wir konnten | wir mußten |
| ihr könnt | ihr müßt | ihr konntet | ihr mußtet |
| sie können | sie müssen | sie konnten | sie mußten |

### Examples.

| | |
|---|---|
| Ich kann heute nicht kommen. | I cannot come to-day. |
| Er konnte nicht laufen. | He was unable to run. |
| Wir müssen bleiben. | We must stay. |
| Sie mußten schwer arbeiten. | They had to work hard. |

Observe : 1. These verbs govern an infinitive (without zu), which comes at the end in a principal sentence.

2. As the English ' must' has no past tense, the German imperfect must be variously rendered as above.

### EXERCISE XV

auf ei'nmal, at once.
die Axt, ⁻e, axe.
bedeckt, covered.

beide, both.
der Berg, –(e)s, –e, hill, mountain.

betrachten, to observe, consider.

das Dach, –(e)s, "er, roof.

der Dampfer, –s, —, steamer.

denn (*conj.*), for.

dort, there, yonder.

ei'nmal, once.

fällen, to fell, cut down.

das Feld, –es, –er, field.

das Gebirge, –s, —, mountain-range, range of hills.

hacken, to hew, chop, cut.

der Hintergrund, –es, "e, background.

das Holz, –es, "er, wood (material).

die Landschaft, –en, landscape.

links, on the (to the) left.

man (*pron.*), one, people, etc.

der Mann, –(e)s, "er, man.

mehrere (*pl.*), several.

morgen, to-morrow.

rechts, on the (to the) right.

das Schloß, –es, "er, castle.

das Segelschiff, –(e)s, –e, sailing-vessel, ship.

sehen, sah, gesehen, to see.

so, so.

das Stroh, –(e)s, straw.

das Tal, –(e)s, "er, valley.

der Taler, –s, —, thaler (3s.).

der Vordergrund, –es, "e, foreground.

was für? what kind (sort) of?

zerfallen, ruined, in ruins.

*A.* 1. Decline throughout like Dorf: der Wald, welches Haus, dieses Schloß, mein Buch, kein Mann. 2. Decline like Maler: unser Lehrer, das Badezimmer, kein Fenster, dieses Mädchen. 3. Decline like Vater: dieser Garten, unsere Mutter, Ihr Bruder. 4. Supply the remaining cases of the following: Garten (*m.*), –s, " ; Arzt (*m.*), –es, "e ; Landhaus (*n.*), –es, "er ; Feld (*n.*), –es, –er ; Schiff (*n.*), –es, –e ; Taler (*m.*), –s, — ; Tal (*n.*), –es, "er ; Gebirge (*n.*), –s, — ; Hand (*f.*), —, "e. 5. Continue: Ich kann meine Bücher nicht finden, du . . . deine, 2c. Ich konnte heute morgen meine Aufgabe nicht machen, du . . . deine, 2c. Ich muß morgen zur Schule gehen. Ich mußte gestern Briefe schreiben.

*B.* 1. Betrachten Sie diese Landschaft. 2. Hier können wir so viel auf einmal sehen: Einen Fluß, eine Stadt mit vielen Häusern, und hinter der Stadt Felder und Wälder, Berge und Täler. 3. Im Vordergrunde liegt die Stadt an

den Ufern eines Flusses.  4. Auf dem Flusse fahren Segel=
schiffe, Dampfer und Kähne.  5. Im Hintergrunde kann man
ein Gebirge sehen.  6. Hinter der Stadt liegen mehrere Dör=
fer.  7. Die Dächer der Häuser in diesen Dörfern sind mit
Stroh bedeckt.  8. Dort arbeiten die Männer fleißig in ihren
Gärten und Feldern.  9. Rechts auf dem Berge hinter den
Dörfern können Sie einen Wald sehen.  10. In diesem Walde
müssen die Knechte Bäume fällen und mit ihren Äxten Holz
hacken.  11. Im Hintergrunde links kann ich auch zwei
Schlösser sehen.  12. Diese Schlösser müssen sehr alt sein,
denn sie sind beide ganz zerfallen.

*C.*  Oral: 1. Was liegt in dem Tale?  2. Was kann man
auf dem Berge rechts sehen?  3. Wer wohnt da?  4. Was für
Dächer haben die Häuser?  5. Wer arbeitet hier?  6. Wo
arbeiten sie?  7. Was steht hinter den Dörfern?  8. Wer
arbeitet dort?  9. Was müssen sie tun?  10. Was können Sie
auf dem Berge links sehen?

*D.*  1. This landscape is very fine.  2. One can see hills
and valleys, towns and villages.  3. In the foreground on the
right lie two villages.  4. The windows of the houses are small,
and the roofs are covered with straw.  5. The houses in the
villages in Germany are often covered with straw.  6. In the
valley on the left lie two towns; can you see them?  7. The
houses in the towns are larger and finer than the houses of the
villages, but the gardens are smaller.  8. In the background
one can see hills.  9. On the hills to the right stand two castles.
10. Castles usually stand on hills.  11. These castles are in
ruins, for they are very old.  12. I can see two steamers on
the river and also three row-boats.  13. In the fields [there]
are cows and horses.  14. They are standing under the trees,
for it is very hot.  15. The labourers are working in the fields
and in the woods.  16. They are making hay, and felling trees
with their axes.

*E.* Lesestück : Ein Maler hatte ein Bildnis vom Sohne eines
Kaufmanns gemalt.  Der Künstler war einmal bei dem Kaufmann auf Besuch.  Der Kaufmann zeigte ihm das Bild seines
Sohnes und sagte : "Dieses Bild ist meinem Sohne sehr ähnlich."  Der Maler antwortete : "Das freut mich sehr, aber ich
habe noch kein Geld von ihm für das Bild erhalten."  Der
Vater erwiderte : "Das ist ihm auch sehr ähnlich."

## LESSON XVI

**46.**                **Present Indicative of werden.**

| | |
|---|---|
| ich werde | wir werden |
| du wirst | ihr werdet |
| er wird | sie werden |

Formal : Sie werden.

OBSERVE : The **i** of the second and third singular.

**47.**          **Future Indicative of haben, machen.**

I shall have (make), thou wilt, etc.

| | |
|---|---|
| ich werde haben (machen) | wir werden haben (machen) |
| du wirst haben (machen) | ihr werdet haben (machen) |
| er wird haben (machen) | sie werden haben (machen) |

Formal : Sie werden haben (machen).

OBSERVE : This tense is formed by adding the infinitive to
the present indicative of werden, as auxiliary.

**48.**           **Future Perfect of haben, machen.**

I shall have had (made), etc.

| | |
|---|---|
| ich werde gehabt (gemacht) haben | wir werden gehabt (gemacht) haben |
| du wirst gehabt (gemacht) haben | ihr werdet gehabt (gemacht) haben |
| er wird gehabt (gemacht) haben | sie werden gehabt (gemacht) haben |

Observe : This tense is formed by inserting the past participle of the verb before the infinitive of the future of the auxiliary.

### 49. Word Order.

| | |
|---|---|
| Wir werden Zeit haben. | We shall have time. |
| Er wird Zeit gehabt haben. | He will have had time. |

Observe : In these tenses the infinitive comes at the end, preceded by the past participle if both occur.

### 50. Separable Prefixes.

| | |
|---|---|
| Ausschicken, abreisen. | To send out, to set out. |
| Zumachen, ausgehen. | To close, to go out. |
| Ich schickte das Kind aus. | I sent the child out. |
| Reist er heute ab? | Does he set out to-day? |
| Machen Sie die Tür zu. | Close the door. |
| Ich wünsche auszugehen. | I wish to go out. |
| Er wird morgen fortgehen. | He will go away to-morrow. |
| Wer hat die Tür aufgemacht? | Who opened the door? |

Observe : 1. Certain prepositions and adverbs (such as aus, mit, nach, fort) are much used as prefixes to verbs, and are always stressed.

2. In the simple tenses these particles come at the end of principal sentences (including direct questions and commands).

3. They precede and are written as one word with the infinitive (with or without zu) and the past participle, wherever these occur.

### 51. Inseparable Prefixes. 1. The prefixes be-, er-, emp-, ent-, ge-, ver-, zer-, are always inseparable and unstressed.

2. Verbs with these prefixes omit the ge- of the past participle :

| | |
|---|---|
| Betrachten Sie das Bild. | Observe the picture. |
| Er hat das Haus verkauft. | He has sold the house. |

**52.** Compound verbs are conjugated like the simple verbs from which they are derived: ausſchicken, ſchickte aus, aus= geſchickt; ausſteigen, ſtieg aus, ausgeſtiegen.

### EXERCISE XVI

aufſtehen (ſtand, geſtanden), to get up, rise.

der Ausflug, –(e)s, ⁾e, excurſion, picnic.

auspacken, to unpack.

ausſteigen, to get off, get out.

ausſuchen, to pick out, select.

der Bahnhof, –(e)s, ⁾e, ſtation.

begleiten, to accompany, go with.

einpacken, to pack up.

einſteigen, to go aboard.

erſt, first, not before.

die Fahrkarte, –n, ticket (for travelling).

früh, early.

das Gaſthaus, –es, ⁾er, hotel, inn.

helfen (*dat.*), half, geholfen, to help.

hoffentlich, it is to be hoped, I hope.

der Kaffee, –s, coffee.

kaufen, to buy.

der Korb, –es, ⁾e, basket.

packen, to pack.

der Platz, –es, ⁾e, place.

der Provia'nt, –(e)s, provisions.

ſchon, already.

der Schutz, –(e)s, shelter, protection.

ſogleich, immediately.

ſteigen, ſtieg, geſtiegen, to mount, climb.

die Straßenbahn, –en, streetrailway, tram.

der Tee, –s, tea.

trinken, trank, getrunken, to drink.

unterdeſſen, meanwhile, in the meantime.

vielleicht, perhaps.

weit, far.

der Zug, –(e)s, ⁾e, train.

zurückkehren, to return.

IDIOM: **Einen Ausflug machen,** to make an excursion, go on a picnic.

*A.* 1. Hoffentlich wird das Wetter morgen ſchön ſein. 2. Dann werden wir einen Ausflug machen. 3. Wir werden früh aufſtehen und mit der Straßenbahn zum Bahnhof fahren. 4. Der Lehrer wird uns begleiten. 5. Dort werden wir erſt die Fahrkarten löſen (buy) und dann einſteigen. 6. In Blu=

menbach werden wir aussteigen. 7. Nicht weit von B. ist ein
Wald neben dem See. 8. Im Walde werden wir uns einen
Platz aussuchen. 9. Dort werden wir sogleich unsere Körbe
auspacken; Marie wird uns helfen. 10. Gestern haben wir
schon Proviant für unseren Ausflug eingepackt. 11. Dann
werden wir Tee und Kaffee machen. 12. Unterdessen wer=
den die Kinder Blumen für den Tisch pflücken. 13. Dann
werden wir essen und trinken. 14. Es wird vielleicht regnen.
15. Was werden Sie dann tun? 16. Im Gasthause des
Dorfes werden wir Schutz suchen. 17. Des Abends werden
wir mit dem Zuge zur Stadt zurückkehren.

*B.* Continue: Ich mache heute einen Ausflug, du, 2c.; ich
machte gestern . . . 2c.; ich habe heute . . . gemacht, 2c.;
ich hatte gestern . . . gemacht, 2c.; ich werde morgen . . .
machen, 2c.; ich werde . . . gemacht haben, 2c. Similarly
continue in all the six tenses: 1. Ich spiele im Walde, 2c.
2. Ich kaufe meine Fahrkarte, du . . . deine, 2c. 3. Ich
suche im Gasthause Schutz. 4. Ich packe Proviant ein.
5. Ich suche einen Platz aus.

*C.* Oral: 1. Wird es morgen regnen? 2. Wird das Wetter
morgen schön sein? 3. Was werden Sie dann tun? 4. Machen
Sie gern Ausflüge? 5. Wer wird die Körbe packen? 6. Wer
wird sie zum Bahnhof bringen? 7. Wie werden Sie fahren?
8. Wer wird den Platz aussuchen? 9. Werden Sie sogleich
essen? 10. Was werden Sie erst tun? 11. Was werden die
Kinder unterdessen tun? 12. Wann werden Sie zur Stadt
zurückkehren? 13. Wie werden Sie zurückkehren?

*D.* 1. It is to be hoped it will not rain to-morrow. 2. No,
it will be fine to-morrow. 3. Then I shall go on an excursion
with my teacher. 4. He likes to go on excursions with us.
5. Many friends will accompany us. 6. Mother will pack the
baskets this evening. 7. My sister will help her. 8. I shall go to
the station in (mit) the tramcar. 9. Father and mother can

drive to the station.   10. The teacher will pick out a place in the woods.   11. My aunt will make the coffee.   12. Mother will unpack the baskets.   13. We shall eat and drink and play in the woods.   14. Then the children will sing and dance under the trees.   15. We shall enjoy ourselves very much. 16. Shall you return with the train to the city?   17. No, we must return with the steamer.

*E.* Lesestück: Der Dichter Rossetti war auch als Maler berühmt. Ein Fürst aus Indien besuchte ihn einmal und sagte zu ihm: "Können Sie mir ein Bildnis von meinem Vater malen?" "Ist Ihr Herr Vater jetzt in London?" fragte der Künstler. "Nein, mein Vater ist tot," antwortete der Fürst. "Haben Sie vielleicht eine Photographie von ihm?" "Nein, wir haben gar kein Bildnis von ihm." "Wie kann ich denn sein Bildnis malen? Das ist unmöglich. Es ist lächerlich. Das kann ich nicht tun." "Weshalb ist es lächerlich?" erwiderte der Fürst. "Sie haben Cäsar, Hannibal und die zwölf Apostel gemalt; warum können Sie denn meinen Vater nicht malen?"

## LESSON XVII

**53.**                **Weak Declension of Nouns.**

### VII. der 𝔎𝔫𝔞𝔟𝔢, boy.

| *Singular.* | *Plural.* |
|---|---|
| *N.* der Knabe | die Knabe n |
| *G.* des Knabe n | der Knabe n |
| *D.* dem Knabe n | den Knabe n |
| *A.* den Knabe n | die Knabe n |

### VIII. der 𝔊𝔯𝔞𝔣, count.

| *Singular.* | *Plural.* |
|---|---|
| *N.* der Graf | die Graf en |
| *G.* des Graf en | der Graf en |
| *D.* dem Graf en | den Graf en |
| *A.* den Graf en | die Graf en |

### IX. die **Blume,** flower.

| *Singular.* | *Plural.* |
|---|---|
| *N.* die Blume | die Blume n |
| *G.* der Blume | der Blume n |
| *D.* der Blume | den Blume n |
| *A.* die Blume | die Blume n |

NOTES. — 1. For classes of nouns so declined, see Lesson XIX.
2. Herr drops **e** before –n in the singular: Genitive, Herrn, 2c.

REMARKS: 1. These models are all variations of the same type of declension, called the 'weak declension.'

2. In masculines all cases of the singular, except the nominative, end in –n or –en.

3. The plurals end in –n or –en throughout.

**54.**               Mixed Declension of Nouns.

### X. der **Name,** name.

| *Singular.* | *Plural.* |
|---|---|
| *N.* der Name | die Name n |
| *G.* des Name ns | der Name n |
| *D.* dem Name n | den Name n |
| *A.* den Name n | die Name n |

### XI. der **Vetter,** cousin.

| *Singular.* | *Plural.* |
|---|---|
| *N.* der Vetter | die Vetter n |
| *G.* des Vetter s | der Vetter n |
| *D.* dem Vetter | den Vetter n |
| *A.* den Vetter | die Vetter n |

### XII. das **Ohr,** ear.

| *Singular.* | *Plural.* |
|---|---|
| *N.* das Ohr | die Ohr en |
| *G.* des Ohr(e)s | der Ohr en |
| *D.* dem Ohr(e) | den Ohr en |
| *A.* das Ohr | die Ohr en |

NOTE. — For classes of nouns so declined, see Lesson XIX.

REMARKS: 1. Model X. is a variation of the Knabe model (§ 53), adding –s in the genitive singular.

2. Model XI. follows the Maler model (§ 43) in the singular and the Knabe model in the plural.

3. Model XII. follows the Hund model (§ 33) in the singular and the Graf model (§ 53) in the plural.

**55. Rules of Gender.** 1. Nouns in –ei, –heit, –keit, –schaft, –ung, –in, are always feminine.

NOTE. — The ending –in is used to form feminine nouns from masculines, often with umlaut; they double –n in the plural: Freund, Freundin, plur. Freundinnen; Graf, Gräfin, Gräfinnen.

2. Foreign nouns in –age, –ie, –if, –enz, –tät, –(t)ion, –ur, are always feminine.

### EXERCISE XVII

anrichten, to do (damage).

der Apfel, –s, ", apple.

der Apfelbaum, –(e)s, "e, apple-tree.

der Bauer, –n, –n, peasant, countryman, farmer.

das Beet, –es, –e, garden-bed.

der Birnbaum, –(e)s, "e, pear-tree.

die Birne, –n, pear.

blühen, to blossom, be in bloom, be in flower.

der Blumengarten, –s, ", flower-garden.

die Blüte, –n, blossom.

die Bohne, –n, bean.

die Erbse, –n, pea.

graben, grub, gegraben, to dig.

das Insekt, –es, –en, insect.

die Kirsche, –n, cherry.

der Mensch, –en, –en, man (human being).

das Obst, –es, fruit (of garden or orchard).

reif, ripe.

der Russe, –n, –n, Russian (noun).

säen, to sow.

der Same, –ns, –n, seed.

der Schade, –ns, –n or ", damage.

der Spaten, –s, —, spade.

der Teil, –(e)s, –e, part, portion.

die Tomate, –n, tomato.

umgraben, to dig up, dig over.

unentbehrlich, indispensable.

zuerst (adv.), first.

IDIOM : **Junge** is used for **Knabe** in addressing a boy.

F

*A.* 1. Decline like Knabe: mein Junge, dieser Bauer.
2. Like Blume: meine Kirsche, die Kartoffel. 3. Like Graf:
kein Mensch, welche Frau? 4. Like Name: der Same.
5. Like Ohr: dieses Insekt. 6. Like Vetter: unser Nachbar.
7. Supply the remaining cases of the following: Rose (*f.*), —,
–n; Russe (*m.*), –n, –n; Mann (*m.*), –es, ⁀er; Erbse (*f.*), —,
–n; Feder (*f.*), —, –n; Bett (*n.*), –es, –en; Spaten (*m.*),
–s, —; Aussicht (*f.*), —, –en.

*B.* 1. Hinter unserem Hause haben wir einen Garten.
2. Hier hat unser Gärtner diese Woche mit einem Knaben
gearbeitet. 3. Dieser Knabe ist ein Russe, der Sohn eines
Bauern. 4. Der Junge hat die Beete mit einem Spaten umgegraben und der Gärtner hat gesät und gepflanzt. 5. Mein
Vater hatte ihnen den Samen gegeben. 6. Der Teil des
Gartens rechts ist für das Gemüse und der Teil links für die
Blumen. 7. Gestern haben sie Kartoffeln und Tomaten gepflanzt, und auch Erbsen und Bohnen. 8. Im Blumengarten
werden die Veilchen bald blühen. 9. Die Apfel- und Birn-
bäume werden auch bald in Blüte stehen. 10. Die Kirschen
werden im Juni reif sein; die Birnen und Äpfel im Oktober.
11. Hoffentlich werden die Insekten dieses Jahr nicht viel
Schaden anrichten. 12. Wir haben mehr Obst und Gemüse
als unsere Nachbarn. 13. Gemüse und Obst sind dem Menschen unentbehrlich.

*C.* Oral: 1. Wann beginnen die Menschen im Garten zu
arbeiten? 2. Was tun sie zuerst? 3. Wie graben sie den
Garten um? 4. Wo liegt Ihr Garten? 5. Wer hat diese
Woche im Garten gearbeitet? 6. Wer hat mit ihm gearbeitet?
7. Was haben sie getan? 8. Was für Blumen sind in Ihrem
Garten? 9. Hat der Junge Englisch gelernt? 10. Wie alt
ist er? 11. Wessen Sohn ist er? 12. Was für Obst haben
Sie? 13. Wann wird das Obst reif? 14. Was tun die
Insekten?

*D.* 1. Vegetables and fruit are indispensable to (the) men.
2. They must have gardens.   3. They dig up the garden with
a spade.   4. Then the gardeners sow and plant.   5. Our gardener is a Russian.   6. His father and mother were peasants.
7. Here on the left he will plant the cabbage and tomatoes.
8. Yonder he will plant the beans and peas.   9. He bought the
seed yesterday.   10. He has already planted the potatoes.
11. In which month do people plant them?   12. The pear-trees
are in flower in April or May.   13. We have picked the
cherries already.   14. We had more cherries this year than
our neighbours.   15. In October we shall pick our apples and
pears.   16. The insects do much damage in the garden.

*E.* Lesestück:

Sonnenschein und Blütenduft,       Und die Schmetterlinge sich
Das ist ein Vergnügen!             Auf den Halmen wiegen:
Wenn in blauer Maienluft           Ach, wie ist es da so schön
Hoch die Lerchen fliegen.          Tief im Gras zu liegen
Wenn des Baches Wellen sich        Und zum Himmel aufzusehn!
Durch die Blumen schmiegen,        Das ist ein Vergnügen!

# LESSON XVIII

**56. Declension of Attributive Adjectives.**  1. When not preceded by a determinative, they take the endings of the dieser
model (§ 31) throughout (Strong Form).

NOTE. — The articles, possess., interrog., demonstr., and indef. adjs. are
called 'determinatives.'

2. When preceded by the definite article or a determinative
of the dieser model they take the ending -e in the nominative
singular of all genders, and in the accusative singular feminine
and neuter; otherwise -en throughout (Weak Form).

3. When preceded by a determinative of the mein model
they take the endings -er, -e, -es in the nominative singular,
and -en, -e, -es in the accusative singular; otherwise -en
throughout (Mixed Form).

*der, dieser*　　*ein — mein*

*no determinative*

|  | I. STRONG FORM. | | | II. WEAK FORM. | | | III. MIXED FORM. | | |
|---|---|---|---|---|---|---|---|---|---|
|  | *M.* | *F.* | *N.* | *M.* | *F.* | *N.* | *M.* | *F.* | *N.* |
| *Sing. N.* | –er | –e | –es | –e | –e | –e | –er | –e | –es |
| *G.* | –es | –er | –es | –en | –en | –en | –en | –en | –en |
| *D.* | –em | –er | –em | –en | –en | –en | –en | –en | –en |
| *A.* | –en | –e | –es | –en | –e | –e | –en | –e | –es |

| | *All genders.* | *All genders.* | *All genders.* |
|---|---|---|---|
| *Plur.*　*N.* | –e | –en | –en |
| *G.* | –er | –en | –en |
| *D.* | –en | –en | –en |
| *A.* | –e | –en | –en |

NOTE. — In the mixed form, the adj. follows the bieſer model only in the three places where the mein model lacks distinctive endings, namely, nom. sing. masc. and neut. and acc. sing. neut.; otherwise it is like the weak form.

### 57.　　　　　　Paradigms with Nouns.

#### I. STRONG FORM.

##### *Singular.*

| | Good wine. | | Good soup. | | Good glass. | |
|---|---|---|---|---|---|---|
| *N.* | gut er | Wein | gut e | Suppe | gut es | Glas |
| *G.* | gut es(en) | Weines | gut er | Suppe | gut es(en) | Glaſes |
| *D.* | gut em | Weine | gut er | Suppe | gut em | Glaſe |
| *A.* | gut en | Wein | gut e | Suppe | gut es | Glas |

##### *Plural.*

Good wines, etc.

| | | |
|---|---|---|
| *N.* | gut e | Weine, Suppen, Gläſer |
| *G.* | gut er | Weine, Suppen, Gläſer |
| *D.* | gut en | Weinen, Suppen, Gläſern |
| *A.* | gut e | Weine, Suppen, Gläſer |

NOTES. — 1. Before a gen. in –s, the adj. usually has –en.

2. The ending –es of the nom. and acc. sing. neut. is often dropped in poetry and sometimes in prose.

3. Adjs. after pers. prons. are strong, exc. in dat. sing. and nom. plur., where weak endings are commoner: Mir armen Manne.

## II. Weak Form.

### Singular.

|   | The good man. | The good woman. | The good child. |
|---|---|---|---|
| N. | der gute Mann | die gute Frau | das gute Kind |
| G. | des guten Mannes | der guten Frau | des guten Kindes |
| D. | dem guten Manne | der guten Frau | dem guten Kinde |
| A. | den guten Mann | die gute Frau | das gute Kind |

### Plural.

#### The good men, etc.

| N. | die guten Männer, Frauen, Kinder |
|---|---|
| G. | der guten Männer, Frauen, Kinder |
| D. | den guten Männern, Frauen, Kindern |
| A. | die guten Männer, Frauen, Kinder |

## III. Mixed Form.

### Singular.

|   | My good hat. | My good axe. |
|---|---|---|
| N. | mein guter Hut | meine gute Axt |
| G. | meines guten Hutes | meiner guten Axt |
| D. | meinem guten Hute | meiner guten Axt |
| A. | meinen guten Hut | meine gute Axt |

#### My good book.

| N. | mein gutes Buch |
|---|---|
| G. | meines guten Buches |
| D. | meinem guten Buche |
| A. | mein gutes Buch |

### Plural.

#### My good hats, etc.

| N. | meine guten Hüte, Äxte, Bücher |
|---|---|
| G. | meiner guten Hüte, Äxte, Bücher |
| D. | meinen guten Hüten, Äxten, Büchern |
| A. | meine guten Hüte, Äxte, Bücher |

REMARK : Two or more adjectives qualifying the same noun
follow the same form : Guter, alter, roter Wein ; des guten,
alten, roten Weines, ꝛc.

### 58.            Adjectives used Substantively.

| | |
|---|---|
| Ein altes Buch und ein neues. | An old book and a new one. |
| Der Alte; die Alte. | The old man ; the old woman. |
| Die Alten. | The old people (ancients). |
| Das Gute und das Schöne. | The good and the beautiful. |

OBSERVE : 1. The English 'one' after adjectives, as in the
first example, is not to be translated into German.

2. Attributive adjectives may be used substantively, and are
then written with a capital.

### EXERCISE XVIII

also, so, thus, accordingly.

ankommen (kam, gekommen),
to arrive.

der Appeti't, –(e)s, appetite.

arm, "er, poor.

die Arzenei', –en, medicine,
physic.

berühmt, celebrated, famous.

bitter, bitter.

breit, broad, wide.

das Brot, –es, –e, bread, loaf.

darauf, thereupon, then.

der Diener, –s, —, servant.

der Doktor (Dr.), –s, –en,
doctor (academic degree).

eintreten (trat, getreten), to
enter.

endlich, at last, finally.

essen, aß, gegessen, to eat.

das Essen, –s, meal, dinner.

fehlen (dat.), to be missing, ail.

fragen, to ask.

fühlen, to feel.

ganz (adj.), whole.

gar nicht, not at all.

gehen, ging, gegangen, to go,
walk.

heißen, hieß, geheißen, to be
called, named.

der Kopfschmerz, –es, –en,
headache (usually pl.).

lieb, dear.

nächst, next.

der Patie'nt, –en, –en, patient.

der Puls, –es, –e, pulse.

pünktlich, punctual.

der Schulkamerad, –en, –en,
school-fellow, school-mate.

die Straße, –n, street.

der Traum, –(e)s, "e, dream.

u'ngeduldig, impatient.

verschreiben, verschrieb, ver=
  schrieben, to prescribe.

vorig (*adj.*), last, former.

warten, to wait (for, auf, *acc.*).

winken (*dat.*), to beckon.

zeigen, to show.

die Zunge, –n, tongue.

IDIOMS: 1. **Arzt** = physician, medical man; **Doktor** is the academic degree in any faculty.

2. **Wie geht es Ihnen, Herr Doktor?**  How are you, doctor?

3. **Ich heiße Karl,** My name is Charles; **Wie heißt er?** What is his name?

*A.* 1. Decline in the singular in German: White bread, good cabbage, red ink.   2. In the plural: Ripe apples, old books, beautiful hands.   3. In full: Which great river, my good friend, this fine view, your white rose, the small child, my little room.   4. Continue with similar examples.

*B.* 1. Vorigen Dienstag ging ich zum Arzte, Herrn Dr. Aue. 2. Ich war gar nicht wohl.  3. Ich hatte heftige Kopfschmer= zen.  4. Dieser gute Herr ist ein alter Freund und Schul= kamerad meines lieben Vaters.  5. Sein neues Haus steht in einer schönen breiten Straße.  6. Ich kam pünktlich an, aber schon warteten viele Ungeduldige.  7. Diese waren arme Pa= tienten des berühmten Arztes.  8. Also mußte ich eine ganze Stunde warten.  9. Endlich winkte mir der alte Diener und ich trat ein.  10. „Was fehlt Ihnen, mein junger Freund?" fragte der Arzt.  11. „Das kann ich Ihnen nicht sagen, Herr Doktor, das müssen Sie mir sagen."  12. „Haben Sie guten Appetit?"  13. „Nein."  14. „Haben Sie Kopfschmerzen nach dem Essen?"  15. „Jawohl, sehr heftige.  16. Ich schlafe nicht gut und habe oft böse Träume."  17. Dann mußte ich ihm meine Zunge zeigen und er fühlte meinen Puls. 18. Darauf verschrieb er mir eine bittere Arzenei und sagte: „Kommen Sie nächste Woche wieder."

*C.* Continue: 1. Vorige Woche ging ich zum Arzte, . . . gingst du, 2c.  2. Ich kam pünktlich an.  3. Was fehlte mir?

... dir, ꝛc.  4. Ich mußte lange warten.  5. Ich habe den Garten umgegraben.

*D*. Oral: 1. Was fehlte Ihnen?  2. Zu wem gingen Sie? 3. Wann?  4. Wie heißt er?  5. Ist er ein berühmter Arzt? 6. Wo wohnt er?  7. Waren schon viele da?  8. Wer war da?  9. Was taten sie?  10. Wie lange mußten Sie warten? 11. Was sagten Sie zum Arzte?  12. Was tat er darauf? 13. Wann werden Sie wieder zu ihm gehen?

*E*. 1. My elder brother often has violent headaches.  2. Last week he went to an old friend.  3. This good gentleman is a famous physician.  4. He and our dear father are old school-mates.  5. My poor brother did not arrive punctually.  6. Accordingly he had to wait a long time.  7. The old servant at last beckoned to him to enter.  8. The kind old gentleman asked : "What is the matter with you?"  9. My brother replied : "I often have violent headaches, and do not sleep very well.  10. I also have bad dreams."  11. "Do you enjoy (use schmecken) your (the) dinner?"  12. "O, yes."  13. "Show me your tongue."  14. Then the doctor felt the patient's pulse, and said : "You have been eating too much.  15. Take a walk every morning in the fresh air.  16. Here is also a bitter medicine.  17. It is bitter, but it is very good.  18. Come again next Thursday."

*F*. Lesestück : Man muß kleinen Kindern immer die Wahr-heit sagen.  Dies erfuhr unser guter Großvater einmal.  Einer von seinen Enkeln fragte ihn : "Großvater, warum ist dein Haar so weiß?"  "Ich bin sehr alt," antwortete er.  "Wie alt bist du denn, Großpapa?" fragte das Kind wieder.  "Ach, ich war schon mit Noah in der Arche."  "Dann bist du wohl einer von seinen Söhnen?"  "Nein, das bin ich nicht." "Aber du kannst doch nicht seine Frau sein; also mußt du eins von den Tieren in der Arche sein."

# LESSON XIX

**59.**      **Summary of Noun Declension.**

*A.* STRONG DECLENSION.

I. Hund ⎫
II. Sohn ⎬ Models.    IV. Dorf Model.    V. Maler ⎫
III. Hand ⎭                                 VI. Vater ⎬ Models

[Primary Form.]      [Enlarged Form.]      [Contracted Form.]

| | | | |
|---|---|---|---|
| *Sing.* N. — ⎫ | N. — | N. — ⎫ | |
| G. -(e)s ⎬ Fems. un-changed. | G. -(e)s | G. -s ⎬ Fems. un-changed. | |
| D. -(e) ⎪ | D. -(e) | D. — ⎪ | |
| A. — ⎭ | A. — | A. — ⎭ | |
| *Plur.* N. -e ⎫ | N. -er ⎫ | N. — ⎫ | |
| G. -e ⎬ Many with umlaut. | G. -er ⎬ Umlaut. | G. — ⎬ Some with umlaut. | |
| D. -en ⎪ | D. -ern ⎪ | D. -n ⎪ | |
| A. -e ⎭ | A. -er ⎭ | A. — ⎭ | |

After I. are de-
clined : Masc. mon-
osylls. in App. A, 1 ;
neut. monosylls. in
App. A, 2 ; nouns in
-at, -ich, -ig, -ing,
-nis, -sal ; foreign
mascs. in -al, -an,
-ar, -ier ; also in -or
stressed. After II.
are declined : Masc.
monosylls., exc. as
in App. A, 1 and A,
4 ; the neuts. Floß,
Chor, and some-
times Boot ; those
in -ast ; those in -al,
-an, -ar sometimes.
After III., fems. in
App. A, 3.

After IV. are
declined : Mascu-
lines in App. A,
4 ; neuter mono-
syllables, except
those in App. A,
2 ; nouns in -tum ;
das Regiment,
das Hospital (or
Spital); no fem-
inines ; stems
having a, o, u,
take umlaut in
the plural.

After V. are de-
clined : Masculines
and neuters in -el,
-en, -er (except those
in App. A, 5) ; di-
minutives in -chen and
-lein ; neuter collec-
tives beginning with
Ge- and ending in
-e ; der Käse. After
VI. are declined :
The nouns in App.
A, 5, and the
feminines Mutter,
Tochter.

*B.* Weak Declension.  *C.* Mixed Declension.

| VII. Knabe | Models. | X. Name Model. | XI. Vetter | Models. |
|---|---|---|---|---|
| VIII. Graf | | | XII. Ohr | |
| IX. Blume | | | | |

| | | | | |
|---|---|---|---|---|
| *Sing.* N. –(e) | Fems. un-changed. | N. –(e) | N. — | |
| G. –(e)n | | G. –(e)ns | G. –(e)s | |
| D. –(e)n | | D. –(e)n | D. –(e) | |
| A. –(e)n | | A. –(e)n | A. — | |
| *Plur.* N. –(e)n | No umlaut. | N. –(e)n | No umlaut. | N. –(e)n | No umlaut. |
| G. –(e)n | | G. –(e)n | | G. –(e)n | |
| D. –(e)n | | D. –(e)n | | D. –(e)n | |
| A. –(e)n | | A. –(e)n | | A. –(e)n | |

Thus are de-clined: After VII., mascs. in –e; after VIII., mascs. of App. A, 6, many for-eign mascs., all fems. (except as in App. A, 3, and those in –e); after IX., all fems. in –e.

Thus are de-clined: Those in App. A, **7**.

Thus are de-clined: After XI., the nouns in App. A, 8, rejecting e throughout; after XII., those in App. A, 9, foreign mascs. in unstressed –or.

### EXERCISE XIX

das Abendbrot, –(e)s, supper.
die Abendluft, "e, evening air.
alle (*pl.*), all.
anfangen (fing, gefangen), to begin.
der Arbeiter, –s, —, workman.
aufhören, to cease, stop.
aufsteigen (stieg, gestiegen), to rise, mount.

ausruhen, to rest, repose.
einschlafen (schlief, geschlafen), to go to sleep.
feucht, damp.
das Futter, –s, fodder, food.
die Hitze, heat.
hungrig, hungry.
in (*acc.*), into.

kommen, kam, gekommen, to
  come.

letzt, last.

leuchten, to shine.

müde, tired, fatigued.

der Nebel, –s, —, fog, mist.

der Ochse, –n, –n, ox.

rauchen, to smoke.

die Ruhe, rest, repose.

ruhen, to rest.

der Schornstein, –(e)s, –e,
  chimney.

der Stall, –(e)s, ⁓e, stable.

der Stern, –(e)s, –e, star.

süß, sweet.

der Tau, –(e)s, dew.

der Teich, –(e)s, –e, pond.

der Vogel, –s, ⁓, bird.

der Wagen, –s, —, wagon, carriage.

die Wolke, –n, cloud.

der Zweig, –(e)s, –e, branch,
  bough.

IDIOM: **Ich bin satt,** I have had enough to eat.

Review Lessons XIII, XV, XVII, XVIII.

*A.* 1. Es wird Abend. 2. Die Wolken und der Himmel
werden rot. 3. Die Hitze hat aufgehört. 4. Vom Wasser
des Teiches steigt ein Nebel auf. 5. Das Gras ist feucht vom
Tau. 6. In der Abendluft spielen viele Insekten. 7. Die
Vögel auf den Zweigen der Bäume singen ihr letztes, süßes
Lied. 8. Die Arbeiter kommen vom Felde nach Hause.
9. Ochsen und Kühe, Pferde und Schafe gehen in den Stall.
10. Alle sind müde und wünschen auszuruhen. 11. Aber
Menschen und Tiere sind auch hungrig und warten auf ihr
Abendbrot. 12. Bald werden sie aber alle satt sein, denn der
Schornstein raucht und die Wagen bringen Futter. 13. Dann
können sie zur Ruhe gehen und einschlafen. 14. Die Sterne
werden bald anfangen zu leuchten.

*B.* 1. Decline the following nouns throughout, prefixing a
possessive pronoun and an appropriate adjective: Kuh, Baum,
Bett, Haus, Vogel, Wagen, Schaf, Stall. 2. Decline with
definite article or dieser and an adjective: Mensch, Luft, Gras,
Wolke, Himmel, Abend, Arbeiter, Insekt. 3. Decline with
an adjective only: Nebel, Teich, Stern, Lied, Pferd, Ochse,
Stall, Tier, Schornstein.

*C.* Oral on *A.*

*D.* 1. It (es) is a beautiful evening. 2. Red clouds are in (an) the sky. 3. It is no longer so hot. 4. A white mist is rising from the water of a large pond. 5. The little birds are singing sweet songs in the green trees. 6. The tired workmen are returning from their work in the fields. 7. They are hungry; but a bright fire is burning, and a good supper will be waiting for them. 8. Then they can go to (the) rest. 9. Soon the bright stars will begin to shine.

*E.* Lesestück:

### Klein-Marie.

Marie auf der Wiese,
Auf der Wiese Marie,
Alle Gräser und Blumen
Sind größer als sie.

Mir wird schon ganz bang',
Weil ich nirgend sie seh',
Ich hab' sie verloren,
Verloren im Klee.

Zwischen den Sternblumen weiß
Und den Glocken so blau
Und den gold'nen Ranunkeln,
Ei, was ich da schau'!

Das ist keine Sternblum'—
Ein Köpflein ist das.
Ich hab' sie gefunden,
Gefunden im Gras.

— Johannes Trojan.

## LESSON XX

**60.**  Compound Tenses of sein.

| *Perf. Indic.* | *Pluperf. Indic.* |
|---|---|
| I have been, etc. | I had been, etc. |
| ich **bin** gewesen | ich **war** gewesen |
| du bist „ | du warst „ |
| er ist „ | er war „ |
| wir sind „ | wir waren „ |
| ihr seid „ | ihr wart „ |
| sie sind „ | sie waren „ |

*Fut. Perf. Indic.*

I shall have been, etc.

> ich werde gewesen sein
> du wirst      „      „
> er wird       „      „
> wir werden    „      „
> ihr werdet     „      „
> sie werden     „      „

*Perf. Infin.* gewesen (zu) sein, to have been.

**61.**       **Compound Tenses of kommen.**

| *Perf. Indic.* | | *Pluperf. Indic.* | |
|---|---|---|---|
| I have come, etc. | | I had come, etc. | |
| ich **bin** | gekommen | ich **war** | gekommen |
| du bist | „ | du warst | „ |
| er ist | „ | er war | „ |
| wir sind | „ | wir waren | „ |
| ihr seid | „ | ihr wart | „ |
| sie sind | „ | sie waren | „ |

*Fut. Perf. Indic.*

I shall have come, etc.

> ich werde gekommen sein
> du wirst     „      „
> er wird      „      „
> wir werden    „      „
> ihr werdet     „      „
> sie werden     „      „

*Perf. Infin.* gekommen (zu) sein, to have come.

**62.** **Verbs with sein.** The following classes of verbs are conjugated with sein as an auxiliary of tense:

**1.** The two verbs of rest:

> sein, be.                bleiben, remain.

2. Verbs of motion, such as :

| | | |
|---|---|---|
| begegnen, meet. | fallen, fall. | kommen, come. |
| eilen, hasten. | folgen, follow. | laufen, run. |
| fahren, drive, etc. | gehen, go. | |

NOTE.— Some of these also admit **haben** when action rather than destination is expressed: Der Kutscher **hat** zu schnell gefahren, 'The coachman has been driving too quickly.'

3. Those expressing a change of condition, such as :

sterben, die.　　wachsen, grow.　　werden, become.

4. The following impersonal verbs :

gelingen, succeed.　　geschehen, happen.　　glücken, succeed.

NOTE.— Verbs conjugated with **sein** are indicated in the vocabularies and dictionary by (f.).

### 63.　　Present and Imperfect Indicative of wollen.

| *Present Indicative.* | | *Imperfect Indicative.* | |
|---|---|---|---|
| I will, etc. | | I would, etc. | |
| ich will | wir wollen | ich wollte | wir wollten |
| du willst | ihr wollt | du wolltest | ihr wolltet |
| er will | sie wollen | er wollte | sie wollten |

### 64.　　Use of wollen.

| | |
|---|---|
| Ich will heute abreisen. | I will (mean to) go to-day. |
| Er will nicht kommen. | He doesn't intend to come. |
| Wir wollten dahin gehen. | We wanted to go there. |

OBSERVE : 1. This verb renders the English 'will,' 'would,' when the latter expresses more than mere futurity (an exertion of the will of the subject).

2. It often equals 'want to,' 'intend to,' 'mean to,' etc.

### 65.　　Infinitive of Purpose.

| | |
|---|---|
| Ich gehe aus, um ein Buch zu kaufen. | I am going out (in order) to buy a book. |

Observe: Purpose is often expressed by an infinitive with
zu, governed by um.

### EXERCISE XX

abfahren (f., fuhr, gefahren),
to depart, set off, set out.

anfehen (fah, gefehen), to look
at.

das Auge, –s, –n, eye.

außerhalb (*gen.*), outside of.

ausgehen (f., ging, gegangen),
to go out.

begegnen (f., *dat.*), to meet.

das Bild, –es, –er, picture.

die Bildergalerie', –n, picture-
gallery.

bleiben (f.), blieb, geblieben,
to remain, stay.

dahin, thither, to that place,
there.

die Droschke, –n, cab.

das Eis, –es, ice.

fallen (f.), fiel, gefallen, to
fall.

gelingen (f., *impers.*, *dat.*),
gelang, gelungen, to suc-
ceed.

herauskommen (f., kam, ge=
kommen), to come out.

hinausfahren (f.), to drive out.

italienisch, Italian (*adj.*).

laufen (f.), lief, gelaufen, to
run.

mehrmals, several times.

mieten, to hire, engage.

die Minute, –n, minute.

mitbringen (brachte, gebracht),
to bring along (with).

nachher, afterwards.

der Park, –s, –e or –s, park.

der Saal, –(e)s, Säle, hall.

der Schlittschuh, –(e)s, –e,
skate.

Schlittschuh laufen (f.), to
skate.

die Viertelstunde, –n, quarter
of an hour.

werden (f.), ward or wurde, ge=
worden, to become, be.

weshalb? why?

zu (*adv.*), too.

*A.* Continue the following : 1. Ich bin neulich krank gewesen.
2. Ich war müde geworden. 3. Ich bin ausgegangen, um
einen Besuch zu machen. 4. Ich werde morgen abgefahren
sein. 5. Ich bin (war) schnell gelaufen. 6. Ich bin (war)
meiner Schwester begegnet. 7. Ich bin (war) auf dem Eise
gefallen. 8. Es ist (war) mir gelungen, das Buch zu finden,
es ist (war) dir, 2c. 9. Ich bin (war) viel zu spät geblieben.

*B.* 1. Ich bin gestern mit meinem alten Freunde, Karl Löffler, in der Stadt gewesen, um den Tag dort zu verbringen. 2. Wir sind zuerst mit der Straßenbahn zur großen Bildergalerie gefahren. 3. Mein Freund war schon mehrmals dort gewesen. 4. Wir sind in den italienischen Saal gegangen. 5. In diesem Saale sind wir eine Stunde geblieben und haben die Bilder angesehen. 6. Dann sind wir wieder herausgekommen, denn unsere Augen waren müde geworden. 7. Mein Freund wollte den großen Park außerhalb der Stadt besuchen. 8. Wir haben eine Droschke gemietet, um hinauszufahren. 9. In zwanzig Minuten sind wir dort angekommen. 10. Dann sind wir durch den schönen Park gegangen. 11. Nach einer Viertelstunde sind wir zum kleinen See gekommen. 12. Es war sehr kalt gewesen und das Eis war prächtig. 13. Wir hatten unsere Schlittschuhe mitgebracht und sind eine Stunde Schlittschuh gelaufen. 14. Auf dem Eise sind wir einem Schulkameraden begegnet. 15. Nachher sind wir zur Stadt zurückgekehrt, denn wir waren müde und hungrig geworden. 16. Wir wollen nächste Woche wieder zur Stadt fahren.

*C.* Oral: 1. Wo sind Sie gestern gewesen? 2. Wer war mit Ihnen? 3. Wie sind Sie dahingekommen? 4. Weshalb sind Sie dahingefahren? 5. Wie lange sind Sie in der Bildergalerie geblieben? 6. Weshalb sind Sie nicht länger geblieben? 7. Weshalb sind Sie zum Park hinausgefahren? 8. Was haben Sie nachher getan?

*D.* (Render the past tense in this exercise by the German perfect.) 1. Where were you yesterday, Albert? 2. I was in the city. 3. I was there too, but I did not meet you. 4. I was sorry not to have met you. 5. Did you go to the park first? 6. No, I went with my sister to the picture-gallery to see the German pictures. 7. How long did you stay there? 8. We stayed there two hours. 9. Are you fond of the German painters? 10. Many of their pictures are splendid; I admire them very [much]. 11. Had you been in the picture-gallery before (ſchon)? 12. Oh yes, I had been there several times. 13. Did you go into the hall of the Italian painters? 14. No, we had no time; we wished to visit the park. 15. Did you drive there (dahin)? 16. Yes, we drove in a cab. 17. Afterwards we walked through the park. 18. We also skated. 19. We then returned home to eat and rest.

*E.* Leſeſtück:

Es blüht ein ſchönes Blümchen     Es weiß nicht viel zu reden,
Auf unſrer grünen Au',           Und alles was es ſpricht,
Sein Aug' iſt wie der Himmel    Iſt immer nur dasſelbe,
So heiter und ſo blau.           Iſt nur: „Vergiß mein nicht."

                   — Hoffmann von Fallersleben.

# LESSON XXI

**66. Adjective Stems in –e, –el, –en, –er.** 1. Adjective stems in –e drop e before the endings: müde, 'tired'; der (die, das) müd-e; die müd-en, etc.

2. Adjectives in –el drop e of the inflectional ending before a final –n, and drop e of the stem before other terminations; so usually also adjectives in –er preceded by a vowel: edel, 'noble,' edeln, edle, edler, edles; teuer, 'dear,' teuern, teure, etc.

3. Adjectives in –er preceded by a consonant usually drop e of the inflectional ending before –m or –n only: heiſer, 'hoarse,' heiſerm, heiſern.

4. Adjectives in –en may drop e of the stem before any termination: golden, 'golden,' gold(e)nen, gold(e)ne, gold(e)nes, etc.

NOTE.—The above changes are euphonic, and serve to obviate the repetition of the weakened e sound in successive syllables (see p. xiv).

**67. Special Cases.** 1. The adjective hoch, 'high,' drops e when inflected:

        Der hohe Baum.           The high tree.

G

2. After etwas, 'something,' nichts, 'nothing,' viel, 'much,' wenig, 'little,' the adjective follows the strong declension, and is written with a capital:

Etwas (nichts) Gutes.    Something (nothing) good.
Mit wenig Gutem.    With little that is good.

3. After the plurals alle, 'all,' einige, etliche, 'some,' manche, 'many,' mehrere, 'several,' solche, 'such,' viele, 'many,' wenige, 'few,' the adjective may be weak or strong in nom. and acc.:

Alle gute(n) Menschen.    All good men.

4. Adjectives in –er from names of cities are indeclinable, and are written with a capital:

Die Londoner Zeitungen.    The London newspapers.
Pariser Moden.    Paris fashions.

## 68.    Adjectives as Nouns.

| The stranger (*m.*). | The stranger (*f.*). | The strangers. |
|---|---|---|
| *N.* der Fremde | die Fremde | die Fremden |
| *G.* des Fremden | der Fremden | der Fremden |
| *D.* dem Fremden | der Fremden | den Fremden |
| *A.* den Fremden | die Fremde | die Fremden |

| A stranger (*m.*). | A stranger (*f.*). | Strangers. |
|---|---|---|
| *N.* ein Fremder | eine Fremde | Fremde |
| *G.* eines Fremden | einer Fremden | Fremder |
| *D.* einem Fremden | einer Fremden | Fremden |
| *A.* einen Fremden | eine Fremde | Fremde |

OBSERVE: Adjectives and participles used as nouns vary their declension according to the rules for adjective declension (Lesson XVIII), but are written with capital letters.

NOTE.—Many adjectives and participles are thus used in German, the English equivalents of which are nouns only: fremd, 'strange,' der (die) Fremde, 2c., 'the stranger'; reisend, 'travelling,' der Reisende, 2c., 'the traveller'; verwandt, 'related,' der Verwandte, 2c., 'the relative.'

### EXERCISE XXI

abreifen (f.), to set out, start, depart, go away.

der Beamte, official.

der Bediente, servant.

blind, blind.

die Dame, –n, lady.

deutfch (*adj.*), German.

edel, noble.

ehrlich, honest.

erft (*adj.*), first.

Frankreich, *n.*, –8, France.

fremd, strange, foreign.

Freude machen, to give pleasure.

der Gefandte, ambassador.

glücklich, happy.

golden, golden, gold (*adj.*).

heifer, hoarse.

Pari's, *n.*, Paris.

reich, rich.

der Reifende, traveller.

fchlafen, fchlief, gefchlafen, to sleep.

fchlecht, bad, poor.

das Spita'l, –(e)8, "er, hospital.

der Staat, –e8, –en, state.

stattfinden (fand, gefunden), to take place.

sterben (f.), starb, gestorben, to die.

teuer, dear, costly.

übera'll, everywhere.

u'nglücklich, unhappy, unfortunate.

der Verwandte, relative.

der Wein, –(e)8, –e, wine.

die Weltausstellung, –en, international exhibition.

Wien, *n.*, –8, Vienna.

willko'mmen, welcome.

die Wurst, "e, sausage.

*A.* 1. Viele Deutfche wohnen in unferer Stadt. 2. Unfer Lehrer ift ein Deutfcher; feine Frau ift eine Deutfche. 3. Die Deutfchen lernen gern Englifch. 4. Meine Verwandten wollen auf dem Lande wohnen. 5. Ein Reifender muß oft in fchlechten Betten fchlafen. 6. Diefer arme Blinde hat meiner Mutter zwei hübfche Körbe gemacht, denn fie hat ihm viel Gutes getan. 7. Er tat es, um ihr eine Freude zu machen. 8. Die erfte Londoner Weltausstellung fand im Jahre 1851 ftatt. 9. Parifer Handfchühe und Wiener Würfte find überall berühmt. 10. Diefe Reifenden bewunderten die fchöne Landfchaft. 11. Frau Mofer ift eine Ver-

wandte unseres alten Arztes. 12. Ein Fremder ist nicht
immer willkommen. 13. Der alte Bediente meines guten
Onkels ist gestorben. 14. Der deutsche Gesandte ist abgereist,
um Verwandte zu besuchen. 15. Die Gesandten von Frank=
reich und England sind angekommen. 16. Beamte sind die
Diener des Staates. 17. Ein Beamter muß ehrlich sein.
18. Die Reichen sind nicht immer glücklich. 19. Auch Arme
können glücklich sein. 20. Der Arzt will dem unglücklichen
Kranken guten, alten Wein geben. 21. In diesem Spital
sind viele Kranke.

*B.* Oral on the above.

*C.* Supply the proper termination of the following stems:
1. Ein Deutsch–. 2. Meinem Verwandt–. 3. Zwei Rei=
send–. 4. Ihr Bedient–. 5. Des armen Blind–. 6. We=
nig Schön–. 7. Der berühmten Reisend–. 8. Ein reicher
Verwandt–. 9. Die armen Fremd–. 10. Den guten Be=
dient–. 11. Des deutschen Gesandt–. 12. Viele unglück=
liche Krank–.

*D.* Inflect, and give the proper orthographical form of the
adjectives: 1. Ein (golden) Ring. 2. Mein (teuer) Sohn.
3. Die (edel) Dame. 4. Dem (edel) Gesandten. 5. Den
(heiser) Schülern.

*E.* 1. I have many relatives in this village. 2. Where do
your relatives intend to live? 3. The son of this German is a
celebrated physician. 4. The blind are not always unhappy.
5. This noble German has done much good. 6. The London
cabs drive very fast. 7. My aunt likes Paris gloves very
much. 8. Our old physician is a relative of (von) Mrs. Moser.
9. This German [woman] is a friend of my aunt. 10. Strangers
and poor people were always welcome at our house. 11. The
German ambassador was a very noble man. 12. Ambassadors
are the servants of the state. 13. The young may (können)
die; the old must die; the patient has died. 14. I have sold

my house [to] a rich man.   15. We have bought this dear wine
for the patients in the hospital.   16. Good old wine costs
a great deal.   17. Do you like (to eat) Vienna sausages?
18. This honest official was our neighbour.   19. Officials are not
always honest.   20. Honest officials are not always rich.

*F.* Lesestück: Die Menschen wohnen in Häusern.   Viele
Häuser zusammen bilden eine Stadt oder ein Dorf.   Eine Stadt
hat lange und breite Straßen.   Die Stadt ist groß.   Die Häuser
sind sehr schön gebaut.   Die Straßen der Stadt sind gepfla-
stert.   Zu beiden Seiten stehen Laternen.   Abends zündet man
sie an.   In den Häusern sind oft Läden; diese haben große,
schöne Schaufenster.   In den Straßen und auf den Plätzen
sieht man stets viele Menschen.

## LESSON XXII

**69.**              Word Order of Objects, etc.

| | |
|---|---|
| 1. Ich schickte **ihm** gestern ein Buch. | I sent him a book yesterday. |
| 2. Ich schicke **Ihnen** dieses. | I send you this. |
| 3. Er hat **es mir** geschickt. | He sent it to me. |
| 4. Ich schickte **meinem Sohne** ein Buch. | I sent my son a book. |
| 5. Ich schickte gestern ein Buch **an ihn** (an meinen Sohn). | I sent a book to him (to my son) yesterday. |
| 6. Ich habe ihm **gestern** ein gutes Buch geschickt. | I sent him a good book yester- day. |

OBSERVE: 1. Pronoun objects without prepositions precede
all other objects, adverbs, etc.

2. Personal pronouns precede other pronouns.

3. Of several personal pronouns, the accusative precedes.

4. Of noun objects without prepositions, the person precedes
the thing.

5. Prepositional objects follow other objects and adverbs.

6. Adverbs of time usually precede everything, except pronouns not governed by a preposition.

### 70.    Word Order in Dependent Sentences.

| | |
|---|---|
| Ich arbeite nicht, weil ich müde bin. | I am not working, because I am tired. |
| Ich hoffe, daß er uns besuchen wird. | I hope that he will visit us. |
| Ich glaube, daß er Zeit gehabt haben wird. | I think that he will have had time. |
| Da ich müde bin, arbeite ich nicht. | As I am tired I am not working. |
| Er sagt, daß er keine Zeit gehabt (hat). | He says he has had no time. |

OBSERVE: 1. The verb comes last in a dependent sentence.

2. In compound tenses, the participle and infinitive immediately precede the verb, *i.e.* the auxiliary.

3. If both participle and infinitive occur, the participle precedes the infinitive.

4. The place of the subject in a dependent sentence is usually the same as in English.

5. The dependent is always separated from the principal sentence by a comma.

6. When a dependent sentence precedes the principal sentence, the subject of the latter is thrown after the verb.

7. The tense auxiliary haben or sein is frequently omitted in a daß clause.

### 71.    Use of wenn, als, wann.

| | |
|---|---|
| Wenn ich meine Pflicht tue (getan habe), bin ich glücklich. | When I do (have done) my duty, I am happy. |
| Ich besuchte immer meine Freunde, wenn ich in der Stadt war. | I always visited my friends when(ever) I was in town. |

Ich ging gestern aus, **als** es　I went out yesterday when it
　zehn geschlagen hatte.　　　　had struck ten.
**Als** ich jung war, war ich stark.　When I was young I was
　　　　　　　　　　　　　　　strong.
**Wann** war sein Vater hier?　When was his father here?

OBSERVE: 1. 'When' = **wenn** always with present or perfect.

2. 'When' = **wenn** with imperfect and pluperfect of a habitual or repeated occurrence, state, or condition (= 'whenever').

3. 'When' = **als** with imperfect and pluperfect only, of a single, definite occurrence, or of a state or condition once occurring.

4. 'When?' interrogative = **wann?**

NOTE. — Remember that **wenn** also = 'if.'

## EXERCISE XXII

besonders, especially, particu-
　larly.
da (conj.), as, when, since.
daß, that (conj.).
enttäuscht, disappointed.
die Enttäuschung, –en, disap-
　pointment.
erkältet sein, to have a cold.
etwas, something, somewhat.
geben, to act, present (a play).
gefallen, gefiel, gefallen, to
　please, suit.
glauben, to believe, think.
herrlich, magnificent, splendid.
hoffen, to hope.
liegen, lag, gelegen, to lie, be.
die Rolle, –n, part.

das Schauspiel, –(e)s, –e, play.
der Schauspieler, –s, —, actor.
die Schauspielerin, –nen, ac-
　tress.
das Spiel, –(e)s, –e, play, act-
　ing.
sprechen, sprach, gesprochen, to
　speak.
das Stück, –(e)s, –e, piece,
　play.
das Theater, –s, —, theatre.
überne'hmen (übernahm, über=
　nommen), to undertake.
warum? why? wherefore?
weil, because.
zurück, back (adv.).

IDIOMS: **Im Theater,** at the theatre; **ins Theater gehen,** to go to
the theatre.

A. 1. Wann sind Sie im deutschen Theater gewesen? 2. Wir
sind gestern abend dort gewesen. 3. Warum sind Sie dahin

gegangen? 4. Weil man Shakespeares Hamlet gab. 5. Wir
wollten besonders gern die berühmte Schauspielerin Fräulein M.
in der Rolle der Ophelia sehen. 6. Wie hat Ihnen ihr Spiel
gefallen? 7. Wir waren etwas enttäuscht, da unsere Plätze
so weit zurück lagen, daß wir nicht gut hören konnten. 8. Aber
ich kann Ihnen sagen, daß das Stück uns sonst sehr gut
gefallen hat. 9. Hat der berühmte Schauspieler S. den Hamlet gespielt? 10. Nein, Herr B. mußte diese Rolle über-
nehmen, da Herr S. nicht spielen konnte. 11. Das war auch
eine große Enttäuschung, aber ich hoffe, daß er morgen abend
spielen wird. 12. Und weshalb konnte er nicht spielen?
13. Ich glaube, daß er erkältet war und nicht sprechen konnte.
14. Finden Sie nicht, daß dieses Schauspiel herrlich ist?
15. Jawohl! Besonders wenn ein guter Schauspieler den
Hamlet spielt. 16. Wir wollen nächste Woche wieder ins
Theater gehen, um Herrn S. zu sehen.

*B.* Oral exercise on the above.

*C.* Complete the following sentences: 1. Ich kann heute
nicht kommen, weil . . . 2. Wir werden müde, wenn . . .
3. Wir konnten heute keine Besuche machen, denn . . .
4. Mein Freund glaubt, daß . . . 5. Ich werde Sie morgen
besuchen, wenn . . . 6. Ich hoffe, daß . . . 7. Der Schüler
kommt nicht, da . . . 8. Er konnte die Aufgabe nicht machen,
weil . . . 9. Ich bin ihm begegnet, als . . . 10. Ich will
morgen zur Stadt fahren, um . . .

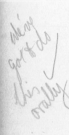

*D.* 1. I like to go to the theatre when I have time. 2. I
wanted to go to the theatre yesterday evening, for Miss M. was
playing the part of (the) Ophelia. 3. But I was obliged to stay
at home, because I had headache. 4. I was very [much] disappointed, as Miss M. is a celebrated actress. 5. People say
that she plays this part especially well. 6. Were you there yesterday evening? 7. Yes, but my seat was so far back that I
couldn't hear well. 8. I was disappointed, as the celebrated

actor S. didn't play.   9. They (man) say that he had a cold
and couldn't speak.   10. I do not believe that he had a cold.
11. When he was here last year he had a cold and couldn't
play.   12. Perhaps he doesn't like to play in a small town.
13. If he is well to-morrow evening, I hope that he will play
(the) Hamlet.   14. When will Miss M. play again in this town?

*E.* Lesestück : Ein Schauspieler spielte die Rolle des Geistes
im Hamlet sehr schlecht und wurde ausgezischt.   Nachdem er
dies eine Zeitlang ertragen hatte, versetzte er die Zuhörer
dadurch wieder in gute Laune, daß er sagte : "Meine Damen
und Herren !  Es tut mir sehr leid, daß ich bei Ihnen keinen
Erfolg habe ; wenn Sie nicht zufrieden sind, so muß ich den
Geist aufgeben."

# LESSON XXIII

**72.**          **The Relative Pronoun der.**

| SINGULAR. | | | PLURAL. |
|---|---|---|---|
| *Masc.* | *Fem.* | *Neut.* | *All Genders.* |
| *N.* der | die | das | die, who, which, that. |
| *G.* dessen | deren | dessen | deren, whose, of which. |
| *D.* dem | der | dem | denen, (to, for) whom, which. |
| *A.* den | die | das | die, whom, which, that. |

OBSERVE : These forms are the same as those of the definite
article, except the added –en of the genitive singular and plural
and the dative plural.

**73.**          **The Relative Pronoun welcher.**

| SINGULAR. | | | PLURAL. |
|---|---|---|---|
| *Masc.* | *Fem.* | *Neut.* | *All Genders.* |
| *N.* welcher | welche | welches | welche, who, which, that. |
| *G.* — | — | — | — |
| *D.* welchem | welcher | welchem | welchen, (to, for) whom, etc. |
| *A.* welchen | welche | welches | welche, whom, etc. |

Observe : Welcher follows the dieser model, but lacks the genitive, which is replaced by the genitive forms of der (dessen, 2c.).

## 74.                    Relative Clauses.

Das ist der Arzt, der (welcher) hier war.

That is the doctor who was here.

Hier ist der Stock, den (welchen) Sie gehabt haben.

Here is the stick which you have had.

Hier sind Bücher, die (welche) nützlich sind.

Here are books that are useful.

Kennen Sie die Dame, der (welcher) wir begegneten?

Do you know the lady we met?

Das Haus, worin (= in dem) ich wohne.

The house in which I live.

Observe : 1. The relative agrees with its antecedent in gender and number ; the case depends on its use in its own clause.

2. Since all relative clauses are dependent, the verb comes last (§ 70).

3. Der and welcher refer to both persons and things ; der is more common than welcher, which is chiefly used to avoid repetitions of der.

4. Der and welcher, referring to inanimate objects, are sometimes replaced by wo (wor before a vowel) preceding a preposition.

5. The relative is never omitted in German.

Note. — The gen. dessen, 2c. always precedes the word on which it depends: Ein Baum, dessen Blätter grün sind, ' A tree, the leaves of which are green.'

### EXERCISE XXIII

Abschied nehmen, nahm, ge= nommen, to take leave.

empfangen, empfing, emp= fangen, to receive.

bringen, brachte, gebracht, to bring.

die Erfrischung, –en, refresh- ment.

einladen (lud, geladen), to invite.

das Erlebnis, –ses, –se, experi- ence.

der Gast, –es, ⁿe, guest.

das Gedicht, –(e)s, –e, poem.

die Gemahlin, –nen, wife.

die Gesellschaft, –en, company,
  party.

interessa'nt, interesting.

kennen, kannte, gekannt, to
  know, be acquainted with.

lustig, gay, merry.

die Mitternacht, ⁿe, midnight.

schlagen, schlug, geschlagen, to
  strike.

singen, sang, gesungen, to
  sing.

vortragen (trug, getragen), to
  recite.

zubringen, to spend, pass (time).

zugegen, present.

*A.* 1. Ich bin gestern abend in einer Gesellschaft gewesen,
zu welcher man mich eingeladen hatte. 2. Der Herr des
Hauses, in dem ich war, ist Herr Heinze, dessen Gemahlin
eine Verwandte von mir (of mine) ist. 3. Als wir ankamen,
empfingen uns die Damen des Hauses. 4. Eine junge Dame,
die ich sehr gut kenne, war auch zugegen. 5. Sie spielte auf
einem Klavier, welches Herr Heinze seiner Frau neulich ge=
schenkt hat. 6. Ein Bruder der Dame, welche gespielt hatte,
sang ein hübsches Lied. 7. Dann spielten und sangen mehrere
Herren und Damen, die ich nicht kenne. 8. Ein Schauspieler,
den ich schon im Theater gesehen hatte, trug ein schönes Ge=
dicht von Goethe vor. 9. Viele Gäste waren zugegen, welche
in Deutschland gewesen waren. 10. Einer von ihnen erzählte
mir seine Erlebnisse, die sehr interessant waren. 11. Als es
elf geschlagen hatte, brachten die Bedienten Erfrischungen.
12. Die jungen Herren und Damen, die sehr lustig geworden
waren, fingen an zu tanzen. 13. Die Gäste, welche einen
sehr angenehmen Abend zugebracht hatten, nahmen erst zwei
Stunden nach Mitternacht Abschied.

*B.* Complete orally, supplying suitable relative pronouns:
1. Die Gäste, — zugegen waren. 2. Die Gäste, — er eingeladen
hatte. 3. Der Freund, — ich ein Geschenk schicke. 4. Das
Buch, — auf dem Tische liegt. 5. Der Schauspieler von —
ich spreche. 6. Die Dame, — wir begegnet sind. 7. Die

Damen, — wir Blumen schickten.   8. Der Herr, — Haus ich
gekauft habe.   9. Das Haus, in — er wohnt.   10. Die Nachbarn, mit — Kindern wir spielen.   11. Das Schauspiel, von
— ich Ihnen erzählte.   12. Der Schüler, — der Lehrer lobt.
13. Der Lehrer, — den Schüler lobt.   14. Die Lehrerin, —
Mutter gestorben ist.

*C.* 1. Mr. and Mrs. Heinze, whom I know very well, invited me to a party.   2. The party of (von) which I am speaking took place yesterday evening.   3. The house in which
these good friends live is large and handsome.   4. Many ladies
and gentlemen, whom I had never (yet) seen, were also present.   5. A young lady played on the piano and sang a song
which pleased the guests very much (ſehr gut).   6. The piano
on which she played was a new one, which Mr. Heinze pre-
sented to his wife lately.   7. When she had sung, a celebrated
actor recited a very beautiful poem.   8. The poem he recited
was by (von) Goethe.   9. A friend of mine, beside whom I was
sitting, and who had been in Germany, related his experiences
to me.   10. When the servants had brought refreshments, many
of (von) the older guests wanted to go home.   11. The young
gentlemen and ladies, who remained in order to dance, took
leave two hours after midnight.

*D.* Lesestück : Der Kronprinz Olaf von Norwegen ist ein rei-
zender kleiner Bengel, ist aber zuweilen unartig.   Seine Mutter,
die Königin, züchtigt ihn immer selbst, wenn es nötig ist.
Eines Tages war der Kleine sich bewußt, Strafe verdient zu
haben.   Als die königliche Mutter ihn suchte, war er nirgends
zu finden.   Auch seine Großmutter, die Königin Alexandra
von England, half mitsuchen.   Als sie nun in ihr Schlafzimmer trat, rief eine helle Kinderstimme unter dem Bette :
"Großmutter, suchen sie dich auch?   Komm her zu mir;
ich will dich beschützen."

# LESSON XXIV

**75.**     The Passive with **werden.**

| *Present Indicative.* | *Imperfect Indicative.* |
|---|---|
| I am (being) praised, etc. | I was (being) praised, etc. |

| | | | | | |
|---|---|---|---|---|---|
| ich | werde | gelobt | ich | ward   or wurde | gelobt |
| du | wirst | „ | du | wardst or wurdest | „ |
| er | wird | „ | er | ward   or wurde | „ |
| wir | werden | „ | wir | wurden | „ |
| ihr | werdet | „ | ihr | wurdet | „ |
| sie | werden | „ | sie | wurden | „ |

*Pres. Infin.*  gelobt (zu) werden, to be praised.

### EXAMPLES.

| | |
|---|---|
| Er wird oft von uns gelobt. | He is often praised by us. |
| Der Boden wird durch den Regen fruchtbar gemacht. | The soil is made fertile by the rain. |

OBSERVE : 1. The past participle of a transitive verb added to the verb werden forms the passive voice of that verb, whenever agency is implied or specified.

2. The personal agent of the passive takes the preposition **von** = 'by' (+dative); other agency is expressed by **durch** or **mit.**

NOTES. — 1. The past part. of a verb added to **sein** denotes a permanent condition resulting from the action of the verb, no agency being implied ; a participle so used is often purely adjectival in character (see Lesson XLIX): Das Feld ist gepflügt, 'The field is ploughed'; Ich bin befriedigt, 'I am satisfied.'

2. **Man** with the active voice often replaces the passive when there is no definite personal agent: Man bestellt den Boden im Frühling, 'The ground is prepared in spring.'

**76. Prepositions with Accusative.** The following preposi-tions govern the accusative only :

| | | | | | | |
|---|---|---|---|---|---|---|
| bis | durch | für | gegen | ohne | um | wider |

**77.**          **Bis,** till, until (time), as far as (space).

Bis Abend; bis Rom.          Till evening ; as far as Rome.

NOTES. — 1. **Bis** is more commonly used as an adverb followed by a prep. of direction: Bis gegen Abend, 'till towards evening'; bis zur Stadt, 'as far as the town.'

2. With numerals **bis** ='or': Vier bis fünf, 'four or five.'

**78.**          **Durch,** through, by (means of).

Er reitet durch den Wald.          He rides through the wood.

Durch einen Brief gewarnt.          Warned by a letter.

**79.**          **Für,** for, on behalf of.

Der Brief ist für ihn.          The letter is for him.

Ich spreche für Sie.          I speak on your behalf.

**80.**          **Gegen,** towards, against.

Er reitet gegen die Brücke.          He rides towards the bridge.

Gegen acht Uhr.          Towards eight o'clock.

Stellen Sie den Stuhl gegen          Place the chair against the
die Wand.                                      wall.

Wir kämpfen gegen den Feind.          We fight against the enemy.

**81.**          **Ohne,** without.

Ohne Freunde; ohne Sie.          Without friends ; without you.

**82.**          **Um,** round, around, at.

1. Of Place :

Er geht um die Stadt herum.          He walks round the town.

NOTE. — The adverb **herum** is usually added after the object in this sense.

2. Of Time :

Um diese Zeit; um zwei Uhr.          At this time; at 2 o'clock.

**83.**          **Wider,** against, contrary to.

Wider meinen Wunsch.          Against my wish.

Wider mein Erwarten.          Contrary to my expectation.

**84. Contractions.** Durch, für, and um are generally contracted with the neuter of the unemphasized definite article, as follows:

durchs (= durch das)     fürs (= für das)     ums (= um das)

**85. Da for Pronoun.** With personal pronouns of the third person referring to inanimate objects, the pronoun is replaced by da (before vowels dar) prefixed to the preposition (except bis and ohne) and written with it as one word:

Dies ist mein Hut; ich habe       This is my hat; I gave ten
   zehn Mark dafür gegeben.          marks for it.

### EXERCISE XXIV

ander, other.
die Arbeit, –en, work, labour.
ausstreuen, to scatter.
bereiten, to make ready, prepare.
bestellen, to till, prepare.
der Boden, –s, ground, soil.
da'mals, then, at that time.
die Egge, –n, harrow.
das Ende, –s, –n, end.
fruchtbar, fruitful, fertile.
das Getreide, –s, grain, corn.
der Hafer, –s, oats.
heutzutage, nowadays, in these days, now.
hin und her, to and fro, backwards and forwards.
lockern, to loosen.
der Mais, –es, Indian corn.
die Maschine, –n, machine.
noch nicht, not yet.
pflügen, to plough.
die Saat, –en, sowing, green crop.
der Säemann, –(e)s, ⁻er, sower.
der Sonnenschein, –(e)s, sunshine.
verhindern, to hinder, prevent.
wachsen (s.), wuchs, gewachsen, to grow.
der Weizen, –s, wheat.
ziehen, zog, gezogen, to draw.
zudecken, to cover (up).

*A.* 1. Das Feld wird gegen Ende März oder im April für die Saat bereitet. 2. Um diese Zeit werden Weizen, Hafer und anderes Getreide gesät. 3. Später pflanzt man Kartoffeln, Mais, ꝛc. 4. Zuerst wird der Boden gepflügt. 5. Der Boden wird dann mit einer Egge gelockert. 6. So wird er durch den Regen und den Sonnenschein fruchtbar

gemacht. 7. Ohne Regen und Sonnenschein kann die Saat
nicht wachsen. 8. Nachher wird der Same heutzutage mit
einer Maschine gesät, welche von Pferden oder Ochsen hin und
her gezogen wird. 9. Früher tat man das ohne Maschine.
10. Damals wurde der Same vom Säemann gesät, der hin
und her ging und den Samen ausstreute. 11. Nachher wurde
der Same durch die Egge zugedeckt. 12. Ist das Feld schon
bestellt, welches Sie voriges Jahr kauften? 13. Nein, es ist
noch nicht bestellt. 14. Die Arbeit wurde oft durch das
schlechte Wetter verhindert.

*B.* Oral: 1. Um welche Zeit wird der Weizen gesät? 2. Ist
Ihr Weizen schon gesät? 3. Wann werden die Kartoffeln
gepflanzt? 4. Wann pflanzt man Kartoffeln? 5. Was tut
man zuerst, wenn man ein Feld für die Saat bereiten will?
6. Was tut man dann? 7. Wie wird der Boden gelockert?
8. Weshalb wird der Boden gelockert? 9. Wie wurde der
Same früher gesät? 10. Wie wird die Maschine gezogen?
11. Ist Ihr Feld schon gepflügt? 12. Weshalb ist es noch
nicht gepflügt? 13. Wollten Sie es vorige Woche bestellen?
14. Wann wollen Sie Ihren Hafer und Ihre Erbsen säen?
15. Was wollen Sie in diesem Beete pflanzen?

*C.* Turn the following orally into the passive voice: 1. Das
schlechte Wetter verhindert die Arbeit. 2. Der Bauer bestellte
das Feld. 3. Die Egge deckt den Samen zu. 4. Die Egge
deckte den Samen zu. 5. Der Säemann streute den Samen
aus. 6. Die Pferde ziehen die Egge hin und her. 7. Der
Regen macht den Boden fruchtbar. 8. Man pflanzt jetzt die
Kartoffeln. 9. Der Knecht pflügt das Feld. 10. Die Knechte
pflügten die Felder.

*D.* 1. Grain is sown towards [the] end [of] March or in
April. 2. The field must first be prepared (use man).
3. The soil is ploughed, and then a harrow is drawn to and
fro. 4. It is drawn by horses or oxen. 5. The soil is loos-
ened by the harrow. 6. It is made fruitful by the rain and

sun. 7. Without rain and sunshine the wheat cannot grow. 8. In these days the seed is not scattered by the sower. 9. That used to be done (use man) formerly, but now it is sown with a machine. 10. Our field is not yet ploughed, because we were hindered by the bad weather. 11. We wanted to plough it earlier, in order to sow our wheat. 12. We mean to begin to plough it to-morrow, if the weather is fine. 13. We shall plant our potatoes and our Indian corn next week. 14. Our cabbage and our tomatoes are planted already.

*E.* Lesestück: Es ging ein Säemann aus, zu säen. Und indem er säete, fiel etliches an den Weg; da kamen die Vögel und fraßen es auf. Etliches fiel in das Steinichte, wo es nicht viel Erde hatte, und ging bald auf, darum, daß es nicht tiefe Erde hatte. Als aber die Sonne aufging, verwelkte es, und weil es nicht Wurzel hatte, ward es dürre. Etliches fiel unter die Dornen und die Dornen wuchsen auf und erstickten es. Etliches fiel auf gutes Land und trug Frucht, etliches hundertfältig, etliches sechzigfältig, etliches dreißigfältig.

## LESSON XXV

**86.** **The Time of Day.**

| | |
|---|---|
| Wie viel Uhr ist es? | What time is it? |
| Es ist eins (ein Uhr). | It is one o'clock. |
| Um zwölf Uhr mittags (nachts). | At twelve o'clock noon (at night). |
| Es ist ein Viertel auf zwei. | It is a quarter past one. |
| Es ist halb zwei. | It is half-past one. |
| Es ist drei Viertel auf zwei. | It is a quarter to two. |
| Um halb eins (ein Uhr). | At half-past twelve. |
| Um 23 Minuten nach eins. | At 23 minutes past one. |
| Es ist 21 Minuten vor zwei. | It is 21 minutes to two. |
| Acht Uhr morgens (vormittags). | Eight o'clock A.M. |
| Drei Uhr nachmittags. | Three o'clock P.M. |
| Sechs Uhr abends. | Six o'clock P.M. |

H

Observe: 1. The verb fein in these expressions is singular.

2. Uhr remains uninflected, and may be omitted.

3. 'At' = um.

4. Ein remains uninflected, but eins is used when Uhr is omitted.

5. The 'quarter past' is expressed by ein Viertel auf + the number of the hour following.

6. The 'half-past' is expressed by halb + the hour following.

7. The 'quarter to' is expressed by drei Viertel auf + the hour following.

8. The 'minutes past' is expressed by nach; the 'minutes to' by vor.

9. The abbreviation 'A.M.' = morgens or vormittags (abbreviated Vm.); 'P.M.' = nachmittags (abbreviated Nm.), abends, or nachts, according to the lateness of the hour.

Notes. — 1. Colloquially auf is often omitted after Viertel.

2. The time may also, as always in railway time-tables, be expressed thus: Ein Uhr fünfzehn = 1.15; ein Uhr dreißig = 1.30; ein Uhr fünf=undfünfzig = 1.55.

## 87.                    Genitive of Time.

| | |
|---|---|
| Des Tages; des Abends. | By day; in the evening. |
| Ich ging eines Tages im Park. | I was walking one day in the park. |
| Mittwochs haben wir nach=mittags keine Schule. | On Wednesdays we have no school in the afternoon. |

Observe: 1. Point of time is often expressed by an adverbial genitive singular, when denoting indefinite time, or time with reference to a habitual action, but only with Tag, 'day,' days of the week, and divisions of the day, used with or without article.

2. When the article is omitted, the genitive is not usually written with a capital, except with days of the week.

Notes. — 1. With determinatives other than the art., the acc. must be used, except in the expression dieser Tage (gen. plur.) = 'of late.'

2. Nacht, though fem., is similarly used, with or without the masc. art.: (Des) Nachts schläft man, 'We sleep by night.'

### EXERCISE XXV

bedeuten, to signify, mean.
beinahe, almost, nearly.
damit, with that, with it, etc.
doch, yet, still, however.
freilich, certainly, to be sure.
der Minutenzeiger, –s, —,
　minute-hand, long hand.
der Pulsschlag, –(e)s, ˮe, pulse-
　beat.
die Runde, –n, round, circuit.
der Sekundenzeiger, –s, —,
　second-hand.
stehen, stand, gestanden, to
　stand.

der Strich, –(e)s, –e, stroke,
　mark.
der Stundenzeiger, –s, —,
　hour-hand, short hand.
die Tasche, –n, pocket.
tragen, trug, getragen, to
　bear, carry, wear.
die Zahl, –en, number, figure.
zählen, to count.
der Zeiger, –s, —, hand (of
　a time-piece).
die Ziffer, –n, figure.
das Zifferblatt, –(e)s, ˮer, dial,
　face.

*A.* 1. Tragen Sie eine Uhr? 2. Jawohl, ich habe eine in
der (my) Tasche. 3. Zeigen Sie mir das Zifferblatt Ihrer
Uhr. 4. Was sehen Sie auf dem Zifferblatt? 5. Ich sehe
Zahlen oder Ziffern, von eins bis zwölf. 6. Was bedeuten
diese Ziffern? 7. Sie bedeuten die Stunden des Tages.
8. Aber ein Tag hat doch 24 Stunden, und hier stehen nur
zwölf. 9. Freilich; aber der kleine Zeiger, der Stundenzeiger,
macht zweimal die Runde in 24 Stunden und 2 × 12 macht 24.
10. Was bedeuten die kleinen Striche zwischen den Stunden?
11. Diese bedeuten die Minuten; in jeder Stunde sind 60
Minuten. 12. Weshalb sind nur 5 Striche zwischen den
Stunden? 13. Der große Zeiger, der Minutenzeiger, macht
die Runde einmal in einer Stunde und 5 × 12 macht 60.
14. Uhren haben gewöhnlich auch einen Sekundenzeiger.
15. Dieser wird vom Arzte gebraucht, um die Pulsschläge eines
Kranken zu zählen.

*B.* Oral: 1. Wie viele Stunden hat ein Tag? 2. Wie viele
Ziffern hat eine Uhr? 3. Was für Zeiger hat sie? 4. Wie viel

Uhr ist es, wenn beide Zeiger auf 12 stehen (are at twelve)?
5. Wie viel Uhr ist es, wenn der Minutenzeiger auf 6 und der
Stundenzeiger zwischen eins und zwei steht? 6. Wenn der
Minutenzeiger auf 9 steht und der Stundenzeiger beinahe auf 4?
7. Um wie viel Uhr gehen Sie gewöhnlich zu Bett? 8. Wann
sind Sie heute morgen aufgestanden? 9. Wie viel Uhr ist es,
wenn der Minutenzeiger auf 4 steht und der Stundenzeiger
zwischen 6 und 7? 10. Wenn der Minutenzeiger auf 8 und
der Stundenzeiger zwischen 8 und 9 steht?

*C.* 1. Can you tell me what time it is? 2. Yes, I have a
watch in my pocket. 3. I will show you the dial. 4. I see
that it is a quarter to eight, for the long hand is (ſteht) at nine,
and the short hand almost at eight. 5. What time is it when the
minute-hand is at 6 and the hour-hand between 9 and 10?
6. It is then half-past nine. 7. How many hands has a watch?
8. Mine has three, one for the hours, one for the minutes, and
one for the seconds. 9. Not all watches have a second-hand,
but it is used by physicians in order to count the pulse-beats of
their patients. 10. At what o'clock do you usually get up in
the morning? 11. I usually rise at half-past seven. 12. Yesterday evening I was working until after midnight. 13. I was
too tired this morning to rise at the usual hour. 14. It was 20
minutes past eight when I got up. 15. Goethe, the great German poet, usually rose at 5 o'clock or at half-past 5 in the summer, when he was (still) young. 16. The train for (nach)
Berlin will leave at 9.10 A.M. and will arrive at 2.48 P.M.

*D.* Leſeſtücke:

1.                              Rätſel.

    Wie heißt das Ding dort an der Wand?
    Es ſchlägt und hat doch keine Hand;
    Es hängt und geht doch fort und fort;
    Es geht und kommt doch nicht vom Ort.

                                    [Die Uhr.]

2. Um ſechs Uhr morgens werden die Schüler durch die

Glocke geweckt; sie wachen auf und müssen dann sofort aufstehen; dann waschen sie Hände und Gesicht und ziehen die
Kleider an.   Bis halb acht Uhr lernen sie ihre Aufgaben; um
drei Viertel auf acht frühstücken sie; nach dem Frühstück haben
sie eine halbe Stunde frei.   Um neun Uhr gehen sie in das
Schulzimmer und bleiben bis elf Uhr dort.   Von elf Uhr bis
halb zwölf ist Pause.   Dann haben sie Zeichenstunde oder
arbeiten im Studierzimmer.   Um ein Uhr wird zu Mittag
gegessen.

## LESSON XXVI

**88.    Pres. and Impf. Subj. of haben, sein, werden.**

*Present.*                              *Imperfect.*

I have, may have, etc.              I had, might have, etc.

| ich habe | wir haben | ich hätte | wir hätten |
|----------|-----------|-----------|------------|
| du habest | ihr habet | du hättest | ihr hättet |
| er habe | sie haben | er hätte | sie hätten |

I am, may be, etc.                  I was, might be, etc.

| ich sei | wir seien | ich wäre | wir wären |
|---------|-----------|----------|-----------|
| du seiest | ihr seiet | du wärest | ihr wäret |
| er sei | sie seien | er wäre | sie wären |

I become, may become, etc.      I became, might become, etc.

| ich werde | wir werden | ich würde | wir würden |
|-----------|------------|-----------|------------|
| du werdest | ihr werdet | du würdest | ihr würdet |
| er werde | sie werden | er würde | sie würden |

OBSERVE: 1. The persistent **e** of the present endings; also
the umlaut of the imperfect.

2. These tenses of haben, sein, and werden serve to form the
compound tenses of other verbs, as below.

**89.**    Subjunctive of **machen, sprechen, fallen.**

### Present.

| I make, may make, etc. | I speak, may speak, etc. | I fall, may fall, etc. |
|---|---|---|
| ich mache | ich spreche | ich falle |
| du machest | du sprechest | du fallest |
| er mache | er spreche | er falle |
| wir machen | wir sprechen | wir fallen |
| ihr machet | ihr sprechet | ihr fallet |
| sie machen | sie sprechen | sie fallen |

### Imperfect.

| I made, might make, etc. | I spoke, might speak, etc. | I fell, might fall, etc. |
|---|---|---|
| ich machte | ich spräche | ich fiele |
| du machtest | du sprächest | du fielest |
| er machte | er spräche | er fiele |
| wir machten | wir sprächen | wir fielen |
| ihr machtet | ihr sprächet | ihr fielet |
| sie machten | sie sprächen | sie fielen |

### Perfect.

| I have (may have) made, spoken, etc. | I have (may have) fallen, etc. |
|---|---|
| ich habe  gemacht, gesprochen | ich sei  gefallen |
| du habest gemacht, gesprochen | du seiest gefallen |
| er habe  gemacht, gesprochen, 2c. | er sei  gefallen, 2c. |

### Pluperfect.

| I had (might have) made, spoken, etc. | I had (might have) fallen, etc. |
|---|---|
| ich hätte  gemacht, gesprochen | ich wäre  gefallen |
| du hättest gemacht, gesprochen, 2c. | du wärest gefallen, 2c. |

*Future.*

I shall make, speak, fall, etc.

ich werde machen, sprechen, fallen
du werdest machen, sprechen, fallen
er werde machen, sprechen, fallen, 2c.

*Future Perfect.*

I shall have made (spoken), etc.

ich werde gemacht (gesprochen) haben
du werdest gemacht (gesprochen) haben, 2c.

I shall have fallen, etc.

ich werde gefallen-sein
du werdest gefallen sein, 2c.

OBSERVE: 1. The persistent **e** of the endings.

2. The imperfect subjunctive of all regular weak verbs is the same as the imperfect indicative.

3. Strong verbs with **a, o, u** in the imperfect indicative stem take umlaut in the imperfect subjunctive.

4. The compound tenses are formed by adding the past participle or the infinitive, or both, to the auxiliary, precisely as in the indicative (for word order, see § 49).

**90. Use of Subjunctive.** 1. The use of this mood is confined almost entirely to dependent sentences.

2. The English forms with 'may' and 'might' in the paradigms only partially and occasionally represent the exact force of the German subjunctive:

| | |
|---|---|
| Er sagte, daß er Geld habe. | He said he had money. |
| Ich habe oft gewünscht, daß ich Geld hätte. | I have often wished that I had (might have) money. |

**91.**       **Indirect Statements and Questions.**

| | |
|---|---|
| Er sagt: „Ich bin müde." | He says: "I am tired." |
| Er sagt, daß er müde ist. | He says (that) he is tired. |

| | |
|---|---|
| Er sagte : „Ich bin müde." | He said : " I am tired." |
| Er sagte, daß er müde sei (wäre). | He said (that) he was tired. |
| Er fragte : „Wer ist da?" | He asked : " Who is there?" |
| Er fragte, wer da sei (wäre). | He asked who was there. |
| Ich fragte, ob er müde sei (wäre). | I asked if (whether) he was tired. |
| Sie sagten, daß sie ihren Vater liebten. | They said that they loved their father. |
| Er sagte, er sei (wäre) müde. | He said (that) he was tired. |

OBSERVE : 1. Indirect statements and questions are always dependent clauses, and have the word order of such clauses (§ 70).

2. The verb of the dependent clause is usually in the subjunctive if the verb of the governing clause be in a past tense, and, unlike English, has regularly the same tense which it would have if the statement or question were direct.

NOTE. — The indic. is used in indir. statement to express a fact as undisputed or as vouched for by the speaker.

3. Where the present subjunctive of a verb has no forms distinct from those of its present indicative, the imperfect subjunctive is used instead of the present, as in the last example but one above.

4. 'If' or 'whether' in dependent questions = **ob**.

5. The conjunction **daß** may be omitted in clauses of indirect statement, which then have the word order of a principal sentence (verb second).

## EXERCISE XXVI

annehmen (nahm, genom=
  men), to accept.
befehlen, befahl, befohlen,
  (*dat.*), to order, command.
berühren, to touch.
dick, thick.

die Einladung, –en, invitation.
einst, once (upon a time).
entdecken, to discover.
französisch, French.
fürchten, to fear, be afraid of.

gedenken, gedachte, gedacht, to intend.

holen, to get, fetch, bring.

imstande sein, to be in a position to, be able to.

laden, lud, geladen, to invite.

lebe'ndig, living.

der Löwe, –n, –n, lion.

Nord=Afrika, n., –s, North Africa.

reisen (s., h.), to travel, journey; go (away), set out (on a journey).

der Revolver, –s, —, revolver.

der Schädel, –s, —, skull.

der Scheik, –s, –e, sheik.

sofort, immediately.

sondern (*after neg.*), but.

töten, to kill.

trotzdem, in spite of this (that), nevertheless.

die Überra'schung, –en, surprise.

u'nangenehm, disagreeable, unpleasant.

die Waffe, –n, weapon.

warnen, to warn.

IDIOMS: 1. **Bei Tisch,** at table, at meals.
2. **Zu Tisch laden,** to invite to dinner.

*A.* Ein französischer Offizier, der in Nord=Afrika reiste, wurde einst von einem Scheik zu Tisch geladen. Man warnte ihn, daß dieser seinen Gästen oft unangenehme Überraschungen bereite. Trotzdem sagte der Offizier, er werde die Einladung annehmen, da er diesen Mann nicht fürchte. Als er nachher bei Tisch war, fühlte er, daß seine Füße etwas Lebendiges berührten. Bald entdeckte er, daß es ein großer Löwe war. Sofort befahl er seinem Diener, seinen Revolver zu holen. Der Scheik fragte, was das bedeute. Er sagte auch, daß man mit dieser kleinen Waffe nicht imstande sei, den Löwen zu töten, der einen sehr dicken Schädel habe. Der Gast antwortete, er gedenke den Revolver nicht gegen das Tier, sondern gegen den Scheik zu brauchen. Er sagte, er werde den Scheik sofort töten, wenn der Löwe unangenehm würde.

*B.* Oral: Turn the following direct statements and questions into the indirect form, prefixing 'man sagte, daß' to the statements, and either 'man fragte' or 'man fragte, ob' to the questions. 1. Sie sind müde. 2. Der Offizier wird die Einladung annehmen. 3. Das ist ein großer Löwe. 4. Dies sind große Löwen. 5. Das waren große Löwen. 6. Der Diener wird den Revolver holen. 7. Hat er den Revolver geholt? 8. Wer hat den Revolver geholt? 9. Ist der Diener imstande, einen Löwen zu töten? 10. Wer gedenkt, die Waffe zu brauchen. 11. Wird er den Löwen töten?

*C.* 1. The officer told me that the sheik had invited him to dinner. 2. I warned him that the sheik was an unpleasant man. 3. The officer answered that he didn't fear the sheik. 4. He discovered that a big lion was under the table. 5. At once he asked the sheik why the lion was there. 6. He (dieſer) replied that it (eŝ) was a pleasant surprise which he had prepared for his guest. 7. The officer then said that he also had a pleasant surprise for the sheik. 8. Thereupon he beckoned to his servant, and the servant got the revolver. 9. As (alŝ) he was giving it to his master, he warned him that a lion had a very thick skull. 10. He said that it was impossible (unmöglich) to kill him with this weapon. 11. The officer replied that he would be in a position to kill the sheik if the lion became disagreeable.

*D.* Lesestück : Es kam einmal ein Bauer in die Stadt gefahren, hielt vor einer Apotheke an und lud eine große Stubentür vom Wagen ab. Als er die Tür in den Laden trug, machte der Apotheker große Augen und fragte ihn, was er hier wolle ; der Tischler wohne nebenan. Der Bauer aber sagte, er wolle nicht zum Tischler, sondern zum Apotheker. Der Arzt sei bei seiner kranken Frau gewesen und habe ihr eine Arzenei verschrieben. Als der Herr Doktor aber das Rezept aufschreiben wollte, sei weder Feder, noch Tinte, noch Papier im Hause gewesen ; da habe er es mit Kreide an die Stubentür geschrieben. Der Apotheker lachte, bereitete aber dem Bauern die Arzenei, der damit nach Hause zurückfuhr und sie der Frau eingab.

# LESSON XXVII

**92. Prepositions with Dative.** The following nine prepositions govern the dative only:

| | | | |
|---|---|---|---|
| aus | bei | nach | von |
| außer | mit | seit | zu |
| | gegenüber | | |

**93.**　　　　　　　**Aus,** out of, of, from.

1. Out of (motion):

Er kommt aus dem Hause.　　　He comes out of the house.

2. Of (material):

Das Haus ist aus Holz gebaut.　　The house is built of wood.

3. From (origin):

Er kommt aus England.　　　He comes from England.

4. From (cause):

Ich tue es aus Furcht.　　　I do it from fear.

**94.**　　　　　　　**Außer,** outside of, except.

1. Outside of (rest), more commonly **außerhalb** + genitive:

Er wohnt außer der Stadt.　　He lives outside the town.

2. Except, besides, but:

Nichts außer einem Stocke.　　Nothing but (except) a cane.

**95.**　　　　　　　**Bei,** near (by), beside, at, with.

1. Near (by), beside:

Er stand bei der Tür.　　　He stood by (near) the door.

2. At (the house, etc., of = French *chez*), with:

Er wohnt beim Onkel.　　　He lives at his uncle's.

3. About (one's person), with:

Ich habe Geld bei mir.　　　I have money about me.

NOTE. — **Bei** is generally contracted with unemphasized **dem: beim =**
**bei dem.**

**96.** **Mit,** with, along with.

1. With (instrument):

Ich schreibe mit der Feder.      I am writing with the pen.

2. (Along) with, in company with:

Er kommt mit ihnen.      He is coming with them.

**97.** **Nach,** after, to, according to.

1. After (time, order):

Nach der Schule.      After school.

Er kommt nach mir.      He comes after (next to) me.

2. To (with proper names of places):

Er reist nach Rom (China).      He is going to Rome (China).

3. According to (may follow its case in this sense):

Nach meiner Meinung.      According to my opinion.

Meiner Meinung nach.      According to my opinion.

**98.** **Seit,** since.

Seit dem Kriege.      Since the war.

Er ist seit acht Tagen hier.      He has been here for a week.

NOTE. — Observe the use of the pres. tense in this idiom.

**99.** **Von,** from, of, about, by.

1. From:

Er kommt von der Stadt.      He comes from the town.

2. Of, about:

Wir redeten von Ihnen.      We were speaking of you.

3. Of (replacing genitive case):

Vater von vier Kindern.      Father of four children.

NOTES. — 1. The Eng. prep. ' of ' with a noun must generally be rendered in Ger. by a gen. without a prep., whenever it can be turned into
the Eng. poss., otherwise by **von** : Der Kopf eines Hundes, 'The head of
a dog (a dog's head)'; Die Mutter dieser Kinder, 'The mother of these
children'; Wir reden **von** dem Mädchen, 'We are talking of the girl.'

2. **Von** replaces the gen. with unqualified plur. nouns, as in the example
under 3, above ; also to avoid repetition of genitives, and usually after
partitives: Das Haus **vom** Bruder meines Vaters ; einer **von** meinen
Freunden.

4. By (with personal agent after the passive voice):

Er wurde vom König gelobt.        He was praised by the king.

**100.**                  Zu, to, at, for.

1. To (persons):

Er redet zu mir.                  He is speaking to me.

Er geht zu seinem Freunde.        He is going to his friend (*or*
                                  to his friend's house).

NOTE. — The Eng. prep. 'to' with a noun must be rendered in Ger. by
the dat. without a prep., whenever the noun can be turned into the Eng.
indir. obj., otherwise generally by a prep., as in the examples above: Geben
Sie mir das Buch: 'Give the book to me (= Give me the book).'

2. To (places, if not proper names):

Er geht zur Stadt.                He is going to town.

3. At (with names of towns, etc.):

Er wohnt zu Berlin.               He lives at Berlin.

4. At (of time, with Zeit and Stunde, and with names of
festivals):

Zur rechten Zeit (Stunde).        At the right time (hour).

Zu Weihnachten (Ostern).          At Christmas (Easter).

5. At, of (price and measure):

Tuch zu M. 3.— das Meter.         Cloth at 3 marks a metre.

Ein Braten zu 10 Pfund.           A roast of 10 pounds.

6. For (of purpose):

Zum Vergnügen.                    For pleasure.

**101.**               Gegenüber, opposite.

Meinem Hause gegenüber.           Opposite my house.

Gegenüber meinem Hause.           Opposite my house.

NOTE. — This preposition usually follows its case.

**102.** Da with prepositions replaces inanimate objects (compare § 85), but not with außer, seit, or gegenüber.

NOTE. — For other preps. with dat., see App. B, 2, 3; for idioms, App. B, 4, 5

### EXERCISE XXVII

absteigen (s.), to dismount, get out of (a vehicle).
die Bank, -en, bank.
besehen, besah, besehen, to look at, view, see.
besteigen, bestieg, bestiegen, to mount, ascend, get into (a vehicle).
die Börse, -n, Exchange.
die Freundin, -nen, friend.
der Gasthof, -(e)s, ⁻e, hotel.
das Gebäude, -s, —, building.
das Gedränge, -s, crowd, throng, crush.
der Kutscher, -s, —, coachman, driver.
längs (*gen.*, *dat.*, or *acc.*), along.
möglich, possible.
nachdem (*conj.*), after.
niemand, nobody, no one.
der Omnibus, —, -sse, omnibus.
Ostern, Easter.
das Rathaus, -es, ⁻er, town-hall, Guildhall.
die Reise, -n, journey, voyage, trip; eine — machen, to take (go on) a journey.
die Restauratio'n, -en, restaurant.
schauen, to look, gaze.
sitzen, saß, gesessen, to sit.
sobald wie, as soon as.
die Tasse, -n, cup.
verbringen, verbrachte, verbracht, to spend, pass (time).
Zeitlang (eine), for a while.
zu Fuß, on foot.
zu Mittag essen, to dine.

*A.* 1. Ich bin seit vier Jahren Lehrerin in Boston; zu Ostern dieses Jahres machte ich eine Reise nach England. 2. Eine Freundin begleitete mich. 3. Unser Schiff fuhr von Montreal nach London. 4. Nach sieben Tagen kamen wir in London an. 5. Sobald wie möglich fuhren wir zu unserm Gasthofe bei Charing Croß. 6. Da es spät abends war, gingen wir bald zu Bett, nachdem wir eine Zeitlang aus dem Fenster geschaut hatten. 7. Früh morgens gingen wir aus, um die Stadt ein wenig zu besehen. 8. Wir bestiegen einen Omnibus, und saßen auf dem Oberdeck. 9. Der Omnibus fuhr längs dem „Strand“ bis zur Bank von England. 10. Das Gedränge in dieser Straße war sehr groß, besonders bei der

Bank. 11. Diesem Gebäude gegenüber steht die Börse, die
berühmte Londoner „Exchange." 12. Hier stiegen wir ab und
gingen zu Fuß zum Rathaus oder „Guildhall," wie es heißt.
13. Vom Rathause gingen wir zu einer Restauration, wo wir
zu Mittag aßen. 14. Dann fuhren wir mit einer Droschke
zu einem Verwandten. 15. Bei ihm war niemand zu Hause,
außer seiner Frau Gemahlin. 16. Nachdem wir bei ihr eine
Tasse Tee getrunken hatten, kehrten wir zum Gasthofe zurück.
17. So verbrachten wir den Tag sehr angenehm.

*B*. Oral: 1. Wann machtest du die Reise, wovon du er-
zählst? 2. Wohin fuhr das Schiff? 3. Wo kam das Schiff an?
4. Wo steht der Gasthof, wo ihr abstiegt? 5. Wie fuhrt
ihr dahin? 6. Weshalb seid ihr früh zu Bett gegangen?
7. Weshalb schaut man aus den Fenstern? 8. Wo war das
Gedränge besonders groß? 9. Welches Gebäude steht der
Börse gegenüber? 10. Sitzst du gern beim Kutscher? 11. Hat
der Kutscher viel mit euch gesprochen? 12. Sprechen die
Kutscher gern mit Fremden? 13. Wohin fuhr der Omnibus?
14. Längs welcher Straße fuhr er? 15. Gehst du gern zu
Fuß? 16. Weshalb seid ihr zur Restauration gegangen?
17. Warst du heute bei deinen Verwandten? 18. Bei wem
habt ihr Tee getrunken?

*C*. 1. Miss Klein has told me of her journey to London.
2. She had not been in England for five years. 3. A lady,
a friend of her[s], went with her. 4. Their ship did not go
very fast, and only (erst) after ten or twelve days did they
arrive in London. 5. They were tired from the journey,
and went at once to their hotel at (bei) Charing Cross. 6. The
next morning they mounted an omnibus, in order to see the
city. 7. One can learn a great deal about the town, if one
sits on the top. 8. With the omnibus they drove through the
streets as far as the **Guildhall**. 9. Opposite this building stands
a restaurant, where they drank a cup of tea. 10. Afterwards
they went on foot to the Exchange and the Bank of England.

11. At the bank the crush was so great that they had to take a cab. 12. They then drove to the house of an aunt of (von) Miss Klein, with whom they dined. 13. Thus they spent their first day in London very agreeably.

*D.* Lesestück: Ein Reisender war stundenlang durch eine öde Gegend gefahren, ohne einem menschlichen Wesen zu begegnen. Endlich erblickte er eine elende Hütte, vor deren Tür eine hagere Gestalt gegen den Türpfosten lehnte. " Mein Freund," fragte der Reisende, " haben Sie Ihr ganzes Leben hier zugebracht? " " Noch nicht ! " lautete die Antwort.

# LESSON XXVIII

**103.**      The Simple Conditional.

| I should have, | | make, | be, | fall, etc. |
|---|---|---|---|---|
| ich würde | haben | machen | sein | fallen |
| du würdest | „ | „ | „ | „ |
| er würde | „ | „ | „ | „ |
| wir würden | „ | „ | „ | „ |
| ihr würdet | „ | „ | „ | „ |
| sie würden | „ | „ | „ | „ |

OBSERVE : The simple conditional of all verbs is formed by adding their infinitive to the imperfect subjunctive of werden.

**104.**     The Compound Conditional with haben.

I should have had (made), thou wouldst, etc.

> ich würde   gehabt (gemacht) haben
> du würdest gehabt (gemacht) haben
> er würde   gehabt (gemacht) haben, ꝛc.

OBSERVE : The compound conditional of a verb conjugated with haben is formed by adding its past participle to the simple conditional of haben (for word order, compare § 49).

**105.**        The Compound Conditional with sein.

I should have been (fallen), thou wouldst, etc.

> ich würde   gewesen (gefallen) sein
> du würdest gewesen (gefallen) sein
> er würde   gewesen (gefallen) sein, ꝛc.

OBSERVE: The compound conditional of a verb conjugated with sein (see § 62) is formed by adding its past participle to the simple conditional of sein (for word order, compare § 49).

**106.**               Conditional Sentences.

| | |
|---|---|
| Wenn ich Geld hätte, (so) würde ich ein Haus kaufen. | If I had money, I should buy a house. |
| Ich würde ein Haus gekauft haben, wenn ich Geld gehabt hätte. | I should have bought a house, if I had had money. |
| Hätte ich Zeit, so würde ich es tun. | If I had (had I) time, I should do it. |
| Wenn ich Geld hätte, könnte ich ein Haus kaufen. | If I had money, I could buy a house. |
| Hätte ich Zeit gehabt, so hätte ich es getan. | If I had had (had I had) time, I should have done it. |
| Er wird kommen, wenn er kann. | He will come if he can. |

OBSERVE: 1. Conditional sentences regularly consist of two parts: the condition and the result; and either part may come first.

2. The subjunctive mood is required in the imperfect or pluperfect of the 'if' clause, the result being then expressed by the conditional; with other tenses the verb is in the indicative in both clauses (see last example above).

3. The imperfect or pluperfect subjunctive may replace the conditional in the result clause, if the latter follows.

NOTE. — These shorter forms are used to avoid complicated constructions, as for example in the modal auxiliaries; see Lesson XXXVII.

I

4. When the 'if' clause precedes, the subject of the result clause is thrown after the verb (as in the first example above), the particle ſo being usually inserted before the verb, but not translated into English.

5. Wenn, = 'if,' may be omitted when the condition precedes the result, in which case the verb begins the sentence, and the result clause is introduced by ſo.

### EXERCISE XXVIII

abgehen (ſ.), to go away, set out, start, depart.

abweſend, absent.

ach! ah! oh!

Berli'n, *n.*, Berlin.

beſetzt, occupied, full.

beſorgen, to take care of, see to, look after.

deshalb, for this or that reason, therefore, on that account.

erkranken (ſ.), to fall ill.

der Fall, –(e)s, ⁔e, fall, case.

die Gelegenheit, –en, occasion, opportunity.

geneſen (ſ.), genas, geneſen, to get well, recover.

genug, enough.

das Geſchäft, –(e)s, –e, business.

koſtſpielig, costly, expensive.

mitkommen (ſ.), to come along (with).

mitreiſen (ſ.), to travel with, go with, come along (with).

die Mittel (*pl.*), means.

natürlich, naturally, of course.

U'nkoſten (*pl.*), expenses.

wahr, true.

wohl, probably, I suppose.

IDIOMS: 1. **Kommen Sie doch mit!**  Do come along.
2. **Das Wetter iſt ſchön, nicht wahr?**  The weather is fine, isn't it?

*A.* Würden Sie eine Reiſe nach Deutſchland machen, wenn Sie Gelegenheit hätten? — Jawohl! Wäre mein Vater nicht erkrankt, ſo wäre ich jetzt ſchon abgereiſt. — Müſſen Sie deshalb zu Hauſe bleiben? — Wenn mein Vater krank oder abweſend iſt, muß ich ſeine Geſchäfte beſorgen. — Da er wieder geneſen iſt, werden Sie bald abreiſen, nicht wahr? — Ich würde ſchon dieſe Woche reiſen, wenn die Dampfer nicht alle beſetzt wären.

— Jetzt müssen Sie wohl bis nächste Woche warten. — Ja!
Ich will mit dem Dampfer fahren, der nächsten Mittwoch ab=
geht. Wenn Sie Luft hätten mitzureisen, so wäre es mir sehr
angenehm. — Wenn ich die Mittel hätte, würde ich Sie gerne
begleiten, aber ich fürchte, die Reise würde zu kostspielig
werden. — Ach! Die Unkosten sind wohl nicht so groß, wie Sie
glauben. — In diesem Falle würde es mir vielleicht möglich
sein. — Dann kommen Sie mit; das wäre prächtig! — Sie
würden natürlich zuerst Berlin besuchen, nicht wahr? — Ja;
wenn ich Zeit und Geld genug hätte, so würde ich später nach
England reisen.

*B.* Continue the following: 1. Ich würde kommen, wenn
ich Zeit hätte, du . . . , wenn du, 2c. 2. Wenn ich Gelegen=
heit hätte, so würde ich eine Reise machen. 3. Ich will zu
Hause bleiben, wenn ich kann. 4. Hätte ich Geld genug ge=
habt, so hätte ich das Haus gekauft. 5. Wäre ich nicht krank
gewesen, so würde ich gestern gekommen sein. 6. Würde ich
gefallen sein, wenn ich Schlittschuh gelaufen wäre? 7. Wenn
ich morgen wohl bin, so werde ich abreisen.

*C.* Complete the following orally by adding a clause expressing condition or result: 1. Wenn die Kinder artig sind,
so . . . 2. Hätte ich Feder und Tinte, so . . . 3. Ich
würde Berlin schon besucht haben, wenn . . . 4. Wenn sie
nicht erkältet gewesen wäre, so . . . 5. Er würde schon
abgereist sein, wenn . . . 6. Wenn es morgen regnet, so . . .
7. Wir hätten gestern unser Feld gepflügt, wenn . . . 8. Wenn
die Unkosten nicht so groß wären, so . . . 9. Wir müssen
bis nächste Woche warten, wenn . . . 10. Es würde uns sehr
angenehm sein, wenn . . . 11. Wenn ich morgen nicht zu
müde bin, so . . . 12. Ich hätte Sie gern begleitet, wenn . . .

*D.* 1. I have a mind to take a trip to Europe this summer.
2. If I had had time and money enough, I should have gone
(abreisen) at Easter. 3. If one has no money and no time,

one must stay at home.　4. I should travel much more, if I had the means.　5. Would it be possible for you to accompany me?　6. I should accompany you gladly, if my father had not been ill.　7. I hope he will soon be well again.　8. Perhaps; and in that case it would be possible for me to go with [you].　9. If the steamers are not all full, we can start next month.　10. I should have started already, if the steamers had not all been full.　11. We should of course visit Germany, should we not?　12. Certainly; and afterwards we should take a trip to London, where I have relatives.　13. That would be splendid.　14. We should be very welcome at their house.　15. You would enjoy yourself very much in London.

*E.* Leſeſtück:

Glöcklein, Abendglöcklein, läute
Frieden, Freude
Allen Menſchen zu!
Helle laß dein Lied erſchallen
Und bring' allen
Eine ſanfte Ruh'.

Ruhe dem, der ſorgt und weint,
Ruh' dem Freund und auch dem
　Feind!
Allen Lieben bringe du
Ruhe und auch mir dazu!

# LESSON XXIX

**107.**　　Article with Noun in General Sense.

Der Menſch iſt ſterblich.　　Man is mortal.
Das Glas iſt durchſichtig.　　Glass is transparent.
Die Muſik iſt eine Kunſt.　　Music is an art.
Der Hund iſt der treue Freund　The dog is the faithful friend
　des Menſchen.　　　　　　　of man.

OBSERVE: A noun used in a general sense ('in general,' 'all,' 'every,' etc., being implied with it) regularly has the definite article in German, though not usually in English.

NOTES. — 1. This art. is frequently omitted in the plur.; also in enumerations and proverbs: Eltern lieben ihre Kinder, 'Parents love their children'; Gold und Silber sind Metalle, 'Gold and silver are metals.'

2. The art. is omitted when the sense is partitive, *i.e.* when 'some' or 'any' is implied: Haben Sie Brot? 'Have you (any) bread?' Er studiert Musik, 'He is studying music.'

## 108.           Article with Proper Names.

| | |
|---|---|
| Der Vesuv. | Mount Vesuvius. |
| Der Ontario. | Lake Ontario. |
| Der Rhein. | The (river) Rhine. |
| Die Schweiz; die Türkei'. | Switzerland; Turkey. |
| Das schöne Frankreich. | Beautiful France. |
| Der kleine Karl. | Little Charles. |

OBSERVE: 1. Geographical names always take the article when masculine or feminine.

2. Place names are neuter, except countries in -ei and -z (which are feminine), and a few others.

3. All proper names require the article when preceded by an adjective.

## 109.             Various Uses of Article.

| | |
|---|---|
| Im Sommer; im August. | In summer; in August. |
| Am Montag. | On Monday. |
| In der Königstraße. | In King Street. |
| Bei dem Mittagsessen. | At dinner. |
| Zur Schule gehen. | To go to school. |

OBSERVE: The article is required before seasons, months, days of the week, streets, meals, and places of public resort.

NOTE.—The art. is also used before Stadt, Himmel, Erde, and Hölle.

## 110.             Article for Possessive.

| | |
|---|---|
| Geben Sie mir die Hand. | Give me your hand. |
| Alle haben das Leben verloren. | They all lost their lives. |

OBSERVE: 1. The definite article usually replaces the possessive adjective when no ambiguity would result as to the possessor.

2. With plurality of possessor, the object possessed is usually singular, if it is singular as regards the individual possessor.

### 111.　　　Omission of Indefinite Article.

| | |
|---|---|
| Er ist (wurde) Arzt. | He is (became) a doctor. |
| Er ist ein guter Arzt. | He is a good doctor. |

OBSERVE: The indefinite article is usually omitted before the unqualified predicate after ſein and werden when it indicates calling or profession.

### EXERCISE XXIX

das Abendeſſen, –s, supper.
abnehmen, to take away, take off.
die Chemie', chemistry.
du'rchſichtig, transparent.
das Eiſen, –s, iron.
Europa, n., –s, Europe.
der Feiertag, –(e)s, –e, holiday.
die Friedrichſtraße, Frederick Street.
das Glas, –es, "er, glass.
das Gold, –es, gold.
grüßen (acc.), to greet, bow to.
halb (adj.), half.
hierzulande, in this country.
hinabfahren (ſ., acc.), to go (etc.) down.
höflich, polite.
die Leute (pl.), people.
die Medizi'n, medicine.

der Nachmittag, –(e)s, –e, afternoon.
der Ontario, –s, Lake Ontario.
die Phyſi'k, physics.
der Rhein, –(e)s, the (river) Rhine.
die Schweiz, Switzerland.
ſchwer, heavy, hard, difficult.
die Seeküſte, –n, sea-coast.
ſtecken, to thrust, put, stick.
der Stude'nt, –en, –en, student.
ſtudieren, ſtudierte, ſtudiert, to study.
das Studium, –s, –ien, study.
treten (ſ.), trat, getreten, to walk, go, come.
die Vergnügungsreiſe, –n, pleasure-trip.

A. 1. Das Glas iſt durchſichtig; man macht Fenſter aus Glas. 2. Das Gold iſt ſchwerer als das Eiſen. 3. Unſere Kinder gehen früh des Morgens zur Schule; ſie ſind jetzt in der Schule. 4. Ihre Schule ſteht in der Friedrichſtraße. 5. Am

Mittwoch und Sonnabend haben sie des Nachmittags einen halben Feiertag.  6. Nach dem Abendessen machen sie gewöhnlich ihre Aufgaben.  7. Wenn sie in die Schulstube treten, nehmen sie den Hut ab und grüßen den Lehrer höflich.  8. Höfliche Knaben stecken die Hände nicht in die Tasche.  9. Der kleine Karl ist ein höflicher Junge.  10. Ich bin Maler, aber mein Vetter ist Student; er studiert jetzt Physik und Chemie.  11. Er findet das Studium der Physik besonders interessant.  12. Nächsten Winter wird er in Deutschland Medizin studieren.  13. In den Ferien wird er eine Reise nach der Schweiz machen.  14. Hierzulande macht man eine Vergnügungsreise nach dem Ontario oder nach der Seeküste.  15. In Europa fahren viele Leute den Rhein hinab oder besuchen die Schweiz.  16. Andere reisen nach England oder nach dem schönen Frankreich.

*B.* Oral: 1. Weshalb werden Fenster aus Glas gemacht? 2. Welches ist schwerer, das Eisen oder das Glas? 3. Gehst du heute zur Schule? 4. In welcher Straße steht eure Schule? 5. In welchem Monate habt ihr Ferien? 6. An welchem Tage der Woche habt ihr einen halben Feiertag? 7. Wie grüßen Sie eine Dame, wenn Sie ihr begegnen? 8. Ist es höflich, die Hände in die Tasche zu stecken? 9. Sind Sie Student? 10. Was studieren Sie jetzt? 11. Welches Studium haben Sie gern? 12. Was wollen Sie sonst studieren? 13. Wohin wollen Sie im Sommer reisen? 14. Wie bringen die Deutschen die Ferien zu? 15. Und die Leute hierzulande?

*C.* 1. Gold is dearer than iron. 2. Rings are made of gold. 3. Windows are made of glass, because it is transparent. 4. Children learn; students study. 5. I am a student; little Max, my brother, is only (erst) a pupil. 6. He goes to school every morning in King Street. 7. He intends to become a painter. 8. I am studying physics and chemistry now, for I mean to be (werden) a doctor. 9. The study of medicine is interesting; it is also very useful to man. 10. When we

meet ladies in (auf, *dat.*) the street, we take off our hats and
bow to them.   11. They bow to us, but they do not take off
their hats.   12. In this country people generally take a pleasure-
trip in summer.   13. A pleasure-trip is often better (besser) for
the health than a bitter medicine.   14. Last winter I visited
Germany with my mother.   15. We intend to pass this summer
in Switzerland.   16. If we have time afterwards, and if we have
enough money, we shall go down the Rhine.

*D.* Sprichwörter:   1. Übermut tut selten gut.   2. Übung
macht den Meister.   3. Kleider machen Leute.   4. Borgen
macht Sorgen.   5. Die Not ist die Mutter der Erfindung.
6. Hunger ist der beste Koch.

*E.* Lesestück :  Ein Tourist, der einen entlegenen Teil von
Irland bereiste und die Nacht in einem kleinen, wenig be-
suchten Wirtshaus verbracht hatte, klagte dem Wirte am Morgen, daß seine Stiefel, die er vor die Zimmertür gesetzt habe,
nicht angerührt seien.  "Ach," sagte der Wirt, " in diesem Hause
könnten Sie sogar Ihre goldene Uhr vor die Zimmertür legen,
und kein Mensch würde sie anrühren."

## LESSON XXX

**112.**          **Expressions of Quantity.**

| | |
|---|---|
| Vierundzwanzig Zoll machen zwei Fuß. | Twenty-four inches make two feet. |
| Vier Pfund; tausend Mann. | Four pounds ; a thousand men. |
| Zwei Flaschen; zwölf Ellen. | Two bottles ; twelve yards. |
| Fünf Mark, zwanzig Pfennig. | Five marks, twenty ' pfennigs.' |
| Fünf Glas Bier. | Five glasses of beer. |
| Mit zwei Paar Schuhen. | With two pairs of shoes. |
| Sechs Meter von diesem Tuch. | Six metres of this cloth. |
| Der Stock ist einen Fuß lang. | The stick is a foot long. |

OBSERVE:  1. Nouns expressing measure, weight, or number
(except feminines in –e) retain the uninflected form of the
singular, even when the sense is plural.

2. Feminines in –e add –n in the plural.

3. The noun, the quantity of which is expressed, is usually in apposition to the noun expressing the quantity, unless preceded by a determinative.

4. The measure of distance, weight, etc., is in the accusative.

### 113.   Distributive Article.

| | |
|---|---|
| Zweimal des Jahres. | Twice a year. |
| Dreimal die Woche. | Three times a week. |
| Drei Mark die Elle. | Three marks a yard. |

OBSERVE: The English indefinite article is replaced by the definite article in German when used distributively (= 'each').

NOTE. — In expressions of time, as above, masc. and neut. nouns are in the genitive, fems. in the accusative; in those of price the noun is in the accusative.

### 114. Remarks on Numerals.   1. Ein is used adjectively after a determinative:

| | |
|---|---|
| Der eine Bruder; mein einer Schuh. | The one brother; one of my shoes. |

2. Ein is also used substantively with the definite article, in both singular and plural:

| | |
|---|---|
| Der eine oder der andere. | The one or the other. |
| Die einen sagten dies, die andern das. | Some said this, (the) others that. |

3. Beide, 'both,' is used substantively and adjectively; substantively it also has the neuter singular form beides:

| | |
|---|---|
| Meine Eltern sind beide hier. | My parents are both here. |
| Die (meine) beiden Brüder. | The (my) two brothers. |
| Beides ist wahr. | Both (things) are true. |

### EXERCISE XXX

| | |
|---|---|
| die Abteilung, –en, department. | bestellen, to order. |
| ausreichen, to be enough, suffice. | bezahlen, to pay |
| bekommen, bekam, bekommen, to get, receive, obtain. | billig, cheap. |

die Bonbons (*pl.*), candy, sweets.

die Cousine, –n, cousin (*f.*).

das Damenkleid, –(e)s, –er, lady's dress.

das Dutzend, –es, –e, dozen.

der Einkauf, –(e)s, ⁀e, purchase.

fertig, ready ; — sein, to have finished (done).

die Flasche, –n, bottle.

grau, grey.

die Mark, mark (about one shilling ; *abbr*. M. or Mk.).

das Meter, –s, —, metre.

das Mittagsessen, –s, dinner.

das Muster, –s, —, pattern, sample.

das Paar, –(e)s, –e, pair.

der Pfennig, –s, –e, 'pfennig,' ($\frac{1}{100}$ part of a mark).

das Pfund, –es, –e, pound.

die Rechnung, –en, bill, account.

die Reihe, –n, row ; turn.

die Rosine, –n, raisin.

der Rotwein, –(e)s, –e, red wine, claret.

die Sache, –n, thing, matter, affair.

die Schachtel, –n, box (of cardboard, etc.).

das Sommerkleid, –(e)s, –er, summer-dress.

sowie, as well as, and also.

das Taschentuch, –(e)s, ⁀er, handkerchief.

ungefähr, about, nearly.

die Verkäuferin, –nen, saleswoman, shopgirl.

das Waarenhaus, –es, ⁀er, departmental store, shop.

das Zeug, –(e)s, –e, stuff, material.

der Zoll, –(e)s, –e, inch.

der Zucker, –s, sugar.

zuletzt, last.

zunächst, next, then.

IDIOMS: 1. **Einkäufe machen,** to make purchases, go shopping.
      2. **An der Reihe sein** (**an die Reihe kommen**), to be one's turn.

*A.* Vorige Woche war eine Cousine vom Lande bei uns auf Besuch. Sie kommt gewöhnlich zweimal des Jahres zur Stadt, um Einkäufe zu machen. Am Donnerstag gingen wir also zum großen Waarenhause von Hartmann und Sohn. Dort kann man fast alle Sachen bekommen, die man braucht, ohne weiter zu gehen. Zuerst gingen wir in die Abteilung für Damenkleider. Die Verkäuferin zeigte uns ein Muster zu einem Sommerkleide zu M. 3.— das Meter. Sie sagte, daß

ungefähr 6 Meter davon ausreichen würden, da das Muster
50 Zoll breit sei. Meine Cousine kaufte 8 Meter davon, da
es so billig war. Zunächst kaufte sie auch 6 Taschentücher für
ihren Bruder und bezahlte M. 12.50 das Dutzend dafür.
Dann kaufte sie zwei Paar Handschuhe für die Mutter. Sie
waren beide sehr schön. Die einen waren grau, die andern
weiß. Nachdem die Cousine fertig war, kam ich an die Reihe.
Ich bestellte 5 Pfund Rosinen, und 10 Pfund Zucker zu 25
Pfennig das Pfund, sowie ein Dutzend Flaschen Rotwein für den
Onkel. Als wir fertig waren, kauften wir zwei Schachtel Bonbons für die Kinder und bezahlten die Rechnung. Dann fuhren
wir mit der Straßenbahn zum Mittagsessen nach Hause.

*B.* Oral: 1. Wo steht das große Waarenhaus von Hartmann und Sohn? 2. Machen Sie gern Einkäufe dort?
3. Weshalb? 4. Wie oft gehen Sie dahin? 5. Wie fahren
Sie dahin? 6. Wann waren Sie zuletzt da? 7. In welche
Abteilung gingen Sie zuerst? 8. Wie viele Meter Zeug braucht
man für ein Sommerkleid? 9. Wie breit ist dieses Zeug?
10. Wie viel kosten Taschentücher das Dutzend? 11. Wie
viel bezahlt man für drei Paar Handschuhe, zu M. 2.50 das
Paar? 12. Wie viel kostet guter Tee? 13. Wie viel Pfund
Rosinen brauchen wir? 14. Für wen ist die Schachtel Bonbons, die Sie gekauft haben? 15. Für wen sind die beiden
Paar Handschuhe?

*C.* 1. Hartmann and Son have a large departmental store.
2. You (man) can buy many things very cheap at Hartmann's.
3. My mother goes shopping there usually twice a week. 4. We
can go there (dahin) by the tramcar and come home before
dinner. 5. Here is the ladies' dress department. 6. Please
show us several patterns for a summer-dress. 7. The
material must be about 48 inches wide. 8. If it is wide
enough, 7 metres will suffice. 9. This material costs 4
marks [and] 50 pfennigs a metre. 10. Give me 7 metres of it.
11. Next show us handkerchiefs, if you please. 12. They must

not be too dear ; about 10 marks a dozen.    13. I shall take
two dozen of these.    14. How much are (cost) these gloves
a pair?    15. We sell them at 7 marks for 2 pairs.    16. Now it
is mother's turn.    17. Send me 2 pounds of tea and 3 pounds
of raisins.    18. How much is the sugar?    19. Twenty-five
pfennigs a pound.    20. That is too dear.    21. We have also
sugar at 22 pfennigs.    22. Then send me 10 pounds of it.
23. We must buy two or three boxes of sweets for my little
sisters.    24. I have finished now.    25. So have I (= I also).

*D.*  Lesestück: Können Sie mir dieses Goldstück wechseln?
— Was für eine Münze ist das? — Es ist ein amerikanisches Fünf-
dollarstück. — Ich bedauere ; das müssen Sie zur Bank tragen.
— Haben Sie die Güte, mir vorher den Wert des deutschen
Geldes zu erklären. — Sehr gern.  Hundert Pfennig machen eine
Mark (in Silber), und eine Mark ist ungefähr so viel wert wie
24 Cents amerikanisch oder wie ein Shilling sterling.  Außer
der Mark gibt es folgende Silbermünzen : Zweimarkstücke,
Dreimarkstücke (oder Taler), Fünfmarkstücke und Fünf-
zigpfennigstücke.  Wir haben auch Goldstücke zu je 10 und 20
Mark, sowie Papiergeld in Scheinen.  Endlich gibt es Nickel-
münzen zu 5 und 10 Pfennig, sowie ein paar Kupfermünzen von
kleinerem Betrage.  Also bekommen Sie ungefähr M. 20.80 für
Ihr Goldstück, je nach dem Kurse.

# LESSON XXXI

### 115.    The Imperative of haben, fein, werden.

| | |
|---|---|
| habe (du), have (thou). | fei (du), be (thou). |
| er habe, <br> habe er, } let him have. | er fei, <br> fei er, } let him be. |
| haben wir, let us have. | feien wir, let us be. |
| habt (ihr), have (ye). | feid (ihr), be (ye, you). |
| haben fie, let them have. | feien fie, let them be. |
| haben Sie, have (you). | feien Sie, be (you). |

werde (bu), become (thou).

er werde, ⎫
werde er, ⎭ let him become.

werden wir, let us become.
werdet (ihr), become (ye, you).
werden sie, let them become.
werden Sie, become (you).

**116.**        Imperative of machen, singen.

mache (bu), make (thou).

er mache, ⎫
mache er, ⎭ let him make.

machen wir, let us make.
macht (ihr), make (ye, you).
machen sie, let them make.
machen Sie, make (you).

singe (bu), sing (thou).

er singe, ⎫
singe er, ⎭ let him sing.

singen wir, let us sing.
singt (ihr), sing (ye, you).
singen sie, let them sing.
singen Sie, sing (you).

OBSERVE: 1. The only true imperative forms are the 2nd singular and the 2nd plural; the remaining forms are present subjunctives used with imperative force.

2. The imperative of most verbs (weak and strong) is formed as above.

3. The pronoun of the 3rd singular more commonly precedes, but Sie always follows; the 3rd plural (='let them') is very rare.

4. The pronouns bu, ihr are not expressed, except for contrast or emphasis.

**117. Imperative with lassen.** The imperative of the verb lassen, 'let,' is used as an auxiliary, with the force of an imperative, to replace the 3rd singular and plural and the 1st plural, as follows:

laß     (2nd sing.) ⎫
laßt    (2nd plur.) ⎬ uns bleiben, let us remain.
lassen Sie (formal) ⎭

*wir wollen bleiben*

**118.**                    Infinitive.

*Present.*                              *Perfect.*

(zu) haben, to have.          gehabt   (zu) haben, to have had.
(zu) sein, to be.             gewesen  (zu) sein, to have been.
(zu) werden, to become.       geworden (zu) sein, to have become.
(zu) machen, to make.         gemacht  (zu) haben, to have made.

OBSERVE : The perfect infinitive is formed by prefixing the past participle to the present infinitive.

**119.**                          **Participles.**

| *Present.* | | *Past.* | |
|---|---|---|---|
| hab enb, having. | | ge hab t, had. | |
| fei enb, being. | | ge wef en, been. | |
| mach enb, making. | | ge mach t, made. | |
| fing enb, singing. | | ge fung en, sung. | |

OBSERVE :  1. The present participle of all verbs ends in –enb.

2. The past participle of weak verbs is formed by prefixing ge– to the stem and adding –t; the past participle of strong verbs has ge– prefixed and ends in –en, usually also with change of stem vowel.

NOTES. — 1. Both the present and the past participles are also used as attributive adjs.

2. For the fut. passive part., see § 296.

**120. Omission of ge–.** Foreign verbs in –ieren and verbs with inseparable prefixes (see § 51) omit the prefix ge– of the past participle :

| ftubieren, study, | ftubiert | bezahlen, pay, | bezahlt |
|---|---|---|---|
| entbecfen, discover, | entbecft | vergeffen, forget, | vergeffen |

**121.**                    **Present of follen.**

| *Indicative.* | | *Subjunctive.* | |
|---|---|---|---|
| ich foll | wir follen | ich folle | wir follen |
| bu follft | ihr follt | bu folleft | ihr follet |
| er foll | fie follen | er folle | fie follen |

**122.**                    **Use of follen.**

| | |
|---|---|
| Jch foll (wir follen) ausgehen. | I am to (we are to) go out. |
| Soll ich bleiben? | Shall I (am I to) stay? |
| Du follft nicht ftehlen. | Thou shalt not steal. |
| Er foll fommen. | He is to (shall) come. |

OBSERVE :  1. In the first person follen = 'am to,' etc., in statements, and in questions 'shall' or 'am to,' etc.

2. In the other persons, follen is equivalent to an emphatic imperative (= 'shall' or 'are to,' etc.), unless interrogative.

### EXERCISE XXXI

auf Deutsch, in German.
aufmachen, to open.
auswendig, by heart.
das Blümlein, –s, —, little flower.
der Dichter, –s, —, poet.
erlauben (dat.), to permit, allow.
Friedrich, Frederick.
die Frühlingszeit, spring-time.
das Grün, –s, green.
hersagen, to recite, repeat.
die Höhe, –n, height.
lauten, to sound, run, read.
lesen, las, gelesen, to read.
mit einem Mal, all at once.
nennen, nannte, genannt, to name.
noch einmal, once more, again.
nun, now.
die Regenzeit, –en, rainy weather.

der Satz, –es, ⁻e, sentence.
schallen, to resound.
schön (adv.), well, very well.
die Seite, –n, page.
sich, himself, herself, etc.
der Sonnenstrahl, –(e)s, –en, sunbeam.
sprießen (f.), sproß, gesprossen, to sprout, bud.
volle'nden, to finish, complete.
vorbei, past, gone.
vorlesen, to read aloud.
die Winterqual, hard winter weather.
das Wort, –(e)s, ⁻er, word.
die Zeile, –n, line (of writing).
das Zeitwort, –(e)s, ⁻er, verb.
zerfließen (f.), zerfloß, zerflossen, to melt (away).
zu Ende, at an end.
zuhören (dat.), to listen.
zumachen, to close, shut.

A. Kinder, macht die Bücher auf und laßt uns das Gedicht auf Seite 132 lesen. Sagt mir, wie das Gedicht heißt. — Das Gedicht heißt „Der Frühling" und der Dichter heißt Friedrich Bodenstedt. — Marie, fange an, es mir vorzulesen. — Bitte, entschuldigen Sie mich, Fräulein Bauer, ich bin erkältet. — Gut, mein Kind; also fange du an, Klara. — Erlauben Sie mir, es herzusagen; ich habe es auswendig gelernt. — Schön; hört aufmerksam zu, Kinder. —

Wenn der Frühling auf die Berge steigt
Und im Sonnenstrahl der Schnee zerfließt,
Wenn das erste Grün am Baum sich zeigt
Und im Gras das erste Blümlein sprießt,
Wenn vorbei im Tal nun mit einem Mal
Alle Regenzeit und Winterqual,
Schallt es von den Höh'n bis zum Tale weit:
O wie wunderschön ist die Frühlingszeit!

—Das hast du sehr gut hergesagt, mein Kind.  Jetzt sollt
ihr die Bücher wieder aufmachen.  Lest noch einmal Zeile
5 und 6.  Hier fehlt etwas, nicht wahr?  Rudolf, nenne mir
das fehlende Wort.—Das Zeitwort „sind" fehlt, Fräulein
Bauer.—Ganz richtig, mein Junge; jetzt vollende den Satz.—
Der vollendete Satz würde lauten: „Wenn alle Regenzeit,
usw., vorbei sind."—Nun, Kinder; die Stunde ist zu Ende;
ihr sollt jetzt nach Hause gehen.—Bitte, erzählen Sie uns erst
ein Märchen auf Deutsch, Fräulein Bauer.—Jetzt habe ich
keine Zeit, aber morgen will ich das gern tun, da ihr so artig
gewesen seid.

*B.* Continue the following: 1. Ich soll heute morgen ein
Gedicht hersagen, du . . . ꝛc.  2. Soll ich das Gedicht vorlesen oder hersagen?  3. Er sagte, ich solle nicht so viel Lärm
machen, er sagte, du . . . ꝛc.  4. Ich habe zu viel für das
Buch bezahlt.  5. Ich habe (hatte) fleißig studiert.

*C.* Oral: 1. Sollen wir die Bücher nicht jetzt aufmachen?
2. Wer hat dieses schöne Gedicht geschrieben?  3. Wie nennt
man einen, der Gedichte schreibt?  4. Wer soll zuerst lesen?
5. Wer soll das Gedicht hersagen?  6. Soll Marie jetzt anfangen, oder Rudolf?  7. Sollen wir die Bücher wieder aufmachen? 8. Wer hat die Tür aufgemacht?  9. Wer soll sie
wieder zumachen?  10. Wer will die Fenster zumachen?
11. Was sagt der Lehrer, wenn die Stunde zu Ende ist?
12. Wohin sollen wir jetzt gehen?

*D.* 1. Tell me what poem you read yesterday, Clara.
2. Please excuse me, Miss Bauer, I was not at school.
3. Then you tell me (it), Charles. 4. It was a poem about
(über, *acc.*) spring, Miss B. 5. Do you know it by heart?
6. Not yet, Miss B. 7. Then learn it this evening, and recite
it to me to-morrow, my boy. 8. Open your books, and let us
read line[s] one to (bis) eight. 9. Now close them again, and
you recite me these lines, Mary. 10. You are to listen, children; Mary is to recite them. 11. Please tell us, Miss B.,
what word is missing in line six. 12. The missing word is
'sind.' 13. Don't make so much noise, children. 14. Now
go home. 15. Take your books with [you], and read the poem
attentively. 16. You are to learn it by heart to-morrow.
17. Please read the poem aloud to us first, and show us the
pictures you brought from Germany. 18. I shall do so (es)
to-morrow if you are good. 19. Charles, please shut the door
when you go out (hinaus).

## LESSON XXXII

**123.** **Prepositions with Dative or Accusative.** The following
nine prepositions govern the dative when they indicate locality
merely, and answer the question 'where?' or 'in what place?'
the accusative when they imply motion, direction, or tendency
towards the object of the preposition, and answer the question
'whither?' or 'to what place or person?'

| an | hinter | neben | unter | zwischen |
|------|--------|-------|-------|----------|
| auf | in | über | vor | |

**124.** **Contractions.** An and in are generally (in expressions of time always) contracted with the unemphasized dem
and das: am=an dem, im=in dem, ans=an das, ins=in das;
auf is contracted with das only: aufs=auf das.

**125.**　　　　　**An,** on, upon, to, at, in.

1. Of place (surface non-horizontal):

K

(*a*) With dative = on, upon (adjacent to), at —

Das Bild hängt an der Wand.      The picture hangs on the wall.
Ich sitze am Tische.             I am sitting at the table.

(*b*) With accusative = on, to (towards) —

Er hängt das Bild an die         He hangs the picture on the
  Wand.                            wall.
Er geht ans Fenster.             He goes to the window.

2. Of time and date, with dative only = on, upon, in :

Am Vormittag (Abend).            In the forenoon (evening).
Am zweiten Juli.                 On the second of July.

**126.**          **Auf,** on, upon, to, for.

1. Place (surface horizontal) :

(*a*) With dative = on, upon, on top of —

Das Buch ist auf dem Tische.     The book is on the table.

(*b*) With accusative = on, to —

Legen Sie das auf den Tisch.     Lay that on the table.
Er geht auf den Markt.           He is going to the market.

2. Of future time, with accusative only = for :

Er kommt auf zwei Tage.          He is coming for two days.

NOTE. — Bis auf + acc. = 'except,' 'but': Er aß alle Äpfel bis auf
einen, 'He ate all the apples but one.'

**127.**          **Hinter,** behind.

Der Hund liegt hinter dem        The dog lies behind the stove.
  Ofen.
Er kriecht hinter den Ofen.      He creeps behind the stove.

**128.**          **In,** in, into.

1. Of place, with dative = in ; with accusative = into :

Er arbeitet im Garten.           He works in the garden.
Er geht ins Zimmer.              He goes into the room.

2. Of time, with dative only = in :

Er tat es in einer Stunde.          He did it in an hour.

**129.**              Neben, beside, by, near.

Er steht neben dem Tische.          He stands beside the table.
Stelle es neben die Tür.            Put it by (near) the door.

**130.**      über, over, across, of, about, concerning.

1. Of place, with dative = over (above); with accusative = over (across).

Die Wolke hängt über dem            The cloud hangs over the hill.
  Berge.
Die Brücke führt über den           The bridge leads across the
  Fluß.                               river.

2. Of excess, with accusative only = over :

Das kostet über einen Taler.        That costs over three shillings

3. With accusative only = of, about, concerning :

Er redete über seine Reise.         He spoke of his journey.

**131.**              Unter, under, among.

1. Of place, with dative or accusative = under (beneath, below) :

Die schwarze Katze war unter        The black cat was under the
  dem Tische.                         table.
Sie kroch unter den Tisch.          She crept under the table.

2. Of number, with dative or accusative = among :

Der grausame Wolf ist unter         The cruel wolf is among the
  den Schafen.                        sheep.
Er ist unter die Schafe gegan-      He went among the sheep.
  gen.

**132.**         Vor, before, in front of, ago.

1. Of place, with dative or accusative = before, in front of :

| | |
|---|---|
| Der Stuhl steht vor der Tür. | The chair stands before the door. |
| Stelle ihn vor die Tür. | Put it in front of the door. |

2. Of order, with dative only = before (ahead of):

| | |
|---|---|
| Sie kommen vor mir. | You come before (precede) me. |

3. Of time, with dative only = before, ago:

| | |
|---|---|
| Er kommt vor nächster Woche. | He comes before next week. |
| Er kam vor zwei Tagen an. | He arrived two days ago. |

**133.** **Zwischen,** between.

| | |
|---|---|
| Der Stuhl steht zwischen der Tür und dem Fenster. | The chair stands between the door and the window. |
| Stellen Sie ihn zwischen die Tür und das Fenster. | Put it between the door and the window. |

**134.** **Da** with all these prepositions replaces pronouns used for inanimate objects (compare § 85).

### EXERCISE XXXII

das Andenken, –s, memory.

der Ausländer, –s, —, foreigner.

die Bank, ̈e, bench.

die Brücke, –n, bridge.

einige, a few, several.

der Einwohner, –s, —, inhabitant.

führen, to lead.

der Fußgänger, –s, —, pedestrian.

die Hauptstadt, ̈e, capital.

die Hauptstraße, –n, main street.

der Kaiser, –s, —, emperor.

königlich, royal.

die Linde, –n, linden.

der Lustgarten, –s, ̈, pleasure-garden, park.

die Mitte, middle, centre.

das National=Denkmal, –s, ̈er, or –e, National Monument.

östlich, eastern.

das Reich, –(e)s, –e, empire.

die Schildwache, –n, sentry.

das Schloß, –es, ̈er, castle, palace.

die Schloßfreiheit, Precincts of the Palace.

der Schloßplatz, –es, Palace    das Tor, –(e)s, –e, gate.
  Square.                         die Universitä't, –en, univer-
die Spree, the (river) Spree.      sity.
der Springbrunnen, –s, —,       vorbeigehen (f.), to go past
  fountain.                       (an + dat.).
der Tiergarten, –s, ", deer-    der Weg, –(e)s, –e, way, road.
  park, park.                    westlich, western.

*A.* Berlin liegt an der Spree und ist seit 1871 die Haupt=
stadt des Deutschen Reiches. Jetzt hat es über drei Mil=
lionen Einwohner. Die Hauptstraße Berlins heißt Unter den
Linden. In dieser Straße stehen vier Reihen Linden und
deshalb heißt sie so. In der Mitte zwischen den Linden liegt
ein breiter Weg für Fußgänger. Unter den Bäumen stehen
Bänke, auf denen man sitzen kann. Am östlichen Ende der
Straße liegt das königliche Schloß. Vor dem Schlosse,
zwischen zwei Armen des Flusses, ist der Lustgarten. An der
Schloßfreiheit neben dem Schlosse steht das National=Denkmal
zum Andenken an Kaiser Wilhelm den Ersten. Hinter dem
Schlosse ist der Schloßplatz, auf dem ein großer Springbrunnen steht. Eine schöne Brücke führt vom Schlosse über
den Fluß zur Hauptstraße. Dann geht man weiter und an
der Universität vorbei. Auf der Universität studieren neun bis
zehntausend Studenten. Bis auf einige hundert Ausländer
sind diese Deutsche. Am westlichen Ende der Straße steht
das berühmte Brandenburger Tor. Durch dieses Tor geht
man in den Tiergarten. Eine Schildwache steht immer
darunter.

*B.* Oral : 1. Wann waren Sie zuletzt in Europa? 2. In
welchen Ländern waren Sie? 3. Wie heißt die Hauptstadt des
Deutschen Reiches? 4. Wie nennt man die Hauptstraße Berlins? 5. Weshalb? 6. Wo liegt der Weg für Fußgänger?
7. Wo steht das königliche Schloß? 8. Wer wohnt darin?
9. Wie kommt man aus dem Tiergarten in die Hauptstraße?

10. Sind Sie gestern an der Universität vorbeigegangen?
11. Wie viele Studenten hat die Universität? 12. Studieren
auch Ausländer auf der Universität? 13. Zum Andenken an
wen ist das National-Denkmal? 14. Wo steht es? 15. Wohin
führt diese schöne Brücke? 16. Wo liegt der Lustgarten?

*C.* 1. I was standing between my two (beide) friends.
2. He did that exercise a month ago. 3. Put (stellen) my
chair in front of the door. 4. Don't put your hands into your
pockets. 5. Let us put (stecken) the letter under the door.
6. We can see clouds above the hills. 7. They went past me
on the street. 8. Let the coachman drive behind the palace.
9. Let us go to the market. 10. They will come in the evening. 11. We are sitting at the table.

*D.* 1. I spent six months in Berlin last year. 2. I was
studying at the University. 3. Accordingly I know this city
very well. 4. It is situated on the Spree. 5. The Spree flows
(fließt) into the Havel (*f.*). 6. The main street of Berlin is called
Unter den Linden. 7. It is celebrated among the streets of
great capitals. 8. The royal palace is at the eastern end of the
street. 9. At the western end stands the Brandenburg Gate.
10. I used to go past the palace every day on the way to the
university. 11. Among the celebrated buildings in this street
is the Berlin University. 12. The University has now more
than 9000 students. 13. Among these are several hundred
women. 14. In the middle of the street [there] are four
rows of lindens. 15. One can sit on the benches under these
trees. 16. The middle of the street is only for pedestrians.
17. A fine park is situated in front of the royal palace. 18. Between the palace and an arm of the river stands a monument
in memory of the first German Emperor. 19. From the palace
you (man) go over a bridge which leads into the main street.

*E.* Lesestück:

Treue Liebe bis zum Grabe
Schwör' ich dir mit Herz und Hand,

Was ich bin und was ich habe
Dank' ich dir, mein Vaterland!

Nicht in Worten nur und Liedern
Ist mein Herz zum Dank bereit;
Mit der Tat will ich's erwidern
Dir in Not, in Kampf und Streit.

In der Freude, wie im Leide,
Ruf' ich's Freund und Feinden zu:
Ewig sind vereint wir beide
Und mein Trost, mein Glück bist du.

— Hoffmann von Fallersleben.


# LESSON XXXIII

*N.B.* Before studying this and the following lessons, review carefully the verb paradigms of previous lessons, and remember that the compound tenses of all verbs are formed with either **haben** or **sein** (§ 62) as auxiliary.

**135.**                    Verb Stems.

| | | |
|---|---|---|
| mach en | rechn en | tadel n |
| red en | ruder n | sing en |

OBSERVE: The stem of a verb is what is left when the ending –en or –n is dropped from the infinitive.

**136.**                    Principal Parts.

| | *Infin.* | *Impf. Indic.* | *Past Part.* |
|---|---|---|---|
| Weak Verb : | machen | mach te | ge mach t |
| Strong Verb : | singen | sang | ge sung en |

OBSERVE: From the principal parts may be inferred the various forms of the stem, which is regularly changeable only in strong verbs.

**137.**          Special Forms of Weak Verbs.

1. Reden, 'speak': reben, rebete, gerebet.

*Present Indicative.*

| | |
|---|---|
| ich rede | wir reden |
| du redeft | ihr redet |
| er redet | fie reden |

OBSERVE : Verb stems ending in –d, –t (*e.g.* reben, arbeiten), or in any combination of consonants after which –t or –ft cannot be pronounced (*e.g.* atmen, rechnen), retain e of the ending throughout.

2. Tadeln, 'blame': tadeln, tadelte, getadelt.
   Bewundern, 'admire': bewundern, bewunderte, bewundert.

*Present Indicative.*          *Imperative.*

| | | | |
|---|---|---|---|
| ich tadle | wir tadeln | | tadeln wir |
| du tadelft | ihr tadelt | table | tadelt |
| er tadelt | fie tadeln | er tadle | tadeln fie |

*Present Indicative.*

| | |
|---|---|
| ich bewundere | wir bewundern |
| du bewunderft | ihr bewundert |
| er bewundert | fie bewundern |

OBSERVE : Verb stems in –el drop e of the stem in the first singular present indicative, and in the second and third singular imperative; verb stems in –el and –er drop e of the ending –en.

NOTE. — Stems in –el drop e of the stem in the pres. subj.

3. Tanzen, 'dance'; reifen, 'travel.'
   *Pres. Indic.* du tanzeft, du reifeft.

OBSERVE : Verb stems in a sibilant (s, sch, ß, x, z) insert e in the ending of the second singular, but these forms are usually spoken and often written du tanzt, du reift, ꝛc.

**138.**    Irregular Weak Verbs.

| Infin. | Impf. Indic. | Impf. Subj. | Past Part. |
|---|---|---|---|
| brennen, burn. | brannte | brennte | gebrannt |
| kennen, know. | kannte | kennte | gekannt |
| nennen, name. | nannte | nennte | genannt |
| rennen, run. | rannte | rennte | gerannt |
| senden, send. | sandte / sendete | sendete | gesandt / gesendet |
| wenden, turn. | wandte / wendete | wendete | gewandt / gewendet |
| bringen, bring. | brachte | brächte | gebracht |
| denken, think. | dachte | dächte | gedacht |

OBSERVE: 1. The change of the stem vowel to **a** in the imperfect indicative and past participle.

2. Except in the last two verbs, the imperfect subjunctive has the same stem vowel as the infinitive.

3. The shorter forms of senden and wenden are more usual.

4. The last two verbs have also a consonant change, and umlaut in the imperfect subjunctive.

5. Otherwise these verbs are conjugated regularly.

### EXERCISE XXXIII

die Absicht, –en, intention.
begrüßen, to greet.
bekannt, well-known.
einstecken, to pocket.
enthalten, enthielt, enthalten, to contain.
erfüllen, to fulfil.
erkennen, to recognize.
erwidern, to reply.
folgen (s., *dat.*), to follow.
freundlich, friendly, kind.

füllen, to fill.
die Gabe, –n, gift, present.
das Geldstück, –(e)s, –e, coin.
gewiß, certain.
die Handarbeit, –en, needlework, knitting, etc.
die Herzensgüte, kindliness.
Italien, *n.*, –s, Italy.
jedermann, –s, everybody, every one.
die Königin, –nen, queen.

lächeln, to smile.

die Majestä't, –en, majesty.

reden, to speak, talk.

seiden, silken, (of) silk.

Signora, madam.

stricken, to knit.

der Strumpf, –es, ᵘe, stocking.

tadeln, to blame.

die Träne, –n, tear.

verbrennen, to burn (tr.).

wegen (gen.), on account of.

wegnehmen, to take away.

IDIOM: **Was ist aus ihm geworden?**   What has become of him?

*A.* Die Königin Helena von Italien ist wegen ihrer Her=
zensgüte überall bekannt.  Sie denkt immer an die Armen und
Unglücklichen.  Jedermann bewundert diese königliche Frau.
Eines Tages machte Ihre Majestät einen Spaziergang im
Park.  Dort begegnete ihr ein kleines Mädchen.  Die Königin
begrüßte das Mädchen freundlich und fragte: „Was für Hand=
arbeit kannst du machen?"  „Ich kann Strümpfe stricken," er=
widerte die Kleine.  „Kennst du mich, Kleine?" fragte die
Königin lächelnd.  „Gewiß, Signora, ich habe Sie sofort er=
kannt; Sie sind die Königin."  Die Königin sagte, die Kleine
solle ihr ein Paar Strümpfe stricken und sie aufs Schloß
bringen.  Nach einigen Tagen wurden ihr die Strümpfe ge=
bracht.  Die Königin dachte, dem Kinde eine große Freude zu
machen und sandte ihm ein Paar seidene Strümpfe, sowie einen
Brief.  Der eine davon war mit Bonbons gefüllt; der andere
enthielt mehrere Geldstücke.  Den nächsten Tag brachte das
Mädchen folgenden Brief aufs Schloß: „Ihre Gabe, Signora,
hat mich viele Tränen gekostet.  Das Geld hat mein Vater
eingesteckt; die Bonbons hat mein Bruder gegessen; die
Strümpfe hat meine Mutter mir weggenommen und den Brief
hat man verbrannt."  Also kann man sehen, daß gute Absichten
nicht immer erfüllt werden.

*B.* Continue: 1. Ich tadle den Jungen, weil er die Bon=
bons gegessen hat, du, ꝛc.  2. Ich bewundere die Herzens=
güte der Königin.  3. Mein Onkel fragt, ob ich gern reise,

. . . ob bu, 2c.  4. Ich rede viel von meiner Reise, du . . .
von deiner, 2c.  5. Ich erkannte das Kind sogleich.  6. Ich
sandte einen Brief aufs Schloß.

*C.* Oral : 1. Was wird hier von guten Absichten gesagt?
2. Bewundern Sie die gute Königin?  3. Wie heißt sie?
4. Warum ist sie bekannt?  5. Kannte Ihre Majestät das
kleine Mädchen?  6. Wer strickte die Strümpfe?  7. Was tat
es nachher?  8. Weshalb sandte Ihre Majestät dem Mädchen
die Strümpfe?  9. Wohin wurde der Brief gebracht?  10. Was
stand darin geschrieben?  11. Weshalb tadeln Sie den Vater?
12. Weshalb tadelte das Kind seinen Bruder?  13. Was ward
aus den Bonbons?  14. Was ward aus dem Briefe?

*D.* 1. I am a poor Italian girl.  2. One day I was taking a
walk in the park.  3. I met a beautiful lady who greeted
me.  4. I recognized her at once.  5. Everybody knows (the)
Queen Helena.  6. Her kindliness is [well-]known in Italy,
as also in other countries.  7. She asked me if I knew her.
8. She asked me also where my father and mother lived.
9. Finally she said, smiling: "Can you knit stockings?"
10. "Certainly, signora, I often knit stockings."  11. Then
she bowed to me and went on (weiter).  12. I knitted her
a pair of stockings at once, and sent them to her.  13. The next
day a servant of the queen brought me a pair of silk stockings,
which she had sent me.  14. He also brought me sweets and
several pieces of money.  15. The queen thought I should be
very happy.  16. But good intentions are not always fulfilled.
17. The letter was burnt, and the sweets were eaten by my
brother.  18. My father pocketed the money, and the stockings
were sold by my mother.

*E.* Lesestück : Als Charles Lamb im "India-House" war,
sagte ein Vorgesetzter eines Morgens zu ihm : "Herr Lamb,
ich habe bemerkt, daß Sie jeden Morgen sehr spät ins Bureau
kommen." "Das gebe ich zu," erwiderte der Dichter, "vergessen Sie aber nicht, daß ich jeden Nachmittag sehr früh
fortgehe."

## LESSON XXXIV

**139.**    **Declension of Personal Pronouns.**

|  | | FIRST PERSON. | SECOND PERSON. |
|---|---|---|---|
| *Sing.* | N. | ich, I. | du, thou. |
|  | G. | meiner, of me. | deiner, of thee. |
|  | D. | mir, (to, for) me. | dir, (to, for) thee. |
|  | A. | mich, me. | dich, thee. |
| *Plur.* | N. | wir, we. | ihr, ye, you. |
|  | G. | unfer, of us. | euer, of you. |
|  | D. | uns, (to, for) us. | euch, (to, for) you. |
|  | A. | uns, us. | euch, you. |

THIRD PERSON.

*Singular.*

| | Masc. | Fem. | Neut. |
|---|---|---|---|
| N. | er, he. | fie, she. | es, it. |
| G. | feiner, of him. | ihrer, of her. | feiner, of its. |
| D. | ihm, (to, for) him. | ihr, (to, for) her. | ihm, (to, for) it |
| A. | ihn, him. | fie, her. | es, it. |

*Plural.*

| | |
|---|---|
| N. | fie, they. |
| G. | ihrer, of them. |
| D. | ihnen, (to, for) them. |
| A. | fie, them. |

NOTES. — 1. In poetical and archaic language, the following forms of the genitive are found: mein, dein, fein, ihr, unfrer, eurer.

2. The gen. and dat. of the 3rd sing. neut. do not occur, except when referring to persons (*e.g.* Mädchen, Männlein, etc.).

3. Deſſen (gen. of das) replaces the neut. gen. feiner, referring to things: Ich erinnere mich **deſſen** nicht, 'I don't remember it.'

4. For the use of **da** before preps. instead of pers. prons. of 3rd pers., see § 85.

**140. Agreement.** The pronouns of the third singular must agree in gender and number with the nouns to which they refer.

NOTE. — Fräulein, 'young lady,' requires the fem. pron. fie (as also the fem. poss.).

**141.** Pronouns of Address.

| | |
|---|---|
| Wie geht es dir, Tante? | How are you, aunt? |
| Bist du es, lieber Freund? | Is it you, dear friend? |
| Was macht ihr, Kinder? | What are you doing, children? |
| Was machst du, mein Hündchen? | What are you doing, doggie? |
| Gott, ich erkenne Dich! | I acknowledge thee, O God! |
| Wie geht es Ihnen, Herr S.? | How are you, Mr. S.? |

OBSERVE: 1. Du is used in familiar address, as to a near relative, an intimate friend, a child, an animal.

2. Du is used in exalted or archaic language, as in addressing the Supreme Being, and in poetry; also in fables and fairy tales.

3. Ihr (plur. of du) is used in addressing a number of persons, each of whom would be addressed by du.

4. In all other cases 'you,' whether singular or plural, is expressed by Sie (Ihrer, Ihnen, Sie), the pronoun of formal address, the verb agreeing in the third plural.

NOTES. — 1. All pronouns of address, as well as the corresponding poss. adjs., are spelled with capitals in writing a letter.

2. Er, Sie (3rd sing. fem.), Ihr (2nd plur.) are used in archaic and rustic speech as prons. of address.

**142.** Impersonal Verbs.

| | |
|---|---|
| Es friert (schneit, regnet). | It is freezing (snowing, raining). |
| Wie geht's dir? | How are you? |
| Was gibt's? | What's the matter? |
| Es ist (tut) mir leid. | I am sorry. |
| Mich hungert (friert). | I am hungry (cold). |
| Er sagte, daß ihn hungere. | He said he was hungry. |

OBSERVE: 1. Impersonal verbs are used only in the third singular with es as subject.

2. Many verbs are used impersonally with a special sense.

3. Those denoting bodily or mental affection drop es if the object precedes the verb of a principal sentence, and also in dependent sentences.

**143. Idiomatic Uses of es.** 1. Es is often placed before a verb (especially ſein) to represent the real subject, which follows the verb, and with which the verb agrees; thus used it frequently = 'there':

| | |
|---|---|
| Wer iſt es? Es iſt die Tante. | Who is it? It is aunt. |
| Es waren meine Vettern. | It was my cousins. |
| Es leuchten die Sterne. | The stars are shining. |
| Es iſt ein Vogel im Käfig. | There is a bird in the cage. |
| Es liegen Bücher hier. | There are books lying here. |

2. Whenever indefinite existence is to be expressed, or when the assertion is general, 'there is,' 'there were,' etc., must be rendered by es gibt, es gab, ꝛc., and the English subject becomes the direct object (*acc.*) in German:

| | |
|---|---|
| Es gibt einige Vögel, die nicht ſingen. | There are some birds which do not sing. |
| Letztes Jahr gab es viele Birnen. | There were a great many pears last year. |
| Es gibt nur einen Goethe. | There is only one Goethe. |

3. With ſein, 'to be,' when the real subject is a personal pronoun, the English order is inverted, and the verb agrees with the real subject:

| | |
|---|---|
| Ich bin es; du biſt es, ꝛc. | It is I; it is you, etc. |
| Sind Sie es? | Is it you? |

4. After a verb, es often represents a predicate or clause, and corresponds to the English 'one,' or 'so':

| | |
|---|---|
| Iſt er Arzt? | Is he a doctor? |
| Ja, er iſt es. | Yes, he is (one). |
| Biſt du frei? Ich bin es. | Are you free? I am (so). |
| Wir wollen kommen und ihr ſollt es auch. | We will come, and you shall (do so) too. |

### EXERCISE XXXIV.

allerdi'ngs, certainly, indeed.

behilflich, helpful, of assistance.

der Beruf, –(e)s, –e, calling, profession.

bitten, bat, gebeten, to beg, ask.

dankbar, thankful.

denn (*adv.*), then.

ermöglichen, to make possible.

die Fähigkeit, –en, capacity.

freuen, to gladden; es freut mich), I am glad.

gedenken (*gen.*), to be mindful of.

herein! come in!

jederzeit, always.

klopfen, to knock.

nötig, necessary, needful.

der Rat, –(e)s, advice.

raten, riet, geraten, to advise.

der Umstand, –es, ⁻e, circumstance.

verdienen, to earn.

vorziehen, to prefer.

wählen, to choose, select.

das Zutrauen, –s, trust, confidence.

IDIOMS: 1. **Wie geht es Ihnen?**　How are you?

2. **Ich bin müde. — Ich (bin es) auch,** I am tired. — So am I.

*A.* **Lehrer.** Es klopft; herein! Bist du es, Robert? **Robert.** Ja, ich bin es, Herr Lehrer. **L.** Es freut mich, dich zu sehen, Robert; was gibt es denn? **R.** Ich wollte Sie bitten, mir einen guten Rat zu geben. Es ist hohe Zeit, daß ich einen Beruf wähle, denn ich bin schon sechzehn Jahre alt. **L.** Warum glaubst du denn, daß ich dir in dieser Sache raten kann? **R.** Es ist niemand, der meine Umstände und meine Fähigkeiten so gut kennt, wie Sie. **L.** Es freut mich, daß du so viel Zutrauen zu mir hast. Welchen Beruf würdest du vorziehen? **R.** Ich würde das Studium der Medizin vorziehen, aber es fehlen mir die Mittel dazu. **L.** Das ist allerdings ein kostspieliges Studium, aber andere sind es auch. Heutzutage gibt es aber viele Gelegenheiten, das nötige Geld zu verdienen. **R.** Das würde es mir vielleicht ermöglichen, Arzt zu werden; ich habe es mir lange gewünscht. **L.** Schön; es wird mich jederzeit freuen, dir in dieser Sache behilflich zu sein. **R.** Ich bin Ihnen sehr dankbar dafür, daß Sie meiner so freundlich gedenken.

*B.* Oral: 1. Hat es geklopft? 2. Wer war da? 3. War es Robert oder sein Bruder? 4. Ist es schwer, einen Beruf zu wählen? 5. Was sagte Robert darüber? 6. Freute es den Lehrer, seinem Schüler zu helfen? 7. Wird der Lehrer immer dieses Jungen gedenken? 8. Ist Roberts Vater Arzt? 9. Willst du auch Arzt werden? 10. Fehlen dir die Mittel dazu? 11. Wird es Robert möglich sein, Arzt zu werden? 12. Wollen Sie mir einen guten Rat geben?

*C.* 1. There is a book lying on the table. 2. There are six chairs in this room. 3. How are you to-day, dear friends? 4. How are you to-day, Mr. Aue? 5. I am always glad to see you. 6. I am unhappy; so am I; so are we. 7. We praise Thee, O God! Thou art always mindful of us. 8. Was it you, dear aunt? I didn't think it was you. 9. Sing, little birds, sing. 10. Do you hear me, dog? 11. Is Mr. Aue very celebrated? He is. 12. There are always enough doctors, but there are never enough good ones.

*D.* 1. Robert's teacher, Mr. Aue, was sitting at the table. 2. There was a knock [at the door]. 3. "Who is there? Come in," said he. 4. It was one of his pupils. 5. "I am glad to see you, my boy; what can I do for you?" 6. "You can perhaps give me (a) good advice, Mr. Aue. 7. I must choose a profession; it is high time now, for I am over sixteen years old." 8. Mr. A. asked him what profession he preferred. 9. "I prefer the study of medicine," replied the boy, "but I haven't the means." 10. "It is an expensive study, to be sure, but so are others. 11. But there are many opportunities to earn money nowadays." 12. "Perhaps it will be possible," replied Robert. 13. "My father was a doctor, and I mean to become one also, if I can. 14. It is a noble calling." 15. His teacher said he would help him.

*E.* Lesestück: Ein Pfarrer in Schottland fiel eines Abends in ein tiefes Loch und rief um Hilfe. Ein vorbeigehender Arbeiter hörte ihn rufen und fragte, wer es sei. Der Pfarrer

nannte seinen Namen, worauf der Arbeiter erwiderte : " Na !
Regen Sie sich nicht unnötig auf; Sie haben bis nächsten
Sonntag Zeit und heute ist erst Mittwoch."

## LESSON XXXV

**144.**　　　　　The Strong Conjugation.

*Prin. Parts :* bleiben, remain.　　blieb　　geblieben
　　　　　　　singen, sing.　　　sang　　gesungen
　　　　　　　frieren, freeze.　　fror　　gefroren

OBSERVE : Strong verbs form the imperfect indicative by a
change of stem vowel, without adding a tense ending; for the
past participle see § 119.

NOTE. — Remember that, apart from the lack of tense ending in the
imperfect indicative and subjunctive, the simple tenses of strong verbs have
the same endings as those of machen, and that their compound tenses are
formed exactly like those of weak verbs.

**145.**　　　　Vowel Changes of Present Stem.

| Sprechen, speak. | Stehlen, steal. | Fallen, fall. |
|---|---|---|
| *Pres. Indic.* | *Pres. Indic.* | *Pres. Indic.* |
| ich spreche | ich stehle | ich falle |
| du sprichst | du stiehlst | du fällst |
| er spricht | er stiehlt | er fällt |
| wir sprechen | wir stehlen | wir fallen |
| ihr sprecht | ihr stehlt | ihr fallt |
| sie sprechen | sie stehlen | sie fallen |
| *Imperative.* | *Imperative.* | *Imperative.* |
| sprich | stiehl | falle |
| er spreche | er stehle | er falle |
| sprechen wir | stehlen wir | fallen wir |
| sprecht | stehlt | fallt |
| sprechen sie | stehlen sie | fallen sie |

L

OBSERVE: 1. Many strong verbs change short **e** of the infinitive stem vowel to **i**, and long **e** to **ie**, in the second and third singular present indicative and the second singular imperative, and also drop –**e** of the latter.

2. Some strong verbs with **a, o**, of the infinitive stem take umlaut in the second and third singular of the present indicative, but not in the imperative.

3. Hence the principal parts of such verbs are as follows:

| Infin. | Impf. Ind. | Past Part. | 2 Sg., 3 Sg. Pr. Ind. | Impve. |
|--------|-----------|-----------|----------------------|--------|
| geben | gab | gegeben | gibſt, gibt | gib |
| ſprechen | ſprach | geſprochen | ſprichſt, ſpricht | ſprich |
| ſehen | ſah | geſehen | ſiehſt, ſieht | ſieh |
| ſtehlen | ſtahl | geſtohlen | ſtiehlſt, ſtiehlt | ſtiehl |
| fallen | fiel | gefallen | fällſt, fällt | falle |
| ſchlagen | ſchlug | geſchlagen | ſchlägſt, ſchlägt | ſchlage |

NOTE. — The whole pres. indic. and impve. should be practised.

**146.**                    Stems in –**d**, –**t**, ꝛc.

*Present Indicative.*

| Binden, bind. | Bitten, beg. | Fechten, fight. | Raten, advise. | Beißen, bite. |
|---------------|--------------|-----------------|----------------|----------------|
| ich binde | bitte | fechte | rate | beiße |
| du bindeſt | bitteſt | fichtſt | rätſt | beißt |
| er bindet | bittet | ficht | rät | beißt |
| wir binden | bitten | fechten | raten | beißen |
| ihr bindet | bittet | fechtet | ratet | beißt |
| ſie binden | bitten | fechten | raten | beißen |

OBSERVE: 1. Stems in –**d**, –**t**, without vowel change in the present indicative, retain –**e** before –**ſt**, –**t**.

2. Stems in –**d**, –**t**, with vowel change, drop –**e** of the ending in the second singular and –**et** in the third; in other forms they retain the –**e** and –**et**.

3. Stems in sibilants usually drop –**es** of the second singular.

**147.**　　　Formation of Imperfect Subjunctive.

ich bliebe　　　ich fänge　　　ich fröre　　　ich fchlüge

OBSERVE : The stem of the imperfect indicative regularly
serves for the imperfect subjunctive, but with added umlaut
when the imperfect stem vowel is **a, o,** or **u.**

NOTE. — In some verbs the vowel of the impf. subj. does not correspond
with that of the impf. indic.: helfen, 'help,' half, imp. subj. hülfe ; some
have double forms: gewinnen, 'win,' gewann, impf. subj. gewänne or
gewönne ; such forms occur only in Classes 9, 10, 11 (§ 148); see also
Alphabetical List in App. D.

**148.** Classes of Strong Verbs.　For convenience of reference,
the principal strong verbs are arranged here in classes, according to their vowel changes, exceptional forms and peculiarities
being given in the notes :

1.　**Beißen** Model.

*Parts :*　　beißen[1]　　**biß**　　gebiffen　　　bite

gleichen, resemble.　reißen,[1] tear.　　fchneiden,[3] cut.
gleiten,[2] glide.　reiten,[2] ride.　　fchreiten,[2] stride.
greifen,[2] grasp.　fchleichen, sneak.　ftreichen, stroke.
kneifen,[2] pinch.　fchleifen,[2] grind.　ftreiten,[2] contend.
leiden,[3] suffer.　fchmeißen,[1] fling.　weichen, yield.
pfeifen,[2] whistle.

[1] Stem –ß becomes ſſ after shortened vowel in the parts, unless final.
[2] After short i stems –f and –t are doubled.　[3] Stem –d becomes –tt.

2.　**Bleiben** Model.

*Parts :*　　bleiben　　blieb　　geblieben　　remain

gedeihen, thrive.　fcheiden, part.　　fchweigen, be silent.
leihen, lend.　fcheinen, shine.　　fteigen, mount.
meiden, avoid.　fchreiben, write.　　treiben, drive.
preifen, extol.　fchreien, scream.　　weifen, show.
reiben, rub.

### 3. Frieren Model.

*Parts:*        frieren        fror        gefroren        freeze

| | | |
|---|---|---|
| biegen, bend. | heben,[1] lift. | wägen, weigh (*tr.*). |
| bieten, offer. | schieben, push. | wiegen, weigh (*intr.*). |
| fliegen, fly. | schwören,[2] swear. | ziehen,[3] pull (*tr.*), |
| fliehen, flee. | verlieren, lose. | move (*intr.*). |

[1] hob or hub.        [2] schwor or schwur.        [3] zog, gezogen.

### 4. Schießen Model.

*Parts:*        schießen        schoß        geschossen        shoot

| | | |
|---|---|---|
| erschallen, resound. | kriechen, creep. | schließen,[1] lock. |
| fließen,[1] flow. | riechen, smell. | triefen,[1] drip. |
| genießen,[1] enjoy. | saufen,[2] drink | verdrießen,[1] vex. |
| gießen,[1] pour. | (of beasts). | |

[1] Consonant changes of stem as in beißen model.        [2] soff, gesoffen ; 2 and 3 sing. pres. indic., säufst, säuft.

### 5. Fechten Model.

*Parts:*        fechten        focht        gefochten        fichtst        ficht        fight
                                                                        ficht

| | | |
|---|---|---|
| erlöschen, become | melken, milk. | schmelzen, melt. |
| extinguished. | quellen, gush. | schwellen, swell. |
| flechten, weave. | | |

### 6. Essen Model.

*Parts:*        essen        aß        gegessen[1]        ißt        iß        eat
                                                                ißt

| | | |
|---|---|---|
| fressen, eat (of | messen, measure. | treten,[3] tread. |
| beasts). | sitzen,[2] sit. | vergessen, forget. |
| geben, give. | | |

[1] Note the inserted g.        [2] saß, gesessen.        [3] Pres. trittst, tritt, impve. tritt, p. pple. getreten.

### 7. Sehen Model.

*Parts:*  sehen   sah   gesehen   siehst   sieh   see
                                          sieht

bitten, beg.           liegen, lie.            geschehen, happen.
lesen, read.           genesen,[1] recover.

> [1] Pres. genesest, genest, impve. genese.

### 8. Sprechen Model.

*Parts:*  sprechen   sprach   gesprochen   sprichst   sprich   speak
                                                      spricht

brechen, break.        nehmen,[2] take.       treffen,[3] hit.
erschrecken,[1] be     stechen, sting.
frightened.

> [1] Impf. erschrak.        [2] nahm, genommen, nimmst, nimmt, nimm.
> [3] Impf. traf.

### 9. Stehlen Model.

*Parts:*  stehlen   stahl   gestohlen   stiehlst   stiehl   steal
                                                   stiehlt

befehlen, command.  empfehlen, recommend.  kommen,[1] come.

> [1] kam, kommst, kommt (rarely with umlaut).

### 10. Spinnen Model.

*Parts:*  spinnen      spann       gesponnen        spin
beginnen, begin.    rinnen, flow.       sinnen, think.
gewinnen, win.      schwimmen, swim.    *werfen - throw*

### 11. Helfen Model.

*Parts:*  helfen   half   geholfen   hilfst   hilf   help
                                     hilft

dreschen,[1] thresh.   schelten, scold.      verbergen, hide.
gelten, be worth.      sterben, die.         verderben,[2] spoil.
                                             werden,[2] become.

> [1] Impf. drasch or drosch.      [2] Impf. ward or wurde in sg., pl. wurden,
> etc., only; pres. 2 sg. and 3 sg. wirst, wird ; impve. werde.

12. **Singen** Model.

*Parts :*  singen    sang    gesungen    sing

binden, bind.          ringen, wring.              springen, spring.
dringen, press.        schlingen, twine; swallow.  trinken, drink.
finden, find.          schwinden, vanish.          winden, wind.
gelingen, succeed.     schwingen, swing.           zwingen, force.
klingen, sound.        sinken, sink.

13. **Schlagen** Model.

*Parts :*  schlagen  schlug  geschlagen  schlägst  schlage    strike
                                         schlägt

backen,[1] bake.       laden,[2] load ; invite.    tragen, carry.
fahren, drive.         schaffen,[3] create.        wachsen, grow.
graben, dig.           stehen,[4] stand.           waschen, wash.

[1] Impf. buk, or more usually backte.    [2] 2 sg. and 3 sg. lädst, lädt or
ladest, ladet.    [3] schuf, schaffst, schafft.    [4] stand (stund, obsolete),
gestanden.

14. **Fallen** Model.

*Parts :*  fallen  fiel  gefallen  fällst  falle    fall
                                   fällt

blasen, blow.          hangen,[3] hang.            raten, advise.
braten, roast.         hauen,[4] hew.              rufen,[5] call.
fangen,[1] catch.      heißen, bid ; be called.   schlafen, sleep.
gehen,[2] go, walk.    lassen, let.                stoßen, knock.
halten, hold.          laufen, run.

[1] Impf. fing.    [2] ging, gegangen.    [3] Impf. hing.    [4] hieb, haust,
haut.    [5] rufst, ruft.

15. Anomalous Verbs.

*Parts :*  sein    war    gewesen    be
           tun     tat    getan      do

## EXERCISE XXXV

*N.B.* It is not intended that the following exercise should be completed at this stage, but that its various parts should be used from time to time at the discretion of the teacher, for drill in the conjugation of strong verbs. For the vocabulary of this and following exercises, see end of volume.

*A.* Review § 148, 1, and translate : 1. As the woodcutter was grinding his axe, it slipped out of his hand. 2. When I was young I suffered much from (an, *dat.*) toothache. 3. Mary has torn (zerreißen) her new dress. 4. The thief was seized (ergreifen) as he was sneaking into the house. 5. That bad boy has pinched his little brother. 6. Charles was punished because he whistled in school. 7. The boys have flung their books on the ground. 8. Two officers were riding with the emperor through the park. 9. The farmers were cutting their wheat last week.

*B.* Review § 148, 2, and translate : 1. The emperor ascended the throne in the year 1888. 2. You thought I was in the wrong because I was silent. 3. Would you stay here if I stayed with you? 4. The poor girl screamed when the dog bit her. 5. Where are the books which I (have) lent you? 6. The tree was not thriving, because the soil was too poor. 7. The teacher has proved to us that we were wrong. 8. He seemed to be angry with (auf, *acc.*) us. 9. I stayed at home because I was suffering from headache. 10. The sheep were being driven to the pasture. 11. I have already copied my exercises. 12. I hope I have avoided (vermeiden) all mistakes this time.

*C.* Review § 148, 3, and translate : 1. The birds have flown into the wood. 2. The students have lost much time this winter. 3. The witness swore that he recognized the thief. 4. The enemy fled when they were attacked. 5. I picked up a book which was lying on the table. 6. Robert weighed more a year ago than he weighs now. 7. I have offered a thousand marks for this picture. 8. The children are not dressed yet.

9. My parents have (are) moved into another street.   10. This pen is bent; I cannot write with it.   11. I should be sorry if I lost this beautiful ring.

*D*. Review § 148, 4, 5, and translate: 1. Has the gardener watered the flowers and cut the grass?   2. A river swells when the ice melts.   3. This river is always swollen in spring.   4. This basket was woven by a blind man.   5. The cows are already milked and have been driven to the pasture. 6. The doors are locked; I locked them myself.   7. It vexed me that this pretty bird had been shot (use man).   8. Have you smelled those roses?   They smell very fine.   9. The cat drank the milk which I poured into a cup.   10. The dog has (is) crept behind the stove because he was cold (frieren). 11. We have not swum in the river, because it was flowing so fast.

*E*. Review § 148, 6, 7, and translate: 1. Have you seen my gloves?   2. Yes; they are lying on the table.   3. What has happened to your little sister?   4. She stepped on a piece of glass and cut her foot.   5. This happened in the holidays, and she recovered very slowly.   6. She has now quite recovered. 7. Don't forget, my boy, that the door is locked at ten.   8. It often happens that the professor forgets his umbrella.   9. This student reads many books, but he soon forgets what he has read.   10. The horse was eating his oats in the stable, while his master was dining.   11. Don't step on the ice, Robert; it is very thin, the sun has melted it.   12. Charles, please give this letter to your uncle.   13. The stranger trod on my foot, but at once begged my pardon.   14. Please read (vorlesen) this poem to me, Sarah.   15. The newspapers tell us what is happening in the world.   16. See, my child, how brightly the sun shines.

*F*. Review § 148, 8, 9, and translate: 1. One officer commands many soldiers.   2. The officer commanded his soldiers to shoot, and they shot.   3. Thin ice breaks when one treads on it; take care, child.   4. The child was frightened when it saw the soldiers.   5. Speak louder, my boy, I cannot hear you. 6. I spoke as loud as I could.   7. This man speaks French and German well.   8. I have often met this gentleman; I met him yesterday at my brother's.   9. You have taken my book, Mary; take this one.   10. My watch was stolen from (aus) my room. 11. The doctor has recommended me to go (ziehen) to a warmer climate.

*G.* Review § 148, 10, 11, and translate :   1. That fruit is bad (spoiled); throw it away, my child.   2. Honour is worth more than life.   3. This coin is not current here.   4. The good man repays evil with good.   5. Why do you scold us, dear mother?   6. One gladly helps one (einem) who helps himself. 7. This boy has swum over the river.   8. You have reflected long enough.   9. The boy was ashamed, and hid his face.   10. The farmer is threshing his oats to-day.   11. The wheat is already threshed.   12. When did your uncle die?   13. When a good king dies, the people (Volk, *n.*) mourn.   14. My youngest brother won a prize at (bei) the examination.   15. One should always finish what one has begun.

*H.* Review § 148, 12, and translate :   1. Have you succeeded in learning (to learn) German?   2. The traveller jumped from his horse and tied him to (an) a tree.   3. I have found the money I lost yesterday.   4. The telephone was invented by Mr. Bell.   5. My pen has disappeared; do you know where it is?   6. Here it is; I have brought it to you.   7. I should be much obliged to you if you sang that song again.   8. The women on the shore screamed and wrung their hands, when the boat sank, in which their husbands were (sich befinden). 9. They were at once swallowed up by the waves and were drowned.   10. I have been forced to sell my house.   11. Clara's voice sounded very hoarse, as she had a cold.

*J.* Review § 148, 13, and translate :   1. Has the clock struck yet?   2. It is just striking ten.   3. This train goes

very slowly.    4. Are you invited (einlaben) to the ball at Mrs.
Braun's?    5. The gardener is digging a large hole in the garden.    6. Yesterday he was digging (umgraben) a flower-bed.
7. This tree is growing fast.    8. It grew two or three feet
last year, but it bore no fruit.    9. God created the earth and
all that is therein.

*K.* Review § 148, 14, and translate : 1. The ship struck on
a rock and sank.    2. The wind was blowing violently.    3. The
captain did not leave (verlassen) his ship until it was sinking.
4. The child fell and knocked its head on the ice.    5. The
woodcutter was cutting down a big tree.    6. What was the
name of the gentleman whom we met yesterday?    7. Are you
still asleep, John?    I have called you twice.    8. My father
never lets me sleep later than seven o'clock.    9. Our doctor
advises me to rise early.    10. Mine advised me to rise late.
11. My father's picture hangs over my writing-table.    12. How
do you like this town?    13. When did you begin (anfangen) to
learn German?    14. This train stops at all stations (Station, *f.*).
15. If you had run more quickly, you would have won the
prize.    16. Adolf runs quicker than you.

## LESSON XXXVI

**149.**          Reflexive Pronouns and Verbs.

Sich loben, to praise one's self.     Sich einbilden, to imagine.

| *Pres. Indic.* | *Pres. Indic.* |
|---|---|
| ich lobe mich | ich bilde mir ein |
| du lobst dich | du bildest dir ein |
| er lobt sich | er bildet sich ein |
| wir loben uns | wir bilden uns ein |
| ihr lobt euch | ihr bildet euch ein |
| sie loben sich | sie bilden sich ein |
| Sie loben sich | Sie bilden sich ein |

| *Perf. Indic.* | *Perf. Indic.* |
|---|---|
| ich habe mich gelobt, 2c. | ich habe mir eingebildet, 2c., 2c. |

OBSERVE: 1. The pronouns of the 1st and 2nd persons have no special form for reflexive action.

2. Those of the 3rd person (including the formal Sie) have the form fid) for both dative and accusative of all genders and both numbers.

NOTE.—Transitive verbs in English are frequently also used intransitively; such verbs are usually reflexive in German: Das Wetter hat fid) geändert, 'The weather has changed'; Die Tür öffnete fid), 'The door opened.'

### 150.          Government of Reflexives.

| | |
|---|---|
| Id) fdjämte mid) feiner. | I was ashamed of him. |
| Erbarme did) der Armen. | Take pity on the poor. |
| Begnügen Sie fid) damit. | Content yourself with that. |
| Id) kann mir das denken. | I can imagine that. |

OBSERVE: 1. The reflexive object is usually in the accusative, the remote object being in the genitive, or governed by a preposition.

2. The reflexive object is sometimes in the dative and the remote object in the accusative.

### 151.          Reciprocal Pronouns.

| | |
|---|---|
| Sie werden fid) wieder fehen. | They will see each other again. |
| Wir begegneten uns (*dat.*). | We met each other. |
| Wir lieben **einander.** | We love one another. |

OBSERVE: Reflexive pronouns are used in the plural to express reciprocal action; but in case of ambiguity einander replaces them for all persons.

### 152.          Emphatic Pronouns.

| | |
|---|---|
| Du fagft es felbft. | You say so yourself. |
| Erkennt euch felber. | Know yourselves (not others). |
| Selbft der Lehrer fagt es. | Even the teacher says so. |

OBSERVE: The indeclinable felbft or felber is used to emphasize pronouns and nouns; felbft is also used adverbially (=aud) or fogar, 'even'), and then precedes.

## EXERCISE XXXVI

Idioms: 1. **Haben Sie sich gut unterhalten?** Did you enjoy yourself?
2. **Wie hat Ihnen das Essen geschmeckt?** How did you enjoy
your dinner?
3. **Sich auf den Weg machen,** to set out (on a walk, etc.).

*A.* Heute erwachte ich schon um halb sechs Uhr. Ich stand
sofort auf und kleidete mich schnell an, denn ich hatte beschlossen,
einen Spaziergang zu machen. Mutter riet mir, mich warm
anzuziehen, sonst würde ich mich erkälten. Ich meinte aber,
das sei nicht nötig. „Du irrst dich, liebe Klara," sprach sie,
„das Wetter hat sich geändert; es ist sehr kalt geworden." Als
ich durch den Park ging, begegnete ich meiner Freundin Else.
Das wunderte mich nicht, denn wir treffen uns oft an dieser
Stelle. Wir begrüßten uns und freuten uns über dieses
Zusammentreffen, denn Else hatte sich auch zu einem frühen
Spaziergang entschlossen. Auf dem Wege unterhielten wir
uns prächtig. Nachdem wir eine Stunde gegangen waren,
setzten wir uns auf eine Bank am Wege, um uns ein wenig
auszuruhen. Da es aber anfing zu schneien, erhoben wir uns
bald und machten uns auf den Heimweg. Unterwegs trennten
wir uns und ich kehrte allein nach Hause zurück.

*B.* Continue the following: 1. Ich kann mich selbst ankleiden, du . . . dich, ꝛc. 2. Ich werde mich warm anziehen.
3. Ich habe mich sehr darüber gewundert. 4. Ich konnte
mich nicht dazu entschließen. 5. Wir haben uns oft hier getroffen. 6. Ich schäme mich meines Betragens, du . . .
deines, ꝛc. 7. Ich befand mich gar nicht wohl.

*C.* Oral: 1. Wie geht es Ihnen heute? 2. Wie befindet
sich Ihr Herr Vater? 3. Glaubst du, daß das Wetter sich
heute ändern wird? 4. Haben die Kinder sich schon ange-
kleidet? 5. Können sie sich selbst anziehen? 6. Wo haben
sich die beiden Freundinnen getroffen? 7. Wozu hatten sie

sich beide entschlossen?   8. Wollen Sie sich nicht auf diese Bank setzen?   9. Hast du deine Aufgabe nicht selbst geschrieben?   10. Schämst du dich nicht deines Betragens?

*D.* 1. The weather has changed.   2. We must dress more warmly, if we mean to go out.   3. Otherwise we shall catch cold.   4. I think you are mistaken; the weather is warmer now.   5. I don't wonder at that.   6. The weather often changes quickly in this country.   7. Well (nun), have you made up your mind to take a walk?   8. Certainly; and I shall be glad to accompany you.   9. We shall set out at once. 10. Who is that lady you bowed to?   11. Oh, that is a friend of my sister's.   12. They know each other very well.   13. She and I always bow to each other when we meet.   14. I am tired.   15. So am I.   16. Sit down on this bench and rest a little.   17. I fear it will begin to snow soon.   18. In that case we must go home.   19. I am sorry that we must part now, but we have enjoyed ourselves very much (gut).   20. It is to be hoped we shall meet again this evening.

*E.* Lesestück:

> Brichst du Blumen, sei bescheiden,
> Nimm nicht gar so viele fort!
> Sieh', die Blumen müssen's leiden,
> Doch sie zieren ihren Ort.
>
> Nimm ein paar und laß die andern
> Stehn im Gras und an dem Strauch!
> Andre, die vorüber wandern,
> Freu'n sich an den Blumen auch.
>
> Nach dir kommt vielleicht ein müder
> Wand'rer, der des Weges zieht
> Trüben Sinns; — der freut sich wieder,
> Wenn er auch ein Röslein sieht.
>
> — Johannes Trojan.

## LESSON XXXVII

**153.**                    **Mixed Conjugation.**

| Infin. | Impf. Indic. | Past Part. | Pres. Indic. | Meaning. |
|--------|--------------|------------|--------------|----------|
| wiſſen | wußte | gewußt | weiß | know |
| dürfen | durfte | gedurft | darf | may |
| können | konnte | gekonnt | kann | can |
| mögen | mochte | gemocht | mag | may |
| müſſen | mußte | gemußt | muß | must |
| ſollen | ſollte | geſollt | ſoll | shall |
| wollen | wollte | gewollt | will | will |

Observe: The imperfect indicative and past participle have the weak endings –te, –t, without umlaut.

Note. — The imperative is wanting in all, except wiſſen, wiſſe, ?c., and wollen, wolle, ?c.

**154.**                    **Present Indicative.**

| ich weiß | darf | kann | mag | muß | ſoll | will |
|----------|------|------|-----|-----|------|------|
| du weißt | darfſt | kannſt | magſt | mußt | ſollſt | willſt |
| er weiß | darf | kann | mag | muß | ſoll | will |
| wir wiſſen | dürfen | können | mögen | müſſen | ſollen | wollen |
| ihr wißt | dürft | könnt | mögt | müßt | ſollt | wollt |
| ſie wiſſen | dürfen | können | mögen | müſſen | ſollen | wollen |

Observe: 1. The vowel change in the singular (except ſollen) and the absence of personal terminations in the first and third singular.

2. The plural is formed regularly from the infinitive stem.

**155.**                    **Subjunctive.**

*Pres.* ich wiſſe, dürfe, könne, möge, müſſe, ſolle, wolle,
     ?c.    ?c.    ?c.    ?c.    ?c.    ?c.    ?c.

*Impf.* ich wüßte, dürfte, könnte, möchte, müßte, ſollte, wollte,
     ?c.    ?c.    ?c.    ?c.    ?c.    ?c.    ?c.

Continue the paradigm with regular subjunctive endings.

Observe: The absence of umlaut in ſollte and wollte.

**156.**　　　　Compound Tenses.

| | | | |
|---|---|---|---|
| *Perf. Ind.* | ich habe, | du haft, ꝛc. | gewußt, gedurft, ꝛc. |
| *Perf. Subj.* | ich habe, | du habest, ꝛc. | gewußt, gedurft, ꝛc. |
| *Plupf. Ind.* | ich hatte, | du hattest, ꝛc. | gewußt, gedurft, ꝛc. |
| *Plupf. Subj.* | ich hätte, | du hättest, ꝛc. | gewußt, gedurft, ꝛc. |
| *Fut. Ind.* | ich werde, du wirst, ꝛc. | | wissen, dürfen, ꝛc. |
| *Fut. Subj.* | ich werde, du werdest, ꝛc. | | wissen, dürfen, ꝛc. |
| *Fut. Perf. Ind.* | ich werde, du wirst, ꝛc. | | gewußt, ꝛc., haben. |
| *Fut. Perf. Subj.* | ich werde, du werdest, ꝛc. | | gewußt, ꝛc., haben. |
| *Simp. Condl.* | ich würde, du würdest, ꝛc. | | wissen, dürfen, ꝛc. |
| *Comp. Condl.* | ich würde, du würdest, ꝛc. | | gewußt, ꝛc., haben. |
| *Perf. Infin.* | gewußt haben, gedurft haben, ꝛc. | | |

**157. Modal Auxiliaries.** The verbs dürfen, können, mögen, müssen, sollen, wollen, with the verb lassen, are called 'modal auxiliaries,' since they form constructions equivalent to various moods; they all govern an infinitive without zu:

| | |
|---|---|
| Ich kann lesen. | I can read (*potential*). |
| Ich möchte gehen. | I should like to go (*optative*). |
| Lassen Sie uns gehen. | Let us go (*imperative*). |

**158. General Remarks on Modals.** 1. These verbs, unlike their English equivalents, have an infinitive and past participle, and are hence capable of forming a complete set of tenses:

| | |
|---|---|
| Ich werde arbeiten müssen. | I shall be obliged to work. |
| Er wird nicht kommen können. | He will not be able to come. |

2. After a governed infinitive, in the compound tenses, the past participle takes the form of an infinitive:

| | |
|---|---|
| Er hat nicht spielen **können**. | He was unable to play. |
| Er hat es schicken **lassen**. | He caused it to be sent. |

NOTE. — The verbs **hören** and **sehen** (and less commonly heißen, helfen, lehren, lernen, machen) also share this peculiarity: Ich habe ihn kommen hören (sehen), 'I heard (saw) him come.'

3. They may also be used independently (without a governed infinitive), and even as transitive verbs, and have then the regular forms of the past participle in compound tenses:

| | |
|---|---|
| Er hat nicht **gewollt.** | He was not willing. |
| Ich habe nie Wein **gemocht.** | I have never liked wine. |

4. Owing to the defective conjugation and limited meaning of the English modals, German modal constructions are variously rendered into English (see next section and §§ 174–180).

5. The imperfect subjunctive is regularly used for the simple conditional:

| | |
|---|---|
| Ich dürfte es tun. | I should be allowed to do it. |
| Ich möchte es tun. | I should like to do it. |

6. Distinguish carefully between 'could' (='was able'), konnte (indic.) and 'could' (='would be able'), könnte (condl.):

| | |
|---|---|
| Er konnte es nicht tun, da er krank war. | He couldn't (was unable to) do it, as he was ill. |
| Er könnte es nicht tun, wenn er auch wollte. | He couldn't (would be unable to) do it, even if he would. |

NOTE.—The infin. of a verb of motion (especially kommen, gehen) is often omitted after the modals when an adverb or adverbial phrase denoting 'whither' is present: Ich will herein, 'I wish to come in'; Er soll nach Hause, 'He is to go home.'

**159. Primary Signification of Modals.** The following paragraphs contain examples of the commoner uses of modals; for the construction of the compound tenses and the more idiomatic distinctions, see Lesson XL:

1. Dürfen (permission, concession):

| | |
|---|---|
| Darf ich Sie begleiten? | May I accompany you? |
| Wir dürfen Romane lesen. | We are allowed to read novels. |

2. Können (ability, possibility):

| | |
|---|---|
| Er konnte nicht schwimmen. | He could not swim. |
| Das kann sein. | That may (possibly) be so. |
| Können Sie Deutsch? | Do you know German? |

3. Mögen (preference, concession) :

| | |
|---|---|
| Er mochte nicht arbeiten. | He did not like to work. |
| Er möchte (gern) bleiben. | He would like to stay. |
| Er mag bleiben. | He may (let him) stay. |

4. Müssen (necessity, obligation) :

| | |
|---|---|
| Wir müssen alle sterben. | We must all die. |
| Wir werden warten müssen. | We shall have to wait. |

5. Sollen (obligation, duty) :

| | |
|---|---|
| Ich soll morgen abreisen. | I am to start to-morrow. |
| Was sollten wir tun? | What were we to do? |
| Das sollte er nicht tun. | He ought not to do that. |

NOTE. — The obligation is that imposed by the will of another.

6. Wollen (resolution, intention) :

| | |
|---|---|
| Er will nicht warten. | He is unwilling to wait. |
| Ich will morgen schreiben. | I mean to write to-morrow. |

7. Lassen (with imperative force, § 117) :

| | |
|---|---|
| Lassen Sie mich bleiben. | Let me stay. |

### 160.     English 'shall' and 'will.'

| | |
|---|---|
| Ich **werde** ertrinken und nie= mand **wird** mich retten. | I shall be drowned, and no-body will save me. |
| Ich **will** ertrinken und nie= mand **soll** mich retten. | I will be drowned, and nobody shall save me. |

OBSERVE: 1. The English 'shall' and 'will' must both be rendered by werden when they express mere futurity.

2. But if they express obligation or resolution, they must be rendered by sollen and wollen respectively.

### EXERCISE XXXVII

*A.* Ich will zur Stadt fahren; willst du mit, Emil? — Das möchte ich wohl, wenn ich dürfte, aber eigentlich sollte ich arbeiten. Ich muß den Vater erst fragen, ob ich mitfahren darf.

M

—Dann müssen wir uns beeilen. —Sollen wir zum Bahnhof
gehen oder fahren? —Laß uns lieber fahren, sonst möchten wir
den Zug versäumen. —Da sind wir am Bahnhof. —Laß uns
jetzt die Fahrkarten kaufen; es ist hohe Zeit. —Ach, ich muß
mein Portemonnaie zu Hause gelassen haben; könntest du mir
etwas Geld vorschießen? —Mit Vergnügen, aber ich habe nur
wenig bei mir. —Dann müssen wir dritter Klasse fahren, sonst
möchte es nicht ausreichen. —Weißt du wie viel Zeit wir in
der Stadt haben? —Über drei Stunden. —Dann werden wir
dem Fußballspiel beiwohnen können. —Das möchte ich nicht;
ich mag diesen Sport nicht; ich möchte lieber das Museum be=
suchen. —Ach! ich wußte nicht, daß du dich für so etwas inte=
ressiertest. —Wir werden uns also am Bahnhof trennen müssen.
—Wann und wo sollen wir uns wieder treffen? —Um 5.45
auf dem Bahnhof. —Gut; also auf Wiedersehen!

*B.* Continue: 1. Ich weiß nicht, was das bedeuten soll.
2. Ich wußte nicht was ich wollte, du . . . du, 2c. 3. Ich
möchte ausgehen, wenn ich dürfte, du . . . du, 2c. 4. Ich
kann sehr gut Deutsch. 5. Ich könnte eine Reise machen,
wenn ich wollte, du . . . du, 2c. 6. Ich werde morgen nicht
kommen können. 7. Ich habe diesen Menschen nie gemocht.
8. Ich war krank und konnte nicht arbeiten. 9. Ich werde
diese Aufgabe machen müssen. 10. Ich sollte das eigentlich
jetzt tun.

*C.* Oral: 1. Können Sie Deutsch? 2. Kann Ihr Bruder
Deutsch lesen? 3. Könnte er diesen deutschen Brief lesen?
4. Wohin möchten Heinrich und Emil gehen? 5. Dürfen wir
mit (gehen)? 6. Möchten Sie nicht lieber erster Klasse fahren?
7. Darf ich mich auf diese Bank setzen? 8. Mögen Sie das
Fußballspiel nicht? 9. Werden Sie heute dem Spiel beiwohnen
können? 10. Dürften Sie nicht ausgehen, wenn Sie wollten?
11. Wo könnte ich Sie wieder treffen? 12. Wissen Sie, wie
viel Uhr es jetzt ist? 13. Wußten Sie nicht, wie viel Uhr es
war?

*D.* 1. Henry and Emil mean to go to town.  2. They would like to attend the football match.  3. They don't know whether they may.  4. They really ought to work to-day.  5. Father, may I go to town?  6. Might Emil and Robert go with [me]? They would like [to go] along (mit).  7. Yes, but you will have to come back early.  8. I don't know whether we can; we will come home as soon as possible.  9. Emil wanted to buy a ticket, but couldn't find his purse.  10. Henry had to advance him some money.  11. Will they be obliged to travel third class? 12. I think (glauben) not; they must have money.  13. Robert doesn't wish to attend the football match; he doesn't like the game.  14. He has never liked it.  15. Neither have I (ich auch nicht).  16. He prefers to visit (besucht lieber) the museum when he is in town.  17. We didn't know that; we thought he meant to accompany us.  18. Here we are at the station. 19. We must part here.  20. But we could meet again at the (am) museum, couldn't we?  21. Certainly, and let us go home at 6 o'clock.  22. We have to be at home before seven.

*E.* Lesestück: Der türkische Gesandte in London wohnte einst einem lebhaften Fußballspiel bei.  Er folgte dem Spiel mit großem Interesse.  Als es vorüber war, fragte ihn sein Begleiter: "Nun, was denken Sie vom Fußballspiel?"  Der Gesandte antwortete: "Ich bin noch nicht im klaren darüber; für ein Spiel scheint es mir ein bißchen zu viel und für eine Schlacht ein bißchen zu wenig."

## LESSON XXXVIII

**161. Possessive Pronouns.**  They are formed as follows from the stems of the corresponding possessive adjectives: —

1. With endings of bieser model, without article (see § 31, 2).

2. With definite article and weak adjective endings:

*Singular.*

| Masc. | Fem. | Neut. |
|-------|------|-------|
| *N.*  der meine | die meine | das meine |
| *G.*  des meinen, ꝛc. | der meinen, ꝛc. | des meinen, ꝛc. |

*Plural.*

die meinen
der meinen, ꝛc.

3. With definite article and ending –**ig** + weak endings:

*Singular.*

| Masc. | Fem. | Neut. |
|-------|------|-------|
| *N.*  der meinige | die meinige | das meinige |
| *G.*  des meinigen, ꝛc. | der meinigen, ꝛc. | des meinigen, ꝛc. |

*Plural.*

die meinigen
der meinigen, ꝛc.

NOTE. — In unſrige and eurige the **e** of the stem is always omitted.

## 162.                    Use of Possessive Pronouns.

Der Hut ist meiner (der meine,    The hat is mine.
der meinige).

Ich habe meinen Hut, aber sie    I have my hat, but she has not
hat (den) ihr(ig)en nicht.          hers.

OBSERVE: 1. The three forms given in the previous section
are interchangeable, without difference of meaning, the first (or
shortest) form being the most usual.

2. The stem of the possessive pronoun depends on the
gender, number, and person of its antecedent.

NOTES. — 1. A possessive pron. used as predicate may also have the
uninflected form: Dieſe Bücher ſind ſein, 'These books are his.'

2. Observe the following idiomatic uses of the possessive pronoun: Die
Mein(ig)en, die Sein(ig)en, 'My (his) friends, family,' etc.; Ich werde
das Mein(ig)e tun, 'I shall do my part.'

*is invariable in the sense of
'belonging to me'*

3. The forms **meinesgleichen** (deinesgleichen, etc.), meaning 'a person, or persons, like me, you,' etc., are used as indeclinable substs. : **Wir werden seinesgleichen** nie wieder erblicken, ' We ne'er shall look upon his like again.'

## 163.                    Possessive Dative.

| | |
|---|---|
| Es fiel **ihm auf den** Kopf. | It fell on his head. |
| Ein Nagel zerriß **mir den** Rock. | A nail tore my coat. |
| Er schüttelte **seinem** alten Freunde **die** Hand. | He shook the hand of his old friend. |
| Er schnitt **sich den** Finger ab. | He cut off his (own) finger. |

OBSERVE : 1. With parts of the person, clothing, etc., the possessive adjective is commonly replaced by the dative of the personal pronoun or of a noun + the definite article.

2. If the possessor is the subject, the reflexive pronoun is used when the action is reflexive.

NOTE. — But when there is no reflexive action, the refl. pron. is omitted : Er schüttelte den Kopf, ' He shook his head.'

### EXERCISE XXXVIII

*A.* Als ein armer Holzhauer eines Tages am Ufer eines Flusses Bäume fällte, glitt ihm die Axt aus der Hand und fiel ins tiefe Wasser. „Ich Unglücklicher," rief er, „wie soll ich jetzt Brot für die Meinigen verdienen?" Er setzte sich hin und weinte laut. Da rauschte das Wasser ; eine Nixe erschien und fragte ihn, was ihm geschehen sei. „Ach!" erwiderte der Arme, „die Axt ist mir ins Wasser gefallen." „Sei ruhig," sprach sie, „ich will das Meinige tun, dir die Axt wieder zu verschaffen." Dann tauchte sie unter und kam mit einer goldnen Axt herauf. „Ist diese Axt dein?" fragte sie. „Ach nein!" erwiderte der Holzhauer, „das ist die meinige nicht." Wieder verschwand die Nixe und brachte eine silberne herauf. „Ist das die deine?" fragte sie. „Auch das ist nicht meine," versetzte er ; die meinige ift aus Eifen." Noch einmal tauchte fie unter und erfchien mit der richtigen. „Weil du fo ehrlich gewefen bift, will ich dir auch die goldne und die filberne Axt fchenken," fprach fie. Froh dankte ihr der Holzhauer und kehrte zu den Seinen zurück.

*B.* Emil macht jetzt Toilette. Zuerft zieht er den Rock aus. Zunächft wäfcht er fich forgfältig die Hände und das Geficht. Dann bürftet er die Zähne und kämmt fich die Haare. Geftern zerriß ihm ein Nagel den Rock. Heute wird er wohl einen andern anziehen müffen. Karl, bift du fertig, auszugehen? Ich ziehe mir foeben den Überzieher und die Handfchuhe an. Wenn Freunde einander begegnen, fo nehmen fie den Hut ab oder geben fich die Hand. Das Trottoir ift heute fehr glatt; man könnte leicht ausgleiten und fich das Bein brechen.

*C.* Continue : 1. Mir ift die Axt aus der Hand geglitten, dir, 2c. 2. Ich habe mir fchnell den Rock angezogen, du . . . dir, 2c. 3. Ich werde mir jetzt die Hände wafchen, du . . . dir, 2c. 4. Ich bin ausgeglitten und habe mir ein Bein gebrochen, du . . . dir, 2c. 5. Ich will das Meinige tun, du . . . das Deinige, 2c.

*D.* 1. The woodcutter sat on the bank of a river and wept aloud. 2. A water-sprite appeared and said : "What has happened to you? Why are you weeping?" 3. He replied that his axe had slipped from his hand and fallen into the river. 4. The unhappy man had no axe, and could earn no bread for his [family]. 5. Thereupon the sprite dived and brought up a silver axe. 6. She asked him if this axe was his. 7. He said it was not his, since his was of iron. 8. Then she showed him a gold axe, which she had brought up out of the water. 9. The woodcutter was very honest, and would not accept this one. 10. He wanted only [what was] his [own]. 11. At last she brought up his and gave it to him.

*E.* 1. This book is mine. 2. I have my pencil, and you have yours. 3. Emil has eaten his pear and also (a) part of mine.   4. Everybody loves his own [relatives, etc.].   5. Henry, have you washed your face and combed your hair?   6. We shake hands with one another.   7. How did Robert break his leg?   8. Take off your hat, Emil.   9. Henry has torn my coat.   10. Put on your gloves.   11. A stone fell (*perf.*) on my foot.   12. It hurt me very much.

*F.* Lefeſtück:

> Steht ein Kirchlein im Dorf,
> geht der Weg dran vorbei,
> und die Hühner, die machen
> am Weg ein Geſchrei.

> Und der Wagen voll Heu,
> der kommt von der Wieſe,
> und oben darauf
> ſitzt der Hans und die Lieſe.

> Die jodeln und juchzen
> und lachen alle beid',
> und das klingt durch den Abend,
> es iſt eine Freud'!

> Und wär' ich der König,
> gleich wär' ich dabei
> und nähme zum Thron mir
> einen Wagen voll Heu.

> — Robert Reinick.

# LESSON XXXIX

**164.**          Degrees of Comparison.

| *Positive.* | *Comparative.* | *Superlative.* |
|---|---|---|
| reich, rich | reicher | reichſt |
| neu, new | neuer | neueſt |
| ſüß, sweet | ſüßer | ſüßeſt |
| breit, broad | breiter | breiteſt |

| Positive. | Comparative. | Superlative. |
|-----------|--------------|--------------|
| edel, noble | edler | edelst |
| teuer, dear | teurer | teuerst |
| müde, tired | müder | müdest |
| angenehm, agreeable | angenehmer | angenehmst |
| schnell, quickly | schneller | schnellst |

Observe: 1. Adjectives and adverbs form their comparative and superlative stems by adding –(e)r and –(e)st to the positive stem.

2. Stems ending in a vowel (except e), a sibilant, –d or –t, retain e in the superlative.

3. Those in –el, –en, –er, drop e in the stem of the comparative.

4. Those in –e add –r and –st only.

5. The endings are added regardless of length.

## 165.          Umlaut in Monosyllables.

| | | | | | |
|--|--|--|--|--|--|
| groß, great | größer | größ(es)t | klug, wise | klüger | klügst |
| arm, poor | ärmer | ärmst | oft, often | öfter | öftest |

Observe: Most monosyllables with a, o, u (not au) in the stem take umlaut; for exceptions, see dictionary.

## 166.          Irregular Comparison.

| | | | | | |
|--|--|--|--|--|--|
| bald, ehe, soon | eher | ehest | hoch, high | höher | höchst |
| gern(e), gladly | lieber | liebst | nahe, near | näher | nächst |
| gut, good, well } | besser | best | viel, much | mehr | meist |
| wohl, well } | | | wenig, little | minder | mindest |

Notes.—1. **Mehr** and **minder** are invariable.

2. **Wenig** has usually the regular forms weniger, wenigst.

## 167.   Declension of Comparative and Superlative.

| | |
|--|--|
| Ein fleißigerer Schüler. | A more diligent pupil. |
| Der fleißigere Schüler. | The more diligent pupil. |
| Der fleißigste Schüler. | The most diligent pupil. |

OBSERVE : The attributive adjective has the same endings in the comparative and superlative as in the positive (see Lesson XVIII).

**168.**        **The Comparative.**

| | |
|---|---|
| Er ist älter, als ich. | He is older than I. |
| Ich bin (eben) so alt, wie er. | I am (just) as old as he. |
| Je (desto) länger die Nacht ist, desto (umso) kürzer ist der Tag. | The longer the night is, the shorter is the day. |

OBSERVE : 1. 'Than' = als in a comparison of inequality.

2. 'As . . . as,' 'so . . . as' = so . . . wie in a comparison of equality.

3. 'The . . . the' before comparatives = je or desto . . . je, desto or umso, and in complete clauses the former clause has the word order of a dependent sentence (verb last), the latter of a principal sentence (verb second).

NOTES. — 1. The form with mehr, 'more,' is used when two qualities of the same object are compared : Sie ist mehr klug als schön, 'She is more clever than pretty.'

2. The English 'more and more' = immer + comparative : Der Sturm wird immer heftiger, 'The storm grows more and more violent.'

**169.**        **The Superlative Relative.**

| | |
|---|---|
| Der See ist breiter als der Fluß, aber das Meer ist am breitesten. | The lake is broader than the river, but the sea is the broadest. |
| Im Juni ist der Tag am längsten. | The day is longest in June. |
| Dieser Fluß ist der breiteste (Fluß) in Amerika. | This river is the broadest (river) in America. |
| Er liest am besten. | He reads best. |

OBSERVE : 1. The relative superlative of adjectives does not occur in uninflected form, even in the predicate.

2. When no previously expressed noun can be supplied, the

superlative adjective is expressed in the predicate by the form with **am**, which is also the superlative form of the adverb.

3. If a noun can be supplied from the context, the superlative is expressed in the predicate by the definite article + the superlative with adjective inflection.

NOTE.— The superl. adj. is regularly preceded by the def. art. or other determinative.

### 170. The Superlative Absolute.

| | |
|---|---|
| Er ift äußerft gütig. | He is most (exceedingly) kind. |
| Er hat fehr klug gehandelt. | He has acted most wisely. |

OBSERVE : English ' most,' indicating a quality in a very high degree, but without comparative force, is expressed in German by an adverb of eminence.

NOTES.— 1. The superl. absolute of advs. may be expressed also by **aufs** (= auf das) prefixed to a superl. adj.: Er beforgt alles **aufs befte,** 'He attends to everything in the best possible manner.' 2. Advs. in **–ig, –lich, –fam,** and a few monosylls., use the uninflected form in the superl. absolute : Er läßt freundlichft grüßen, 'He wishes to be most kindly remembered'; höchft, längft, 'most highly, long since.' 3. A few superl. advs. end in **–ens** with special meanings: Höchftens, 'at most'; meiftens, 'for the most part'; nächftens, 'shortly'; wenigftens, 'at least.' 4. There is also a compar. absolute : Ein längerer Spaziergang, 'A somewhat long walk.'

### EXERCISE XXXIX

*A.* Sie haben fehr viel gereift, nicht wahr, Herr M. ?— Jawohl, aber meiftens in Europa. — Glauben Sie nicht, daß man auf amerikanifchen Eifenbahnen fchneller und bequemer reift als in Europa?— Nein, fchneller nicht; die fchnellften Züge trifft man in England, fo fagt man wenigftens. — Und wie ift es in Frankreich?— Auch der Schnellzug von Calais nach Paris gehört zu den fchnellften der Welt. — Finden Sie die kleinen Abteile nicht höchft unangenehm, in welche die europä= ifchen Eifenbahnwagen eingeteilt find ?— Nicht im geringften ; im Gegenteil, man reift auf diefe Weife viel ruhiger und wird

viel weniger von den Mitreisenden gestört, als bei uns. — Sind
unsere Schlafwagen nicht besser als die europäischen? — Größer
freilich sind sie, aber in den Schlafwagen drüben haben je zwei
Reisende einen Abteil für sich, wo sie aufs bequemste schlafen
und auch ihre Toilette machen können. — In Bezug auf die
Beförderung des Gepäcks haben wir es hier doch mit unsern
Gepäckscheinen bequemer, nicht wahr? — In England findet
man allerdings diese Einrichtung auf sehr wenigen Zügen,
aber in den meisten europäischen Ländern erhält der Reisende jetzt immer einen Gepäckschein. — Kann man dort
ebenso billig reisen, wie hier? — Sogar billiger, wenn man
zweiter oder dritter Klasse fährt; am billigsten und am lang-
samsten fährt man mit dem sogenannten „Bummelzug," welcher an jeder Station anhält. Je langsamer man fährt, desto
billiger fährt man. — Besten Dank, Herr B., für Ihre höchst
interessante Mitteilung.

*B.* Oral exercise on the above.

*C.* Insert comparative and superlative forms respectively in
the blanks : 1. Ich bin müde, du bist —, er ist —. 2. Die breite
Straße, die — Straße, die — Straße. 3. Wir arbeiten gut,
ihr arbeitet —, sie arbeiten —. 4. Ich spiele wenig, du spielst
—, Karl spielt —. 5. Eine angenehme Reise, eine — Reise,
die — Reise. 6. Klara ist klug, Marie ist —, aber Karl ist —.

*D.* 1. I find travelling (das Reisen) most interesting.
2. Travelling is most agreeable in summer. 3. The days are
longest then, one can see more, and it is much pleasanter.
4. I like to take a somewhat long journey by (zu) water.
5. The fastest steamers go in less than five days from New York
to Europe. 6. Germans travel a great deal, but in this country
people travel still more. 7. One can travel second class very
comfortably in Europe. 8. Most people (die meisten Leute) in
Germany travel second class, even the wealthiest. 9. Over
there you (man) can travel as comfortably second class as first

class in America.　10. Besides, it is much cheaper.　11. You can travel cheapest third class, but the mixed trains (Perſonen-zug, *m.*) often go very slowly.

*E.*　1. The European express trains are among (gehören zu) the fastest in the world.　2. Is it not very disagreeable to travel with baggage?　3. Not at all; in most countries you now get checks.　4. In England, however, this arrangement is found on very few trains.　5. I find the compartments most pleasant.　6. You are much less disturbed by your (the) fellow-travellers.　7. The European sleeping-cars are smaller than ours, but one can at least sleep most comfortably in them.　8. I hope to be able to take a trip to Europe next summer.　9. You will find travelling just as cheap as in America and not less comfortable.　10. In Germany as in America, the farther you travel the more it costs.

*F.* Lesestück: Ich packe meinen Koffer und meine Hand-tasche.　Ich miete einen Wagen.　Ich fahre nach dem Bahn-hof.　Ich bezahle den Kutscher.　Ich gehe an den Schalter. Ich löse eine Fahrkarte nach Berlin.　Ich rufe einen Gepäck-träger.　Ich gebe mein Gepäck auf.　Ich bekomme einen Gepäckschein.　Ich trete in den Wartesaal.　Ich warte auf die Abfahrt des Zuges.　Ich gehe auf den Bahnsteig.　Ich steige in einen Wagen.　Ich setze mich.　Der Zug fährt ab.

# LESSON XL

**171. Compound Tenses of Modal Auxiliaries.** 1. The fol-lowing condensed paradigm illustrates the compound tense forms of the modal auxiliaries (including laſſen) with a governed infinitive:

| | | | | |
|---|---|---|---|---|
| *Perf. Indic.* | ich habe | ſpielen dürfen, | können, | mögen, ꝛc. |
| | du haſt | „　　　„ | „ | „　　　„ |
| *Perf. Subj.* | ich habe | „　　　„ | „ | „　　　„ |
| | du habeſt | „　　　„ | „ | „　　　„ |
| *Plupf. Indic.* | ich hatte | „　　　„ | „ | „　　　„ |
| *Plupf. Subj.* | ich hätte | „　　　„ | „ | „　　　„ |

OBSERVE: The past participle here has the form of an infinitive.

NOTE.— The last form above replaces the compound conditional, which is not in use.

2. The following examples show the use of the pluperfect subjunctive as a shorter compound conditional :

| | |
|---|---|
| Ich hätte es tun dürfen. | I should have been allowed to do it. |
| Ich hätte es tun können. | I could have done it. |
| Ich hätte es tun mögen. | I should like to have done it. |
| Ich hätte es tun müssen. | I should have been obliged to do it. |
| Ich hätte es tun sollen. | I ought to have done it. |

OBSERVE: In all these examples, except the fourth, the German modal has the compound tense, and the governed infinitive the simple tense ; whereas in English the modal has the simple, and the infinitive the compound tense.

3. These verbs have also another form of the perfect and the pluperfect, with the modal in a simple and the infinitive in a compound tense. The following parallel examples show the respective meanings of the two forms :

| | |
|---|---|
| Er hat es nicht tun können. | He has been unable to do it. |
| Er kann es getan haben. | He may possibly have done it. |
| Er hat es nicht tun mögen. | He didn't like to do it. |
| Er mag es getan haben. | He may possibly have done it. |
| Er hat es tun müssen. | He has had to do it. |
| Er muß es getan haben. | He must have done it. |
| Er hat es tun wollen. | He meant to have done it. |
| Er will es getan haben. | He pretends to have done it. |

**172. Word Order.** In a dependent sentence with compound tense and governed infinitive, the auxiliary of tense (haben or werden) does not come last, but precedes both the participle and the governed infinitive :

| | |
|---|---|
| Er sagte, daß er es nicht habe tun mögen. | He said that he had not cared to do it. |
| Wenn er hätte kommen wollen. | If he had wanted to come. |
| Ich weiß nicht, ob ich werde kommen können. | I don't know whether I shall be able to come. |

**173. Various Uses of Modals.** The following sections contain, for reference, examples of the idiomatic uses of the modal auxiliaries.

**174.**                    **Dürfen.**

| | | |
|---|---|---|
| 1 | Darf ich fragen, was er will? | May I ask what he wants? |
| 2 | Dürfte ich Sie bitten? | Might I request you? |
| 3 | Du darfst jetzt gehen. | You may go now. |
| 4 | Das dürfte schon sein. | That might possibly be. |
| 5 | Ich darf behaupten, daß diese Nachricht nicht wahr ist. | I venture to assert that this news is not true. |
| 6 | Das darf ich nicht. | I am not allowed to do that. |

Observe : 1–3 indicate permission ; 4, 5, modest assertion ; 6 shows the absolute use.

Note.—**Dürfen** renders the English 'may,' 'might' in questions, as in 1 and 2 above.

**175.**                    **Können.**

| | |
|---|---|
| Ich hätte kommen können. | I could have come. |
| Das kann sein. | That may be. |
| Er kann die Lektion nicht. | He doesn't know the lesson. |
| Ich habe nicht gekonnt. | I have not been able. |

Observe : 1 denotes ability ; 2, possibility ; 3, the transitive use ; 4, absolute use.

**176.**                    **Mögen.**

| | |
|---|---|
| Möge der Himmel das geben! | May Heaven grant that! |
| Ich möchte gern bleiben. | I should like to stay. |
| Er hat nie arbeiten mögen. | He has never liked working. |
| Ich hätte das sehen mögen. | I should like to have seen that. |
| Du magst den Ball behalten. | You may keep the ball. |

| Sie möchten sich doch wohl irren. | Perhaps you are mistaken after all. |
| Er mag zehn Jahre alt sein. | He may be ten years old. |
| Das mag sein. | They may be (but I doubt it). |
| Ich mag dieses Buch nicht. | I don't like this book. |
| Ich gehe morgen aus, mag es regnen oder nicht. | I am going out to-morrow whether it rains or not. |
| Wie dem auch sein mag. | No matter how that may be. |

OBSERVE: 1 denotes a wish; 2–4, preference or liking; 5, permission; 6, modest assertion; 7, 8, concession; 9, transitive use; 10, 11, special idioms.

NOTE.—The adverb **gern** further emphasizes the idea of liking or preference, as in the second example above.

### 177.　　　　　　Müssen.

| Alle Menschen müssen sterben. | All men must die. |
| Ich habe ausgehen müssen. | I have had to go out. |
| In Rom muß es schön sein. | It must be beautiful in Rome. |
| Es muß sehr kalt gewesen sein, da der See zugefroren ist. | It must have been very cold, as the lake is frozen over. |
| Ich habe gemußt. | I have been obliged to. |

OBSERVE: 1 denotes necessity; 2, compulsion by another person; 3, 4, inference; 5, absolute use.

NOTE.— 'To be obliged, compelled,' after a negative in simple tenses, is usually rendered by **brauchen**: Er braucht nicht zu gehen, 'He is not obliged to go.'

### 178.　　　　　　Sollen.

| Du sollst nicht töten. | Thou shalt not kill. |
| Er soll nicht ausgehen. | He shall not go out. |
| Er hätte gehen sollen. | He ought to have gone. |
| Was soll geschehen? | What is to be done? |
| Was sollte ich tun? | What was I to do? |
| Er soll sehr reich sein. | He is said to be very rich. |
| Ich weiß nicht, was ich soll. | I don't know what I am to do. |
| Wenn er kommen sollte. | If he should (were to) come. |
| Was soll das? | What does that mean? |

Observe: 1, 2 denote command; 3, duty or obligation; 4, 5, submission of the speaker's will; 6, statement not vouched for by the speaker; 7, absolute use; 8, conditional use; 9, special idiom.

## 179. Wollen.

| | |
|---|---|
| Er will nicht gehorchen. | He won't (refuses to) obey. |
| Er will morgen abreisen. | He means to go to-morrow. |
| Er wollte eben gehen. | He was just about to go. |
| Das Eis will brechen. | The ice threatens to break. |
| Er will in Indien gewesen sein. | He asserts that he has been in India. |
| Ich will das Buch nicht. | I don't want the book. |
| Ich habe nicht gewollt. | I didn't want to. |

Observe: 1 denotes exertion of will on the part of the subject; 2, intention; 3, 4, impending action or event; 5, assertion or claim not vouched for by the speaker; 6, transitive use; 7, absolute use.

## 180. Laffen.

| | |
|---|---|
| Laffen Sie uns fortgehen. | Let us go away. |
| Man hat ihn reden laffen. | He has been allowed to speak. |
| Der Hauptmann ließ den Soldaten beftrafen. | The captain ordered the soldier to be punished. |
| Ich ließ das Buch binden. | I had the book bound. |
| Es läßt sich nicht leugnen. | It cannot be denied. |
| Es läßt sich leicht machen. | It is easily done. |

Observe: 1, imperative use; 2, permission; 3, 4, causative use; 5, 6, impersonal reflexive use.

Note.— After laffen the infinitive of transitive verbs has passive force, as in examples 3, 4, 5, 6, above.

### EXERCISE XL

A. 1. Als ich jung war, konnte ich sehr gut Schlittschuh laufen. 2. Ich hätte gestern ins Theater gehen können, wenn ich gewollt hätte. 3. Als Kind mußte ich immer früh zu Bett gehen. 4. Wenn wir unsere Aufgaben nicht machten, so würden wir zu Hause bleiben müssen. 5. Wir haben unsere Aufgaben sorgfältig schreiben müssen. 6. Wir werden noch zwei Stunden daran arbeiten müssen. 7. Wir würden sie abschreiben müssen, wenn wir sie schlecht machten. 8. Möchten Sie nicht gern Paris besuchen, wenn Sie Gelegenheit hätten? 9. Ich habe nie Romane lesen dürfen. 10. Ich hätte sie gern gelesen, wenn ich gedurft hätte. 11. Emil, du hättest dem Bruder helfen sollen. 12. Das wollte ich wohl, aber ich konnte es leider nicht. 13. Wenn du ihm hättest helfen wollen, so hättest du es leicht tun können. 14. Lassen Sie die Uhr nicht fallen.

*B.* 1. Lassen Sie den Kaffee jetzt hereinbringen. 2. Bei welchem Schneider haben Sie diesen Überzieher machen lassen? 3. Ich habe diese Woche nicht ausgehen können; ich war krank. 4. Wir hätten dieses Haus für M. 20,000 kaufen können, wenn wir gewollt hätten. 5. Jetzt könnten wir es nicht so billig bekommen. 6. Wir haben nicht gewollt, aber wir haben gemußt. 7. Könnten Sie mir wohl eine Feder leihen? Ich möchte gern an meinen Vater schreiben. 8. Ich wäre zur Stadt mitgefahren, wenn ich gedurft hätte. 9. Der Lehrer sagte, daß ich nicht mit dürfe. 10. Wenn jedermann täte, was er sollte, so würde die Welt viel besser sein. 11. Diese Dame soll sehr re'ch sein. 12. Sie will viele Jahre in Indien gelebt haben. 13. Man hätte den Dieb nicht entkommen lassen sollen.

*C.* Continue: 1. Ich dürfte diesen Roman lesen, wenn ich wollte, du . . . wenn du, etc. 2. Ich hätte es ihm sofort sagen können. 3. Ich hätte ihn das nicht tun lassen sollen. 4. Dies ist der Überzieher, den ich mir habe machen lassen, . . . den du dir, etc. 5. Ich hätte so einen Brief nicht schreiben mögen. 6. Ich werde mir ein Sommerkleid machen lassen. 7. Ich

N

möchte heute gern spazieren gehen. 8. Ich habe das nicht tun wollen. 9. Ich muß es wohl getan haben. 10. Das mag ich vielleicht gesagt haben.

*D.* 1. I could write better if I had a better pen. 2. You have never been able to write well. 3. I should have had to stay at home if I hadn't done my exercises. 4. I should not have been able to go with you to-day. 5. As [a] child I didn't like to go to school, but I had to. 6. I have not cared to go out to-day. 7. These children were never allowed to stay up late. 8. I might stay up late this evening, if I wanted to. 9. Shall we be allowed to go out to-morrow? 10. The teacher said we ought not to go out in (bei) this cold weather. 11. Where is the overcoat which you have had made? 12. The tailor will have it sent to me to-morrow. 13. He has not been able to send it to-day.

*E.* 1. Mary could have written her exercise, if she had wanted to. 2. Charles has had to write his. 3. We always had to copy our exercises when we had done them badly. 4. When I was young, I could have learnt German, but I wouldn't. 5. Now I should like to learn it if I could, but I can't. 6. If the weather had been cold, we should have been compelled to stay at home. 7. We have never been allowed to stay out late. 8. We always had to come home earlier than we liked. 9. You should have dressed more warmly. 10. The weather has changed, and you might easily have caught cold. 11. Don't play when you should study. 12. This man is said to have learnt German, but he knows nothing of it. 13. He pretends to have been two years in Germany. 14. Where is the house which this gentleman has had built for himself?

*F.* Lesestück: Der Dichter Gilbert begegnete eines Tages einem aufgeregten Herrn, der ihn fragte: "Haben Sie einen Herrn mit einem Auge namens B. gesehen?" "Nein," erwiderte Gilbert, "wie heißt denn eigentlich sein anderes Auge?"

## LESSON XLI

**181.**          **Declension of Place Names.**

*N.* der Rhein, the Rhine.      *N.* die Schweiz, Switzerland.
*G.* des Rhein(e)s.            *G.* der Schweiz.
*D.* dem Rhein(e).             *D.* der Schweiz.
*A.* den Rhein.               *A.* die Schweiz.

*N.* Deutschland, Germany.     *N.* Berlin, Berlin.
*G.* Deutschlands.            *G.* Berlins.

OBSERVE: 1. Proper names of places which are never used without an article (§ 108) are declined like common nouns.

2. If not generally used with an article or determinative, they take no ending except –s in the genitive singular.

NOTE. — Von may replace this gen., and must do so if the noun ends in a sibilant: Die Straßen von Paris, 'The streets of Paris.'

**182.**               **Apposition.**

*N.* die Stadt London, the city    *N.* das Königreich Preußen,
      of London.                        the Kingdom of Prussia.
*G.* der Stadt London.             *G.* des Königreichs Preußen.

OBSERVE: When a place name is defined by a common noun preceding it, the two nouns are in apposition, but the common noun only is inflected.

NOTE. — The word Fluß is regularly omitted in names of rivers: Der Rhein, die Elbe, 'The (river) Rhine, Elbe.'

**183. Adjectives and Nouns of Nationality. — 1.** Adjectives of nationality end in –isch, except deutsch, and are used substantively only of the language, being then written with a capital:

Deutsch; Französisch.          German; French (the language).

NOTE. — They are also written with a capital when forming part of a proper name: Das Deutsche Meer, 'The German Ocean.'

2. After the preposition **auf,** language names are used without article, and remain undeclined; after other prepositions they take the article, and are declined:

Auf Deutsch; im Deutschen.      In German.

3. Nouns of nationality end either in -e (Knabe model), or in -er (Maler model), except Deutsch, which follows the adjective declension:

Der Franzose; ein Preuße.      The Frenchman; a Prussian.
Ein Engländer (Amerikaner).    An Englishman (American).
Der Deutsche; ein Deutscher.   The German; a German.

NOTE. — The Eng. plur. adjectival noun, indicating all people of a particular nationality, is always, except in the case of Deutsch, rendered in German by the noun of nationality: Die Franzosen sind lebhafter als die Engländer oder die Deutschen, 'The French are more vivacious than the English or the Germans.'

## EXERCISE XLI

*A.* (Mit der Landkarte zu studieren.)  Das Deutsche Reich, oder Deutschland, wie es gewöhnlich heißt, ist im Norden von der Nordsee, von Dänemark und von der Ostsee begrenzt; im Osten von Rußland und Österreich=Ungarn; südlich von Österreich und der Schweiz; die westliche Grenze bilden Frankreich, Belgien und Holland.  Das Deutsche Reich wurde während des deutsch= französischen Krieges im Jahre 1871 gegründet und Wilhelm der Erste, König von Preußen, wurde damals als erster Deutscher Kaiser proklamiert.  Es umfaßt vier Königreiche, nämlich: Preußen, Bayern, Sachsen, Württemberg und neun= zehn kleinere Staaten, sowie die drei freien Reichsstädte, Ham= burg, Bremen und Lübeck.  Die Hauptstadt Deutschlands, sowie des Königreichs Preußen, ist Berlin.  Berlin übertrifft schon an Einwohnerzahl die Stadt Paris, ist aber noch nicht so groß wie die Stadt London.  Die Hauptstadt Bayerns ist München, und heißt auf Englisch „Munich." Die Hauptstadt des Königreichs Sachsen ist Dresden.　Die zwei größten Flüsse von Deutschland sind der Rhein und die Elbe.

*B.* Oral on the map of Germany (see p. xxvi).

*C.* 1. The inhabitants of Germany are called Germans; those (die) of (von) England, Englishmen; those of France, Frenchmen. 2. Englishmen speak English, Frenchmen speak French, and Germans speak German. 3. Do you speak German? 4. Not very well, but I can read it a little. 5. Then you should know something about Germany and the Germans. 6. We will take a look at (sich ansehen) the map of the German Empire. 7. You see that Germany is situated between France, Belgium and Holland on (in) the west and Russia on the east. 8. Yes, and to the south lie Austria and Switzerland. 9. The Baltic, Denmark and the North Sea form the northern boundary. 10. Of the rivers of Germany the two largest are the Rhine and the Elbe, which both flow into the North Sea. 11. The Rhine is celebrated for (wegen, *gen.*) its beautiful shores, its ruined castles and its excellent wines.

*D.* 1. William the First was the first German Emperor. 2. The German Empire consists of four kingdoms, three free imperial cities and many smaller states. 3. Bayern is called "Bavaria" in English, Preußen is called "Prussia," etc. 4. The city of Berlin is situated on the Spree. 5. It is the capital of the kingdom of Prussia; it is also the capital of the German Empire. 6. Berlin is not yet as large as the city of London. 7. Dresden, the capital of the kingdom of Saxony, is celebrated for its picture-gallery.

*E.* Lesestück:

Die Wacht am Rhein.

Es braust ein Ruf wie Donnerhall,
Wie Schwertgeklirr und Wogenprall:
Zum Rhein, zum Rhein, zum deutschen Rhein!
Wer will des Stromes Hüter sein?

Lieb Vaterland, magst ruhig sein!
Fest steht und treu die Wacht am Rhein!

So lang' ein Tröpflein Blut noch glüht,
Noch eine Faust den Degen zieht,
Und noch ein Arm die Büchse spannt,
Betritt kein Feind hier deinen Strand!

Der Schwur erschallt, die Woge rinnt,
Die Fahnen flattern hoch im Wind,
Am Rhein, am Rhein, am deutschen Rhein,
Wir alle wollen Hüter sein!

# LESSON XLII

**184.**　　　　　　**Ordinals.**

| | |
|---|---|
| Der zweite, vierte, fünfte Tag. | The second, fourth, fifth day. |
| Das erste, dritte, achte Kind. | The first, third, eighth child. |
| Heute ist der hundertundfünfte Tag des Jahres. | To-day is the hundred and fifth day of the year. |
| Neunundzwanzigster Band. | Twenty-ninth volume. |
| Erstens, drittens. | In the first place, thirdly. |

OBSERVE: 1. The stem of ordinal adjectives is formed from the cardinals by adding –t, up to 19 (except erst–, 'first,' dritt–, 'third,' acht–, 'eighth'), and –st from 20 upwards.

2. Compound ordinals add the suffix to the last component only.

3. Ordinal adverbs are formed by adding –ens to the ordinal stem.

NOTE. — The numeral before Band, 'volume,' Kapitel, 'chapter,' Seite, 'page,' etc., is read as an ordinal when it precedes, and as an undeclined cardinal when it follows; Numero, 'number,' is followed by the cardinal: Das dritte Kapitel, 'The third chapter'; Kapitel drei, 'Chapter three'; Numero fünf, 'Number five.'

**185.**　　　　　　　**Dates.**

| | |
|---|---|
| Der wieviel(s)te ist heute? | What day of the month is it? |
| Den wieviel(s)ten haben wir? | "　"　"　"　　"　　"　" |
| Was für ein Datum ist heute? | What is the date? |
| Es ist der zehnte. | It is the tenth. |
| Wir haben den zehnten. | "　"　"　　" |
| Am 1. (= ersten) Januar. | On the 1st of January. |
| London, 3. April (= London, den dritten April). | London, 3rd April. |
| Goethe starb (im Jahre) 1832. | Goethe died in 1832. |

OBSERVE: 1. In dates, the ordinals are used adjectively before the names of the months, the figures, 1, 2, 3, etc., being read as ordinals with the definite article and the proper adjective termination.

NOTE. — In correspondence, the ordinals are often written as follows: den (or d.) 1sten, 3ten, 23sten, etc.

2. The year number is either preceded by **im Jahre** or written and read without the preposition **in**.

**186. House Numbers and Addresses.**　1. In street names, the preposition and article are omitted in giving an address and in addressing letters, and the street name is written as one word with –straße; the house number follows the street name:

| | |
|---|---|
| Mein Freund wohnt Schiller-straße 13. | My friend lives at number 13 Schiller Street. |

2. In addressing letters, the name of the town precedes that of the street and number:

> Herrn Karl Schneider,
> 　　Heidelberg,
> 　　　　Schloßstraße 15/IV.

NOTE. — The Roman numeral after the house number indicates the story (Etage, *f.*, or Stock, *m.*).

## EXERCISE XLII

*A.*                    Hamburg, Friedrichſtr. 21/III.
                         23. Oktober, 1909.

Liebe Klara!

Entſchuldige, bitte, daß ich Dir ſo lange nicht geſchrieben
habe. Ich bin ſehr beſchäftigt geweſen, wie Du gleich ſehen
wirſt. Erſtens ſind wir am 11. ds. (= dieſes Monats) aus
unſerer alten Wohnung, Schillerſtraße 155, nach der obigen
Adreſſe umgezogen, wobei es natürlich ſehr viel zu tun gab.
Zweitens feierten wir am 19. des lieben Vaters Geburtstag.
Er erhielt viele hübſche Geſchenke, darunter eine ſchöne Aus=
gabe von Shakeſpeares Werken in 10 Bänden, wovon die erſten
drei die Trauerſpiele, der vierte, fünfte und ſechſte die Luſt=
ſpiele, und Band 7 bis 9 die hiſtoriſchen Schauſpiele enthalten,
während ſich im 10. Bande die Gedichte befinden. Es war
ſein 49. Geburtstag, da er am 19. Oktober 1858 geboren
wurde. Am wievielten November haſt Du eigentlich Geburts=
tag? Ich habe leider den Tag vergeſſen. Heute über acht
Tage, den 30. ds., erwarten wir meinen älteſten Bruder aus
England. Hoffentlich werde ich ſpäteſtens am 10. Dezem=
ber zu Dir kommen können, um Dir den lange verſprochenen
Beſuch abzuſtatten. Alſo auf Wiederſehen! Mit herzlichen
Grüßen an Deine lieben Eltern verbleibe ich ſtets
           Deine Dich innig liebende Freundin
                         Eliſabeth Meyer.

*B.* Oral: 1. Was iſt jetzt die Adreſſe Ihres Bruders?
2. In welchem Stock wohnt er? 3. Am wievielten gedenken
Sie umzuziehen? 4. Den wievielten haben wir heute?
5. Der wievielte iſt morgen? 6. Was für ein Datum iſt
heute über acht Tage? 7. Wann wird der Geburtstag Ihres
älteſten Bruders gefeiert? 8. In welchem Jahre wurde er

geboren? 9. In welchem Bande dieser Ausgabe findet man
die Trauerspiele? 10. Welche Bände enthalten die Lustspiele?
11. Welche Bände haben Sie schon gelesen? 12. Können Sie
mir sagen, wann Goethe gestorben ist?

*C.* 1. What day of the month is it to-day? 2. What date
is this day week? 3. Of what date is Elizabeth's letter? 4. I
have read the first and the second volume, but not the third.
5. Bring volume[s] three to (bis) five with [you] when you
come. 6. Sunday is the first day of the week, Monday the
second, etc. 7. January is the first month of the year, February the second, etc. 8. Goethe was born in seventeen hundred
and forty-nine, on the 12th of August. 9. Give the ordinals
corresponding to the cardinals in § 41.

*D.*　　　　　　　　　　40 Hall St., **Liverpool,**
　　　　　　　　　　　　　August 27th, 1910.
My dear friend (*f.*) :
　　　You will certainly wonder why I have not written you
sooner, as your interesting letter from Leeds arrived on the
15th of this month. But I must tell you that I have been
extremely busy in the last two weeks. In the first place, my
eldest brother's birthday was celebrated on the 20th, and we
had a great many visitors (*sing.*). Secondly, we intend to move
on the 1st September. Our new address is No. 115 Farewell St.,
second story. There is (gibt) a great deal to do, but the work
will be finished by the (bis zum) 3rd or 4th of September.
You will then pay us the promised visit, will you not? Mother
hopes you will come on the 10th, or still earlier. With kind
regards to your dear mother,
　　　　　　　　　　Your loving friend,
　　　　　　　　　　　　Anna Lehmann.

*E.* Lesestück : Im allgemeinen sind die Deutschen im brief-
lichen Verkehr viel umständlicher als wir. Erstens, was die
Anrede betrifft, so redet man in Briefen nie einen Herrn als
" Herr " oder " lieber Herr " an. Man schreibt " Sehr geehr-

ter Herr" oder "Verehrter Herr." Eine verheiratete Dame
wird als "Gnädige Frau" oder "Verehrte Gnädige Frau" ange-
redet; eine unverheiratete als "Gnädiges Fräulein," oder auch
"Sehr geehrtes Fräulein" (Bauer, usw.). Wenn man an Verwandte oder Freunde schreibt, so gebraucht man ungefähr die-
selben Redensarten wie im Englischen. Zweitens, was Schluß
und Unterschrift betrifft, so schreibt man an einen Fremden
ungefähr so: Indem ich mich ergebenst empfehle,

Verbleibe ich hochachtungsvoll

W. H.

oder kürzer: Ergebenst (der Ihrige)

W. H.

Die englische Redensart: "Yours affectionately," von einem
Sohne z. B. an seine Mutter, lautet etwa wie folgt: Dein Dich
innig liebender Sohn

Wilhelm.

# LESSON XLIII

**187**　　　　Declension of Person Names.

| | |
|---|---|
| Ich habe Georgs Feder. | I have George's pen. |
| Hier ist Saras Puppe. | Here is Sarah's doll. |
| Das ist Maxens (Luisens) Buch. | That is Max' (Louisa's) book |
| Ich habe es Max gegeben. | I have given it to Max. |
| Des großen Cäsars Taten. | Great Cæsar's deeds. |
| Die Briefe des Cicero. | The letters of Cicero. |
| Das Buch des kleinen Karl. | Little Charles' book. |

OBSERVE: 1. Names of persons are inflected only in the
genitive singular, usually by adding –s.

2. Those ending in a sibilant add –ens, and feminines in -e
add –ns.

3. The genitive usually precedes its governing noun, and is
then inflected; if the genitive follows, it has the article and
remains uninflected.

NOTES. — 1. The name "Jesus Christ" is usually declined thus:
*N.* Jesus Christus, *G.* Jesu Christi, *D.* Jesu Christo, *A.* Jesum Christum,
*Voc.* Jesu Christe.

2. Family names are used in the plur. with added –s, but without art.:
Schmidts sind nach Paris gereist, 'The Schmidts have gone to Paris.'

## 188. Person Names with Titles.

| | |
|---|---|
| König Heinrichs Söhne. | King Henry's sons. |
| Die Söhne des Königs Karl. | The sons of King Charles. |
| Der Fächer der Frau Braun. | Mrs. Braun's fan. |

OBSERVE: 1. Person names in the genitive, preceded by a
common noun as a title, take the genitive ending, the title
remaining uninflected and without article, if the governing word
follows.

2. If the governing word precedes, the title has the article,
and, if masculine, the genitive ending, the proper name remaining uninflected.

NOTE. — The title Herr always takes –n in the sing., except in the nom.;
throughout the plur. it takes the art. and –en: Herrn Schmidts Haus,
'Mr. Schmidt's house'; die Herren S. und B., 'Messrs. S. and B.'

## 189. Ordinals with Person Names. The ordinals after proper
names of sovereigns, etc., are written with a capital letter, and
must be declined throughout, as well as the article:

| | | |
|---|---|---|
| *N.* | Karl der Erste. | Charles the First. |
| *G.* | Karl(s) des Ersten. | Of Charles the First. |
| *D.* | Karl dem Ersten. | (To, for) Charles the First. |
| *A.* | Karl den Ersten. | Charles the First. |

NOTE. — The Roman numerals I, II, etc., after such names, must be
read as above: Karl V. = Karl der Fünfte, 2c.

## EXERCISE XLIII

*A.* Otto Eduard Leopold v. (= von) Bismarck wurde unter
der Regierung König Friedrich Wilhelms III. am 1. April 1815
zu Schönhausen in der Mark Brandenburg geboren. Er war

der älteste Sohn Ferdinands v. Bismarck und Wilhelminens, geborener Mencken. Vom 17. bis zum 19. Lebensjahre studierte er zuerst in Göttingen, später in Berlin. Im Jahre 1847 heiratete er Fräulein Johanna v. Puttkamer, obgleich Johannas Vater anfangs sehr dagegen war. König Wilhelm I., Nachfolger Friedrich Wilhelms IV., bestieg 1861 den preußischen Thron und am 28. September 1862 wurde Bismarck erster Minister. Während seiner Amtstätigkeit fanden drei große Kriege statt: der dänische 1864, der österreichische 1866, und in den Jahren 1870–1871 der größte Krieg unserer Zeit, der deutsch=französische. Nachdem am 18. Januar 1871 der König von Preußen Deutscher Kaiser geworden war, wurde Bismarck der erste Kanzler des Deutschen Reiches und erhielt zugleich den Titel eines Fürsten. Bis nach dem Tode Kaiser Friedrichs III. behielt Bismarck dieses Amt, wurde aber vom jetzigen Kaiser Wilhelm II. am 18. März 1890 entlassen und starb den 30. Juli 1898 in seinem 83. Lebensjahre.

*B.* Oral on the above.

*C.* (Titles and numerals in full.) 1. William II, King of Prussia and German Emperor, was born at Berlin on the 27th of January, 1859. 2. He is the eldest son of the Emperor Frederick III. 3. He passed several years as a student in the University [of] Bonn. 4. In 1881 he married Augusta Victoria, daughter of Frederick, Duke (Herzog) of Schleswig-Holstein-Augustenburg. 5. On the 15th of June, 1888, he ascended the throne. 6. The great Prince Bismarck was then Chancellor of the German Empire, an office which he had retained during the reigns of William I and Frederick III. 7. Bismarck had been appointed as (als) first minister of Prussia by William I, September 28th, 1862, and had remained in office since that time. 8. On March 18th, 1890, Emperor William II dismissed the prince and gave (verleihen) him the title of (a) Duke of Lauenburg. 9. The eldest son of William II and of Augusta Victoria is Frederick William, the present crown-prince of the German Empire.

*D.* Lesestück: Kaiser Wilhelm I war äußerst pflichtgetreu. Als er schon hochbetagt war, hatte er einmal sein Erscheinen bei einer Parade angekündigt. Sein Leibarzt riet ihm dringend abzusagen, da bei dem schlechten Wetter das Schlimmste zu befürchten sei. "Dann sterbe ich im Dienste," antwortete der Kaiser. "Ein König von Preußen, der nicht mehr die Pflichten seines Amtes erfüllen kann, müßte die Regierung niederlegen," und er ging zur Parade.

## LESSON XLIV

**190.** **Demonstratives.**

1. dieser, this, that.
2. jener, that (yonder). *(formal)*
3. der, that, the one.
4. derjenige, that, the one.
5. derselb(ig)e, the same.
6. solcher, such.
7. dergleichen, of that kind. *(that sort of thing)*

**191.** **Dieser, jener.** 1. Both follow the dieser model, whether used as adjectives or pronouns.

2. The English demonstrative 'that' is not rendered by jener, unless when remoteness or contrast is indicated.

3. Dieser = 'the latter,' the nearer or last mentioned of two objects; jener = 'the former,' the more remote:

| | |
|---|---|
| Marie und Klara sind Schwestern; diese ist älter als jene. | Mary and Clara are sisters; the latter is older than the former. |

**192.** **Declension of der.** 1. As adjective der is declined precisely like the definite article, but is always stressed:

| | |
|---|---|
| Der Ma'nn. | The man. |
| De'r Mann. | That man. |
| Die Leu'te. | The people. |
| Die Leute. | Those people. |

2. **Der** as pronoun is declined thus :

|  | *Singular.* |  |  | *Plural.* |
|  | Masc. | Fem. | Neut. | All Genders. |
| N. | der | bie | das | bie |
| G. | deffen | deren | deffen | derer (deren) |
| D. | dem | der | dem | denen |
| A. | den | bie | das | bie |

Observe the enlarged forms in the genitive, and in the dative plural.

**193.   Use of der.**   1. As pronoun it has the force of an emphasized personal pronoun of the 3rd person, and often implies contempt or depreciation :

Kennen Sie den?                Do you know that man?

Dem würde ich kein Geld leih=   I wouldn't lend that fellow any
en; der bezahlt nie.              money ; he never pays.

2. **Der** or **derjenige** (§ 194) renders the English 'that' before a genitive, and before a relative clause :

Mein Hut und der meiner        My hat and that of my wife.
Frau.

Dieser Band und der, welcher   This volume and that (the one)
hier liegt.                      which is lying here.

NOTES. — 1. The form **deren** (gen. plur.) = 'of them': Wie viele Kinder hat er? Er hat **deren** drei, 'How many children has he? He has three (of them).'

2. It is also used as substitute for a plur. possess. (comp. § 199): Unsere Vettern und **deren** Kinder, 'Our cousins and their children.'

**194.                  Declension of derjenige.**

|  | *Singular.* |  |  | *Plural.* |
|  | Masc. | Fem. | Neut. | All Genders. |
| N. | derjenige | diejenige | dasjenige | diejenigen |
| G. | desjenigen | derjenigen | desjenigen | derjenigen |
| D. | demjenigen | derjenigen | demjenigen | denjenigen |
| A. | denjenigen | diejenige | dasjenige | diejenigen |

OBSERVE : These forms are made up of the definite article and **jenig** with weak adjective endings.

**195. Use of derjenige.** It may replace der (for emphasis or clearness) before a genitive, and before a relative clause :

Dies ist mein Buch, nicht das=  | That is my book, not that of
jenige meiner Frau. | my wife (my wife's).
Dieser Band und der(jenige), | This volume and the one that
der dort liegt. | is lying there.

NOTE.—The idiomatic omission of the demonstrative before a possessive in English is permissible in German only before a person name: Mein Haus und Wilhelms, ' My house and William's.'

**196. Derselbe.** It is declined like derjenige (derselbe, die= selbe, dasselbe, 2c.), and is used as adjective or pronoun :

Das ist derselbe Mann. | That is the same man.
Welchen Rock tragen Sie? | Which coat are you wearing?
Denselben, den ich gestern trug. | The same I wore yesterday.

**197. Solch.** When used alone, solch follows the dieser model ; after ein, it follows the mixed declension of adjectives ; before ein, it is undeclined :

Solcher Wein; ein solcher | Such wine ; such a wine ; such
Wein; solch eine Frau! | a woman !

NOTE. — Solch with ein is often replaced by so : So ein Wein ; ein so guter Wein.

**198. Dergleichen.** It is used as indeclinable neuter substantive or adjective :

Dergleichen geschieht oft hier= | That sort of thing often hap-
zulande. | pens in this country.
Dergleichen Wein(e). | Wine(s) of that sort.

**199. Demonstratives as Substitutes.**   1. Dieser and der= selbe are used instead of a personal pronoun of the 3rd person to avoid ambiguity, particularly in reported speech :

Der Redner bemerkte, Herr A. | The speaker remarked that Mr.
habe gesagt, daß er (der | A. had said that he (the
Redner) diesen (or denselben) | speaker) had slandered him
verleumdet habe. | (Mr. A.).

NOTE. — Similarly also the gen. of **der,** referring to things (§ 139, n. 3): Ich erinnere mich **dessen** nicht, 'I don't remember it.'

2. **Derselbe** is used instead of a personal pronoun to avoid awkward combinations of sounds, such as ihn . . . Ihnen, Sie . . . sie, ꝛc.:

Der Käse ist gut; ich kann     The cheese is good; I can
Ihnen **denselben** empfehlen.     recommend it to you.

3. The genitive of **der** and **derselbe** is used instead of the possessive adjective of the 3rd person, to avoid ambiguity:

Er kam mit Georg und **dessen**     He came with George and with
Bruder (or dem Bruder     his (George's) brother.
desselben).

**200. Da and hier for Demonstratives.** Das and jenes are replaced by **da** (dar before a vowel), and dies by **hier,** prefixed to a preposition and written as one word with it:

Davon weiß ich nichts.     I know nothing of that.
Hiermit will ich schließen.     With this I will close.

NOTE. — This substitution of **da** for **das** is not made before a relative: Ich dachte an **das,** was Sie sagten, 'I was thinking of what you were saying.'

### EXERCISE XLIV

*A.* Jungens, Jungens! rief der Lehrer, jetzt bin ich böse auf euch. Hat es jemals solche Aufgaben gegeben? Ich habe deren schon mehr als drei Dutzend verbessert und keine gefunden, die ganz richtig ist. Zum Beispiel, ich finde in dieser wenigstens sechsmal „mir" statt „mich" geschrieben. Denkt einmal, ist es nicht schrecklich, denselben Fehler sechsmal in einer und derselben Aufgabe zu machen? Die, welche ich jetzt in die Hand nehme, hat „laß mir gehen" statt „laß mich gehen" u. dgl. m. (und dergleichen mehr). Jene Aufgabe, die ich eben in den Papierkorb werfen wollte, ist die schlimmste von allen. So eine schlechte habe ich noch nie gesehen; ich glaube die ist Roberts; die wimmelt von Fehlern. Jetzt muß ich euch eine tüchtige Strafe auferlegen. Zuerst gebe ich euch die Auf= gaben zurück und dann soll jeder mir sagen, wie viele Fehler er hat. Der, welcher von zehn bis fünfzehn hat, soll die Auf= gabe einmal abschreiben; derjenige, welcher von sechzehn bis zwanzig hat, soll sie zweimal abschreiben; und diejenigen, die mehr als zwanzig Fehler haben, müssen dieselbe dreimal ab= schreiben und eine Stunde nachsitzen.

*B.* Oral : 1. Weshalb war der Lehrer auf die Schüler böse ? 2. Hatten die Schüler denselben Fehler oft gemacht? 3. In welcher Aufgabe fand er 'laß mir' statt 'laß mich'? 4. Fand er sonst dergleichen Fehler darin? 5. Welche Aufgabe war die schlimmste? 6. Was sagte der Lehrer davon? 7. Wessen Aufgabe war die? 8. Welche Schüler mußten die Aufgabe einmal abschreiben? 9. Welche mußten sie zweimal abschrei- ben?

*C.* 1. I have never seen so fine a ring. 2. It is much finer than my sister's. 3. This is a beautiful flower ; where did you (Sie) find it? 4. These are not my books ; they are my brother's. 5. You are mistaken ; they are George's. 6. He who says that sort of thing is no friend of mine. 7. Those who are richest are not always happiest. 8. Which Mr. Meyer do you know? 9. The one who lives in Hall St. 10. That is the same Mr. Meyer whom I know. 11. Wines of this sort are always dear. 12. The castle on that hill (yonder) is more than five hundred years old. 13. I cannot believe that fellow any more ; he has deceived me so often. 14. George was travelling with my cousin and his (my cousin's) brother. 15. He is ashamed of his conduct ; he is ashamed of it. 16. Mary has written to Clara that her mother was expecting her (Clara). 17. Goethe and Schiller were German poets ; the latter died in 1805 and the former in 1832.

*D.* 1. Our teacher was very angry with us yesterday. 2. He said he had never seen such exercises. 3. Those we had

o

written were the worst he had ever seen. 4. There were more than three dozen of them, and all were bad. 5. The worst exercise was Robert's; it teemed with mistakes. 6. He had written 'mir' instead of 'mich' five or six times. 7. It is very bad (ſchlimm) when one makes the same mistake more than once in the same exercise. 8. I myself had written 'laß mir' twice instead of 'laß mich,' and more [mistakes] of that kind. 9. I don't know how I could make such mistakes. 10. Those of us who had done the exercise worst had to stay in for an hour. 11. Those who had fewer mistakes had to copy it.

*E.* Lesestück : Ein Gelehrter sagte eines Morgens zu einigen Bekannten : "Ich bin soeben von einem Menschen rasiert worden, der in Oxford und Heidelberg die höchsten Ehren davongetragen hatte, und außerdem als sehr gebildeter Mann allgemein bekannt ist. Und doch kann er einen nicht ordentlich rasieren !" "Aber weshalb in aller Welt ist denn ein so ausgezeichneter Mann Barbier?" fragten sie. "Ach! der ist gar kein Barbier ! Ich habe mich heute morgen selbst rasiert."

## LESSON XLV

**201.** Interrogative Adjectives.

1. welcher? which? what?
2. was für ein? what kind of? what?

**202. Declension.** 1. **Welcher?** follows the **dieſer** model.

2. **Was für ein** is declined as follows:

|  | *Singular.* | | | *Plural.* |
| --- | --- | --- | --- | --- |
|  | Masc. | Fem. | Neut. | All Genders. |
| N. | was für ein | was für eine | was für ein | was für |
| G. | „ „ eines | „ „ einer | „ „ eines | „ „ |
| D. | „ „ einem | „ „ einer | „ „ einem | „ „ |
| A. | „ „ einen | „ „ eine | „ „ ein | „ „ |

OBSERVE : **Ein** only is declined, agreeing with its noun, and being omitted in the plural.

**203.**         Use of Interrogative Adjectives.

| | |
|---|---|
| Welcher Mann war hier? | Which man was here? |
| Von welcher Dame spricht er? | Of what lady does he speak? |
| Was für einen Hut hat sie? | What kind of (a) hat has she? |
| Was sind das für Blumen? | What flowers are those? |
| Was für Holz hat er? | What kind of wood has he? |
| Welch(es) Vergnügen! | What pleasure! |
| Was für Wetter! | What weather! |
| Welch ein Sturm! | What a storm! |

OBSERVE : 1. **Was für ein** is often divided, the **für ein** with its noun following the verb.

2. **Ein** is omitted after **was für** with names of materials.

3. **Welcher** and **was für (ein)** are also used in exclamatory sentences, the neuter **welches** often dropping the termination, and always before **ein**.

**204.**          Interrogative Pronouns.

1. **welcher?** which? which one?
2. **wer?** who?
3. **was?** what?

**205. Declension of welcher.** As pronoun it follows the **dieser** model, but lacks the genitive.

**206.**           Use of **welcher?**

| | |
|---|---|
| Welcher von Ihnen ist Arzt? | Which of you is a doctor? |
| Welcher von diesen Damen gehört der Fächer? | To which of these ladies does the fan belong? |
| Welcher (welche) von euch? | Which of you? |
| Welches sind Ihre Brüder? | Which are your brothers? |

OBSERVE : 1. **Welcher?** asks 'which?' of a number of persons or things, and agrees in gender with the noun for which it stands.

2. The neuter singular **welches?** is used directly before the verb **sein**, irrespectively of the gender or number of the subject.

### 207.    Declension of **wer?** and **was?**

*Masc. and Fem.*                        *Neuter.*

*N.*  wer? who?                         was? what?
*G.*  wessen (wes)? whose?              wessen (wes)? of what?
*D.*  wem? (to, for) whom?             —
*A.*  wen? whom?                        was? what?

### 208.    Use of **wer?** and **was?**

| | |
|---|---|
| **Wer** ist dieses Kind? | Who is this child? |
| **Wer** sind diese Männer? | Who are these men? |
| **Wen** meinen Sie? | Whom do you mean? |
| **Was** hat er gesagt? | What did he say? |
| **Wovon** spricht er? | What is he speaking of? |
| **Woran** denken Sie? | What are you thinking of? |
| **Weshalb?** weswegen? | On account of what? |

OBSERVE: 1. **Wer?** is used of persons only, for all genders and both numbers; **was?** is used of things.

2. In the dative or accusative with prepositions, **was?** is replaced by **wo** (**wor** before vowels, except in **warum,** 'what for?' 'why?') prefixed to the preposition and written as one word with it.

3. Prepositions governing the genitive prefix **wes.**

### EXERCISE XLV

*A.* Guten Morgen, Herr Braun. — Guten Morgen; darf ich fragen, mit wem ich die Ehre habe, zu sprechen? — Ich heiße Gustav Meyer und habe einen Empfehlungsbrief an Sie. — Von wem ist der Brief? — Von Ihrem Freunde, dem Herrn Dittmer. — Welchen Herrn Dittmer meinen Sie? Den Weinhändler? — Nein, den Seidenhändler in Hamburg. — Und was wünschen Sie von mir? — Ich suche eine Stellung und möchte

Sie um Rat und Beistand bitten. — Was für eine Stellung?
— Eine Stellung als Buchführer oder auch als Geschäftsrei=
sender. — Was haben Sie sonst für Empfehlungsbriefe? — Ich
habe mehrere sehr gute. — Und was sind Sie für ein Lands=
mann? — Ich bin ein Preuße. — Welcher Sprachen sind Sie
mächtig? — Außer dem Englischen kann ich Französisch und
Spanisch. — In wessen Geschäft waren Sie angestellt? — Ich
war drei Jahre bei Herrn Dittmer. — Aus welchen Gründen
sind Sie ausgetreten? — Weil das Klima von Hamburg meiner
Gesundheit nicht zusagte. — Gut; ich will sehen, was ich für
Sie tun kann. — Wann darf ich Sie wieder bemühen? —
Kommen Sie morgen früh Punkt halb elf.

*B.* 1. Who is knocking?  2. What a noise !  3. Ask the
gentleman what his name is.  4. What is your name?
5. Please tell me also whom you wish to see (fprechen, *tr.*).
6. What (was für ein) letter is this, which you have brought
with [you]?  7. From whom is it?  8. It is a letter of recommendation which Mr. Dittmer has given me.  9. There are
two Mr. Dittmer[s]; I don't know from which it is.  10. It is
from the one in Hamburg.  11. What does the young gentleman want of Mr. Braun?  12. What are they talking about?
13. What is young Mr. Meyer's calling?  14. What is he, an
Englishman or a German?  15. What languages is he master
of?  16. What else has he learned?  17. What other (fonft)
letters of recommendation has he?  18. Kindly (bitte) tell me
in whose business [-house] you have worked.  19. Why did you
leave?  20. What reasons had you?  21. What kind of a climate has Hamburg?  22. What kind of a position are you
seeking?  23. I shall be able to tell you better to-morrow what
I can do for you.  24. At what o'clock can you come to-morrow morning?  25. Between nine and ten, if I may trouble you
again.

*C.* Oral: Answer in German the questions in *B.*

*D.* Lesestück: Im Jahre 1848 drohte überall in Deutschland eine Revolution. Auch in der freien Reichsstadt Hamburg fand ein Aufstand statt. Eine Menge Menschen lief nach dem Rathause und forderte, den Bürgermeister zu sprechen. Dieser erschien denn auch und fragte die Leute, was sie eigentlich wollten. "Eine Republik wollen wir!" "Aber, Kinder, ihr habt ja schon eine!" "Dann wollen wir noch eine," riefen die begeisterten Republikaner.

## LESSON XLVI

**209. Fractions.** 1. They are regularly formed by adding –tel to the ordinal stem minus its final –t, and are neuter nouns :

ein Drittel $= \frac{1}{3}$; drei Viertel $= \frac{3}{4}$; fünf Einundzwanzigstel $= \frac{5}{21}$.   *add st from 19 upwards*

NOTE. — The termination –tel is a weakened form of Teil, 'part.'

2. 'The half' = die Hälfte; 'half' as adjective or adverb = halb; as adjective, halb is inflected and follows the determinative :   *following noun must be in gen.*

Die Hälfte meines Vermögens.   The half of my property.
Mein halbes Vermögen.          Half my property.
Die halbe Schweiz.             The half of Switzerland.

NOTE. — With place names not requiring the article, the uninflected halb may be used: Halb Frankreich, 'The half of France.'

3. The fraction Viertel is prefixed to its noun :

Eine Viertelstunde.            A quarter of an hour.
Drei Viertelstunden.           Three quarters of an hour.

**210. Mixed Numbers with halb.** 1. Invariable adjectives, expressing mixed numbers with the fraction 'half,' are formed by adding –halb to an ordinal: anderthalb $= 1\frac{1}{2}$; dritthalb $= 2\frac{1}{2}$.

NOTE. — The ordinal is one higher than the cardinal of the English idiom, and anderthalb is used for $1\frac{1}{2}$, ander being an old ordinal for 'second.'

2. These numerals, except anderthalb, are now almost universally replaced by zweiundeinhalb, dreiundeinhalb, ꝛc., either as invariable adjectives with noun in the plural, or as variable adjectives with noun in the singular:

| | |
|---|---|
| Wir marschierten dreiund= zwanzig und einhalb Meilen. | We marched twenty-three and a half leagues. |
| *Or:* dreiundzwanzig und eine halbe Meile. | Twenty-three leagues and a half. |

Note. — Other mixed numbers are read as in English; $15\frac{7}{8}$ = fünfzehn und sieben Achtel.

### EXERCISE XLVI

*A.* Anna, wir haben zwei Herren mit deren Damen auf Donnerstag zu Tisch eingeladen und ich möchte das Nötige mit Ihnen besprechen. Sie müssen gleich auf den Markt gehen, da man früh morgens am besten einkaufen kann. — Schön, gnädige Frau; also, was brauchen Sie? — Erstens bestellen Sie $3\frac{1}{2}$ Dutzend Austern; dann zweierlei Fleisch: einen Rin= derbraten zu $10\frac{1}{2}$ bis $12\frac{1}{2}$ Pfund, sowie ein Paar Hühner zu je $3\frac{1}{2}$ bis 4 Pfund und drei Bund Spargel. — Wie vielerlei Pudding gedenken Sie zu geben? — Zweierlei: Schokolade= Pudding, den Sie schon oft gemacht haben, und einen Mais= pudding. Zu letzterem gehören: $\frac{1}{4}$ Tasse Maismehl, $\frac{1}{2}$ Tasse Sirup, $\frac{1}{4}$ Teelöffel Salz, $2\frac{1}{2}$ Eßlöffel Butter, $1\frac{1}{2}$ Tassen Milch, ein Ei, $\frac{1}{4}$ Tasse Wasser und ein wenig Muskatnuß. Beinahe hätte ich den Fisch vergessen; also noch $4\frac{1}{2}$ Pfund Lachs. Ist noch Rheinwein im Keller? — Wir haben ungefähr anderthalb Dutzend Flaschen. — Weniger als die Hälfte davon wird ge= nügen. Wie bald können Sie zurück sein? — In drei Viertel= stunden; es ist ja nicht weit zum Markte.

*B.* Oral (read the following in German, and answer 7): 1. Addieren Sie $\frac{1}{4}$, $\frac{3}{8}$, $\frac{5}{16}$ und $\frac{3}{32}$. 2. Wie viel macht $\frac{31}{50}$, $\frac{72}{100}$ und $\frac{93}{200}$? 3. Subtrahieren Sie $80\frac{2}{7}$ von $100\frac{5}{14}$. 4. Multi-

plizieren Sie $\frac{2}{3}$ mit $\frac{4}{5}$. 5. Wie dividiert man $2\frac{1}{2}$ durch $\frac{2}{3}$?
6. $\frac{1}{5}$ + (plus) $\frac{7}{10}$ — (minus) $\frac{2}{5}$ × $\frac{1}{6}$ ÷ $2\frac{3}{4}$. 7. Der wievielte Teil
von 12 ist 1? 2? 3? 4? 5? 6? 7? 8? 9? 10?

*C.* 1. When one invites guests to dinner, one must purchase
what is necessary. 2. Father had invited two German gentlemen with their wives. 3. After breakfast mother and Anna
were discussing the necessary purchases. 4. Anna was to go
to the market at once. 5. It is better to make purchases in
the morning than in the afternoon. 6. Mother said we required
a roast of beef of eight or eight and a half pounds. 7. Anna
was also to order three and a half dozen oysters, a pair of
chickens of about four and a half pounds apiece, and two and
a half pounds of fish. 8. Anna asked mother how many kinds
of pudding she was going to have. 9. "Two kinds," said
mother, and asked Anna if she could make an Indian meal
pudding. 10. "Yes, mother," said the latter, "you (man) take
two and a half cups of milk, three and a half tablespoons of
cornmeal, half a cup of molasses, a quarter of a teaspoon of
salt and a little nutmeg. 11. Then you let it bake for three
quarters of an hour." 12. Anna then went to the market to
order the meat and vegetables. 13. She returned earlier than
she expected, for she was back in half an hour. 14. She is an
industrious girl, and is always very punctual.

*D.* Lesestück: Hier ist noch ein Tisch frei; bitte, meine
Herren. — Die Speisekarte, bitte. — Hier, mein Herr; Suppe
gefällig? — Ja, bringen Sie uns Suppe. — Wünschen Sie eine
Vorspeise? — Ja, geben Sie uns ein Dutzend Austern. — Schön.
Wünschen Sie Gemüse? — Bringen Sie uns grüne Bohnen und
Kartoffeln. — Was für Fleisch? — Für mich Kalbsbraten. — Was
essen Sie zum Nachtisch? — Käse und Obst. — Was für Obst?
Birnen oder Weintrauben? — Ein paar Weintrauben. — Eine
Tasse Kaffee gefällig? — Ja. Kellner, die Rechnung, bitte. —
Hier, mein Herr, M. 9.25. — Hier sind zehn Mark. Das
übrige ist für Sie. — Danke, meine Herren, Adieu!

# LESSON XLVII

**211.**                  Relative Pronouns.

    1. ber, who, which, that.

    2. welcher, who, which, that.

    3. wer, he (the one) who, whoever.

    4. was, what, that which.

    5. besgleichen, the like of whom, etc.

    6. bergleichen,  "   "   "   "   "

For declension and use of ber and welcher, see §§ 72–74; wer and was are declined like the interrogatives wer? and was? (§ 207).

**212.**                  Use of wer and was.

| | |
|---|---|
| Wer nicht hören will, muß fühlen. | He who (those who) will not hear must feel. |
| Was ich sage, ist wahr. | What (that which) I say is true. |
| Er will nicht studieren, was schade ist. | He will not study, which is a pity. |
| Alles, was er sagt. | All (that) he says. |
| Das Beste, was ich habe. | The best that I have. |

OBSERVE: 1. **Wer** and **was** as relatives are indefinite and compound in meaning, and include the antecedent.

2. 'He who,' 'those who,' are rendered by **wer** in general statements only; otherwise by ber(jenige) + relative (§§ 193–195).

3. **Was** must replace the relative bas or welches when the antecedent is a phrase, and may replace it when the antecedent is a neuter pronoun or adjective.

NOTE.—'Ever' = auch or immer after a relative pronoun for additional emphasis: Wer es auch (immer) gesagt hat, 'Whoever has said it.'

**213.**                  Use of besgleichen, bergleichen

| | |
|---|---|
| Ein Mann, besgleichen (*dat.*) ich noch nie begegnet bin. | A man the like of whom I have never yet met. |
| Ein Mann, besgleichen noch nie gelebt hat. | A man the like of whom has never yet lived. |
| Kinder, bergleichen, ꝛc. | Children the like of whom, etc. |

OBSERVE : These forms are indeclinable, the former referring
to a masculine or neuter noun in the singular, the latter to
feminine or plural nouns.

**214.**          **Agreement in Person.**

| | |
|---|---|
| Der Arzt, welcher hier war. | The doctor who was here. |
| Ich, der ich dein Freund bin. | I who am your friend. |
| O Gott, der Du im Himmel bist! | O God, who art in heaven ! |

OBSERVE : If the antecedent is in the first or second person,
the relative (in this case always **der**) is followed by the personal
pronoun of that person.

NOTE. — The pers. pron. of the 2nd pers. may be omitted, in which case
the verb is in the 3rd pers.: O Gott, der im Himmel ist!

**215. Wie as a Relative.** Solch ein or so ein is often followed in German by wie (=' as ') and a personal pronoun agreeing in gender and number with its antecedent ; the solch or so
may also be omitted :

| | |
|---|---|
| (Solch, so) ein Brief, wie wir ihn erwarteten. | Such a letter as we expected. |
| (Solche) Früchte, wie sie in Indien wachsen. | Such fruits as grow in India. |

**216. Word Order of Relatives.**   1. A relative must immediately follow its antecedent when the latter precedes the verb
of a principal sentence :

| | |
|---|---|
| Der Mann, der gestern hier war, ist wieder gekommen. | The man who was here yester-day has come again. |
| Den Mann, der jetzt redet, kenne ich nicht. | I do not know the man who is speaking now. |

2. So also when a separation would cause ambiguity :

| | |
|---|---|
| Ich traf einen Freund, den ich lange nicht gesehen hatte, bei seinem Bruder. | I met a friend, whom I had not seen for a long time, at his brother's. |

3. Similarly when the antecedent is the subject of a dependent clause :

Ich glaube, der Mann, der, ꝛc.  I think that the man who, etc.

4. In other cases the relative need not immediately follow, and the relative clause should not needlessly interrupt the sentence :

Ich suchte den Hut aus, der  I picked out the hat I liked
mir am besten gefiel.  best.

Er will zur Stadt zurück,  He means to return to the
in welcher er geboren wurde.  town in which he was born.

## EXERCISE XLVII

*A.* Als der persische Dichter Saadi einmal zu Schiff auf dem Meere fuhr, sah man ein Boot, welches auf dasselbe zukam. Ehe dieses aber das Schiff erreichen konnte, brach es entzwei, und zwei Männer, die sich darin befanden, fielen ins Wasser. Ein Matrose sprang vom Schiffe ins Wasser und rettete den einen, während der andere umkam. Saadi fragte den Matrosen: „Weshalb hast du demjenigen, der schwimmen konnte, das Leben gerettet?"  „Was ich tun konnte, das habe ich getan," antwortete jener, „denn ich konnte nur einem helfen. Diese Menschen waren zwei Brüder, die ich kannte: Ibrahim und Ali. Dieser hat mir stets nur Gutes erwiesen, und mich während einer schweren Krankheit gepflegt, was ich ihm jetzt vergolten habe ; jener behandelte mich immer wie einen Hund und ich ließ ihn ertrinken. Wer mein Feind gewesen ist, kann nicht erwarten, daß ich ihm eher helfe, als einem Freunde."  „O Gott, der du gerecht bist!" rief Saadi, „wer anderen Gutes tut, tut sich selber Gutes ; wer aber anderen Böses tut, auf den fällt das Böse zurück, was er an anderen verbrochen hat."

*B.* Oral exercise on the above.

*C.* 1. He who studies much will learn much.  2. Those who study most will learn most.  3. The best that I have is not too

good for you.  4. Whoever has done that is no friend of mine.
5. We had to stay in [after school], which was a pity, as the
weather was so fine.  6. Make a pudding like the one (= such
as) you made last week.  7. Saadi was a poet the like of whom
the world has seldom seen.  8. He lived in a city the name of
which I have forgotten.  9. I do not know the novel the title
of which you have named.  10. What I have said I have said.
11. Ali was the man whose life the sailor saved.  The one
whom he did not help has perished.  12. We praise Thee, O
God, who art in heaven !

*D.*  1. The Persian poet Saadi was once in a ship at (on the)
sea.  2. He saw a small boat which was approaching the ship.
3. This boat, in which were two men, broke to pieces.
4. Only one of the unfortunates who were in it could swim.
5. A sailor who was in Saadi's ship jumped into the sea.
6. He saved the one who could swim, and let the other drown.
7. Saadi asked him why he had saved the one who could
swim, and not the one who could not swim.  8. "The man
whose life I saved," said he, "has always treated me well.
9. The one I allowed to perish was his brother, who always
treated me badly.  10. He who doesn't help me, cannot expect that I should help him."  11. The good that we do to
others is repaid (vergelten) to us.  12. The sailor did what he
could.  13. We should always do what we can to help others.

*E.* Sprichwörter (the forms of wer and was are very common in proverbs and maxims): 1. Wer A sagt, muß auch B
sagen.  2. Wer Gott vertraut, hat wohl gebaut.  3. Wem
nicht zu raten ist, dem ist auch nicht zu helfen.  4. Wer steht,
sehe zu, daß er nicht falle.  5. Wer viel säet, wird viel ernten.
6. Was man nicht hat, kann man nicht geben.  7. Wer anderen
eine Grube gräbt, fällt selbst hinein.  8. Wer zuletzt lacht,
lacht am besten.  9. Wer nicht arbeitet, soll auch nicht essen.
10. Wer seine Arbeit fleißig tut, dem schmeckt auch seine
Suppe gut.  11. Wer lernt am Morgen, hat abends keine
Sorgen.

## LESSON XLVIII

**217.**   The Indefinite Pronouns.

1. man, one, they, people, etc.
2. jedermann, everybody, etc.
3. jemand, anybody, some one, etc.
4. niemand, nobody, not anybody, etc.
5. etwas, something, anything.
6. nichts, nothing.
7. ein paar, a few.
8. einer, one, some one.
9. keiner, no one, none, neither.
10. welcher, some, any.

**218. Man.** 1. This pronoun has the force of 'one,' 'they,' 'we,' 'you,' 'people,' etc. (compare French *on*), and is used only in the nominative :

Man sagt, daß der König krank ist.
They (people) say the king is ill.

Öl und Wasser kann man nicht zusammen mischen.
One (we, you) cannot mix oil and water.

2. Man must not be replaced by a personal pronoun :

Man wird müde, wenn man lange arbeitet.
A man (one) gets tired when he works a long time.

3. Einer sometimes replaces man in the nominative, and always in the other cases :

Wenn einer müde ist, kann er nicht gut arbeiten.
When a man (one) is tired, he cannot work well.

Es tut einem leid, wenn, 2c.
One is sorry when, etc.

4. The possessive adjective and the reflexive pronoun corresponding to man are sein and sich respectively :

Man sollte sich seiner Fehler schämen.
One (we) should be ashamed of one's (our) faults.

5. The man construction may replace the passive forms with werden, but only when the agent is indefinite or unknown :

Wie schreibt man das Wort?
How is the word written?

Man erlaubt uns, zu tanzen.
We are allowed to dance.

**219**. **Jedermann, jemand, niemand.** They are used in the singular only, and have as genitives jedermanns, jemandes, niemandes.

Jedermanns Sache ist nie=  Everybody's business is no-
  mandes Sache.           body's business.

Sagen Sie es niemand(em).    Don't tell it to any one.

Haben Sie jemand(en) gesehen?  Have you seen any one?

NOTE. — Jemand and niemand sometimes take –em or –en in the dat. and –en in the acc.

**220**. **Etwas, nichts.** 1. These are indeclinable forms:

Ich habe **etwas**; er hat  I have something; he has
**nichts**.                 nothing.

2. Etwas = 'some' before nouns in the singular, and also colloquially as a pronoun:

Etwas Brot.             Some bread (*i.e.* not much).

Hat er Geld? Er hat **etwas**.  Has he money? He has some.

**221**. **Ein paar.** This form is indeclinable; paar is not written with a capital:

Mit ein **paar** Talern.      With a few **thalers.**

**222**. **Einer, keiner.** 1. For declension and general use, see § 31.

2. They may replace jemand and niemand, respectively, and always do so before a genitive or von:

Es klopft **einer**.         Somebody is knocking.

**Keiner** von uns glaubt ihm.  Not one of us believes him.

**223**. **Welcher.** For declension, see § 31; it often has the force of 'some,' referring to a preceding noun:

Hat er Wein? Er hat **welchen**.  Has he wine? He has some.

Note. — The indeclinable irgenb is prefixed to a number of words with intensive indefinite force: irgenb jemanb or irgenb einer, 'anybody (at all),' 'somebody (or other)'; irgenb etwas, 'anything (at all),' 'something (or other)'; irgenbwo, 'somewhere (or other),' etc.; gar is similarly used before negatives: gar kein(er), 'none at all,' 'no one at all'; gar nichts, 'nothing at all,' 'nothing whatever.'

## EXERCISE XLVIII

*A.* Wenn irgend einem etwas Großes gelungen ist, so glaubt jedermann, er hätte das auch tun können, wenn er irgend Gelegenheit gehabt hätte. Das meinten auch die spanischen Höflinge, als Kolumbus nach seiner Entdeckung Amerikas allgemein bewundert wurde. Man gab ihm zu Ehren ein großes Gastmahl. Bei dieser Gelegenheit sagte jemand zu Kolumbus: „Das ist nichts Besonderes, eine neue Welt zu entdecken; das hätte irgend einer tun können." Kolumbus nahm ein Ei und fragte den Herrn, der neben ihm saß, ob er dasselbe aufrecht stellen könne. Nach einigen Versuchen gab dieser es auf. Dann versuchten es die anderen Herren der Reihe nach, aber niemanden gelang es. Endlich nahm Kolumbus selber das Ei und setzte es mit einem leichten Stoße auf den Tisch, so daß die Schale nachgab und das Ei aufrecht stand. „So etwas hätten Sie auch wohl tun können, meine Herren," sprach er, „aber keiner von Ihnen hat es getan; das ist der Unterschied zwischen mir und Ihnen," und jedermann mußte ihm recht geben.

*B.* Oral exercise on the above.

*C.* 1. Everybody knows that America was discovered by Columbus in 1492. 2. Before his time people knew nothing of the new world. 3. It was believed (use man) that there was no land beyond the sea. 4. After this discovery people admired and praised him. 5. As usual many people said that this was no great thing (nothing great). 6. Almost everybody thought he could have done the same [thing]. 7. So it is (geht) always when anybody succeeds in doing anything special.  8. When Columbus returned from America a great banquet was given him.  9. At (bei) this banquet he heard somebody say : " I could have done that, too, if I had only had an opportunity."  10. Columbus took an egg and said : " Can any one of you set this egg on end ? "  11. Everybody at the table tried it ; nobody succeeded.  12. At last some one asked Columbus if he could do it himself.  13. " Certainly," said he, " nothing is easier."  14. With a slight blow on the table he set it upright.  15. " (My) gentlemen," he said, " anybody at all could have done it, but why did nobody do it ? "

*D.* 1. Doctors say that people take cold most easily when they are tired.  2. People should assist not only their friends, but (sondern) also their enemies.  3. Is there anybody at the door?  4. I don't see anybody.  5. Will you [have] some meat?  6. No, thank you, I still have some.  7. May I give you anything else?  8. Has he any money?  9. He has some, but only a few marks.  10. I can give him nothing at all.  11. Nobody believed that Columbus could discover America.  12. None of the courtiers could have discovered America.  13. Not one of the gentlemen could set the egg upright.  14. Could any one of you have done it?  15. I believe I could have done it if I had been Columbus.

*E.* Lesestück : Zwei Stunden nach Mitternacht, es war am 12. Oktober, riefen zwei Matrosen: " Land ! Land ! " Sie hatten auch die Küste in der Tat entdeckt.  Sie waren nur noch zwei Meilen davon entfernt.  Bei Tagesanbruch sah man eine schöne flache Insel.  Kolumbus kleidet sich in Scharlach. Er befiehlt, die Anker fallen zu lassen, die Boote zu bemannen, und mit einer Fahne in der Hand, die man zu diesem Zwecke verfertigt hatte, betritt er das Boot.  Kolumbus stieg zuerst ans Land, fiel auf die Knie und betete.  Seinem Beispiele folgte die ganze Mannschaft, die mit ihm gelandet war.  Auf diese Weise wurde Amerika entdeckt.

# LESSON XLIX

**224. The Passive Voice.** The passive voice is the active voice inverted, that is, the direct object of the active becomes the subject of the passive, and the active subject becomes the agent; hence only transitive verbs can have a true passive.

**225. Passive with werden.** 1. This passive is formed by means of werden (= 'become') + the past participle of the verb to be conjugated, as in the paradigm below.

2. In accordance with the meaning of werden, this form of the passive indicates a passing into and continuing in a state or condition.

3. It is used whenever agency is specified or implied; the personal agent is denoted by von + dative; other agency by durch or mit:

| | |
|---|---|
| Kinder werden **von** ihren El= tern geliebt. | Children are loved by their parents. |
| Er **wurde** bestraft. | He was (being) punished. |
| Ein Kind **wird** immer leicht **durch** Güte geleitet. | A child is always easily led by kindness. |

**226.**        Passive of loben, to praise.

PRESENT.

*Indicative.*             *Subjunctive.*

I am being praised, etc.

| | |
|---|---|
| ich werde gelobt | ich werde gelobt |
| du wirst    „   2c. | du werdest    „   2c. |

IMPERFECT.

*Indicative.*             *Subjunctive.*

I was (being) praised, etc.

| | |
|---|---|
| ich wurde (ward) gelobt | ich würde gelobt |
| du wurdest (wardst)   „   2c. | du würdest   „   2c. |

P

### PERFECT.

*Indicative.* *Subjunctive.*

I have been praised, etc.

| | |
|---|---|
| ich bin gelobt **worden** | ich sei gelobt worden |
| du bift „ „ 2c. | du seieft „ „ 2c. |

### PLUPERFECT.

*Indicative.* *Subjunctive.*

I had been praised, etc.

| | |
|---|---|
| ich war gelobt worden | ich wäre gelobt worden |
| du warst „ „ 2c. | du wäreft „ „ 2c. |

### FUTURE.

I shall be praised, etc.

| | |
|---|---|
| ich werde gelobt werden | ich werde gelobt werden |
| du wirst „ „ 2c. | du werdeft „ „ 2c. |

### FUTURE PERFECT.

I shall have been praised, etc.

| | |
|---|---|
| ich werde gelobt worden sein | ich werde gelobt worden sein |
| du wirst „ „ „ 2c. | du werdeft „ „ „ 2c. |

### CONDITIONAL.

*Simple.* *Compound.*

I should be praised, etc. I should have been praised, etc.

| | |
|---|---|
| ich würde gelobt werden | ich würde gelobt worden sein |
| du würdeft „ „ 2c. | du würdeft „ „ „ 2c. |

### INFINITIVE.

*Pres.* gelobt (zu) werden, to be praised.

*Perf.* gelobt worden (zu) sein, to have been praised.

### IMPERATIVE.

werde gelobt, 2c., be praised, etc.

OBSERVE : The prefix **ge-** of geworden is dropped throughout in the passive.

NOTES.— 1. The impf. and plupf. subj. are usually substituted for the condl. 2. The fut. perf., comp. condl., perf. infin., and impve. passive rarely occur.

**227. The Passive with ſein.** 1. A passive is also formed by means of the various tenses of ſein + the past participle of the verb to be conjugated.

2. This form of the passive indicates a state or condition regarded as complete and permanent, and as resulting from the action of the verb; it is never used when agency is expressed or implied, and must be carefully distinguished from the passive with werden:

| | |
|---|---|
| Die Läden **werden** um zehn Uhr geſchloſſen. | The shops are closed at ten o'clock. |
| Sie ſind ſchon geſchloſſen. | They are closed already. |
| Das Haus iſt verkauft. | The house is sold. |
| Ich bin beſchäftigt **geweſen.** | I have been busy. |

**228. Limitations of the Passive.** 1. When the direct object of a transitive verb is a thing (not a person), the thing becomes the subject in the passive, the person remaining as indirect object:

| | |
|---|---|
| Er verſprach mir Hilfe. | He promised me help. |
| Hilfe wurde mir von ihm verſprochen. | I was promised help by him. |

2. Verbs having only an indirect personal object in German (often transitive in English) have no passive form:

| | |
|---|---|
| Ein Freund begegnete mir. | I was met by a friend. |

3. Purely intransitive verbs can have a passive in the impersonal form only:

| | |
|---|---|
| Es wurde geſtern getanzt. | There was dancing yesterday. |
| Geſtern wurde getanzt. | "　　"　　"　　" |
| Ich glaube, daß jetzt getanzt wird. | I think there is dancing going on now. |

NOTE. — Es of this construction is omitted, unless it immediately precedes the verb; the impers. construction is sparingly used, and is usually replaced by the man constr. (§ 218, 5).

4. The passive is much less used in German than in English, being often replaced by a man construction (§ 218, 5) and occasionally by a reflexive, especially with laſſen:

Es wird ſich ſchon finden.　　　It will doubtless be found.
Das läßt ſich leicht machen.　　That can easily be done.

## EXERCISE XLIX

A. In Rom lebten vor alter Zeit zwei blinde Bettler. Täg=
lich konnte man den einen in den Straßen rufen hören: „Wem
Gott hilft, dem iſt geholfen!" Der andere aber rief: „Wem
der Kaiſer hilft, dem iſt geholfen!" Auch der Kaiſer hörte
das, und ließ ein Brot backen und mit Goldſtücken füllen.
Das Brot wurde auf ſeinen Befehl dem Blinden gegeben, der
des Kaiſers Macht geprieſen hatte. Als jener das ſchwere
Gewicht des Brotes fühlte, verkaufte er es dem anderen
Blinden. Von dieſem wurde es nach Hauſe getragen und
erbrochen. Über das Gold, welches darin enthalten war, war
er zugleich erſtaunt und erfreut. Er dankte Gott und hörte
auf, zu betteln. Der andere Bettler war aber noch immer
gezwungen, zu betteln. Er wurde deshalb zum Kaiſer berufen
und von ihm befragt, warum er noch immer bettle, und was
aus dem Brote geworden ſei, das man ihm habe geben laſſen.
Er antwortete, das Brot ſei von ihm ſeinem Kameraden ver=
kauft worden, da er dasſelbe für teigig gehalten habe. Der
Kaiſer aber rief: „In der Tat, wem Gott hilft, dem iſt ge=
holfen!" und der Blinde wurde fortgejagt.

B. Oral: 1. Von welchen Bettlern wird hier erzählt? 2. Von
welchem wurde Gottes Macht gepriesen? 3. Womit war das
Brot gefüllt, das der Kaiser backen ließ ? 4. Welchem Bettler
ward es gegeben? 5. Wem wurde es verkauft? 6. Was ward
zunächst aus dem Brote? 7. Worüber war der zweite Blinde
erfreut? 8. Wozu war der andere gezwungen? 9. Zu wem
wurde er berufen? 10. Was fragte der Kaiser? 11. Was

wurde ihm geantwortet?   12. Was sagte der Kaiser dazu?
13. Was geschah endlich diesem Bettler?

*C.* Continue:  1. Ich bin vom Lehrer gelobt worden, du,
etc.   2. Ich werde von ihm bestraft werden.   3. Ich wäre dazu
gezwungen worden.   4. Es wird mir nicht erlaubt werden, auszugehen, . . . dir, etc.   5. Mir ist nichts davon gesagt worden,
dir, etc.   6. Man glaubt mir nicht, . . . dir, etc.   7. Meine
Aufgabe ist schon abgeschrieben, deine, etc.   8. Mir wird
geholfen, dir, etc.

*D.*  1. Two blind [men] were forced to beg in the streets
of Rome.   2. One of these continually extolled the power of
the emperor.   3. The power of God was extolled by the other.
4. The emperor had a loaf baked.   5. By his order[s] it was
filled with gold-pieces.   6. This loaf was then sent to the beggar
by whom the emperor had been extolled.   7. When it was
brought (use man) to him, he said it was heavy and doughy.
8. It was sold by him to his comrade.   9. When it had been
broken open by the latter, he was rejoiced at the gold which
was contained in it.   10. He had become rich, and ceased
to beg.   11. The other was still (noch immer) forced to beg.
12. The emperor caused this man to be summoned.   13. The
beggar was asked what he had done (machen) with the loaf.
14. The blind man replied that it had been bought by his
comrade.   15. The unfortunate man was driven away and was
compelled to beg again.

*E.*  1. If I should lose my position, I should be forced to beg.
2. The letter is already written and will be copied at once.
3. Is this house sold?   4. When was it sold?   5. We are not
allowed to go out when it is raining.   6. Are you allowed to
read novels?   7. When I said that, I was not believed.   8. It
was not formerly believed that the earth was round.   9. Nothing
has been said to me of the matter.   10. If they did what they
should, they would be helped.   11. He has been promised
help by everybody.   12. This officer has been thanked by the

emperor.   13. There will be dancing at (in) the party to-morrow.   14. I have been told that Mr. Sauer is ill.

*F.*  Lesestück : Ein Soldat war von einer Flintenkugel ver-
wundet worden.   Die Ärzte machten mehrere Einschnitte, um
sie herauszunehmen.   Der Soldat verlor zuletzt die Geduld und
fragte, warum sie ihn so quälten.   "Wir suchen die Kugel,"
sagten sie.   "Warum haben Sie mir das nicht früher gesagt?
Ich habe sie in der Tasche," erwiderte der Soldat.


# LESSON L

**229.**            **Indefinite Pronominal Adjectives.**

1. all, all (the).

2. ganz, all, whole, the whole
   (of).

3. jeder (jedweder, jeglicher),
   each, every.

4. mancher, many a (one).

5. einige, some, a few.

6. etliche,   "   "   "

7. mehrere, several.

8. genug, enough.

9. mehr, more.

10. viel(e), much (many).

11. wenig(e), little (few).

REMARK : All the above may be used as adjectives or as
pronouns.

**230. All.**  1.  This word expresses number as well as quantity ;
when declined it follows the dieser model :

Alles Brot; alle Kinder.        All the bread ; all(the)children.
Er hat alles, was er wünscht.   He has all he wants.
Die Knaben sind alle hier.      The boys are all here.

NOTE.—All is never followed by the unstressed definite article.

2. With a possessive adjective it always precedes, and remains uninflected in the singular :

All ihr Geld ; alle ihre Hüte.   All her money ; all her hats.

3. **Alí** stands appositively with a noun or pronoun:

Ich kenne sie alle.     I know all of them.

**231. Ganz.** 1. This adjective expresses quantity, not number, and denotes an object as complete and undivided; when, therefore, the English 'all' = 'the whole,' it must be rendered by ganz:

Ich arbeite den **ganzen** Tag.     I work all (the whole) day.

2. Ganz is declined like an adjective, and always follows the determinative:

Der ganze Tag.     The whole day.
Mein ganzes Eigentum.     The whole of my property.

3. Before proper names of places, unaccompanied by an article or other determinative, it may remain uninflected:

Ganz (or das ganze) England.     The whole of England.
*But:* Die ganze Schweiz.     The whole of Switzerland.

**232. Jeder (jedweder, jeglicher).** 1. Jeder (dieser model) is used to denote each individual belonging to a class:

Jeder Baum hat Äste.     Every tree has branches.

2. It is sometimes preceded by ein, and then follows the mixed adjective declension:

Er hat einem jeden gedankt.     He thanked each one.

3. It replaces jedermann before a genitive or **von**:

(Ein) **jeder** von den Herren.     Every one of the gentlemen.

NOTE. — Jedweder, jeglicher are less common substitutes for jeder.

**233. Mancher (dieser model)** may remain uninflected before an adjective:

Manches Jahr ist verflossen.     Many a year has gone by.
Manche waren zugegen.     Many (people) were present.
Mancher gute (manch guter)     Many a good man.
    Mann.

**234. Einige, etliche.**  1. They follow the dieſer model, and denote a small number :

Vor einigen (etlichen) Jahren.  A few years ago.

Einige waren unzufrieden.    Some were dissatisfied.

2. They are used in the singular, but only before nouns of quantity, material, etc., to denote a limited amount :

Ich habe einiges Geld.    I have some money (not much).

NOTE. — Unless the idea of limited quantity is emphasized, 'some' and 'any' are omitted when rendering into German.

**235. Genug, mehr.**  1. They are indeclinable, and are also used adverbially :

Er iſt weit **genug** gegangen.  He has walked far enough.

Ich habe **mehr** Geld als Sie.  I have more money than you.

2. **Genug** always follows its adjective or adverb, but may precede or follow its noun :

Das iſt ſchlimm **genug**.    That is bad enough.

Geld **genug** (*or* genug Geld).  Money enough.

**236. Mehrere** is mostly used in the plural (dieſer model) :

Mehrere (Leute) wurden krank.  Several (people) fell ill.

NOTE. — The neut. sing. mehreres is sometimes used as a pron.: Mehreres iſt geſchehen, 'Several things have happened.'

**237. Viel, wenig.**  1. They usually remain uninflected in the singular when used adjectively :

Ich habe wenig (viel) Geld.  I have little (much) money.

2. Ein wenig (uninflected) = 'a little' :

Mit ein wenig Geld.      With a little money.

Haſt du Geld? Ein wenig.  Have you money?  A little.

3. They are usually declined in the plural, and always so when used pronominally :

Waren viele Leute zugegen?  Were many people present?

Es waren nur wenige da.    There were only a few there.

## EXERCISE L

*A.* Es ist in der Tat schrecklich, wenn die feste Erde einem unter den Füßen bebt und zittert. Ein jedes heftiges Erdbe= ben kostet viele Menschenleben, aber selten so viele Tausende, wie dasjenige, welches am 28. Dezember 1908 in Italien statt= fand und die ganze Welt mit Entsetzen erfüllte. Ganze Städte in Kalabrien und Sizilien wurden dadurch vernichtet und nur wenige Dörfer blieben unbeschädigt. Aus einer Stadt kam die furchtbare Nachricht, daß sämtliche Einwohner ums Leben ge= kommen seien. In Messina waren in kurzer Zeit fast alle großen Gebäude sowie manche von den kleineren Häusern ganz zerstört und manch alter Tempel zerrüttet. An manchen Orten waren so wenige Menschen unverletzt geblieben, daß deren nicht genug waren, um den anderen beizustehen. Viele von diesen Leuten verloren alles, nicht nur all ihre Habe, son= dern auch Weib und Kind, die unter den Trümmern begraben lagen. Dieses Erdbeben hat viel mehr Menschenleben gekostet, als der ganze deutsch=französische Krieg.

*B.* Oral exercise on the above.

*C.* 1. All the pupils have come. 2. All my relatives live in Germany. 3. Mr. B. is quite poor now; he has lost all his money. 4. Could you not lend me some money? 5. I have only a few marks, but I will lend you all I have with me. 6. Pardon me; I had quite forgotten your name. 7. When any part at all of the earth trembles, the whole earth trembles more or less. 8. Every one of the courtiers tried to set the egg upright. 9. Many tried it, but only a few succeeded. 10. If one [man] does evil, many suffer by it (dadurch). 11. Many a good man suffers for others. 12. A little is better than nothing at all. 13. Some of the pupils are here; the others have not come yet. 14. They should be here every morning at 9 o'clock. 15. I visited Sicily some years ago. 16. Money lost, little lost; friends lost, much lost; courage lost, everything lost.

*D.* 1. It is something terrible when the earth trembles under one's feet. 2. Almost every year earthquakes take place in some part or other of the world. 3. Some of them are not very violent. 4. By others whole towns are destroyed and many thousands perish. 5. Among the most violent earthquakes of our time was that of (von) San Francisco in 1906. 6. On that occasion almost the whole of the city was destroyed by fire. 7. Several hundreds of the inhabitants lost their lives. 8. The earthquake in Italy in 1908 was something much more dreadful. 9. Many of the towns and villages of Sicily and Calabria were entirely annihilated. 10. In a few minutes the whole city of Messina lay in ruins. 11. Very few of the inhabitants remained uninjured. 12. Many children lost their parents. 13. Many a father had lost wife and child. 14. Almost all had lost all their possession[s]. 15. All Italy was filled with horror. 16. It cost more human lives than all the earthquakes of the last hundred years.

*E.* Leſeſtück:

> Der du von dem Himmel biſt,
> Alles Leid und Schmerzen ſtilleſt,
> Den, der doppelt elend iſt,
> Doppelt mit Erquickung fülleſt,
> Ach, ich bin des Treibens müde!
> Was ſoll all der Schmerz und Luſt?
> Süßer Friede,
> Komm, ach komm in meine Bruſt!
>
> — Goethe.

## LESSON LI

**238**. **Adverbs.** 1. Most adjectives may be used as adverbs without change ; for comparison of adverbs, see Less. XXXIX.

2. The ordinary rules for the formation and derivation of adverbs are omitted here ; adverbial forms are best learned by observation and from the dictionary.

3. The following sections contain examples of the more difficult idiomatic uses of certain adverbs.

**239.** **Auch.** *(also too even)*

| | |
|---|---|
| Auch ich war gegen ihn. | Even I was against him. |
| Mein Bruder war nicht müde, und ich auch nicht. | My brother was not tired, and I was not tired either. |
| Ich bin müde.—Ich auch. | I am tired.—So am I. |

**240.** **Doch.** *(yet, well, however but after all, etc)*

| | |
|---|---|
| Er wird do'ch kommen. | He will come after all. |
| Er wird doch ko'mmen. | He will come, I hope. |
| Habe ich es doch gesa'gt! | I said so (didn't I)! |
| Hast du es nicht gehört? | Didn't you hear it? |
| Do'ch! | I did. |
| Ich habe es nicht getan. | I didn't do it. |
| Sie haben es do'ch getan. | Yes, you did. |
| Kommen Sie doch herein. | Pray (do) come in. |

OBSERVE: 1. In exclamatory sentences with doch (see third example) the verb often begins the sentence.

2. Doch gives an affirmative reply to a negative statement or question.

**241.** **Eben.** *(just, just now)*

| | |
|---|---|
| Das ist eben, was ich meine. | That is just what I mean. |
| Er ist eben angekommen. | He has just arrived. |

**242.** **Erst.** *(first, only, not before, until)*

| | |
|---|---|
| Erst denken, dann sprechen. | First think, then speak. |
| Er kommt erst am Freitag. | He isn't coming before Friday. |
| Sie ist erst zwei Jahre alt. | She is only two years old. |

**243.** **Gern.**

| | |
|---|---|
| Ich esse gern Fisch. | I am fond of fish. |
| Das mag gern sein. | That may well be. |
| Ich würde es gern tun. | I should gladly do it. |
| Er möchte lieber nicht kommen. | He would rather not come. |
| Er käme gern. | He would like to come. |

**244.**  **Ja.** *be sure / indeed, really / you know*

| | |
|---|---|
| Tun Sie es ja'. | Be sure to do it. |
| Er ist ja mein Vater. | He is my father, you know. |
| Das hatte ich ja vergessen. | Why, I had forgotten that. |

**245.**  **Noch.**

| | |
|---|---|
| Sind Sie noch hier? | Are you still here? |
| Ich war noch nie dort. | I was never there. |
| Noch heute; noch gestern; noch immer. | To-day at the latest; only yesterday; still. |
| Noch eine Tasse; noch zwei. | Another cup; two more. |
| Noch einmal so viel. | As much again. |

OBSERVE: Noch precedes the negatives nie, nicht, ꝛc.

**246.**  **Nur.**

| | |
|---|---|
| Kommen Sie nur herein. | Just come in. |
| Was wünschen Sie nur? | What do you want (anyway)? |

**247.**  **Schon.** *already / not later than / as early as?*

| | |
|---|---|
| Sind Sie schon da? | Are you there already? |
| Schon heute. | Not later than to-day. |
| Ist sie schon in Rom gewesen? | Has she ever been in Rome? |
| Ich bin schon acht Tage hier. | I have been here for a week. |
| Das Schiff ist schon gestern angekommen. | The ship arrived (as early as) yesterday. |
| Er wird schon kommen. | He will surely come. |
| Er ist jetzt schon da. | He is there by this time. |

**248**  **Wohl.**

| | |
|---|---|
| Sie sind wohl müde. | I suppose you are tired. |
| Krank ist er wohl, aber nicht gefährlich. | He is ill, to be sure, but not dangerously. |
| Das ist wohl wahr. | That is no doubt true. |
| Das mag wohl sein. | That is very likely so. |

**249.** 3uerſt. *first*

Dieſes Schiff kam zuerſt an.    This ship arrived first.

Ich gehe zuerſt (erſt) zum    I am going first to the tailor's,
Schneider, dann zum Buch=    then to the bookseller's.
händler.

### EXERCISE LI

*credit ...*

*A.* Ein Gläubiger kam eines Morgens zu einem Dichter,
als dieser noch zu Bett lag, und hatte schon das ganze Zimmer
durchsucht, als derselbe erwachte. — Was wollen Sie nur?
fragte er. — Seien Sie doch so gut, diese Rechnung zu begleichen.
— Sehr gerne, aber sehen Sie erst in jener Schublade nach, ob
da Geld liegt. — Das habe ich erst eben getan. — Dann versuchen
Sie es doch mit der anderen. — Auch da ist nichts; da habe ich
zuerst gesucht. — Auf dem Tische haben Sie wohl nicht nach=
gesehen? — Doch; aber da ist eben so wenig zu sehen. — Haben
Sie auch im Schreibtisch gesucht? — Auch da, aber vergebens. *in order*
— Habe ich's mir doch gedacht! Es war noch gestern abend
nichts darin. Dann müssen Sie wohl meine Taschen durch=
suchen. — Das ist auch schon geschehen. — Das ist ja unglaub=
lich! Na, wenn sich weder in den Schubladen noch sonst irgendwo
Geld befindet, so kann ich Sie unmöglich bezahlen. Kommen
Sie nur noch einmal und vergessen Sie ja nicht die Rechnung
mitzubringen. Also, auf Wiedersehen!

*B.* Oral exercise on the above.

*C.* 1. Speak louder, I pray you; I can't hear you. 2. Just
read the letter, if you wish [to]. 3. Uncle has just arrived;
aunt is not coming till Monday. 4. I would rather not go to
the theatre this evening. 5. First (the) business and then (the)
pleasure. 6. Be sure not to take that book; I have only read
the half of it. 7. Who arrived first, your uncle or your aunt?
8. Your cousin must have arrived in Berlin by this time. 9. I
should like to know whether he is there already. 10. That is

just what I should like to know myself.  11. I have only ten
marks left (= still).  12. Do take another piece of roast, Miss L.
13. Why, I have twice as much as I can eat.  14. You surely
don't mean that!  15. Yes, I do.  16. I haven't seen Mr.
Braun since Easter.  17. Neither have I.  18. I suppose he
isn't in town.  19. Yes, he is ; my wife saw him only yesterday.

*D.* 1. The tailor has come and wants his money.  2. He
should not have come when I am still in bed.  3. I suppose
you didn't tell him I was sleeping.  4. O yes, I did.  5. He
has been here for the last hour.  6. He says he would like to
have his money not later than to-day.  7. I should gladly pay
him if I could.  8. Only yesterday I had to pay several bills.
9. I must pay two or three more to-morrow.  10. They
are twice as large as this one.  11. I shall pay these first and
the tailor's afterwards.  12. He might wait another week.
13. A week is not a (fein) very long time, after all.  14. That
he must [do], I suppose.  15. Just tell him he is to be sure to
come back (wieber) next week.  16. But I shall not be at
home before Friday.  17. I shall surely have enough money
then.


# LESSON LII

**250. Prefixes of Compound Verbs.**  1. The prefixes of compound verbs are either stressed or unstressed, *i.e.* the principal
stress falls either on the prefix or on the verb stem :

Au'sgehen; verge'hen.　　　　To go out; to pass away.

2. Unstressed prefixes are inseparable (see § 51) :

Ich habe es versprochen.　　　I have promised it.

3. Stressed prefixes are separable (for word order, see § 50) :

Ich gehe heute aus.　　　　　I am going out to-day.
Karl ist eben ausgegangen.　　Charles has just gone out.
Kommen Sie doch herein.　　　Pray, do come in.

Note. — The difficulties of detail explained in the following paragraphs depend upon the principles stated above.

**251. Quasi-Prefixes.**  1. Besides the ordinary verb prefixes, many words and phrases in common use have practically the function of separable prefixes, and follow the same rules of word order.

2. Such are nouns as objects, with or without prepositions:

| | |
|---|---|
| Gib darauf acht. | Pay heed to it. |
| Er sagte, daß ich nicht achtgebe. | He said I was not paying attention. |
| Nimm dich in acht. | Take care. |

Note. — Nouns so used are now usually written with a small letter, and often in one word with the governing preposition.

3. So also certain adjectives:

| | |
|---|---|
| Lassen Sie mich los. | Let me go. |
| Er wurde freigesprochen. | He was acquitted. |

Notes. — 1. Some adj. prefixes are insep., even when stressed, and retain the prefix ge-: Er fing an zu weissagen, 'He began to prophesy'; Sie hat sich gerechtfertigt, 'She has justified herself.'

2. **Voll**, except in the literal sense, is unstressed and insep.: Er hat das Werk vollendet, 'He has completed the work'; Er hat das Glas voll=gegossen, 'He has poured the glass full.'

**252. Double Prefixes.**  1. Separable + separable; both separable:

| | |
|---|---|
| Er hat das vorau'sgesagt. | He predicted that. |

2. Separable + inseparable; the former alone separable:

| | |
|---|---|
| Ich gestehe das zu. | I admit that. |
| Er erkannte es an. | He acknowledged it. |

3. Inseparable + separable; both inseparable:

| | |
|---|---|
| Ich bea'bsichtige, es zu tun. | I intend to do it. |
| Er hat das vera'nstaltet. | He has arranged that. |

**253. Her, hin.** 1. The simple prepositional prefixes of direction, ab–, an–, auf–, aus–, ein–, nieder–, über–, um–, unter–, vor–, are used only when the compound verb denotes motion in a general way, without specifying or implying a starting-point or destination, or when there is no idea of motion:

| | |
|---|---|
| Er ist eben ausgegangen. | He has just gone out. |
| Sie kamen gestern an. | They arrived yesterday. |
| Wir reisen morgen ab. | We are off to-morrow. |
| Was ziehen Sie vor? | What do you prefer? |

2. The prefixes her–, 'hither,' and hin–, 'thither,' indicate direction, respectively, to or from the speaker or spectator:

| | |
|---|---|
| Kommen Sie her. | Come here (to me). |
| Er soll hingehen. | He is to go there. |

3. Aus–, vor–, and also ab– in the sense of 'down,' require her– or hin– prefixed, when a <u>starting-point</u> is implied but not specified; the others (an–, auf–, 2c.), when a <u>destination</u> is implied but not specified:

| | |
|---|---|
| Er ging zur Tür hinaus. | He went out at the door. |
| Er zog ein Buch hervor. | He produced a book. |
| Gehen Sie hinunter (hinab). | Go down (stairs). |
| Er ist heraufgekommen. | He has come up (stairs). |

4. When the starting-point or destination is specified, these compound prefixes are used when the preposition and prefix do not correspond:

| | |
|---|---|
| Wir fuhren oft nach Holland hinüber. | We often crossed over to Holland. |
| Er fiel vom Dache herab. | He fell (down) from the roof. |

5. When preposition and prefix correspond, the compound prefix may be used:

| | |
|---|---|
| Er ging aus dem Zimmer (hinaus), als ich eintrat. | He went out of the room as I entered. |

**254. Prefixes with Varying Stress.** 1. The prefixes durch–, über–, um–, unter–, are sometimes stressed (separable) and sometimes unstressed (inseparable).

2. Some of these compounds are used both separably and inseparably, usually with different meaning:

| | |
|---|---|
| Er ift hier du'rchgereift. | He passed through here. |
| Er hat das Land durchrei'ft. | He has traversed the country. |
| Der Strom ift ü'bergetreten. | The stream has overflowed. |
| Er übertra't das Gebot. | He transgressed the command. |

3. Some are used inseparably only:

| | |
|---|---|
| Mein Plan ift durchkreu'zt. | My plan is thwarted. |
| Ich überla'ffe das Ihnen. | I leave that to you. |
| Unterbre'chen Sie mich nicht. | Don't interrupt me. |

4. Others are used separably only:

| | |
|---|---|
| Er ift u'mgekehrt. | He has turned back. |
| Der Keffel kocht ü'ber. | The kettle is boiling over. |

NOTES. — 1. The insep. transitive compound is often replaced by the simple verb + the prefix as prep.: Er durchschritt das Tor or Er schritt durch das Tor, 'He passed through the gate.'

2. Hinter– as prefix is insep.; wieder– is insep. only in wiederho'len, 'repeat': Er hat mich hinterga'ngen, 'He has deceived me'; Er hinterlie ß nichts, 'He left nothing'; Ich habe es wiederho'lt, 'I repeated it.'

3. The prefix miß– has varying stress, but is insep., except in the past part. of some verbs, and in the infin. and past part. of others. For details, see dictionary.

### EXERCISE LII

*A.* Nikolaus I. von Rußland ging oft in seiner Hauptstadt Petersburg auf Abenteuer aus. Auf diese Weise gedachte er, die Lebensweise seiner Untertanen zu beobachten. Nur selten wurde er bei diesen Gängen erkannt, denn er verkleidete sich in einen gewöhnlichen Offiziersmantel. Einmal hatte er sich in eine Vorstadt hinausbegeben, hatte aber dabei nicht auf den Weg achtgegeben. Endlich wurde er gewahr, daß er sich verirrt

Q

hatte. Es blieb ihm also nichts übrig, als sich einer Droschke anzuvertrauen. Er rief eine herbei, stieg ein und bedeutete dem Kutscher, ihn zur Stadt hineinzufahren und ihn am Winterpalais abzusetzen. Dort angekommen, stieg der Zar aus. Als er aber bezahlen wollte, stellte es sich heraus, daß er all sein Geld verausgabt hatte. „Warte nur hier,“ sagte er zum Kutscher und wollte ins Schloß eintreten, „ich will dir das Geld sofort herausschicken.“ „Nein, Väterchen,“ unterbrach ihn der Mann, „so haben mich die Herren Offiziere schon ein paarmal hintergangen. Sie gingen zur Vordertür hinein und dann zur Hintertür wieder hinaus, und so kam ich um mein gutes Geld. Überlaß mir nur deinen Mantel; schickst du mir das Geld heraus, so schicke ich ihn dir sogleich hinein.“ Der Kaiser war also gezwungen, dem Kutscher den Mantel zu überlassen, denn er erkannte an, daß der Mann recht hatte.

*B.* Oral: 1. Weshalb ging der Kaiser oft auf Abenteuer aus? 2. Warum wurde er dabei selten erkannt? 3. Wie kam es, daß er sich verirrte? 4. Wohin hatte er sich begeben? 5. Was tat er also? 6. Welchen Befehl gab er dem Kutscher? 7. Weshalb bezahlte er nicht sogleich den Kutscher? 8. Was versprach ihm der Kaiser? 9. Von wem war dieser oftmals hintergangen worden? 10. Wie hatten sie ihn betrogen? 11. Wozu war Seine Majestät gezwungen? 12. Weshalb tat er das?

*C.* 1. Have you observed the conduct of this man? 2. I shall not be recognized. 3. Take care, or else we shall be recognized. 4. Betake yourself to the country. 5. Take care of (auf, *acc.*) your health when you are young. 6. Take care, the train is coming. 7. I have entrusted all my money to a friend. 8. Get into the carriage. 9. Get out of the carriage. 10. Order the cabman to drive into the city. 11. The Czar got out [of the carriage]. 12. We shall have spent all our money. 13. Do you wish to enter the palace? 14. Come in

at the front-door. 15. Send the cabman in at the back-door.
16. First send me out my money. 17. The emperor did not
cheat the cabman. 18. It is impossible to be in the right
always. 19. The cabman was in the right, and the emperor
was obliged to acknowledge it. 20. Even emperors are not
always in the right.

*D.* 1. Nicholas I once betook himself to a suburb of
St. Petersburg. 2. He didn't give heed to the way, and went
astray. 3. He was forced to trust himself to a cab. 4. The
cabman drove him into the city, and set him down at the
palace. 5. When he had arrived there, it turned out that His
Majesty could not pay. 6. He searched all his pockets and
found nothing. 7. He told the cabman he had spent all his
money. 8. "I will go into the palace and bring you out your
money." 9. "Oh, no ! In this way I have often lost (fommen
um) my money. 10. It is very easy to go in at the front-door
and out at the back-door. 11. I have been cheated only too
often. 12. Just hand over your cloak to me." 13. "You are
right ; I will entrust it to you. 14. But promise to hand it over
to the servant, when I send you out your money." 15. The
Czar sent out the money, and the cloak was handed over to
the servant.

*E.* Lesestück : Am 14. Oktober 1806 saß Hegel, der
berühmte Philosoph, der damals Professor in Jena war, am
Schreibtische und arbeitete an einer Abhandlung, als der
Schreibtisch plötzlich von großen Eisensplittern überstreut
wurde. Er rief das Stubenmädchen und sagte ärgerlich : "Was
ist das für eine Unordnung?" Das Mädchen teilte ihm mit,
daß die Preußen und Franzosen in den Straßen kämpften und
daß dies die Ursache der Störung sei. "Das ist mir gleich,"
sagte Hegel, "das interessiert mich gar nicht ; sorge, daß ich
in Ruhe arbeiten kann." Das war am Tage der großen
Schlacht bei Jena, wo das preußische Heer von Napoleon
beinahe vernichtet wurde.

## LESSON LIII

**255. Conjunctions.** Conjunctions are either coördinative, connecting sentences of the same rank or order, or subordinative, connecting a sentence with another on which it depends.

**256. Connectives.** 1. The coördinative conjunctions proper are the common connectives, and do not affect the word order :

| | | |
|---|---|---|
| aber, but. | denn, for. | sondern, but, on the |
| allein, only, but yet. | oder, or. | contrary. |
| *Nevertheless* | und, and. | |

2. When two principal sentences connected by und have a common subject, the verb of the latter sentence usually follows the conjunction immediately :

Mein Freund ist krank und My friend is ill and has to
  muß das Haus hüten.       stay in the house.

3. If any other member of the sentence introduced by und precedes the verb, a personal pronoun must follow as subject :

Mein Freund ist krank und My friend is ill, and so he must
  deshalb muß er das Haus    stay in the house.
  hüten.

4. Denn never introduces a dependent sentence, except in indirect statements with daß omitted :

Er sagte, daß er nicht käme, He said he wasn't coming,
  denn er sei krank.         for he was ill.

5. Aber often follows the verb of its sentence (especially when another conjunction is present), and then = 'however' :

Er kommt wohl nicht, wenn er He will hardly come; if he
  aber kommt, ꝛc.            should come, however, etc.

6. Sondern corrects or contradicts a preceding negative statement :

Er wird nicht sterben, sondern He will not die, but (on the
  genesen.                    contrary) he will recover.

**257. Adverbial Conjunctions.** 1. Adverbs and adverbial phrases often have the function of a connective conjunction, and introduce a sentence coördinate with the preceding sentence ; they then throw the subject after the verb :

Er ist krank; **also** kommt er
nicht.

He is ill; hence he won't come.

2. These adverbial conjunctions may also follow the verb as ordinary adverbs :

Er ist krank; er kommt **also**
nicht.

He is ill; hence he won't come.

**258. Special Cases.** 1. Auch does not cause inversion of verb and subject when it modifies a member of the sentence which precedes the verb :

Auch mein Vater verließ mich.

Even my father forsook me.

2. Denn = 'unless' never begins a sentence :

Ich komme morgen, es sei **denn**
daß es regnet.

I shall come to-morrow unless it rains.

3. Nun in the sense of 'now' implies a relation to a preceding statement ; jetzt denotes time only :

Nun kommt es oft vor, ᛬c.

Now, it often happens, etc.

Jetzt ist es Zeit.

It is time now.

4. Adversative adverbial conjunctions, *e.g.* also, freilich, nun, ᛬c., followed by a pause (indicated by a comma), cause no inversion :

Freilich, das mag wahr sein.

Of course, that may be true.

### EXERCISE LIII

*A.* Ein gewisser Bankier brauchte einen Laufburschen an seiner Bank und hatte deshalb eine Anzeige in die Zeitung einsetzen lassen. Darauf meldeten sich am andern Tage etwa 50 Knaben. Sogleich schickte er sie alle fort, bis auf einen.

Es hatten zwar einige von ihnen sehr gute Empfehlungsbriefe,
allein er entließ sie und wählte einen, der gar keinen Brief
hatte. Da sagte ein Herr, der zufällig dabei war: „Dieser
Junge hatte doch keinen Empfehlungsbrief, und trotzdem haben
Sie ihn bevorzugt. Warum taten Sie das eigentlich?"
„Briefe hatte er freilich nicht," lautete die Antwort, „dagegen
hatte er eine Menge Empfehlungen. Ich bemerkte, zum Beispiel, daß er die Stiefel abputzte, und außerdem hob er eine
Stecknadel vom Boden auf; folglich ist er zugleich reinlich und
sorgfältig. Auch nahm er die Mütze ab und antwortete mir
schnell und richtig; daher muß er nicht nur höflich, sondern
auch klug und aufmerksam sein. Er drängte sich nicht vor, also
ist er auch bescheiden. Übrigens, ich gebe mehr auf das, was
ich an einem Menschen beobachten kann, als auf die besten
Empfehlungsbriefe."

*B*. 1. The pupils came late, and therefore had to stay in.
2. I did not keep his letter, but threw it into the waste-basket.
3. Don't come in at the front-door, but at the back-door. 4. I
can't come to-day, but I can come to-morrow. 5. My brother
saw the advertisement, and at once made application. 6. The
banker said the boy pleased him, for he was so polite. 7. Many
had good recommendations; nevertheless they didn't get the
position. 8. You have no recommendations; consequently I
can't give you the position. 9. He took off his cap, hence I am
sure he is polite. 10. Besides, he didn't press forward like the
others. 11. Moreover, I observed that he wiped his boots
when he came in. 12. Hence he must be tidy.

*C*. 1. Nearly every one knows the story of M. Laffitte, who
was a celebrated French banker. 2. When he was (still) quite
young, he applied to (bei) a Paris banker, and asked for a position in (an) his bank. 3. It is true he had letters of recommendation. 4. Nevertheless the banker dismissed him, for he
didn't need even an errand-boy. 5. As young Laffitte was going
out, however, the banker observed that he picked up a pin, which

lay on the floor. 6. Consequently he thought: "At least this boy is careful." 7. Accordingly the banker wrote him a letter in which he said: "I find that I have after all (doch) a place for you. 8. It is not a very important (wichtig) one, to be sure, but still it is better than nothing at all. 9. So then, I shall expect you to-morrow morning." 10. Naturally Laffitte accepted the place with pleasure. 11. Afterwards he became a very wealthy man. 12. He was besides one of the most celebrated ministers of France.

## LESSON LIV

**259. Subordinative Conjunctions.** 1. Those most commonly occurring are:

| | |
|---|---|
| als, as, when, than. | obgleich, (al)though. |
| als ob, als wenn, as if. | obschon, " |
| auf daß, (in order) that. | obwohl, " |
| bevor, before. | seit(dem), since. |
| bis, until. | sobald, as soon as. |
| da, as, since, when. | solange, as long as. |
| damit, in order that. | sowie, as soon as, as well as. |
| daß, that. | unterdessen, while. |
| ehe, before. | während, while. |
| falls, in case. | weil, because. |
| indem, while. | wenn, if, when. |
| indessen, " | wenn auch, (al)though, even if. |
| nachdem, after. | wenngleich, " " " " |
| ob, whether, if. | wennschon, " " " " |
| ob auch, (al)though. | wie, as, like. |
| | wiewohl, (al)though. |

2. These conjunctions connect a subordinate sentence with a principal sentence, or with another subordinate sentence, and throw the verb to the end:

| | |
|---|---|
| Ich glaube, daß er kommt. | I think he will come. |
| Ich weiß nicht, ob es wahr ist, daß er verreist. | I don't know whether it is true that he is going away. |

**260. Special Cases.** 1. 'As' in the sense of 'while' = indem (indeſſen, unterdeſſen):

| | |
|---|---|
| Er ſchlief, **indem** ich wachte. | He slept while I watched. |

2. 'As' or 'since' indicating cause = da:

| | |
|---|---|
| Er kann heute nicht kommen, **da** es regnet. | He can't come to-day, as it is raining. |

3. 'Since' as preposition = ſeit; as subordinative conjunction of time = ſeitdem (or ſeit):

| | |
|---|---|
| Er iſt ſchon **ſeit** voriger Woche hier. | He has been here since last week. |
| Ich habe ihn nicht geſehen, **ſeitdem** er angekommen iſt. | I have not seen him since he arrived. |

4. 'Since' as adverb or coördinative adverbial conjunction = ſeitdem:

| | |
|---|---|
| **Seitdem** ſchreibt er nicht. | He hasn't written since. |

5. Als = 'but' after negatives; nichts weniger als = 'anything but':

| | |
|---|---|
| Nichts **als** Unglück. | Nothing but bad luck. |
| **Nichts weniger als** reich. | Anything but rich. |

6. Indeſſen, unterdeſſen are coördinative in the sense of 'meanwhile'; subordinative in the sense of 'while':

| | |
|---|---|
| Ich wachte; **indeſſen** ſchlief mein Freund. | I watched; meanwhile my friend slept. |
| Ich wachte, **unterdeſſen** mein Freund ſchlief. | I watched while my friend slept. |

7. Ob = 'if' or 'whether' in indirect questions:

| | |
|---|---|
| Frage ihn, **ob** er müde iſt. | Ask him if he is tired. |

8. In obgleich (wenngleich, obſchon, ꝛc.), 'though,' 'although,' the latter part may be separated and placed after the subject; auch is always so separated:

| | |
|---|---|
| **Obgleich** er reich iſt. | Although he is rich. |
| **Ob** er **gleich** (auch, ꝛc.) reich iſt. | "　　"　"　" |

9. The ob or wenn may also be omitted in these conjunctions, and in als ob, als wenn; the verb then begins its sentence :

| | |
|---|---|
| Ift er gleich reich. | Though he is rich. |
| Es scheint, als käme er. | It seems as if he would come. |

10. Bevor expresses time only ; ehe also expresses preference :

| | |
|---|---|
| Ehe (bevor) es dunkel wird. | Before it gets dark. |
| Ehe ich das tue, trete ich lieber aus. | Rather than do that, I will resign. |

11. Distinguish carefully between 'after' and 'before' as prepositions and as conjunctions :

| | |
|---|---|
| Nach dem Balle. | After the ball. |
| Nachdem er fort war. | After he had gone. |
| Vor dem Abendessen. | Before supper. |
| Ehe (bevor) ich ihn sah. | Before I saw him. |

**261. Correlative Conjunctions.** 1. These conjunctions consist of two parts, the second being necessary to complete the first ; the following are the most important :

entweder . . . oder, either . . . or.
weder . . . noch, neither . . . nor.
nicht nur . . . sondern auch, not only . . . but also.
sowohl . . . als (auch), both . . . and.

bald . . . bald, at one time . . . at another ; now . . . now (then).
(eben) so . . . wie, (just) as . . . as.
defto (je) . . . desto (je, umso), the . . . the.
so . . . so, as . . . as.

2. In sentences introduced by sowohl . . . als (auch) the verb agrees with the last subject :

| | |
|---|---|
| Sowohl ich als (auch) mein Vetter ist angekommen. | Both my cousin and I have arrived. |

3. **Desto** and **je** are used interchangeably in either member of a proportional clause; the former member is subordinate, the latter principal, but with inversion of subject and verb.

**Je** (desto) eher er kommt,     The sooner he comes, the
**desto** (je) eher kann er gehen.     sooner he can go.

4. **So . . . so** introduce correlative clauses containing adjectives compared together in the positive degree, the former being subordinate:

**So** groß er ist, **so** feige ist er.     He is as cowardly as he is big.
**So** gerne ich käme, **so** un=     Gladly as I would come, it is
    möglich ist es.     quite impossible.

### EXERCISE LIV

*A.* Als ein alter Lotse eines stürmischen Tages mit anderen am Ufer des Meeres stand, sah er draußen ein großes Segel= schiff vorbeifahren. Da er erkannte, daß dasselbe falsch gesteuert ward, rief er aus: „Entweder muß die Brigg einlenken, oder sie wird am Vorgebirge scheitern. Ich muß hinaus, damit ich den Steuermann warne." „Wenn du auch hinausführest," er= widerte man ihm, „so könntest du doch nicht helfen, da dein Boot sofort kentern würde, und du versinken müßtest." „Sollte es gleich mein Leben kosten, so will ich ihm wenigstens zurufen, wie er steuern muß. Wenn es auch mein letzter Ruf ist, so bleibt mir nichts übrig, als den Versuch zu machen." Also holte er sein Sprachrohr und stieg in sein kleines Boot ein. Sobald das Segel aufgehißt war, flog das Boot pfeilschnell vor dem Sturme dahin. Im Augenblicke aber, da dasselbe aus dem Schutze des Vorgebirges herausschoß, schlug es um. Indessen hatte er noch eben dem Steuermann zurufen können: „Links müßt ihr steuern." Während die Brigg weiterfuhr, versank der heldenmütige Alte in die Tiefe. Doch war sein Heldenmut nicht vergebens gewesen, da das Schiff mit Hunderten von

Menſchenleben gerettet war.　So groß das Opfer war, ſo groß war auch der Lohn.

*B.* Oral exercise on the above.

*C.* Complete the following sentences : 1. Ich habe ihn nicht gesehen, seitdem . . . 2. Seit . . . muß meine Tante zu Hause bleiben. 3. Wir studierten, unterdessen . . . 4. Nachdem . . . , muß ich noch eine Aufgabe schreiben. 5. Wir müssen vor . . . abreisen. 6. Der Lotse versank, ehe . . . 7. Wir gehen nicht ins Konzert, da . . .

*D.* 1. It seems as if the ship must (*subj.*) be wrecked. 2. Even if the pilot goes out in his boat, perhaps he will not be able to save it after all. 3. Neither he nor his boat will ever return. 4. While the others were talking, the old man got (holen) his speaking-trumpet. 5. After he had got it, he embarked in his little boat. 6. As soon as everything was ready, he hoisted the sail. 7. Although the storm was very violent, the heroic pilot resolved to make the attempt. 8. If his boat capsizes, he will certainly lose his life. 9. He must warn the steersman, before the latter comes too near the promontory. 10. Even now it seems as if he would be (kommen) too late. 11. Meanwhile the storm became more and more violent. 12. It is anything but easy to steer a small boat through a stormy sea (See, *f.*). 13. Not only will the ship be wrecked, but also hundreds of men will perish. 14. Either the pilot must warn the steersman or the ship will be wrecked. 15. At one time it seemed as if he would succeed, at another it seemed as if his boat would capsize. 16. The greater the danger, the greater is the heroism of the pilot. 17. Before his boat sank, however, he called to the steersman through his speaking-trumpet. 18. As the latter now knew how he should steer, he saved the brig. 19. Even if the old man lost his life, still he had his reward. 20. After he was dead, his heroism was honoured by every one.

*E.* Lesestück:

> Zur Schmiede ging ein junger Held,
> Er hatt' ein gutes Schwert bestellt.
> Doch als er's wog in seiner Hand,
> Das Schwert er viel zu schwer erfand.
>
> Der alte Schmied den Bart sich streicht:
> „Das Schwert ist nicht zu schwer, noch leicht;
> Zu schwach ist euer Arm, ich mein';
> Doch morgen soll geholfen sein!"
>
> „Nein, heut'! bei aller Ritterschaft!
> Durch meine, nicht durch Feuers Kraft!"
> Der Jüngling spricht's, ihn Kraft durchdringt,
> Das Schwert er hoch in Lüften schwingt.

## LESSON LV

**262. Agreement of Verb and Subject.** 1. This agreement is, in general, the same in German as in English; for exceptions, see below.

2. With several subjects, the verb may agree with the nearest singular subject, especially if the subjects follow the verb, or are grouped together, or form a climax:

| | |
|---|---|
| Vorbei ist Wind und Regen. | Wind and rain are past. |
| Geld und Gut ist hin. | Money and wealth are gone. |
| Vermögen, Ruf, Leben steht auf dem Spiele. | Property, reputation, life are at stake. |

3. With titles of rank and compliment, the verb is often in the third plural in address and in official documents:

| | |
|---|---|
| Was wünschen gnädige Frau? | What do you wish, madam? |
| Seine Majestät haben geruht, 2c. | His Majesty has been pleased, etc. |

4. The agreement of a verb with a collective is in general the same as in English.

**263. Appositive Noun.** 1. A noun in apposition with another usually agrees with it in case:

Karl, mein jüngster Bruder, ist krank.

Charles, my youngest brother, is ill.

Die Krankheit Karls, meines jüngsten Bruders.

The illness of Charles, my youngest brother.

Ich begegnete Karl, seinem jüngsten Bruder.

I met Charles, his youngest brother.

2. The case of a noun in apposition after als or wie depends upon the sense, the indefinite article being omitted after als before an unqualified noun:

Ich kannte ihn als Knabe (= als ich ein Knabe war).

I knew him as a boy (when I was a boy).

Ich kannte ihn als Knaben (= als er ein Knabe war).

I knew him as a boy (when he was a boy).

Er hat keinen besseren Freund als mich.

He has no better friend than I.

Einem Manne wie Sie (es sind) ist nicht zu trauen.

A man like you is not to be trusted.

NOTES. — 1. Als indicates identity and wie comparison: Er kommt als König, ' He comes as a king' (and is one ); Er kommt wie ein König, ' He comes like a king' (though he may not be one).

2. For apposition in expressions of quantity, see § 112, 3; in titles and proper names, §§ 182, 188.

**264. Appositive Adjective.** 1. An uninflected adjective or participle may stand in apposition to a noun (usually the subject):

Die Pferde, vom Zuge erschreckt, gingen durch.

The horses, frightened by the train, ran away.

2. Unless the apposition is with the subject, the English appositive construction should be rendered into German by a subordinate clause:

Ich habe die Uhr verloren, die Vater mir schenkte.

I have lost the watch given me by father.

Notes. — 1. The appositive adjectival construction, frequent in English, is but sparingly used in German.

2. The appositive construction may be replaced by the attributive construction, for which see § 298.

## EXERCISE LV

*A.* 1. A large number of guests had been invited to the ball, but only [a] few were present. 2. Not more than a dozen had come at 9 o'clock. 3. Among these was the sister of (the) Count B., the German ambassador. 4. [Your] Majesty is always in the right. 5. Do you want the carriage at once, madam (gnädige Frau)? 6. The eldest daughter of Henry the Seventh, King of England, married James the Fourth, King of Scotland. 7. These were the grandparents of Mary Stuart, Queen of Scotland. 8. The city of Dresden is the capital of the kingdom of Saxony. 9. Have you ever seen William the Second, the present German Emperor? 10. I saw him as a boy, but not since he has become Emperor. 11. When I saw him, he was riding through the park with Prince Henry, his younger brother. 12. A multitude of human beings lost their lives by (durch) the earthquake. 13. The greater part of the inhabitants of Messina perished.

*B.* 1. Dear father and (dear) mother, I am sorry you have had to wait for us so long. 2. I asked you, as my oldest friend, to assist me. 3. You were right; you have no better friend than I. 4. Yes, indeed, one can always trust a friend like you. 5. The name of my brother George's teacher is Moser. 6. To do right and to be happy is one and the same [thing]. 7. The German people (Volk, *n.*) are (is) most intelligent and industrious. 8. I gave the beggar 20 pfennigs, and he went on (weiter) quite happy. 9. A dozen silver spoons costs forty marks. 10. Indignant at (über, *acc.*) his conduct, I went away at once. 11. Messrs. Schmidt and Braun have a large departmental store in Schiller Street. 12. I was not speaking with Elsa, your eldest sister, but with Clara, your youngest sister. 13. The teacher is satisfied with the exercises written by his pupils.

*C.* Lesestück : Ein Professor kam eines Abends nach Hause und sagte zu seiner Frau : "Siehst du wohl, wir Professoren sind doch nicht so vergeßlich, wie man glaubt. Ich habe meinen Regenschirm diesmal doch nicht vergessen ! " "Aber," erwiderte seine Frau, "du hast deinen Regenschirm nicht mitgenommen ; du hast ihn zu Hause gelassen."


## LESSON LVI

**265. Nominative.** 1. The nominative is the case of the subject, and is also used as a vocative.

2. Verbs indicating a state or transition, such as sein, werden, bleiben, heißen, take a predicate nominative :

| | |
|---|---|
| Er blieb Soldat. | He remained a soldier. |
| Er heißt Karl. | His name is Charles. |

NOTE. — With werden, zu is often used to indicate transition : Das Wasser wurde zu Eis, 'The water turned to ice.'

**266. Accusative.** 1. The accusative is the case of the direct object of a verb.

2. Lehren, 'teach,' takes the accusative of the person taught, as well as of the thing taught :

| | |
|---|---|
| Ich lehre sie Physik. | I am teaching them physics. |

NOTE. — When both person and thing are mentioned, unterrichten in + dat. is more usual : Ich unterrichte sie in der Physik.

3. Fragen, 'ask,' takes an accusative of the person, but only a neuter pronoun or clause as accusative of the thing :

| | |
|---|---|
| Ich will Sie etwas fragen. | I want to ask you something. |
| Er fragte, ob ich käme. | He asked if I was coming. |

**267. Predicate Accusative.** 1. Verbs of naming, calling, etc., have a second accusative with predicative force :

| | |
|---|---|
| Ich nannte ihn einen Narren. | I called him a fool. |

2. Some verbs of regarding, considering, declaring, etc., similarly take an accusative with als :

Jch betrachte ihn **als** einen Feind.    I consider him an enemy.

NOTE. — **Halten** takes **für** + acc.: Jch halte ihn **für** einen guten Mann, 'I consider him a good man.'

3. Verbs of choosing, electing, appointing, etc., usually take zu + article, but sometimes have an accusative with als :

Man wählte ihn gestern **zum**    They chose him as chairman
(als) Vorsitzenden.                yesterday.

NOTE. — The predicate acc. in all these constructions becomes a nom. in the passive: Heinrich I. wurde **der** Vogler (Fowler) genannt; Er wurde als Vorsitzender gewählt.

**268. Adverbial Accusative.** The accusative is used adverbially to express time 'when' and 'how long,' price (§ 29), and measure (§ 112, 4) ; also way or road after verbs of motion :

Welchen Weg gehen Sie ?    Which way are you going?

**269. Accusative Absolute.** The accusative is often used absolutely to form adverbial phrases, either with or without an adjective or participle :

Den Hut in der Hand.         Hat in hand.
Die Hände emporgehoben.      With hands uplifted.

### EXERCISE LVI

*A.* 1. As a child I always used to say that I meant to be a soldier.    2. I entered the army at (mit) twenty (years) as lieutenant.    3. I remained a lieutenant ten years, but now I am a captain, and I expect to become a general in the course of (the) time.    4. Among Englishmen the Duke of Wellington is called "the Iron Duke."    5. They regard him as one of the greatest generals that ever lived.    6. The Germans call Bismarck "the Iron Chancellor."    7. In 1862 Prince Bismarck

became prime minister of Prussia and in 1871 chancellor of the
German Empire.   8. He was made (ernennen) a duke by the
Emperor William II, when the latter dismissed him in 1890.
9. Ask that stranger what his name is.   10. He says his name
is Meyer, and that he is a commercial traveller.   11. Here we
must part; you must go your way, and I will go mine.
12. Our neighbour's son is anything but polite; this morning he
came in at the front-door, his hat on his head and his hands in
his pockets.

*B* 1. One of my brothers is a physician and the other is
a merchant.   2. When I was at (auf, *dat.*) the high-school,
Mr. B. taught me English and Mr. S. taught me chemistry.
3. Everybody thought Mr. B. an excellent teacher.   4. On
this account he was chosen headmaster.   5. In the elementary
schools the children are taught reading (*infin.*), writing, and
arithmetic.   6. The fool remains a fool his [whole] life long.
7. When water freezes it turns to ice; when ice melts it turns
to water again.   8. The Niagara Falls are regarded as one of
the wonders of the world.   9. As a young man Abraham Lin-
coln was a clerk in a store; later, however, he became a lawyer.   10. In the year 1860 he was elected President of the
United States.   11. In 1794 Napoleon was appointed general-
in-chief of the French army in Italy.   12. In 1799 he became
first consul and afterwards emperor.

*C.* Lesestücke: 1. Ein Fremder vom Lande auf Besuch in
London wollte einem Konzerte beiwohnen.   Er erkundigte sich
am Schalter nach dem Preise der Sitze.   "Vordersitze, zwei
Shilling; Rücksitze, einen Shilling; Programme, einen Penny."
"Na, dann geben Sie mir ein Programm: darauf sitzt sich's
schon ganz bequem," sagte der Fremde.

2. Ein Dichter sandte einen Band seiner Gedichte an einen
Bekannten und bat denselben, ihm zu sagen, was er davon halte.
Er erhielt folgende Antwort: "Ich habe Ihr Werk gelesen und
habe selten ein Buch mit größerem Vergnügen niedergelegt."

R

## LESSON LVII

**270. Genitive.** The use of the German genitive is much the same as that of the English possessive, or the objective with ' of.'

**271. Position of Genitive.** The genitive more usually follows the governing noun, unless the genitive is a person name :

Das Haus meines Freundes.    My friend's house.
Schillers Werke.    The works of Schiller.

**272. Genitive with Adjectives and Verbs.**   1. Some German adjectives govern a genitive, usually corresponding to an ' of ' construction in English:

Er ist seiner Sache gewiß.    He is sure of his case.
Unserer Achtung würdig.    Worthy of our respect.
Des Mordes schuldig.    Guilty of murder.

NOTE. — Los, 'rid of,' takes acc.: Ich möchte ihn los werden, 'I should like to get rid of him'; with voll, 'full of,' the acc. is more usual: Das Glas ist voll Wein, 'The glass is full of wine'; gewiß, 'certain of,' müde, 'tired of,' take acc. of neut. pron., but gen. of noun: Ich bin es gewiß, 'I am certain of it'; Ich bin des Wartens müde, 'I am tired of waiting.'

2. The German equivalents of many English transitive verbs take a genitive :

Er gedachte dieser Tatsache.    He mentioned this fact.
Ich bedarf Ihrer Hilfe.    I need your help.

3. Verbs of accusing, convicting, acquitting, depriving, and some others, take a genitive of the remoter object:

Man klagt ihn des Mordes an.    He is accused of murder.
Der Pflicht entbunden.    Relieved of duty.

4. Impersonal verbs expressing mental affection take a genitive of the remoter object (the cause of the emotion):

Es jammert mich seiner.    I pity him.
Mich reut meiner Sünden.    I repent of my sins.

NOTES. — 1. Some of these verbs are also used personally with the cause of the emotion as subj. : Er jammert mich ; meine Sünden reuen mich.

2. For the gen. after refl. verbs, see § 150.

**273. Adverbial Genitive.**   1. The genitive may express adverbial relations of place and manner, mostly confined to fixed phrases :

| | |
|---|---|
| Seines Weges gehen. | To go one's way. |
| Linker Hand; trocknen Fußes. | On the left hand ; dryshod. |
| Meines Erachtens. | In my opinion. |
| Zweiter Klasse reisen. | To travel second class. |
| Guter Dinge sein. | To be of good cheer. |

NOTE. — For gen. of time, see § 87.

2. The adverbial genitive with –weise is a common mode of forming adverbs of manner from adjectives :

| | |
|---|---|
| Glücklicherweise. | Fortunately. |

**274. The Dative.**   The dative is the case of the indirect object, and denotes the person for whose advantage or disadvantage a thing is or is done, corresponding not only to the English ' to ' or ' for,' but also to ' from ' :

| | |
|---|---|
| Sie gab dem Kinde Bonbons. | She gave the child sweets. |
| Er kauft mir Bücher. | He is buying books for me. |
| Er hat mir Geld gestohlen. | He stole money from me. |

**275. Dative with Adjectives.**   German equivalents of English adjectives followed by ' to ' (with some others) take the dative :

| | |
|---|---|
| Er blieb mir treu. | He remained faithful to me. |
| Sie ist dem Bruder ähnlich. | She is like her brother. |

**276. Dative with Verbs.**   The dative stands as the personal and only object after many verbs, the equivalents of which are transitive in English :

| | |
|---|---|
| Er begegnete (folgte) mir. | He met (followed) me. |
| Er hat mir gedroht. | He threatened me. |
| Wie kann ich Ihnen dienen? | How can I serve you? |
| Er wird mir beistehen. | He will assist me. |

**277. Ethical Dative.** The dative is used freely in German to denote the person who has some interest in an action or thing, and when so employed is called the 'ethical dative,' or 'dative of interest':

Tu **mir** das nicht.　　　　　　Don't do that (I tell you).

Du bist **mir** ein netter Bursch!　A nice fellow you are!

Seht **mir** nur die schönen Äpfel.　Just look at these fine apples.

NOTE. — For dat. with preps., see Lessons XXVII and XXXII; for possessive dat., see § 163.

### EXERCISE LVII

*A.* Als Benjamin Franklin ein kleiner Junge war, begegnete ihm eines kalten Morgens ein Mann, der eine Axt trug. Er klopfte dem Knaben freundlich auf die Schulter und fragte ihn, ob sein Vater einen Schleifstein habe. „Gewiß," erwiderte ihm der Kleine. „Du bist mir ein hübscher Junge," sagte der Fremde zu ihm, „willst du mir erlauben, meine Axt darauf zu schleifen?" „Seine Worte," erzählt Franklin, „schmeichelten meiner Eitelkeit und ich antwortete ihm: Recht gerne. Dann streichelte der Mann mir die Backe und bat mich, ihm ein wenig heißes Wasser zu holen. Auch das konnte ich ihm nicht abschlagen, da er mir so freundlich zu sein schien, und ich brachte ihm einen Kessel voll. Dann fuhr der Fremde fort: Möchtest du mir wohl ein paar Minuten den Schleifstein drehen? Ich machte mich törichterweise an die Arbeit und drehte, bis mir Kopf, Rücken und Arme weh taten. Als die Axt fertig war, gab mir der Mann unerwartet eine Ohrfeige und rief: Die Schulglocke hat schon längst geläutet! Mache, daß du fortkommst, kleiner Schlingel, sonst geht es dir schlecht. Diese Begebenheit," sagt Franklin weiter, „ist mir im späteren Leben jedesmal eingefallen, wenn ich merkte, daß jemand mir oder anderen zu seinem eigenen Vorteil schmeicheln wollte. Dann dachte ich mir immer: Dem Manne ist nicht zu trauen, der hat dir gewiß eine Axt zu schleifen."

*B.* Oral exercise on the above.

*C.* 1. Good children obey their parents and follow their advice. 2. This house is too expensive for me. 3. I should like to get rid of it, but nobody will buy it from me. 4. A good king is ever mindful of his subjects. 5. His subjects are not always grateful to him. 6. The emperor thanked the chancellor and relieved him of his duty. 7. It is not worth while to read such a book. 8. I am sorry that I began it. 9. In America people don't like to travel second class. 10. Is the gentleman whom we met just now an acquaintance of yours? 11. No, he is an entire stranger (ganz fremd) to me. 12. He resembles my friend Schäfer very much. 13. I should be glad of the opportunity to make his acquaintance.

*D.* 1. My neighbour has been accused of forgery. 2. I do not believe that he is capable of such a crime. 3. He is a man who is worthy of all respect. 4. I am of the same opinion, and I am convinced of (von) his innocence. 5. All his friends are certain of his acquittal. 6. They will do what they can to assist him. 7. What is the matter with you to-day? You seem to me to be very sad. 8. My father has forbidden me to attend the football match. 9. He needs my help at home. 10. I often help him mornings and evenings.

*E.* 1. I met a man one cold morning. 2. He called me a nice little boy and patted me on the shoulder. 3. "Do you think your father would allow me to grind my axe on his grindstone?" 4. "I am certain of it," I answered him. 5. "Wouldn't you like to help me to grind the axe?" 6. As he seemed to me to be so friendly, I could not refuse him this. 7. "Well, just get me a kettle full of hot water. 8. Now turn the grindstone for me a few minutes." 9. I was soon tired of the work, and my back and arms were sore. 10. But he wouldn't allow me to stop till the work was done. 11. As long as he needed my help he flattered my vanity. 12. When the axe was done he wanted to get rid of me at once. 13. So he gave me a box on the ear, and told me I should go to school. 14. The school-bell had already rung, and I went my way sadly. 15. This occurrence often came to my mind afterwards. 16. I said to myself: "Don't trust those who have an axe for you to grind. 17. They will flatter you to their own advantage."

## LESSON LVIII

**278. The Indicative Mood.** The indicative is the mood of reality and direct statement or question.

**279. The Present.** 1. This tense answers to all the English forms of the same tense (*e.g.* id) lobe = 'I praise,' 'am praising,' 'do praise'), and is used to denote action now going on, or to state a general fact or custom.

2. It is used for the imperfect to give greater vividness to historical narrative:

Plötzlich öffnet er das Tor, Suddenly he opens the gate,
und ein Tiger stürzt heraus.    and a tiger rushes out.

3. It is also used to denote what has happened and still continues, especially with schon, seit, and seitdem:

Wie lange ist er schon krank?    How long has he been ill?
Seitdem er krank ist, kann er He has not been able to sleep
nicht schlafen.    since he has been ill.

4. It is often used for the future, as sometimes in English:

Ich komme morgen wieder.    I return to-morrow.

**280. The Imperfect.** 1. This is the past tense of historical narrative; it also denotes customary, repeated, or contemporaneous action, answering to the English forms 'was doing,' 'used to do,' etc.:

In sechs Tagen schuf Gott die In six days God created the
Welt und ruhte am sie=    world, and rested on the
benten.    seventh.
Er ging jeden Tag aus.    He used to go out every day.
Er wachte, während ich schlief. He was watching while I slept.

NOTE.—'Would,' of customary action, must be rendered by the impf. or by pflegen ... zu: Er sagte oft *or* pflegte oft zu sagen, 'He would often say.'

2. It is used with schon and erst to denote what had happened and still continued:

| | |
|---|---|
| Er war schon drei Tage hier, als ich ankam. | He had been here three days when I arrived. |

**281. The Perfect.   1.** This tense indicates an event in past time, continuing up to, but not including, the present:

| | |
|---|---|
| Ich habe meine Uhr verloren. | I have lost my watch. |

2. It often answers to the English past, when referring to a period recently completed; also of an event as a separate and independent fact:

| | |
|---|---|
| Ich bin gestern ausgegangen. | I went out yesterday. |
| Gott hat uns geschaffen. | God created us. |

3. The perfect replaces the German future-perfect, as the present does the future:

| | |
|---|---|
| Ich komme, sobald ich das abgemacht habe. | I shall come as soon as I have attended to that. |

**282. The Pluperfect.** This tense is used of a past action completed before another had begun:

| | |
|---|---|
| Es war geschehen, als ich kam. | It had happened when I came. |

**283. The Future.** This tense corresponds in general to the English future, but is also used to denote probability or conjecture:

| | |
|---|---|
| Er wird heute abend kommen. | He will come this evening. |
| Er wird wohl bald hier sein. | He will probably be here soon. |

**284. The Future-Perfect.** This tense corresponds to the English future-perfect, but also expresses probability, etc.:

| | |
|---|---|
| Ich werde meine Arbeit vollendet haben, ehe sie kommen. | I shall have finished my work before they come. |
| Der Brief wird gestern angekommen sein. | No doubt the letter came yesterday. |

**285. The Subjunctive Mood.** 1. The subjunctive is the mood of indirect statement and of supposed or unreal condition.

2. The present subjunctive also replaces the missing persons of the imperative (§ 116, 1).

3. The imperfect and pluperfect subjunctive may be used to express a wish :

**Wäre ich bei Jhnen (gewesen)!**  Would that I were (had been)
                                              with you !

4. The subjunctive is used in clauses expressing purpose, especially after a past tense in the governing clause, with the conjunctions **daß, auf daß, damit** :

**Er eilte, daß (auf daß, damit)**  He hastened in order not to be
**er nicht zu spät käme.**                too late.

5. The imperfect subjunctive is sometimes used to express possibility :

**Das ginge wohl.**              That might possibly do.
**Jch dächte das wäre gut.**    I should think that might do.

NOTE.— For the use of the subjunctive in indirect statements, see § 91; for its use in conditional sentences, see § 106.

**286. Imperative Mood.** 1. The imperative expresses command or entreaty.

2. For **lassen** with imperative force, see § 117 ; for **sollen** as imperative, see § 122, 2 ; other substitutes for the imperative are the present and future indicative, and, in exclamatory clauses, the infinitive, the past participle, or an adverb or adverbial phrase :

**Du bleibst (wirst bleiben)!**    You stay !
**Alle einsteigen!**                All aboard !
**Still gestanden!**                Stand still !
**Fort mit ihm!**                   Away with him !

### EXERCISE LVIII

*A.* 1. Now I must [be] off (fort), but I return next week.
2. My birthday falls on the (auf den) 30th of (the) next
month. 3. How long has Charles been learning French?
4. He has been learning it since his fifth year. 5. The Schrö-
ders have been visiting at our house for a fortnight, but they
leave us to-morrow. 6. My cousin arrived only yesterday
morning. 7. Yesterday evening he set out again, as he had
promised to be at home to-day. 8. No doubt he has arrived
by this time. 9. I suppose he will write as soon [as] he arrives.
10. I shall have learnt my lessons before the clock strikes nine.
11. I was hastening in order that everything might be finished
before nine o'clock. 12. Some of us had finished half an hour
before the clock struck. 13. All aboard! The train starts in
two minutes.

*B.* 1. We go away to-morrow, and we don't know when we
shall be back. 2. There is a knock [at the door]; no doubt
it is the postman. 3. He comes every day at about this time.
4. My friend Schlegel has been at the University for five
years. 5. When I was at the University, I used to spend my
holidays in the Black Forest every summer. 6. No doubt you
enjoyed yourself very much. 7. Robert would always play
when he should have been working. 8. The telegraph was invented by an American named (namens) Morse. 9. Another
American named Howe invented the sewing-machine. 10. John,
you will bring Mr. B. this letter, and wait for an answer.
11. I had been only twenty-four hours in San Francisco when
the earthquake took place. 12. Only drive quickly, coachman!
Drive quickly!

*C.* 1. The express train arrives this evening at 7.45 and
leaves at 7.55. 2. I suppose you are tired after your long
journey. 3. How long have you been living in this street?
4. For the last three years. 5. Uncle had been a fortnight ill,

before he knew what was the matter with him. 6. God grant that his illness may not be serious! 7. He is not very ill; I doubt not he will get well in a few days. 8. He kept on (fort= fahren zu) working, though he should have been in bed. 9. Would that he had followed my advice! 10. He was just about to set out for Europe when he fell (werden) ill. 11. Make no noise (translate in different ways), children, till I come back

*D.* Review Exercises XXVI and XXVIII.

*E.* Lesestück:

Hallo! Die Türen aufgetan!
Hör' zu, wer hören will,
ich bin der Herbst, ein lust'ger Mann,
ich steh' nicht lange still!

Heut fahr' ich Gerst' und Hafer ein
und trag' den Erntekranz,
und abends dann beim kühlen Wein
mach' ich Musik und Tanz.

Und morgen auf die Bäum' hinauf!—
Kopf weg und aufgepaßt!
Hei! wie das rot und gelb zuhauf
herunterschlägt vom Ast!—

Ich bin der Herbst, ihr kennet mich,
ich steh' nicht gerne still.
Hallo, Hallo! drum tummle sich,
wer fröhlich werden will!

## LESSON LIX

**287.** **Infinitive without zu.** This form is used as follows:—
1. With werden to form the future tense, and with the modal auxiliaries dürfen, können, lassen, ꝛc. (§ 157).

2. With the verbs **bleiben, finden, heißen, helfen, hören, lehren, lernen, machen, nennen, sehen**:

| | |
|---|---|
| **Er blieb stehen.** | He remained standing. |
| **Ich helfe ihm arbeiten.** | I am helping him to work. |
| **Wir sahen sie kommen.** | We saw her come (coming). |

NOTE.—**Helfen, lehren, lernen** also take an infinitive with **zu**, especially with a compound tense: **Ich habe gelernt zu gehorchen,** 'I have learned to obey.'

3. In certain phrases with **gehen** and other verbs of motion:

| | |
|---|---|
| **Ich gehe (fahre) spazieren.** | I go for a walk (drive). |
| **Das Kind muß schlafen gehen.** | The child must go to bed. |
| **Ich gehe morgen fischen.** | I am going fishing to-morrow. |

**288. Infinitive with zu.** This form usually corresponds to the English infinitive with 'to,' and is used:—

1. After verbs requiring an infinitive complement, except those mentioned in § 287:

| | |
|---|---|
| **Es fängt an zu regnen.** | It is beginning to rain. |
| **Er scheint reich zu sein.** | He seems to be rich. |
| **Ich habe viel zu tun.** | I have a great deal to do. |

NOTES.—1. With most of such verbs a **daß** clause may replace the infin., and must do so unless the subject of the two clauses is the same: **Er glaubt, klug zu sein** (*or* **daß er klug ist**), 'He thinks himself clever'; **Er wünscht zu kommen,** 'He wishes to come'; **Er wünscht, daß ich komme,** 'He wishes me to come'; observe from the last example that the English construction of the acc. with infin. is inadmissible in Ger.

2. **Sagen,** 'tell,' requires a **daß** clause with **sollen**: **Sagen Sie ihm, daß er kommen soll,** 'Tell him to come.'

2. After verbs, as adverbial complement denoting purpose, usually preceded by **um**, which heads the infinitive clause:

**Er kam, um mich zu warnen.** He came to warn me.

3. After nouns, as adjectival complement:

**Er hat Lust zu bleiben.** He has a mind to stay.

4. After adjectives as adverbial complement:

**Ich bin bereit zu helfen.** I am ready to help.

NOTE. — Where зu (= 'too') precedes the adjective, um may be used: Er ift зu ftolз, um зu betteln, 'He is too proud to beg.'

5. After fein, ftehen, bleiben, with passive force :

Sie ift nirgends зu finden.     She is nowhere to be found.

Es fteht зu erwarten.     It is to be expected.

Es bleibt viel зu tun.     Much remains to be done.

NOTE. — Observe the following analogous idiom with haben : Ich habe einen Brief зu fchreiben, 'I have a letter to write.'

### EXERCISE LIX

*A.* 1. The man let Franklin turn the grindstone. 2. He would not let him stop till the axe was done. 3. If you see anybody come in, please tell me (it). 4. We heard somebody walking behind us. 5. We stood still (remained standing) at the corner to see who it was. 6. Help me to do this work, and I will help you to do your exercises. 7. My brothers wanted to go fishing, but father bade them stay at home. 8. I wish you to hear what I have to say ; do not expect me to keep silent always. 9. My father wishes me to come home before ten o'clock. 10. Schlegel, my schoolmate, has gone to Berlin to study medicine. 11. We stayed at home yesterday to receive you, but you did not come. 12. My eldest brother has had the misfortune to break an arm. 13. He is very much to be pitied. 14. I have a dozen letters to write. 15. I shall not have time enough to write them all this evening. 16. I should like to go for a walk before dinner. 17. We are always glad to see our friends.

*B.* 1. Who has left these books lying on the table? 2. John ; he says he forgot to bring them upstairs. 3. Young people should not remain sitting while older people are obliged to stand. 4. I am glad to make the acquaintance of (fennen lernen) this gentleman. 5. I have heard (say) that the celebrated statesman M. is coming here. 6. I should like to hear him speak. 7. I am sorry not to have heard him when he was here. 8. Those who have not learned to obey have not yet

learned to command.  9. Everybody believed Mr. Hartmann
to be a rich man, but he has become bankrupt.  10. Yes, he
thought himself to be richer than he really was.  11. If you
wish me to wait, write to me at once.  12. A well-known
proverb says (lauten): " Man (der Mensch) does not live to eat,
but eats to live."  13. You will be glad to learn (erfahren) that
we mean to visit you next week.  14. My sister is still too
young to go to school.  15. Are there any houses to sell in
your street?  16. Whether the prisoner is innocent of this
crime remains to be decided.

*C.* Lesestück : Eines Abends erschien ein würdiger Bürger
auf einer Sternwarte und sagte, er sei gekommen, um den Mond
durchs Teleskop zu sehen.  " Kommen Sie nach fünf Stunden
wieder ; der Mond geht erst gegen zwei Uhr morgen früh auf,
und jetzt ist es doch erst neun Uhr."  " Das weiß ich recht gut,"
antwortete der Besuch.  " Deshalb komme ich ja eben jetzt ;
wenn er erst aufgegangen ist, kann ich ihn auch ohne Teleskop
sehen."

# LESSON LX

**289**. **Substantival Infinitive.**  1. Any infinitive may be used
in the singular as a neuter noun of the Maler model, and takes
a capital :

Sein lautes Reden ist lästig.     His loud talking is annoying.

NOTE. — Such an infinitive has the force of the English form in –ing,
denoting an act, *e.g.* das Lesen, ' (the act of) reading,' or of an Eng.
noun, *e.g.* das Leben, ' life.'

2. This infinitive (with or without adjuncts) often stands as
the subject of a verb, preferably with zu, which must be used
when es precedes the principal verb :

Gute Freunde zu haben ist     To have good friends is better
  besser, als reich zu sein.        than being rich.
Es ist angenehm, gelobt zu     It is pleasant to be praised.
  werden.

**290. Infinitive with Prepositions.** 1. Only the prepositions um, (an)ſtatt, and ohne can govern an infinitive (with zu) directly, and then only with identical subject :

| | |
|---|---|
| Um mich zu beſuchen. | (In order) to visit me. |
| Anſtatt länger zu bleiben. | Instead of staying longer. |
| Ohne ein Wort zu ſagen. | Without saying a word. |

2. Observe from the above that the English gerund, or verbal in –ing, answers to this German construction, except after um.

3. The English gerund is a noun, and may stand as subject or object ; it must be carefully distinguished from the English present participle, which is an adjective, and which must refer to some noun, expressed or understood, *e.g.* Fishing (gerund subj.) is exciting (participial adj.) ; I like fishing (gerund obj.) ; I am tired of fishing (gerund obj. of prep.).

4. The preposition governing an English gerund is not always required in German, and the gerund is then rendered by an infinitive :

| | |
|---|---|
| Die Gabe, gut zu ſprechen. | The gift of speaking well. |
| Er hat Urſache, das zu ſagen. | He has cause for saying that. |

5. But when the German construction requires a preposition, this preposition is put into the governing clause and preceded by da(r), which represents the governed infinitive or daß clause :

| | |
|---|---|
| Profeſſor M. findet Vergnügen daran, Schach zu ſpielen. | Professor M. finds pleasure in playing chess. |
| Das Glück beſteht darin, zu= frieden zu ſein. | Happiness consists in being contented. |
| Ich habe nichts dagegen, daß das Haus verkauft wird. | I have no objection to the house being sold. |

6. A gerund preceded in English by a noun in the possessive, or by a possessive adjective, must be rendered by a daß clause :

Ich habe nichts **dagegen, daß**    I have no objection to your
   Ihr Bruder bleibt.          brother's remaining.
Wir verlassen uns **darauf, daß**    We rely on your coming.
   Sie kommen.

7. When the gerund governed by a preposition expresses an adverbial relation, it must be expanded into a subordinate sentence :

Als er uns sah, lief er fort.    On seeing us, he ran away.
Indem wir andere überreden,    In persuading others, we per-
   überreden wir uns selbst.      suade ourselves.

**291. Interrogative Infinitive.** The English infinitive in indirect questions must be replaced in German by a finite clause :

Ich weiß was ich tun soll.    I know what to do.
Sage mir, wo ich stehen soll.    Tell me where to stand.

**292. Elliptical Infinitive.** 1. The infinitive is used, as in English, in various elliptical constructions :

Warum mich **wecken?**    Why waken me?
Danach **zu urteilen.**    To judge by that.

2. For the elliptical infinitive with imperative force, see § 286, 2.

### EXERCISE LX

*A.* 1. The habit of speaking distinctly is most important. 2. You cannot neglect your work without my knowing it. 3. Before leaving (the) town we must visit our old friend Schulz. 4. It would be a pity to go away without having visited him. 5. I hope nothing will prevent our visiting him to-morrow. 6. If you go swimming without your father's knowing it, he will be very angry. 7. Little Charles was drowned yesterday while swimming in the lake. 8. We were punished for laughing in the class. 9. It is better to think without speaking than to speak without thinking. 10. You will finally succeed in learning French.   11. We learn to speak French while speaking French.   12. His being rich is no excuse for his wasting his money.   13. I have so much to do that I don't know where to begin.   14. I am tired of reading ; it is time to retire to rest.

*B.*   1. Did you ever hear the proverb : "Speech (speaking) is silver ; silence (being silent) is gold " ?   2. A certain man called his sons to him (*refl.*) before dying and told them that there was a treasure buried in his field.   3. After his death they began digging everywhere, without, however, finding the treasure.   4. One of them finally guessed what his father meant.   5. "Since digging the ground," said he, "we have better crops, and that is what father meant."   6. Don't allow yourself to be disturbed by my coming ; don't stop writing.   7. After writing this letter, I shall be able to talk with you.   8. You say that the matter is quite clear, but your saying so makes no difference.   9. Our teacher would always insist on our writing a German exercise every day.   10. Don't make any mistakes in copying your exercise.   11. Instead of scolding us, please show us how to avoid the mistakes.   12. Oh no ! Instead of my helping you always, you must learn to help yourselves.

*C.* Lesestück :

Ich ging im Walde
So für mich hin,
Und nichts zu suchen,
Das war mein Sinn.

Im Schatten sah ich
Ein Blümchen stehn,
Wie Sterne leuchtend
Wie Äuglein schön.

Ich wollt' es brechen,
Da sagt' es fein :
„Soll ich zum Welken
Gebrochen sein?"

Ich grub's mit allen
Den Würzlein aus,
Zum Garten trug ich's
Am hübschen Haus

Und pflanzt' es wieder
Am stillen Ort,
Nun zweigt es immer
Und blüht so fort.

—Goethe.

## LESSON LXI

**293. Participles.** 1. The verb has three participial forms, namely, the present, the past, and the future passive (§ 296).

2. The past participle is a regular part of the compound tenses of the verb, and of the passive voice. For the adjectival use of participles, see below.

**294. Present and Past Participles.** 1. When used as adjectives, they are variable or invariable like ordinary adjectives :

| | |
|---|---|
| Das schlafende Kind. | The sleeping child. |
| Meine verehrten Eltern. | My honoured parents. |
| Sie ist befriedigt. | She is satisfied. |

2. Like other adjectives, they may be used substantively (§ 68) :

Der Reisende; die Verwandten.   The traveller; the relatives.

3. They are also used as adverbs :

| | |
|---|---|
| Er ist bedeutend größer. | He is considerably taller. |
| Ausgezeichnet gelehrt. | Remarkably learned. |

NOTE. — For appositive participle, see § 264.

4. The participle must follow all its adjuncts, and come at the end of the phrase :

Bis auf den höchsten Grad   Enraged to the highest degree.
entrüstet.

**295. Past Participle Idioms.** 1. The past participle is used after kommen to denote the manner of the action :

Er kam gelaufen.   He came running.

2. It occurs in absolute constructions, with or without a substantive (usually in the accusative) :

| | |
|---|---|
| Meinen Bruder ausgenommen. | My brother excepted. |
| Frisch gewagt, halb gewonnen. | Well begun, half done. |

NOTE. — For the imperative use, see § 286, 2.

S

**296. Future Passive Participle.** It has the form of the present participle preceded by зu, is formed from transitive verbs only, and is always used attributively :

Eine zu lobende Handlung.　An action to be praised.

**297. Participle of Time and Cause.** 1. The English present participle often has the force of an adverbial clause of time or cause, and when so used is rendered in German by a sentence introduced by a subordinative conjunction.

2. The conjunctions thus used to express time are da, als, 'when,' indem, während, 'while':

Als (da) ich ihn kommen sah, Seeing him coming, I went to
ging ich ihm entgegen.　　meet him.

Indem er sich sammelte, fuhr Recovering himself, he con-
er fort.　　　　　　　　tinued.

Ich traf ihn, als (während, I met him when (while) travel-
indem) ich in Europa reiste.　ling in Europe.

3. For time, expressed by the English perfect participle, nachdem, 'after,' or als, 'when,' is always used, followed by the pluperfect :

Nachdem (als) ich den Brief Having read the letter, I threw
gelesen hatte, warf ich ihn　it away.
weg.

4. To express cause, da, indem, 'as,' 'since,' or weil, 'be-cause,' is used :

Da ich ihn nicht gefunden hatte, Not having found him, I went
ging ich fort.　　　　　　away.

Indem ich hoffe, Sie zu sehen. Hoping to see you.

Weil er ehrlich ist, kann man Being honest, he is to be
ihm trauen.　　　　　　trusted.

**298. The Adjectival Participle.** 1. The English present participle with the force of a relative clause is rendered in German by a relative clause :

Jd) begegnete einer Frau, die    I met a woman carrying a
ein Kind trug.                    child.

Ein Mann, der vorbeiging,        A man passing by bowed to
grüßte mich.                      me.

2. A German participle used attributively very commonly
replaces the construction employed in the last example above :

Ein **vorbeigehender** Mann      A man passing by bowed to
grüßte mich.                      me.

NOTE. — Attributive participles and adjectives immediately precede the
substantive qualified. This construction is very common in modern jour-
nalistic style : Die Stadt Algier liegt an der Westseite einer geräumigen,
von Kap Pescada im Westen und Kap Matifu im Osten begrenzten, nach
Norden geöffneten herrlichen Bucht, 'The city of Algiers lies on the west
side of a spacious and magnificent bay, bounded by Cape Pescada on the
west and Cape Matifu on the east, and open towards the north.'

### EXERCISE LXI

*A*. 1. The lost ring has been found. 2. The view from our
veranda is charming. 3. Sleeping dogs do not bite. 4. Clara
is a charming little girl. 5. The child stood weeping before
the closed door. 6. A ruined castle stands to the left on the
hill. 7. Our fellow-travellers were all Englishmen. 8. Let
us not think of the past. 9. A soldier came riding along
(daher). 10. Turning to me, the beggar asked for alms.
11. He went away complaining that I had given him very little.
12. Believing what my friends said, I followed their advice.
13. Not having had experience enough, I knew not what
to do. 14. The bad news received yesterday has made us all
very sad. 15. I have found all the letters, yours included.

*B*. 1. This young man has already earned a considerable
sum of money. 2. Honoured Sir : Your long-expected letter
has arrived at last. 3. Our professor is a very learned man.
4. The thief came in through a broken window. 5. We have
not had time to make our intended excursion (in)to the woods.
6. Smiling, he began to read the letter, but before finishing it

he was raging.    7. The coachman came driving up (ɦeran) as
we were at the door.    8. I shall show you the mistakes to be
avoided.    9. It is to be regretted that you did not ask me for
advice before beginning this exercise.    10. Having no hope of
passing the examination, I went home.    11. The famine occa-
sioned by war is often worse (ſdjlimm) than war itself.    12. He
continued praying, his hands raised to heaven.

*C.* On a certain occasion, Frederick the Great found that the
enemy was opposed to him with a superior force.    Being very
anxious regarding (um) the outcome of the battle, which was to
take place on the next day, he resolved to make a round through
the camp by night.    This he did in order to ascertain the state
of mind prevailing among his troops.    While doing so (that)
he observed a soldier seeking to avoid him, and acting generally (überɦaupt) in (auf) a suspicious manner.    Halting, he
called the soldier to him (*refl.*).    The latter, seeing no possibility of escaping, stood still, saluting.    " Where are you (Ér)
going?" asked the king, looking him in the face.    "To tell
the truth, [Your] Majesty, I was just on the point of deserting."
Instead of calling the guard to arrest the soldier, the king said :
"Just try (use Ér) your luck once more with me.    In case of
our losing, we will desert together."

*D.* Lesestück : Die Mäuse hatten einmal Krieg mit den Frö-
schen.    Nach vielen blutigen Schlachten wählte endlich jeder
Teil seinen größten Helden, um den Streit in einem Zweikampfe
auszumachen.    Als alles fertig war, traten die beiden Kämpfer
auf.    Sie griffen einander mit der größten Tapferkeit an.    Der
Frosch teilte Ohrfeigen aus wie ein Bär.    Die Maus biß wie ein
Löwe.    In dieser Kampfwut bemerkten sie aber nicht, daß
ein hungriger Habicht über ihnen schwebte.    Plötzlich stürzt
dieser auf die Kämpfenden herab.    Er packt mit der rechten
Kralle den Frosch, mit der linken die Maus.    Da liefen alle
Zuschauer davon.    Der Krieg hatte ein Ende.

# APPENDIX.

## *A.* REFERENCE LISTS OF NOUNS.

*N.B.* In the following lists words of less common occurrence have been omitted.

### 1. Masculine monosyllables of **Hund** model (§ 33).

Aal, eel.
Arm, arm.
Bord, shelf.
Docht, wick.
Dolch, dagger.
Dom, cathedral.
Grad, degree.
Halm, blade (*grass*).
Huf, hoof.

Hund, dog.
Lachs, salmon.
Laut, sound.
Mord, murder.
Ort, district.
Pfad, path.
Pol, pole.
Puls, pulse.
Punkt, point.

Schuh, shoe.
Stoff, material.
Strauß, ostrich.
Tag, day.
Takt, bar (*music*).
Thron, throne.
Zoll, inch.

NOTE. — The above list contains only nouns with stem vowel a, o, u, au

### 2. Neuter monosyllables of **Hund** model (§ 33).

Band, tie.
Beet, garden-bed.
Beil, hatchet.
Bein, leg.
Boot,[1] boat.
Brod, loaf.
Ding, thing.
Erz, ore.
Fell, hide.
Fest, festival.
Floß,[2] raft.
Gift, poison.
Haar, hair.
Heer, army.
Heft, handle.
Jahr, year.
Joch, yoke.

Knie, knee.
Kreuz, cross.
Land, province.
Los, lot.
Maß, measure.
Meer, sea.
Netz, net.
Öl, oil.
Paar, pair.
Pferd, horse.
Pfund, pound.
Pult, desk.
Recht, right.
Reich, empire.
Riff, reef.
Roß, horse.
Salz, salt.

Schaf, sheep.
Schiff, ship.
Schwein, pig.
Seil, rope.
Sieb, sieve.
Spiel, game.
Stück, piece.
Tau, cable.
Teil, share.
Tier, animal.
Tor, gate.
Werk, work.
Zelt, tent.
Zeug, stuff.
Ziel, goal.

[1] Also Böte.       [2] Also with umlaut.

### 3. Feminines of **Hand** model (§ 33).

| | | |
|---|---|---|
| Angst, anguish. | Haut, skin. | Naht, seam. |
| Ausflucht, evasion. | Kluft, cleft. | Not, need. |
| Art, axe. | Kraft, strength. | Nuß, nut. |
| Bank, bench. | Kuh, cow. | Schnur, string. |
| Braut, bride. | Kunst, art. | Stadt, town. |
| Brust, breast. | Luft, air. | Wand, wall. |
| Faust, fist. | Lust, desire. | Wurst, sausage. |
| Frucht, fruit. | Macht, power. | Zunft, guild. |
| Gans, goose. | Magd, maid-servant. | Zusammenkunft, meet- |
| Gruft, grave. | Maus, mouse. | ing. |
| Hand, hand. | Nacht, night. | |

And nouns ending in –nis and –sal.

### 4. Masculines of **Dorf** model (§ 43).

| | | |
|---|---|---|
| Bösewicht,[1] villain. | Mann, man. | Wald, forest. |
| Geist, spirit. | Ort, place. | Wurm, worm. |
| Gott, god. | Rand, edge. | |
| Leib, body. | Vormund, guardian. | |

And nouns in –tum.

[1] Also of Hund model.

### 5. Nouns of **Vater** model (§ 43).

| | | |
|---|---|---|
| der Acker, field. | der Hafen, harbour. | der Sattel, saddle. |
| der Apfel, apple. | der Hammer, hammer. | der Schnabel, beak. |
| der Boden, floor, soil. | das Kloster, cloister. | der Schwager, brother- |
| der Bogen,[1] bow. | der Laden, shop. | in-law. |
| der Bruder, brother. | der Mantel, cloak. | die Tochter, daughter. |
| der Faden, thread. | die Mutter, mother. | der Vater, father. |
| der Garten, garden. | der Nagel, nail. | der Vogel, bird. |
| der Graben, ditch. | der Ofen, stove. | |

[1] Also of Maler model.

### 6. Nouns of **Graf** model (§ 53).

| | | |
|---|---|---|
| Bär, bear. | Herr,[1] master. | Pfau, peacock. |
| Bursch, lad. | Hirt, herdsman. | Prinz, prince. |
| Christ, Christian. | Husar,[2] hussar. | Spatz, sparrow. |
| Fürst, prince. | Mensch, man. | Tor, fool. |
| Gesell, fellow. | Narr, fool. | Vorfahr, ancestor. |
| Graf, count. | Nerv, nerve. | |
| Held, hero. | Ochs, ox. | |

[1] Sing. adds –n only.  [2] Also of Ohr model

### 7. Nouns of 𝕹𝖆𝖒𝖊 model (§ 54).

Buchstabe, letter of alphabet.
Gedanke, thought.
Name, name.

Fels,[1] rock.
Funke(n),[2] spark.
Same(n),[2] seed.

Friede(n),[2] peace.
Glaube(n),[2] faith.
Schade(n),[3] injury.

Haufe, heap.
Wille, will.

And das Herz, heart, G. Herzens, A. Herz.

[1] Also Felsen (Maler model).  [2] Also of Maler model.
[3] Also of Vater model.

### 8. Nouns of 𝕺𝖊𝖙𝖙𝖊𝖗 model (§ 54).

das Auge, eye.
der Konsul, consul.

der Bauer,[1] peasant.
der Nachbar, neighbour.

das Ende, end.
der Pantoffel,[2] slipper.

der Gevatter, godfather.
der Stachel, sting.

[1] Also adds –n throughout sing.  [2] Also Maler model.

### 9. Nouns of 𝕺𝖍𝖗 model (§ 54).

der Ahn, ancestor.
der Mast, mast.
der Strahl, beam.

das Bett, bed.
das Ohr, ear.
der Untertan,[1] subject.

der Forst, forest.
der Schmerz, pain.
der Zins, interest.

das Hemd, shirt.
der See, lake.

der Husar,[1] hussar.
der Staat, state.

[1] Also of Graf model.

## B. REFERENCE LISTS OF PREPOSITIONS.

### 1. Prepositions with the Genitive.

The prepositions governing the genitive are chiefly nouns used adverbially; they are easily recognizable because, with a few exceptions, the corresponding English locution is followed by 'of.' The following are those of common occurrence:

anstatt, statt, instead of.
oberhalb, above.

außerhalb, outside of.
um . . . willen, for the sake of.

diesseit, on this side of.
ungeachtet, in spite of.

halb(en), halber, for the sake of.
unterhalb, below.

inmitten, in the midst of.
unweit, unfern, not far from.

innerhalb, inside of.
vermittelst, by means of.

jenseit, on the other side of.
vermöge, by means of.

kraft, by virtue of.
während, during.

laut, in accordance with.
wegen, on account of.

mittelst, by means of.

NOTES. — 1. Halb(en), halber always follows the gen. 2. With um ... willen the gen. stands between um and willen. 3. Ungeachtet, wegen, zufolge may precede or follow the gen. 4. Before halb(en), wegen, ... willen, the gens. of the pers. prons. have the forms meinet-, deinet-, seinet-, unsert-, euret-, ihret-, Ihret-: meinethalb(en), unsert= wegen, um Ihretwillen. 5. To the above list may be added a number of adjectival abverbs, such as: gelegentlich, 'on the occasion of'; hinsichtlich, 'in regard of'; unbeschadet, 'notwithstanding.'

## 2. Additional Prepositions with the Dative.

entgegen, contrary to.
gleich, like.
nächst, zunächst, next to.

nebst, samt, together with.
zuwider, contrary to.

NOTE. — Entgegen, zunächst usually follow the dat.; gleich may precede or follow.

## 3. Prepositions with Varying Case.

binnen, within (of time), gen. or dat.
entlang, längs, along, gen., dat., or acc.
gemäß, agreeably to, gen. or dat.
ob, above, at, concerning, gen. or dat.
trotz, in spite of, gen. ; as well as, dat.
zufolge, in consequence of, gen. or dat.

NOTES. — 1. Entlang, längs, may precede or follow. 2. Gemäß takes gen. or dat. when it precedes; dat. only when it follows. 3. Zufolge takes gen. when it precedes; dat. when it follows.

## 4. Equivalents of English Prepositions.

English and German differ widely in the idiomatic use of prepositions. For convenient reference, the most commonly occurring English prepositions are given below in alphabetical order with examples showing their German equivalents.

### About.

| | |
|---|---|
| Haben Sie Geld bei sich? | Have you money about you? |
| Was weißt du von ihm (über ihn)? | What do you know about him? |
| Sie stritten sich ums Geld. | They quarrelled about the money. |
| Ungefähr (etwa) M. 10. | About (nearly) 10 marks. |

## At.

| | |
|---|---|
| In der Schule (Kirche). | At (in) school (church). |
| Im Theater (Konzert). | At the theatre (concert). |
| Am Tische; bei Tisch. | At the table; at table. |
| An der Tür. | At the door. |
| Zu (in) Paris. | At (in) Paris. |
| Auf dem Markte (Balle). | At the market (ball). |
| Auf der Post. | At the post-office. |
| Er studiert auf der Universität. | He is studying at the University. |
| Er ist Professor an der Universität. | He is a professor at the University. |
| Auf alle Fälle. | At all events. |
| In diesem Augenblick. | At this moment. |
| Um halb vier. | At half-past three. |
| Bei Tagesanbruch; bei Nacht. | At daybreak; at night. |
| Zur rechten Zeit (Stunde). | At the right time (hour). |
| Zu Weinachten (Ostern). | At Christmas (Easter). |
| Tee zu M. 5 das Pfund. | Tea at 5 marks a pound. |
| Um den (zum) halben Preis. | At half (the) price. |

## By.

| | |
|---|---|
| Er ward von Räubern getötet. | He was slain by robbers. |
| Durch die Post. | By post. |
| Durch Krankheit verhindert. | Prevented by illness. |
| Mit der Eisenbahn reisen. | To travel by rail. |
| Bei (an) der Hand ergreifen. | To seize by the hand. |
| Bei Tageslicht; bei Nacht. | By daylight; by night. |
| Zu Land; zu Schiff. | By land; by ship. |

## For.

| | |
|---|---|
| Ich tat es für ihn. | I did it for him. |
| Schönes Wetter zum Spazieren. | Fine weather for walking. |
| Er reist zum Vergnügen. | He travels for pleasure. |
| Zum Beispiel. | For example. |
| Er ist seit zwei Tagen hier. | He has been here for two days. |
| Ich verreise auf acht Tage. | I am going away for a week. |
| Er war einen Monat hier. | He was here for a month. |
| Fürs erste. | For the present. |
| Zum zweiten Male. | For the second time. |
| Zum Geburtstag. | For a birthday present. |

### In.

| | |
|---|---|
| Im Hauſe; in einer Woche. | In the house; in a week. |
| Im Himmel; am Himmel. | In heaven; in the sky. |
| Des Abends. | In the evening. |
| Auf der Straße. | In the street. |
| Auf dem Lande. | In the country. |
| Auf dieſe Weiſe. | In this manner. |
| Auf die Dauer. | In the long run. |
| Unter Karl V. | In the reign of Charles V. |
| Zu Wagen; bei kaltem Wetter. | In a carriage; in cold weather. |
| Meiner Meinung nach. | In my opinion. |
| Zum Gedächtniß (zu Ehren). | In memory (honour) of. |

### Of.

| | |
|---|---|
| Ich ſpreche von ihm. | I speak of him. |
| Der König von Spanien. | The king of Spain. |
| Einer von meinen Freunden. | One of my friends. |
| Der Vater von vier Knaben. | The father of four boys. |
| Zur Tür hinaus. | Out of (at) the door. |
| Die Schlacht bei Prag, am Nil. | The battle of Prague, of the Nile. |
| Was ſoll aus mir werden? | What will become of me? |

### On.

| | |
|---|---|
| Auf dem Tiſche (der Bank). | On the table (the bench). |
| Auf der Erde; auf Erden. | On the ground; on earth. |
| Auf der Reiſe; am Finger. | On the journey; on the finger. |
| Den (am) zweiten März. | On the second of March. |
| Die Schiffe auf dem Fluſſe. | The ships on the river. |
| New York liegt am Hudſon und am Meere. | New York is on the Hudson and on the sea. |
| Zu Pferd; zu Fuß. | On horseback; on foot. |
| Mit Fleiß. | On purpose. |
| Im Begriffe. | On the point of. |
| Bei dieſer Gelegenheit. | On this occasion. |
| Unter dieſer Bedingung. | On this condition. |

### To.

| | |
|---|---|
| Ich will zum Vater gehen. | I will go to my father. |
| Nach Europa; nach London. | To Europe; to London. |
| Gehe in die (zur) Stadt. | Go to the city. |

| | |
|---|---|
| **Er** geht **aufs** Land. | He goes to the country. |
| Gehst du **zur** Schule? | Are you going to school? |
| Er ging **ins** (**zum**) Theater. | He went to the theatre. |
| Gehe **ans** (**zum**) Fenster. | Go to the window. |
| **Auf** den (**zum**) Markt gehen. | To go to the market. |
| **Auf** die Universität gehen. | To go to the University (as a student). |
| **Zur** Universität gehen. | To go to the University (building). |

## With.

| | |
|---|---|
| **Mit** einem Stock schlagen. | To strike with a stick. |
| **Von** ganzem Herzen. | With all my heart. |
| **In** dieser Absicht. | With this intention. |

### 5. Prepositions with Verbs, Adjectives, and Nouns.

The object of many verbs, as well as the complement of nouns and adjectives corresponding with them in signification, is indicated by prepositions. The proper use of prepositions in such cases must be learnt from practice and from the dictionary; but below is given, for convenient reference, the regimen of particular classes of verbs, etc., which differ most widely from their English equivalents.

### At, of.

Of joy, vexation, wonder, etc. = über + accusative:

| | |
|---|---|
| Wir ärgern uns **über** ihn. | We are vexed at him. |
| Er klagt **über** die Hitze. | He complains of the heat. |
| Er lachte **über** uns. | He laughed at us. |
| Ihr Erstaunen **über** die Nachricht. | Her surprise at the news. |

Note. — **Böse** takes **auf** + acc. of person: Ich war böse auf ihn, 'I was angry at him.'

### For.

1. Of expectation, etc. = **auf** + accusative:

| | |
|---|---|
| Sie war nicht **darauf** gefaßt. | She was not prepared for that. |
| Wir hoffen **auf** gutes Wetter. | We hope for good weather. |
| Er wartete **auf** Sie. | He was waiting for you. |

2. Of longing, inquiry, etc. = **nach**:

| | |
|---|---|
| Durst **nach** Weisheit. | Thirst for wisdom. |
| Sie sehnt sich **nach** Ruhe. | She longs for rest. |
| Suche **nach** der Wahrheit. | Search for the truth. |

3. Of entreaty, etc. = **um**:

| | |
|---|---|
| Ich bat ihn **um** Geld. | I asked him for money. |
| Mein Kummer **um** ihn. | My concern for him. |

## From.

Of protection, etc. = **vor** + dative:

| | |
|---|---|
| Rette uns **vor** dieser Schmach. | Save us from this disgrace. |

## In.

1. Of plenty, want, etc. = **an** + dative:

| | |
|---|---|
| Arm **am** Beutel. | Poor in purse. |

2. Of confidence, etc. = **auf** + accusative:

| | |
|---|---|
| Vertrauen Sie **auf** mich. | Trust in me. |

## Of.

1. Of plenty, want, doubt, etc. = **an** + dative:

| | |
|---|---|
| Es fehlt **an** Männern. | There is lack of men. |
| Mangel **an** Geld. | Want of money. |
| Ich verzweifle **am** Erfolg. | I despair of success. |

2. Of remembrance, etc. = **an** + accusative:

| | |
|---|---|
| Ich denke **an** Sie. | I am thinking of you. |
| Erinnere ihn **daran**. | Remind him of it. |

3. Of suspicion, envy, pride, etc. = **auf** + accusative:

| | |
|---|---|
| Er ist argwöhnisch **auf** mich. | He is suspicious of me. |
| Er ist **auf** mich neidisch. | He is envious of me. |
| Ich bin stolz **auf** meinen Sohn. | I am proud of my son. |

4. Of fear, etc. = **vor** + dative:

| | |
|---|---|
| Furcht **vor** dem Blitze. | Fear of lightning. |
| Mich graut **vor** dem Tode. | I am in dread of death. |

5. Of disease, etc. = **an** + dative:

| | |
|---|---|
| **Am** Fieber erkrankt. | Sick of a fever. |

## To.

1. Of address, etc. = **an** + accusative:

| | |
|---|---|
| Ich schreibe **an** einen Freund. | I am writing to a friend. |
| Ein **an** mich adressierter Brief. | A letter addressed to me |
| Wenden Sie sich **an** ihn. | Apply to him. |

2. After many nouns and adjectives signifying an affection of the mind = **gegen**:

| | |
|---|---|
| Barmherzig **gegen** die Armen. | Merciful to the poor. |
| Er ist freundlich **gegen** mich. | He is friendly to me. |
| Sei nachsichtig **gegen** ihn. | Be indulgent to him. |

3. Of attention = **auf** + accusative:

| | |
|---|---|
| Gib **auf** meine Worte acht. | Pay attention to my words. |

## C. VERB PARADIGMS.

*N.B.* In the paradigms no special English forms are given for the subjunctive, as such forms are only occasionally correct, and often misleading.

### 1. Auxiliaries of Tense.

#### Haben, to have.

PRINCIPAL PARTS: haben, hatte, gehabt.

##### PRESENT.

| *Indicative.* | | *Subjunctive.* | |
|---|---|---|---|
| I have, etc. | | | |
| ich habe | wir haben | ich habe | wir haben |
| du hast | ihr habt | du habest | ihr habet |
| er hat | sie haben | er habe | sie haben |

##### IMPERFECT.

| | | | |
|---|---|---|---|
| I had, etc. | | | |
| ich hatte | wir hatten | ich hätte | wir hätten |
| du hattest | ihr hattet | du hättest | ihr hättet |
| er hatte | sie hatten | er hätte | sie hätten |

##### PERFECT.

I have had, etc.

| | |
|---|---|
| ich habe gehabt | ich habe gehabt |
| du hast gehabt | du habest gehabt |
| er hat gehabt | er habe gehabt |
| wir haben gehabt | wir haben gehabt |
| ihr habt gehabt | ihr habet gehabt |
| sie haben gehabt | sie haben gehabt |

## PLUPERFECT.

| *Indicative.* | | *Subjunctive.* |
|---|---|---|

I had had, etc.

| | |
|---|---|
| ich hatte gehabt | ich hätte gehabt |
| du hattest gehabt | du hättest gehabt |
| er hatte gehabt | er hätte gehabt |
| wir hatten gehabt | wir hätten gehabt |
| ihr hattet gehabt | ihr hättet gehabt |
| sie hatten gehabt | sie hätten gehabt |

## FUTURE.

I shall have, etc.

| | |
|---|---|
| ich werde haben | ich werde haben |
| du wirst haben | du werdest haben |
| er wird haben | er werde haben |
| wir werden haben | wir werden haben |
| ihr werdet haben | ihr werdet haben |
| sie werden haben | sie werden haben |

## FUTURE PERFECT.

I shall have had, etc.

| | |
|---|---|
| ich werde gehabt haben | ich werde gehabt haben |
| du wirst gehabt haben | du werdest gehabt haben |
| er wird gehabt haben | er werde gehabt haben |
| wir werden gehabt haben | wir werden gehabt haben |
| ihr werdet gehabt haben | ihr werdet gehabt haben |
| sie werden gehabt haben | sie werden gehabt haben |

## CONDITIONAL.

| *Simple.* | *Compound.* |
|---|---|
| I should have, etc. | I should have had, etc. |
| ich würde haben | ich würde gehabt haben |
| du würdest haben | du würdest gehabt haben |
| er würde haben | er würde gehabt haben |
| wir würden haben | wir würden gehabt haben |
| ihr würdet haben | ihr würdet gehabt haben |
| sie würden haben | sie würden gehabt haben |

| IMPERATIVE. | INFINITIVES. | PARTICIPLES. |
|---|---|---|
| Have, etc. | *Pres.*, haben, to have. | *Pres.*, habend, having. |
| habe | *Perf.*, gehabt haben, to | *Past*, gehabt, had. |
| habt | have had. | |
| haben Sie | | |

*for all motion towards*
*verbs*

**Sein,** to be.  **Werden,** to become.

PRINCIPAL PARTS: sein, war, gewesen.
"       "    werden, ward (wurde), geworden.

| PRESENT. | | PRESENT. | |
|---|---|---|---|
| *Indicative.* | *Subjunctive.* | *Indicative.* | *Subjunctive.* |
| I am, etc. | | I become, etc. | |
| ich bin | ich sei | ich werde | ich werde |
| du bist | du seiest | du wirst | du werdest |
| er ist | er sei | er wird | er werde |
| wir sind | wir seien | wir werden | wir werden |
| ihr seid | ihr seiet | ihr werdet | ihr werdet |
| sie sind | sie seien | sie werden | sie werden |

| IMPERFECT. | | IMPERFECT. | |
|---|---|---|---|
| I was, etc. | | I became, etc. | |
| ich war | ich wäre | ich ward (wurde) | ich würde |
| du warst | du wärest | du wardst | du würdest |
| er war | er wäre | (wurdest) | er würde |
| wir waren | wir wären | er ward (wurde) | wir würden |
| ihr wart | ihr wäret | wir wurden | ihr würdet |
| sie waren | sie wären | ihr wurdet | sie würden |
| | | sie wurden | |

| PERFECT. | | PERFECT. | |
|---|---|---|---|
| I have been, etc. | | I have become, etc. | |
| ich bin ⎫ | ich sei ⎫ | ich bin ⎫ | ich sei ⎫ |
| du bist ⎪ | du seiest ⎪ | du bist ⎪ | du seiest ⎪ |
| er ist ⎪ gewesen | er sei ⎪ gewesen | er ist ⎪ geworden | er sei ⎪ geworden |
| wir sind ⎪ | wir seien ⎪ | wir sind ⎪ | wir seien ⎪ |
| ihr seid ⎪ | ihr seiet ⎪ | ihr seid ⎪ | ihr seiet ⎪ |
| sie sind ⎭ | sie seien ⎭ | sie sind ⎭ | sie seien ⎭ |

| PLUPERFECT. | | PLUPERFECT. | |
|---|---|---|---|
| I had been, etc. | | I had become, etc. | |
| ich war ⎫ | ich wäre ⎫ | ich war ⎫ | ich wäre ⎫ |
| du warst ⎪ | du wärest ⎪ | du warst ⎪ | du wärest ⎪ |
| er war ⎪ gewesen | er wäre ⎪ gewesen | er war ⎪ geworden | er wäre ⎪ geworden |
| wir waren ⎪ | wir wären ⎪ | wir waren ⎪ | wir wären ⎪ |
| ihr wart ⎪ | ihr wäret ⎪ | ihr wart ⎪ | ihr wäret ⎪ |
| sie waren ⎭ | sie wären ⎭ | sie waren ⎭ | sie wären ⎭ |

### FUTURE.

*Indicative.*     *Subjunctive.*

I shall be, etc.

| ich | werde | | ich | werde | |
|-----|-------|---|-----|-------|---|
| du | wirſt | | du | werdeſt | |
| er | wird | ſein | er | werde | ſein |
| wir | werden | | wir | werden | |
| ihr | werdet | | ihr | werdet | |
| ſie | werden | | ſie | werden | |

### FUTURE.

*Indicative.*     *Subjunctive.*

I shall become, etc.

| ich | werde | | ich | werde | |
|-----|-------|---|-----|-------|---|
| du | wirſt | | du | werdeſt | |
| er | wird | werden | er | werde | werden |
| wir | werden | | wir | werden | |
| ihr | werdet | | ihr | werdet | |
| ſie | werden | | ſie | werden | |

### FUTURE PERFECT.

I shall have been, etc.

| ich | werde | | ich | werde | |
|-----|-------|---|-----|-------|---|
| du | wirſt | | du | werdeſt | |
| er | wird | geweſen ſein | er | werde | geweſen ſein |
| wir | werden | | wir | werden | |
| ihr | werdet | | ihr | werdet | |
| ſie | werden | | ſie | werden | |

### FUTURE PERFECT.

I shall have become, etc.

| ich | werde | | ich | werde | |
|-----|-------|---|-----|-------|---|
| du | wirſt | | du | werdeſt | |
| er | wird | geworden ſein | er | werde | geworden ſein |
| wir | werden | | wir | werden | |
| ihr | werdet | | ihr | werdet | |
| ſie | werden | | ſie | werden | |

### CONDITIONAL.

*Simple.*     *Compound.*

I should be, etc.     I should have been, etc.

| ich | würde | | ich | würde | |
|-----|-------|---|-----|-------|---|
| du | würdeſt | | du | würdeſt | |
| er | würde | ſein | er | würde | geweſen ſein |
| wir | würden | | wir | würden | |
| ihr | würdet | | ihr | würdet | |
| ſie | würden | | ſie | würden | |

### CONDITIONAL.

*Simple.*     *Compound.*

I should become, etc.     I should have become, etc.

| ich | würde | | ich | würde | |
|-----|-------|---|-----|-------|---|
| du | würdeſt | | du | würdeſt | |
| er | würde | werden | er | würde | geworden ſein |
| wir | würden | | wir | würden | |
| ihr | würdet | | ihr | würdet | |
| ſie | würden | | ſie | würden | |

IMPERATIVE: ſei, ſeid, ſeien Sie, be.
            werde, werdet, werden Sie, become.

INFINITIVE: *Pres.*, ſein, to be.     *Perf.*, geweſen ſein, to have been.
         "    werden, to become.     "    geworden ſein, to have become.

PARTICIPLE: *Pres.*, ſeiend, being.     *Past*, geweſen, been.
         "    werdend, becoming.     "    geworden, become.

## 2. Auxiliaries of Mood.

| PRIN. PARTS: | dürfen | durfte | gedurft | (dürfen, after infin.) |
| --- | --- | --- | --- | --- |
| | können | konnte | gekonnt | (können " " ) |
| | mögen | mochte | gemocht | (mögen " " ) |
| | müssen | mußte | gemußt | (müssen " " ) |
| | sollen | sollte | gesollt | (sollen " " ) |
| | wollen | wollte | gewollt | (wollen " " ) |

### PRESENT INDICATIVE.

| ich | darf | kann | mag | muß | soll | will |
| --- | --- | --- | --- | --- | --- | --- |
| du | darfst | kannst | magst | mußt | sollst | willst |
| er | darf | kann | mag | muß | soll | will |
| wir | dürfen | können | mögen | müssen | sollen | wollen |
| ihr | dürft | könnt | mögt | müßt | sollt | wollt |
| sie | dürfen | können | mögen | müssen | sollen | wollen |

### PRESENT SUBJUNCTIVE.

| ich | dürfe | könne | möge | müsse | solle | wolle |
| --- | --- | --- | --- | --- | --- | --- |
| du | dürfest | könnest | mögest | müssest | sollest | wollest |
| er | dürfe | könne | möge | müsse | solle | wolle |
| | 2c. | 2c. | 2c. | 2c. | 2c. | 2c. |

### IMPERFECT INDICATIVE.

| ich | durfte | konnte | mochte | mußte | sollte | wollte |
| --- | --- | --- | --- | --- | --- | --- |
| du | durftest | konntest | mochtest | mußtest | solltest | wolltest |
| | 2c. | 2c. | 2c. | 2c. | 2c. | 2c. |

### IMPERFECT SUBJUNCTIVE.

| ich | dürfte | könnte | möchte | müßte | sollte | wollte |
| --- | --- | --- | --- | --- | --- | --- |
| du | dürftest | könntest | möchtest | müßtest | solltest | wolltest |
| | 2c. | 2c. | 2c. | 2c. | 2c. | 2c. |

### COMPOUND TENSES.

*Perf.*    ich habe gedurft (gekonnt, gemocht, gemußt, gesollt, gewollt)

"    ich habe bleiben dürfen (können, mögen, müssen, sollen, wollen)

*Plupf.*    ich hatte gedurft (gekonnt, gemocht, gemußt, gesollt, gewollt)

"    ich hatte bleiben dürfen (können, mögen, müssen, sollen, wollen)

*Fut.*    ich werde dürfen (können, mögen, müssen, sollen, wollen)

*Fut. Perf.* ich werde gedurft (gekonnt, gemocht, gemußt, gesollt, gewollt) haben.

T

## 3. Weak Conjugation.

Principal Parts: loben, lobte, gelobt.

Infinitives: *Pres.*, loben, to praise; *Perf.*, gelobt haben, to have praised.

### Present.

*Indicative.* — *Subjunctive.*

I praise, etc.

| | |
|---|---|
| ich lobe | ich lobe |
| du lobst | du lobest |
| er lobt | er lobe |
| wir loben | wir loben |
| ihr lobt | ihr lobet |
| sie loben | sie loben |

### Imperfect.

*Indicative.* — *Subjunctive.*

I praised, etc.

| | |
|---|---|
| ich lobte | ich lobte |
| du lobtest | du lobtest |
| er lobte | er lobte |
| wir lobten | wir lobten |
| ihr lobtet | ihr lobtet |
| sie lobten | sie lobten |

### Perfect.

I have praised, etc.

| | |
|---|---|
| ich habe | ich habe |
| du hast | du habest |
| er hat | er habe |
| wir haben | wir haben |
| ihr habt | ihr habet |
| sie haben | sie haben |

(gelobt)

### Pluperfect.

I had praised, etc.

| | |
|---|---|
| ich hatte | ich hätte |
| du hattest | du hättest |
| er hatte | er hätte |
| wir hatten | wir hätten |
| ihr hattet | ihr hättet |
| sie hatten | sie hätten |

(gelobt)

### Future.

I shall praise, etc.

| | |
|---|---|
| ich werde | ich werde |
| du wirst | du werdest |
| er wird | er werde |
| wir werden | wir werden |
| ihr werdet | ihr werdet |
| sie werden | sie werden |

(loben)

### Future Perfect.

I shall have praised, etc.

| | |
|---|---|
| ich werde | ich werde |
| du wirst | du werdest |
| er wird | er werde |
| wir werden | wir werden |
| ihr werdet | ihr werdet |
| sie werden | sie werden |

(gelobt haben)

### Conditional.

*Simple.* — *Compound.*

I should praise, etc. — I should have praised, etc.

| | |
|---|---|
| ich würde | ich würde |
| du würdest | du würdest |
| er würde | er würde |
| wir würden | wir würden |
| ihr würdet | ihr würdet |
| sie würden | sie würden |

(loben) (gelobt haben)

### Imperative.

lobe, praise.
lobt, praise.
loben Sie, praise.

### Participles.

*Pres.*, lobend, praising.
*Past*, gelobt, praised.

## 4. Strong Conjugation.

Principal Parts: singen, sang, gesungen.

Infinitives: *Pres.*, singen, to sing; *Perf.*, gesungen haben, to have sung.

|  | PRESENT. | | IMPERFECT. | |
|---|---|---|---|---|
|  | *Indicative.* | *Subjunctive.* | *Indicative.* | *Subjunctive.* |
|  | I sing, etc. | | I sang, etc. | |
|  | ich singe | ich singe | ich sang | ich sänge |
|  | du singst | du singest | du sangst | du sängest |
|  | er singt | er singe | er sang | er sänge |
|  | wir singen | wir singen | wir sangen | wir sängen |
|  | ihr singt | ihr singet | ihr sangt | ihr sänget |
|  | sie singen | sie singen | sie sangen | sie sängen |

|  | PERFECT. | | PLUPERFECT. | |
|---|---|---|---|---|
|  | I have sung, etc. | | I had sung, etc. | |

PERFECT. — I have sung, etc.

ich habe · du hast · er hat · wir haben · ihr habt · sie haben ⎱ gesungen

ich habe · du habest · er habe · wir haben · ihr habet · sie haben ⎱ gesungen

PLUPERFECT. — I had sung, etc.

ich hatte · du hattest · er hatte · wir hatten · ihr hattet · sie hatten ⎱ gesungen

ich hätte · du hättest · er hätte · wir hätten · ihr hättet · sie hätten ⎱ gesungen

FUTURE. — I shall sing, etc.

ich werde · du wirst · er wird · wir werden · ihr werdet · sie werden ⎱ singen

ich werde · du werdest · er werde · wir werden · ihr werdet · sie werden ⎱ singen

FUTURE PERFECT. — I shall have sung, etc.

ich werde · du wirst · er wird · wir werden · ihr werdet · sie werden ⎱ gesungen haben

ich werde · du werdest · er werde · wir werden · ihr werdet · sie werden ⎱ gesungen haben

CONDITIONAL.

*Simple.* — I should sing, etc.

ich würde · du würdest · er würde · wir würden · ihr würdet · sie würden ⎱ singen

*Compound.* — I should have sung, etc.

ich würde · du würdest · er würde · wir würden · ihr würdet · sie würden ⎱ gesungen haben

IMPERATIVE.

singe, sing.
singt, sing.
singen Sie, sing.

PARTICIPLES.

*Pres.*, singend, singing.
*Past*, gesungen, sung.

## 5. Conjugation with fein.

PRINCIPAL PARTS: fallen, fiel, gefallen.

INFINITIVES: *Pres.*, fallen, to fall; *Perf.*, gefallen fein, to have fallen.

| PRESENT. | | IMPERFECT. | |
|---|---|---|---|
| *Indicative.* | *Subjunctive.* | *Indicative.* | *Subjunctive.* |
| I fall, etc. | | I fell, etc. | |
| ich falle | ich falle | ich fiel | ich fiele |
| du fällst | du fallest | du fielst | du fielest |
| er fällt | er falle | er fiel | er fiele |
| wir fallen | wir fallen | wir fielen | wir fielen |
| ihr fallt | ihr fallet | ihr fielt | ihr fielet |
| sie fallen | sie fallen | sie fielen | sie fielen |

| PERFECT. | | PLUPERFECT. | |
|---|---|---|---|
| I have fallen, etc. | | I had fallen, etc. | |
| ich bin | ich sei | ich war | ich wäre |
| du bist | du seiest | du warst | du wärest |
| er ist ⎱ gefallen | er sei ⎱ gefallen | er war ⎱ gefallen | er wäre ⎱ gefallen |
| wir sind | wir seien | wir waren | wir wären |
| ihr seid | ihr seiet | ihr waret | ihr wäret |
| sie sind | sie seien | sie waren | sie wären |

| FUTURE. | | FUTURE PERFECT. | |
|---|---|---|---|
| I shall fall, etc. | | I shall have fallen, etc. | |
| ich werde | ich werde | ich werde | ich werde |
| du wirst | du werdest | du wirst | du werdest |
| er wird ⎱ fallen | er werde ⎱ fallen | er wird ⎱ gefallen fein | er werde ⎱ gefallen fein |
| wir werden | wir werden | wir werden | wir werden |
| ihr werdet | ihr werdet | ihr werdet | ihr werdet |
| sie werden | sie werden | sie werden | sie werden |

### CONDITIONAL.

| *Simple.* | *Compound.* |
|---|---|
| I should fall, etc. | I should have fallen, etc. |
| ich würde | ich würde |
| du würdest | du würdest |
| er würde ⎱ fallen | er würde ⎱ gefallen fein |
| wir würden | wir würden |
| ihr würdet | ihr würdet |
| sie würden | sie würden |

### IMPERATIVE.

falle, fall.
fallt, fall.
fallen Sie, fall.

### PARTICIPLES.

*Pres.*, fallend, falling.
*Past*, gefallen, fallen.

## 6. Passive Voice.

INFINITIVES: *Pres.*, gelobt werden, to be praised; *Perf.*, gelobt worden sein, to have been praised.

### PRESENT.

*Indicative.*    *Subjunctive.*

I am praised, etc.

| ich werde | | ich werde | |
|---|---|---|---|
| du wirst | | du werdest | |
| er wird | gelobt | er werde | gelobt |
| wir werden | | wir werden | |
| ihr werdet | | ihr werdet | |
| sie werden | | sie werden | |

### IMPERFECT.

*Indicative.*    *Subjunctive.*

I was praised, etc.

| ich wurde | | ich würde | |
|---|---|---|---|
| du wurdest | | du würdest | |
| er wurde | gelobt | er würde | gelobt |
| wir wurden | | wir würden | |
| ihr wurdet | | ihr würdet | |
| sie wurden | | sie würden | |

### PERFECT.

I have been praised, etc.

| ich bin | | ich sei | |
|---|---|---|---|
| du bist | gelobt worden | du seiest | gelobt worden |
| er ist | | er sei | |
| wir sind | | wir seien | |
| ihr seid | | ihr seiet | |
| sie sind | | sie seien | |

### PLUPERFECT.

I had been praised, etc.

| ich war | | ich wäre | |
|---|---|---|---|
| du warst | gelobt worden | du wärest | gelobt worden |
| er war | | er wäre | |
| wir waren | | wir wären | |
| ihr waret | | ihr wäret | |
| sie waren | | sie wären | |

### FUTURE.

I shall be praised, etc.

| ich werde | | ich werde | |
|---|---|---|---|
| du wirst | | du werdest | |
| er wird | gelobt werden | er werde | gelobt werden |
| wir werden | | wir werden | |
| ihr werdet | | ihr werdet | |
| sie werden | | sie werden | |

### FUTURE PERFECT.

I shall have been praised, etc.

| ich werde | | ich werde | |
|---|---|---|---|
| du wirst | | du werdest | |
| er wird | gelobt worden sein | er werde | gelobt worden sein |
| wir werden | | wir werden | |
| ihr werdet | | ihr werdet | |
| sie werden | | sie werden | |

### CONDITIONAL.

*Simple.*    *Compound.*

I should be praised, etc.    I should have been praised, etc.

| ich würde | | ich würde | |
|---|---|---|---|
| du würdest | | du würdest | |
| er würde | gelobt werden | er würde | gelobt worden sein |
| wir würden | | wir würden | |
| ihr würdet | | ihr würdet | |
| sie würden | | sie würden | |

### IMPERATIVE.

werde gelobt, be praised.
werdet gelobt, be praised.
werden Sie gelobt, be praised.

### PARTICIPLES.

*Fut.*, zu lobend, to be praised (as adjective only).

*Past*, gelobt worden, been praised.

### D. ALPHABETICAL LIST OF STRONG AND IRREGULAR VERBS.

1. The following list contains only verbs in common use.

2. Compound verbs are omitted, as a rule, and their conjugation is to be inferred from that of the corresponding simple verb, *e.g.* verbinden, see binden; betrügen, see trügen; but compounds which have no corresponding simple verbs will be found in the list.

3. The vowel of the 2nd and 3rd sing. pres. indic. and of the 2nd sing. imper. is given only when it differs from that of the infin.

4. The vowel of the impf. subj. is given only when it differs from that of the impf. indic.

5. Forms in parenthesis are less usual.

6. Verbs followed by ſ. are conjugated with ſein only; those followed by ſ., h. are sometimes conjugated with haben (§ 62, 2, note); all others with haben only.

| *Infinitive.* | *Imperfect.* | *P. Part.* | *Pr. Ind.* | *Impve.* | *Impf. Subj.* |
|---|---|---|---|---|---|
| backen, bake | buk or backte | gebacken | ä | | |
| befehlen, command | befahl | befohlen | ie | ie | ö |
| befleißen, *refl.*, strive | befliß | beflissen | | | |
| beginnen, begin | begann | begonnen | | | ä or ö |
| beißen, bite | biß | gebissen | | | |
| bergen, hide | barg | geborgen | i | i | |
| bersten, ſ., burst | barst or borst | geborsten | i(e) | i(e) | ä or ö |
| bewegen,[1] induce | bewog | bewogen | | | |
| biegen,[2] bend | bog | gebogen | | | |
| bieten,[2] offer | bot | geboten | | | |
| binden, bind | band | gebunden | | | |
| bitten, ask | bat | gebeten | | | |
| blasen, blow | blies | geblasen | ä | | |
| bleiben, ſ., remain | blieb | geblieben | | | |
| braten, roast | briet | gebraten | ä | | |
| brechen, break | brach | gebrochen | i | i | |
| brennen, burn | brannte | gebrannt | | | brennte |
| bringen, bring | brachte | gebracht | | | |
| denken, think | dachte | gedacht | | | |
| dreschen, thresh | drasch or drosch | gedroschen | i | i | |

| Infinitive. | Imperfect. | P. Part. | Pr. Ind | Impve | Impf. Subj. |
|---|---|---|---|---|---|
| dringen, f., h., press | drang | gedrungen | | | |
| dünken, seem | deuchte | gedeucht | dünkt or deucht | | |
| dürfen, may | durfte | gedurft | darf, darfst, darf | | |
| empfehlen, recommend; *see* befehlen | | | | | |
| erbleichen, f., turn pale | erblich | erblichen | | | |
| erlöschen,[3] f., be extinguished | erlosch | erloschen | i | | i |
| erschrecken,[4] f., be frightened | erschrak | erschrocken | i | | i |
| essen, eat | aß | gegessen | i | | i |
| fahren, f., h., go, drive | fuhr | gefahren | ä | | |
| fallen, f., fall | fiel | gefallen | ä | | |
| fangen, catch | fing | gefangen | ä | | |
| fechten, fight | focht | gefochten | i | | i |
| finden, find | fand | gefunden | | | |
| flechten, braid | flocht | geflochten | i | | i |
| fliegen,[2] f., h., fly | flog | geflogen | | | |
| fliehen,[5] f., h., flee | floh | geflohen | | | |
| fließen,[2] f., h., flow | floß | geflossen | | | |
| fressen, eat | fraß | gefressen | i | | i |
| frieren, f., h., freeze | fror | gefroren | | | |
| gebären, bear | gebar | geboren | ie | | ie |
| geben, give | gab | gegeben | i | | i |
| gedeihen, f., thrive | gedieh | gediehen | | | |
| gehen, f., go, walk | ging | gegangen | | | |
| gelingen, f., succeed | gelang | gelungen | | | |
| gelten, be worth | galt | gegolten | i | i ' | ä or ö |
| genesen, f., recover | genas | genesen | | | |
| genießen, enjoy | genoß | genossen | | | |
| geschehen, f., happen | geschah | geschehen | ie | | |
| gewinnen, win | gewann | gewonnen | | | ä or ö |
| gießen,[2] pour | goß | gegossen | | | |
| gleichen, be like. | glich | geglichen | | | |
| gleiten, f., glide. | glitt | geglitten | | | |
| graben, dig | grub | gegraben | ä | | |

| Infinitive. | Imperfect. | P. Part. | Pr. Ind. | Impve. | Impf. Subj. |
|---|---|---|---|---|---|
| greifen, seize | griff | gegriffen | | | |
| haben, have | hatte | gehabt | haſt, hat | | |
| halten, hold | hielt | gehalten | ä | | |
| hangen, hang | hing | gehangen | ä | | |
| hauen, hew | hieb | gehauen | | | |
| heben, lift | hob or hub | gehoben | | | |
| heißen, be called | hieß | geheißen | | | |
| helfen, help | half | geholfen | i | i | ü |
| kennen, know | kannte | gekannt | | | kennte |
| klingen, sound | klang | geklungen | | | |
| kneifen, pinch | kniff | gekniffen | | | |
| kommen, ſ., come | kam | gekommen | o(ö) | | |
| können, can | konnte | gekonnt | kann, kannſt, kann | | |
| kriechen,[2] ſ., h., creep | kroch | gekrochen | | | |
| laden, load, invite | lud | geladen | | | |
| laſſen, let | ließ | gelaſſen | ä | | |
| laufen, ſ., h., run | lief | gelaufen | äu | | |
| leiden,[7] suffer | litt | gelitten | | | |
| leihen, lend | lieh | geliehen | | | |
| leſen, read | las | geleſen | ie | ie | |
| liegen, lie | lag | gelegen | | | |
| lügen, lie | log | gelogen | | | |
| meiden, shun | mied | gemieden | | | |
| melken,[8] milk | molk | gemolken | i | i | |
| meſſen, measure | maß | gemeſſen | i | i | |
| mögen, may, like | mochte | gemocht | mag, magſt, mag | | |
| müſſen, must | mußte | gemußt | muß, mußt, muß | | |
| nehmen, take | nahm | genommen | nimmſt, nimm nimmt | | |
| nennen, name | nannte | genannt | | | nennte |
| pfeifen, whistle | pfiff | gepfiffen | | | |
| preiſen, praise | pries | gepriesen | | | |
| quellen, ſ., gush out | quoll | gequollen | i | i | |
| raten, advise | riet | geraten | ä | | |
| reiben, rub | rieb | gerieben | | | |
| reißen, h., ſ., tear | riß | geriſſen | | | |

| Infinitive. | Imperfect. | P. Part. | Pr. Ind | Impve. | Impf. Subj. |
|---|---|---|---|---|---|
| reiten,[9] f., h., ride | ritt | geritten | | | |
| rennen, f., h., run | rannte | gerannt | | | rennte |
| riechen, smell | roch | gerochen | | | |
| ringen,[10] wring | rang | gerungen | | | |
| rinnen, f., flow | rann | geronnen | | | ä or ö |
| rufen, call | rief | gerufen | | | |
| saufen, drink | soff | gesoffen | äu | | |
| saugen, suck | sog | gesogen | | | |
| schaffen,[11] create | schuf | geschaffen | | | |
| schallen,[8] f., h., sound | scholl | geschollen | | | |
| scheiden, h., f., part | schied | geschieden | | | |
| scheinen, shine | schien | geschienen | | | |
| schelten, scold | schalt | gescholten | i | i | ö |
| scheren,[12] shear | schor | geschoren | ie or e | ie or e | |
| schieben, shove | schob | geschoben | | | |
| schießen, shoot | schoß | geschossen | | | |
| schlafen, sleep | schlief | geschlafen | ä | | |
| schlagen,[13] strike | schlug | geschlagen | ä | | |
| schleichen, f., h., creep | schlich | geschlichen | | | |
| schleifen,[11] grind | schliff | geschliffen | | | |
| schließen, shut | schloß | geschlossen | | | |
| schlingen, sling | schlang | geschlungen | | | |
| schmeißen, fling | schmiß | geschmissen | | | |
| schmelzen,[14] f., h., melt | schmolz | geschmolzen | i | i | |
| schneiden, cut | schnitt | geschnitten | | | |
| schreiben, write | schrieb | geschrieben | | | |
| schreien, scream | schrie | geschrien | | | |
| schreiten, f., stride | schritt | geschritten | | | |
| schweigen, be silent | schwieg | geschwiegen | | | |
| schwellen,[4] f., swell | schwoll | geschwollen | i | i | |
| schwimmen, f., h., swim | schwamm | geschwommen | | | ä or ö |
| schwinden, f., vanish | schwand | geschwunden | | | |
| schwingen, swing | schwang | geschwungen | | | |
| schwören, swear | schwor or schwur | geschworen | | | ü |
| sehen, see | sah | gesehen | ie | ie | |
| sein, f., be | war | gewesen | bin, bist, sei ist | | |

| Infinitive. | Imperfect. | P. Part. | Pr. Ind. | Impve. | Impf. Subj. |
|---|---|---|---|---|---|
| senden,[15] send | sandte | gesandt | | | sendete |
| sieden,[16] boil | sott | gesotten | | | |
| singen, sing | sang | gesungen | | | |
| sinken, s., sink | sank | gesunken | | | |
| sinnen, think | sann | gesonnen | | | ä or ö |
| sitzen, sit | saß | gesessen | | | |
| sollen, shall | sollte | gesollt | soll, sollst, soll | | |
| speien, spit | spie | gespien | | | |
| spinnen, spin | spann | gesponnen | | | ä or ö |
| sprechen, speak | sprach | gesprochen | i | i | |
| sprießen, s., h., sprout | sproß | gesprossen | | | |
| springen, s., h., spring | sprang | gesprungen | | | |
| stechen, stick | stach | gestochen | i | i | |
| stecken,[8] stick | stak | gesteckt | e or i | e or i | |
| stehen, stand | stand (stund) | gestanden | | | |
| stehlen, steal | stahl | gestohlen | ie | ie | ä |
| steigen, s., h., mount | stieg | gestiegen | | | |
| sterben, s., die | starb | gestorben | i | i | ü |
| stoßen, h., s., push | stieß | gestoßen | ö | | |
| streichen, stroke | strich | gestrichen | | | |
| streiten, strive | stritt | gestritten | | | |
| tragen, carry | trug | getragen | ä | | |
| treffen, hit | traf | getroffen | i | i | |
| treiben, drive | trieb | getrieben | | | |
| treten, s., h., step | trat | getreten | trittst, tritt | tritt | |
| triefen,[16] s., h., drip | troff | getroffen | | | |
| trügen, deceive | trog | getrogen | | | |
| tun, do | tat | getan | | | |
| verderben,[17] s., h., spoil | verdarb | verdorben | i | i | ü |
| verdrießen, vex | verdroß | verdrossen | | | |
| vergessen, forget | vergaß | vergessen | i | i | |
| verlieren, lose | verlor | verloren | | | |
| wachsen, s., grow | wuchs | gewachsen | ä | | |
| wägen, weigh (tr.) | wog | gewogen | | | |
| waschen, wash | wusch | gewaschen | ä | | |
| weben,[16] weave | wob | gewoben | | | |

| Infinitive. | Imperfect. | P. Part. | Pr Ind. | Impve. | Impf. Subj. |
|---|---|---|---|---|---|
| weichen,[18] f., h., yield | wich | gewichen | | | |
| weisen, show | wies | gewiesen | | | |
| wenden,[15] turn | wandte | gewandt | | | wendete |
| werben, sue, woo | warb | geworben | î | | ü |
| werden, f., become | wurde, ward | geworden | wirst, wird | | würde |
| werfen, throw | warf | geworfen | i | i | ü |
| wiegen, weigh (intr.) | wog | gewogen | | | |
| winden, wind | wand | gewunden | | | |
| wissen, know | wußte | gewußt | weiß, weißt, weiß | | |
| wollen, will | wollte | gewollt | will, willst, will | | wollte |
| zeihen, accuse | zieh | geziehen | | | |
| ziehen,[19] draw (h.), move (f.) | zog | gezogen | | | |
| zwingen, force | zwang | gezwungen | | | |

[1] bewegen, 'move,' is wk.   [2] Has also eu for ie in 2nd and 3rd sing. pres. indic. and 2nd sing. impve. in poetic diction.   [3] löschen, 'extinguish,' is wk.   [4] Wk. when tr.   [5] Also fleuchst, fleucht, fleuch in poetry.   [6] begleiten, 'accompany,' is wk.   [7] verleiden, 'spoil,' is wk.   [8] Usually wk.   [9] bereiten, 'prepare,' is wk.   [10] umringen, 'surround,' is wk.   [11] In other senses wk.   [12] bescheren, 'make a present,' is wk.   [13] ratschlagen, 'deliberate,' is wk.   [14] schmelzen, 'smelt,' is wk.   [15] Also reg. wk.   [16] Also wk.   [17] Wk. or st. when tr.   [18] weichen, 'soften,' is wk.   [19] Also zeuchst, zeucht, zeuch, in poetry.

# GERMAN–ENGLISH VOCABULARY

1. Numerals refer to the sections. 2. Noun inflections are indicated in the usual way; the plural only of feminines is given; umlaut is indicated by "; the e before ß in genitive singular of nouns has been usually given; for rules as to its retention or omission, see § 33, Rem. 2, n. 1. 3. Proper names with identical spelling in both languages have been omitted. 4. For the inflection of adjectival substantives, see § 68. 5. With adjectives, " indicates umlaut in comparison. 6. In the case of words used both as adjective and adverb, the adjectival form only is usually given. 7. Verbs are weak, unless otherwise indicated; those marked *st.* (strong) or *irr.* (irregular) will be found in App. D; the conjugation of a compound verb is given, as a rule, under the simple verb. 8. Verbs followed by ſ. are conjugated with ſein only; those followed by ſ., h. are sometimes conjugated with haben (§ 62, 2, note); all others with haben only. 9. Compound verbs, except those beginning with be–, emp–, ent–, er–, ge–, ver–, zer–, are separable, unless otherwise indicated. 10. The stress ( ′ ) is marked only in exceptional cases. 11. The meanings given are usually confined to those used in this grammar.

## A

**Abend,** *m.,* –es, –e, evening; des Abends *or* abends, in the evening.

**Abendbrot,** *n.,* –es, supper.

**Abendessen,** *n.,* –s, supper.

**Abendglöcklein,** *n.,* –s, —, evening-bell.

**Abendluft,** *f.,* "e, evening air.

**Abenteuer,** *n.,* –s, —, adventure.

**aber,** but; however.

**abfahren,** *st.,* ſ., to depart, set out, start.

**Abfahrt,** *f.,* –en, departure.

**abgehen,** *st.,* ſ., to go away, set out, start, depart.

**Abhandlung,** *f.,* –en, treatise, paper.

**abladen,** *st.,* to unload.

**abnehmen,** *st.,* to take away, take off.

**abputzen,** to clean, wipe.

**abreisen,** ſ., to set out, start, depart, go away.

**absagen,** to decline (an invitation, etc.).

**Abschied,** *m.,* –es, departure; — nehmen, to take leave.

**abschlagen,** *st.,* to refuse, deny.

**abschreiben,** *st.,* to copy (out).

**absetzen,** to set down.

**Absicht,** *f.,* –en, intention.

**abstatten,** to pay (a visit).

**absteigen,** *st.,* ſ., to dismount, descend, get out of (a vehicle).

**Abteil,** *m.,* –es, –e, compartment.

**Abteilung,** *f.,* –en, department.

**a'bwesend,** absent.

**ach!** ah! oh! alas!

**Acht,** *f.,* care, attention.

**achtgeben,** *st.,* to give heed, pay attention.

273

**addieren,** to add (*arith.*).

**adieu** [pr. adjö'], good-bye.

**Adresse,** *f.*, –n, address.

**ähnlich,** like, similar (to).

**all,** all (the), the whole.

**allei'n,** *adj.*, alone; *conj.*, but, only.

**allerdi'ngs,** certainly, indeed.

**allgemei'n,** general, universal; im —en, in general.

**allzumal,** all together.

**als,** than, as (a), when.

**also,** so, thus, accordingly, so then.

**alt,** ⸚er, old; vor —er Zeit, in old(en) times.

**Amerika,** *n.*, –s, America.

**amerikanisch,** American.

**Amt,** *n.*, –es, ⸚er, office.

**Amtstätigkeit,** *f.*, tenure of office.

**an** (*dat. or acc.*), on, upon, to, at, in, beside, by, of, for; — (*dat.*) vorbeigehen, to go past.

**Andenken,** *n.*, –s, memory; zum — an (*acc.*), in memory of.

**ander,** other; die —n, the others, others; den —n Tag, the next day.

**ändern,** *refl.*, to change (*intr.*).

**anderthalb,** one and a half.

**anerkennen,** *irr.*, to acknowledge, recognize.

**anfangen,** *st.*, to begin.

**anfangs,** at first.

**angenehm,** agreeable.

**angreifen,** *st.*, to attack.

**anhalten,** *st.*, to stop, draw up.

**Anker,** *m.*, –s, —, anchor; die — fallen lassen, to cast anchor.

**ankleiden,** *refl.*, to dress one's self.

**ankommen,** *st.*, ſ., to arrive.

**ankündigen,** to announce.

**annehmen,** *st.*, to accept.

**Anrede,** *f.*, –n, (mode of) address.

**anreden,** to address, speak to.

**anrichten,** to do (damage).

**anrühren,** to touch.

**anschauen,** to look at, gaze at.

**ansehen,** *st.*, to look at.

**anstellen,** to appoint; angestellt sein, to have a position.

**Antwort,** *f.*, –en, answer.

**antworten,** to answer, reply.

**anvertrauen,** to entrust.

**Anzeige,** *f.*, –n, advertisement.

**anziehen,** *st.*, to draw on, put on (*of clothing*); sich —, to dress (one's self).

**anzünden,** to kindle, light.

**Apfel,** *m.*, –s, ⸚, apple.

**Apfelbaum,** *m.*, –es, ⸚e, apple-tree.

**Apostel,** *m.*, –s, —, apostle.

**Apotheke,** *f.*, –n, drug-store.

**Apotheker,** *m.*, –s, —, druggist.

**Appeti't,** *m.*, –es, appetite.

**Apri'l,** *m.*, April.

**A'rbeit,** *f.*, –en, work.

**arbeiten,** to work.

**Arbeiter,** *m.*, –s, —, workman, labourer.

**Arche,** *f.*, –n, ark.

**ärgerlich,** angrily.

**Arm,** *m.*, –es, –e, arm; branch (of a river).

**arm,** ⸚er, poor.

**artig,** well-behaved, good.

**Arzenei,** *f.*, –en, medicine, physic.

**Arzt,** *m.*, –es, ⸚e, physician, doctor.

**Ast,** *m.*, –es, ⸚e, bough, branch.

**auch,** also, too, even; — das ist nicht mein, that is not mine either; — da ist nichts, there is nothing there either.

**Aue,** f., –n, meadow.

**auf** (*dat. or acc.*), on, upon, to, for, at, in, by; ein Viertel — zwei, a quarter past one; drei Viertel — zwei, a quarter to two.

**auferlegen,** to impose upon, assign.

**aufessen,** st., to eat up.

**auffressen,** st., to eat up, devour.

**Aufgabe,** f., –n, exercise, lesson.

**aufgeben,** st., to give up, abandon; give in charge.

**aufgehen,** st., s., to rise (*of the sun, etc.*); spring up (*of seed*).

**aufheben,** st., to pick up.

**aufhissen,** to hoist (a sail, etc.).

**aufhören,** to cease, stop.

**aufmachen,** to open.

**aufmerksam,** attentive.

**aufpassen,** to take care, look out.

**aufrecht,** upright; — stellen, to set on end.

**aufregen,** to excite; *refl.*, to become (get) excited.

**aufschlagen,** st., to open.

**aufschreiben,** st., to write down.

**aufsehen,** st., to look up(wards).

**Aufstand,** m., –es, ⸗e, insurrection.

**aufstehen,** st., s., to rise, get up.

**aufsteigen,** st., s., to rise, mount.

**auftreten,** st., s., to come forward, appear.

**auftun,** irr., to open.

**aufwachen,** s., to awake (*intr.*).

**aufwachsen,** st., s., to grow up.

**Auge,** n., –s, –n, eye; große —n machen, to stare.

**Aug(e)lein,** n., –s, —, little eye.

**Augenblick,** m., –es, –e, moment.

**Augu'st,** m., August.

**aus** (*dat.*), out, out of, of, from.

**Ausflug,** m., –es, ⸗e, excursion, picnic.

**Ausgabe,** f., –n, edition.

**ausgehen,** st., s., to go out.

**ausgezeichnet,** eminent, distinguished.

**ausgleiten,** st., s., to slip.

**ausgraben,** st., to dig up.

**Ausländer,** m., –s, —, foreigner.

**ausmachen,** to settle, decide.

**auspacken,** to unpack.

**ausreichen,** to be enough, suffice, be sufficient.

**ausrufen,** st., to call out, exclaim.

**ausruhen,** *intr. or refl.*, to rest, repose.

**außer** (*dat.*), outside of, except, but, besides.

**außerdem,** *adv.*, besides, moreover.

**außerhalb,** *prep.* (*gen.*), outside of.

**äußerst,** extremely.

**Aussicht,** f., –en, view, prospect.

**aussteigen,** st., s., to get off, get out (of a vehicle).

**ausstreuen,** to scatter.

**aussuchen,** to pick out, select.

**austeilen,** to deal out, distribute.

**Auster,** f., –n, oyster.

**austreten,** st., s., to retire, resign.

**auswendig,** by heart.

**ausziehen,** st., to draw out; take off (a coat, etc.).

**auszischen,** to hiss (*tr.*).

**Axt,** f., ⸗e, axe.

## B

**Bach,** *m.,* –es, ⁺e, brook, rivu-
let.

**Backe,** *f.,* –n, cheek.

**backen,** *st.,* to bake.

**Bäcker,** *m.,* –s, —, baker.

**Badezimmer,** *n.,* –s, —, bath-
room.

**Bahnhof,** *m.,* –es, ⁺e, station (railway).

**Bahnsteig,** *m.,* –es, –e, platform
(railway).

**bald,** eher, am ehesten, soon, presently; — . . . —, at one time
. . . at another.

**Ball,** *m.,* –es, ⁺e, ball.

**Band,** *m.,* –es, ⁺e, volume.

**bange,** afraid; mir wird —, I (begin to) feel alarmed, etc.

**Bank,** *f.,* ⁺e, bench.

**Bank,** *f.,* –en, bank, banking-
house.

**Bankier** [*pr.* bankje'], *m.,* –s, –s,
banker.

**Bär,** *m.,* –en, –en, bear.

**Barbier,** *m.,* –es, –e, barber.

**Bart,** *m.,* –es, ⁺e, beard.

**bauen,** to build.

**Bauer,** *m.,* –s *or* –n, –n, peasant,
countryman, farmer.

**Baum,** *m.,* –es, ⁺e, tree.

**Bayern,** *n.,* –s, Bavaria.

**Beamt(er),** *adj. subst.,* official.

**beben,** to quake, tremble.

**bedauern,** *tr.,* to pity; *intr.,* to be
sorry.

**bedecken,** to cover.

**bedeuten,** to signify, mean; order,
instruct (*dat.*).

**Bedient(er),** *adj. subst.,* servant.

**beeilen,** *refl.,* to make haste,
hurry.

**Beet,** *n.,* –es, –e, garden-bed.

**Befehl,** *m.,* –es, –e, order, command.

**befehlen,** *st.* (*dat.*), to order, command.

**befinden,** *st., refl.,* to be found, be
(situated); be (*of health*); wie
— Sie sich? how are you?

**Beförderung,** *f.,* –en, forwarding,
transportation.

**befragen,** to ask, question.

**befürchten,** to fear, apprehend.

**Begebenheit,** *f.,* –en, event, inci-
dent.

**begegnen,** s. (*dat.*), to meet.

**begeistert,** enthusiastic.

**beginnen,** *st.,* to begin, commence.

**begleichen,** *st.,* to pay, settle (an
account).

**begleiten,** to accompany, go with.

**Begleiter,** *m.,* –s, —, companion,
attendant.

**begraben,** *st.,* to bury.

**begrenzen,** to limit, bound.

**begrüßen,** to greet.

**behalten,** *st.,* to keep, retain.

**behandeln,** to treat.

**behilflich;** — sein, to be of assistance.

**bei** (*dat.*), near (by), by, beside,
at, with, about, on, of; —
Tisch, at table; — meinem Onkel,
at my uncle's (house, etc.); —
mir, with me, about me, at my
house; — diesem Wetter, in this
weather.

**beide,** both, (the) two; alle —,
both.

**Bein,** *n.,* –es, –e, leg.

**beinahe,** almost, nearly.

**Beispiel,** *n.,* –es, –e, example.

**beißen,** *st.,* to bite.

**Beistand,** *m.,* –es, assistance, help.

**beistehen,** *st.* (*dat.*), to assist, help.

**beiwohnen** (*dat.*), to be present at, attend.

**bekannt,** well-known.

**Bekannt(er),** *adj. subst.,* acquaintance.

**bekommen,** *st.,* to obtain, get, receive.

**Belgien,** *n.,* –s, Belgium.

**bemannen,** to man.

**bemerken,** to remark, observe.

**bemühen,** to trouble.

**Bengel,** *m.,* –s, —, urchin, chap.

**beob'achten,** to observe, watch.

**beque'm,** comfortable; es — haben, to be convenient, etc.

**berechnen,** to calculate, compute.

**bereisen,** to travel through.

**bereit,** ready, prepared.

**bereiten,** to prepare, provide.

**Berg,** *m.,* –es, –e, hill, mountain.

**Berli'n,** *n.,* –s, Berlin.

**Beruf,** *m.,* –es, –e, calling, profession.

**berufen,** *st.,* to call, summon.

**berühmt,** celebrated, famous.

**berühren,** to touch.

**beschäftigt,** occupied, busy.

**bescheiden,** modest.

**beschließen,** *st.,* to resolve, determine.

**beschützen,** to protect.

**besehen,** *st.,* to look at, view.

**besetzt,** occupied, full.

**besonder,** special, extraordinary.

**besonders,** especially, particularly.

**besorgen,** to see to, look after.

**besprechen,** *st.,* to discuss, talk over.

**besser** (*see* gut).

**bestehen,** *st.;* — auf (*acc.*), to insist on.

**besteigen,** *st.,* to mount, ascend, get into (vehicle).

**bestellen,** to prepare, till; order.

**bestrafen,** to punish.

**Besuch,** *m.,* –es, –e, visit, call; visitor(s); auf — sein, to be on a visit.

**besuchen,** to visit.

**beten,** to pray.

**betrachten,** to look at, consider, observe.

**Betrag,** *m.,* –es, ⁀e, amount, sum.

**Betragen,** *n.,* –s, conduct, behaviour.

**betreffen,** *st.,* to concern, regard; was ihn betrifft, as far as he is concerned.

**betreten,** *st.,* to tread on, enter.

**betrübt,** afflicted, sorrowful.

**betrügen,** *st.,* to cheat, deceive.

**Bett,** *n.,* –es, –en, bed; zu — gehen, to go to bed; zu — liegen, to lie (be) in bed.

**betteln,** to beg.

**Bettler,** *m.,* –s, —, beggar.

**bevorzugen,** *insep.,* to give preference to.

**bewundern,** to admire.

**bewußt,** conscious.

**bezahlen,** to pay.

**Bezug,** *m.,* –es, reference; in — auf, with respect to, regarding.

**Bild,** *n.,* –es, –er, picture.

**bilden,** to form.

U

**Bildergalerie,** *f.*, –n, picture-gallery.

**Bildnis,** *n.*, –es, –e, portrait.

**billig,** cheap.

**Birnbaum,** *m.*, –es, ⸚e, pear-tree.

**Birne,** *f.*, –n, pear.

**bis** (*acc.*), till, until, up to, as far as; — zu, — nach, as far as, even to, up to, until; vier — fünf, four or five; — auf, except.

**bißchen** (ein), a little.

**bitten,** *st.*, to ask, beg, request; (ich) bitte (*lit.* 'I beg'), if you please, please.

**bitter,** bitter.

**blau,** blue.

**bleiben,** *st.*, ſ., to remain, stay, be.

**Bleistift,** *m.*, –es, –e, (lead-)pencil.

**blind,** blind.

**blühen,** to blossom, (be in) bloom.

**Blümchen,** *n.*, –s, —, little flower, floweret.

**Blume,** *f.*, –n, flower.

**Blumengarten,** *m.*, –s, ⸚, flower-garden.

**Blumenkohl,** *m.*, –es, cauliflower.

**Blümlein,** *n.*, –s, —, little flower, floweret.

**Blut,** *n.*, –es, blood.

**Blüte,** *f.*, –n, blossom, bloom.

**Blütenduft,** *m.*, –es, ⸚e, fragrance of flowers.

**blutig,** bloody.

**Boden,** *m.*, –s, ⸚, ground, soil; floor.

**Bohne,** *f.*, –n, bean.

**Bonbons,** *pl.*, candy, **sweets.**

**Boot,** *n.*, –es, –e *or* Böte, boat.

**Borgen,** *n.*, –s, borrowing.

**Börse,** *f.*, –n, Exchange(-building).

**böse,** bad, cross, angry.

**brauchen,** to use, need.

**brausen,** to roar, thunder.

**brechen,** *st.*, to break; pick, gather (flowers, etc.).

**breit,** broad, wide.

**brennen,** *irr.*, to burn.

**Brief,** *m.*, –es, –e, letter.

**brieflich,** epistolary; —er Verkehr, correspondence.

**Brigg** [pr. brigg], *f.*, –s, brig.

**bringen,** *irr.*, to bring, take.

**Brot,** *n.*, –es, –e, bread, loaf.

**Brücke,** *f.*, –n, bridge.

**Bruder,** *m.*, –s, ⸚, brother.

**Brust,** *f.*, ⸚e, breast.

**Buch,** *n.*, –es, ⸚er, book.

**Bücherschrank,** *m.*, –es, ⸚e, book-case.

**Buchführer,** *m.*, –s, —, book-keeper.

**Büchse,** *f.*, –n, rifle.

**Bummelzug,** *m.*, –es, ⸚e, slow train.

**Bund,** *m.*, –es, –e, bundle, bunch.

**Bureau** [pr. büro'], *n.*, –s, –s *or* –r, office.

**Bürger,** *m.*, –s, —, citizen.

**Bürgermeister,** *m.*, –s, —, mayor.

**bürsten,** to brush.

**Butter,** *f.*, butter.

## C

**Cäsar,** *m.*, –s, Cæsar.

**Cent,** *m.*, –s, –s, cent, halfpenny.

**Chemie',** *f.*, chemistry.

**Cousine,** *f.*, –n, cousin.

**D**

**da,** *adv.,* there, in that place; here; then; *conj.,* as, because, since, when.

**dabei,** near it, by it, etc.; at the same time, while doing so; — ſein, to be present, be there.

**Dach,** *n.,* -es, ⸚er, roof.

**dadurch,** through it, by it, etc.

**dafür,** for it, etc.

**dagegen,** against it, etc.; on the other hand.

**daher,** hence, therefore.

**daherziehen,** *st.,* ſ., to come on.

**dahin,** thither, to that place, there.

**dahinfahren,** *st.,* ſ., to drive there.

**dahinfliegen,** *st.,* ſ., to fly away.

**dahinkommen,** *st.,* ſ., to go (get) there.

**da'mals,** then, at that time.

**Dame,** *f.,* -n, lady.

**Damenkleid,** *n.,* -es, -er, lady's dress.

**damit,** with it, etc.; *conj.,* in order that.

**Dampfer,** *m.,* -s, —, steamboat, steamer.

**Dänemark,** *n.,* -s, Denmark.

**dänisch,** Danish.

**Dank,** *m.,* -es, thanks; beſten —, many thanks.

**dankbar,** thankful.

**danken** (*dat.*), to thank; owe; ich danke, no thank you.

**dann,** then, next.

**daran,** on it, at it, etc.

**darauf,** on it, etc.; thereupon.

**darin,** in it, etc.

**darüber,** over it, about it, at it, etc.

**darum,** therefore; —, daß, because.

**darunter,** under it, among it, etc.

**das** (*see* der).

**daß,** that, in order that.

**Datum,** *n.,* -s, Data *or* Daten, date.

**davon,** of it, from it, about it, etc.

**davonlaufen,** *st.,* ſ., to run away.

**davontragen,** *st.,* to win.

**dazu,** to it, for it, etc.; moreover, into the bargain.

**Degen,** *m.,* -s, —, sword.

**dein,** *poss. adj.,* thy, your.

**deiner,** *poss. pron.,* thine, yours.

**deinige** (der, die, das), *poss. pron.,* thine, yours.

**denken,** *irr.,* to think, fancy; — an (*acc.*), think of.

**denn,** *conj.,* for; *adv.,* then.

**der, die, das,** *def. art.,* the; *rel. pron.,* who, which, that; *demonstr. adj.,* that, etc.; *demonstr. pron.,* the one, he, she, it.

**deren,** of them, their; of which, etc.

**dergleichen,** the like of whom, etc.; of the same kind; ſonſt —, others of the same kind.

**derjenige** (die—, das—), *demonstr. pron.,* he, the one, etc.

**derselbe** (die—, das—), the same; he, she, it, etc.

**deshalb,** for this (that) reason, therefore, on that account.

**deutsch,** German; der Deutſche, the German; ein Deutſcher, a German; Deutſch, *n.,* German (*the language*); auf —, in German.

deutſch-franzöſiſch, Franco-German.

Deutſchland, n., -8, Germany.

Dezember, m., December.

dich, thee, you.

Dichter, m., -8, —, poet.

dick, thick.

die (see der).

Dieb, m., -es, -e, thief.

Diener, m., -8, —, servant.

Dienſt, m., -es, -e, service.

Dienstag, m., -8, -e, Tuesday.

dieſer, this, that; the latter; this (man, etc.), he, etc.

Ding, n., -es, -e, thing.

dir, (to, for) thee, you.

dividieren, to divide (arith.).

doch, yet, still, however, but, after all, etc.

Do'ktor, m., -8, Dokto'ren, doctor (academic degree). [shillings].

Dollar, m., -8, -8, dollar (four

Donnerhall, m.,-es, thunder-clap.

Donnerstag, m., -8,-e, Thursday.

doppelt, double.

Dorf, n., -es, ⸗er, village.

Dorn, m., -es, pl. -en, -e or ⸗er, thorn.

dort, yonder, there.

Dr. (see Doktor).

dran (see daran).

draußen, adv., outside.

drehen, to turn.

drei, three.

dreimal, three times.

dreißigfältig, thirty-fold.

dringend, urgent.

drohen, to threaten.

Droſchke, f., -n, cab.

drüben, over there.

drum (see darum).

du, thou, you.

dunkel, dark.

durch (acc.), through, by, with.

durchdri'ngen, st., insep., to penetrate, be infused into.

durchſichtig, transparent.

durchſu'chen, insep., to search, ransack.

dürfen, irr., mod. aux., to dare, be permitted, allowed, etc.; darf ich? may I?

dürre, dry, dried up.

Durſt, m., -es, thirst; — haben, to be thirsty.

durſtig, thirsty.

Dutzend, n., -es, -e, dozen.


## E

eben, just now; erſt —, only just now.

ebenſo, just as, as.

edel, noble.

Eduard, m., -8, Edward.

Egge, f., -n, harrow.

ehe, conj., before.

eher, adv., rather, sooner.

Ehre, f., -n, honour; ihm zu —n, in his honour.

ehren, to honour.

ehrlich, honest.

Ei, n., -es, -er, egg.

ei! ah! why! indeed!

eigen, adj., own.

eigentlich, really, anyway.

ein, art., a, an; num., one.

eina'nder, one another, each other.

einer, pron., one, a man, etc.; der —e, the one; die —en, some.

**einfahren,** *st.,* to haul in.

**einfallen,** *st.,* f., to occur (to one's mind).

**eingeben,** *st.,* to give, administer.

**einige,** a few, several, some.

**Einkauf,** *m.,* –es, ⁻e, purchase; **Einkäufe machen,** to make purchases, go shopping, shop.

**einkaufen,** to make purchases, go shopping, shop.

**einladen,** *st.,* to invite.

**Einladung,** *f.,* –en, invitation.

**einlenken,** to turn, tack.

**einmal,** once; **auf —,** at once; **noch —,** once more, again; **einmal,** once (upon a time); **denken Sie —,** just think; **nicht —,** not even.

**einpacken,** to pack up.

**Einrichtung,** *f.,* –en, arrangement.

**eins,** *num.,* one (*in counting*).

**einschlafen,** *st.,* f., to go to sleep, fall asleep.

**Einschnitt,** *m.,* –es, –e, incision.

**einsetzen,** to put in, insert.

**einst,** once (upon a time).

**einstecken,** to pocket.

**einsteigen,** *st.,* f., to go (get) aboard, get into (a vehicle).

**einteilen,** to divide.

**eintreten,** *st.,* f. (in, *acc.*), to enter.

**Einwohner,** *m.,* –s, —, inhabitant; **—zahl,** *f.,* population.

**Eis,** *n.,* –es, ice.

**Eisen,** *n.,* –s, iron.

**Eisenbahn,** *f.,* –en, railway, railroad.

**Eisenbahnwagen,** *m.,* –s, —, railway-carriage, car.

**Eisensplitter,** *m.,* –s, —, splinter of iron.

**Eitelkeit,** *f.,* –en, vanity.

**e'lend,** miserable, wretched.

**Elisabeth,** *f.,* –s, Elizabeth.

**Else,** *f.,* –ns, Elsa, Elsie.

**Eltern,** *pl.,* parents.

**empfangen,** *st.,* to receive.

**empfehlen,** *st.,* to recommend, commend; *refl.,* to take (one's) leave.

**Empfehlung,** *f.,* –en, recommendation.

**Empfehlungsbrief,** *m.,* –es, –e, letter of introduction (*or* recommendation).

**Ende,** *n.,* –s, –n, end; **zu —,** at an end, over.

**endlich,** at last, finally.

**englisch,** English; **Englisch,** *n.,* English (*the language*); **auf —,** in English.

**Enkel,** *m.,* –s, —, grandson.

**entdecken,** to discover.

**Entdeckung,** *f.,* –en, discovery.

**entfernt,** distant.

**enthalten,** *st.,* to contain.

**entkommen,** *st.,* f., to escape.

**entlang,** along.

**entlassen,** *st.,* to dismiss.

**entlegen,** remote, distant.

**entschließen,** *st., refl.,* to resolve, make up one's mind.

**entschuldigen,** to excuse.

**Entsetzen,** *n.,* –s, horror.

**enttäuscht,** disappointed.

**Enttäuschung,** *f.,* –en, disappointment.

**entweder,** either.

**entzwei,** in two, to pieces; **— brechen,** *st.,* to break up, break to pieces.

**er,** he, it.

**erblicken,** to catch sight of, see, discover.

**erbrechen,** *st.,* to break open.

**Erbse,** *f.,* –n, pea.

**Erdbeben,** *n.,* –s, —, earthquake.

**Erde,** *f.,* earth, ground, soil.

**erfahren,** *st.,* to experience, learn (by report).

**erfinden,** *st.,* to invent; find.

**Erfindung,** *f.,* –en, invention.

**Erfolg,** *m.,* –es, –e, success.

**erfreuen,** to make glad; **erfreut,** delighted.

**Erfrischung,** *f.,* –en, refreshment.

**erfüllen,** to fulfil; fill.

**ergebenst,** (most) humbly, very truly (yours).

**erhalten,** *st.,* to receive, get; preserve, keep.

**erheben,** *st.,* to lift; *refl.,* to rise, get up.

**erkälten,** *refl.,* to catch cold, take cold; **erkältet sein,** to have a cold.

**erkennen,** *irr.,* to recognize; perceive.

**erklären,** to explain.

**erkranken,** *f.,* to fall ill.

**erkundigen,** *refl.,* to make inquiries.

**erlauben,** to permit, allow.

**Erlebnis,** *n.,* –ses, –se, experience.

**ermöglichen,** to render possible.

**ernennen,** *irr.,* to appoint.

**Erntekranz,** *m.,* –es, ⁻e, harvest-wreath, garland.

**ernten,** to reap, harvest.

**Erquickung,** *f.,* –en, comfort.

**erreichen,** to reach, arrive at.

**erschallen,** *wk. or st., f.,* to sound, resound.

**erscheinen,** *st., f.,* to appear.

**Erscheinen,** *n.,* –s, appearance.

**erst,** *adj.,* first; *adv.,* first, only, not before, not until; — **eben,** only just now, not till now; —**ens,** in the first place.

**erstaunen,** to be astonished.

**ersticken,** *intr.,* to choke, smother.

**ertragen,** *st.,* to bear, endure.

**ertrinken,** *st., f.,* to be drowned, drown (*intr.*).

**erwachen,** *f.,* to awake.

**erwarten,** to expect.

**erweisen,** *st.,* to show; do.

**erwidern,** to reply, answer; return (*tr.*).

**erzählen,** to relate, narrate, tell.

**es,** it, etc.; there; so.

**essen,** *st.,* to eat; **zu Mittag —,** to dine.

**Essen,** *n.,* –s, eating, meal.

**Eßlöffel,** *m.,* –s, —, tablespoon.

**etliches,** some.

**etwa,** *adv.,* about.

**etwas,** something, anything, some, any; **so —,** anything (something) of the kind, such a thing; *adv.,* somewhat.

**euch,** you, (to, for) you.

**euer,** *poss. adj.,* your.

**eurer,** *poss. pron.,* yours.

**eurige** (der, die, das), *poss. pron.,* yours.

**Europa,** *n.,* –s, Europe.

**europäisch,** European.

**ewig,** *adj.,* eternal; *adv.,* forever.

# F

**fähig,** capable.

**Fähigkeit,** *f.,* -en, capacity.

**Fahne,** *f.,* -n, flag, banner.

**fahren,** *st.,* f., h., to go, go (in a vehicle), drive, ride, travel, sail, etc.

**Fahrkarte,** *f.,* -n, ticket (for travelling).

**Fall,** *m.,* -es, ⁻e, fall; case.

**fallen,** *st.,* f., to fall.

**fällen,** to fell, cut down.

**falsch,** false, wrong.

**Fami'lie,** *f.,* -n, family.

**fast,** almost, nearly.

**faul,** decayed, bad, stale.

**Faust,** *f.,* ⁻, fist, hand.

**Februar,** *m.,* February.

**Feder,** *f.,* -n, pen.

**fehlen,** to be lacking, missing; be the matter with, ail (*dat.*); —d, missing, lacking.

**Fehler,** *m.,* -s, —, error, mistake.

**feiern,** to celebrate.

**Feiertag,** *m.,* -es, -e, holiday.

**fein,** fine, nice, gentle.

**Feind,** *m.,* -es, -e, enemy.

**Feld,** *n.,* -es, -er, field.

**Fenster,** *n.,* -s, —, window.

**Fe'rien,** *pl.,* holidays, vacation.

**fern,** far (away), remote.

**fertig,** ready; — sein, to be ready, have finished, have (be) done.

**fest,** firm, solid.

**feucht,** damp.

**Feuer,** *n.,* -s, —, fire.

**finden,** *st.,* to find; — Sie nicht? don't you think (consider)?

**Fisch,** *m.,* -es, -e, fish.

**flach,** flat, level.

**Flasche,** *f.,* -n, bottle.

**flattern,** to flutter, wave.

**Fleisch,** *n.,* -es, meat.

**fleißig,** diligent, industrious.

**fliegen,** *st.,* f., h., to fly; soar.

**Flintenkugel,** *f.,* -n, musket-ball.

**Fluß,** *m.,* -es, ⁻e, river.

**folgen** (*dat.*), to follow; —d, (the) following.

**folglich,** hence, therefore, consequently.

**fordern,** to demand.

**fort,** away, off; — und —, continually.

**fortblühen,** to continue to bloom.

**fortfahren,** *st.,* to continue, go on; f., to drive (go, etc.) on.

**fortgehen,** *st.,* f., to go away.

**fortjagen,** to drive away.

**fortkommen,** *st.,* f., to get away; mache, daß du fortkommst, be off with you, begone.

**fortnehmen,** *st.,* to take away.

**fortschicken,** to send away, dismiss.

**fragen,** to ask.

**Frankreich,** *n.,* -s, France.

**Franzose,** *m.,* -n, -n, Frenchman.

**französisch,** French; Französisch, French (*the language*); auf —, in French.

**Frau,** *f.,* -en, woman, wife, lady, madam, Mrs.

**Fräulein,** *n.,* -s, —, young lady, Miss.

**frei,** free; unoccupied.

**Freiherr,** *m.,* -n, -en, baron.

**freilich,** certainly, to be sure, of course.

**Freitag,** m., –δ, –e, Friday.

**fremd,** strange, foreign.

**Fremd(er),** adj. subst., stranger, foreigner.

**Freude,** f., –n, joy, pleasure.

**freuen,** impers., to gladden; das freut mich, I am glad of that, that pleases me; refl., to be glad, rejoice.

**Freund,** m., –es, –e, friend.

**Freundin,** f., –nen, friend (f.).

**freundlich,** friendly; adv., in a friendly manner, kindly.

**Friede,** m., –ns, peace.

**Friedrich,** m., –δ, Frederick.

**Friedrichstraße,** f., Frederick Street.

**frisch,** fresh, cool.

**froh,** glad, joyous.

**fröhlich,** merry, gladsome.

**Frosch,** m., –es, ⸚e, frog.

**Frucht,** f., ⸚e, fruit.

**fruchtbar,** fruitful, fertile.

**früh,** early; — morgens, early in the morning.

**früher,** earlier, formerly.

**Frühling,** m., –es, spring; —szeit, f., springtime, spring.

**Frühstück,** n., –es, –e, breakfast.

**frühstücken,** insep., to breakfast.

**fühlen,** to feel.

**führen,** to lead.

**füllen,** to fill.

**fünf,** five.

**fünfzig,** fifty.

**für** (acc.), for.

**furchtbar,** frightful, terrible.

**fürchten,** to fear, be afraid of.

**Fürst,** m., –en, –en, prince.

**Fuß,** m., –es, ⸚e, foot; zu —, on foot.

**Fußballspiel,** n., –es, –e, football game, match.

**Fußgänger,** m., –δ, —, pedestrian.

**Futter,** n., –δ, food, fodder.

## G

**Gabe,** f., –n, gift, present.

**Gabel,** f., –n, fork.

**Gang,** m., –es, ⸚e, walk, expedition.

**ganz,** whole; quite, wholly.

**gar,** very, at all, etc.

**Garten,** m., –δ, ⸚, garden.

**Gärtner,** m., –δ, —, gardener.

**Gast,** m., –es, ⸚e, guest.

**Gasthaus,** n., –es, ⸚er, hotel, inn.

**Gasthof,** m., –es, ⸚e, hotel.

**Gastmahl,** n., –es, ⸚er, banquet.

**Gaul,** m., –es, ⸚e, horse, nag.

**Gebäude,** n., –δ, —, building.

**geben,** st., to give; present, act, play (theatre); es gibt, there is (are); was gibt es? what is it? what is the matter?; etwas — auf (acc.), to attach importance to.

**gebildet,** educated, cultured.

**Gebirge,** n., –δ, —, mountain-range, range of hills.

**geboren,** born; —e, maiden-name (French née).

**gebrauchen,** to use, employ.

**Geburtstag,** m., –es, –e, birthday; zum —, as a birthday present.

**Gebüsch,** n., –es, –e, thicket, bushes.

**gedenken,** irr., to think of, remember (gen.); intend.

**Gedicht,** *n.,* –es, –e, poem.

**Gedränge,** *n.,* –s, crowd, press, crush.

**Geduld,** *f.,* patience.

**gefallen,** *st.* (*dat.*), to please, suit; wie gefällt Jhnen das? how do you like that?

**gefällig,** agreeable ; (ift Jhnen) Suppe —? do you wish (will you have) soup?

**gegen** (*acc.*), against, towards, about.

**Ge'gend,** *f.,* –en, district, region.

**Gegenteil,** *n.,* –es, –e, contrary, opposite ; im —, on the contrary.

**gegenüber** (*dat.*), opposite (to).

**gehen,** *st.,* f., to go, walk; zu Fuß —, to walk; *impers.*, to fare; wie geht es Jhnen? how are you?; fonft geht es dir schlecht, or it will be the worse for you; fo laut es nur geht, as loud as (I, etc.) can, as loud as possible.

**gehören,** to belong; — zu, be reckoned as, be (among); be necessary (for, zu).

**Geist,** *m.,* –es, –er, spirit, ghost.

**gelb,** yellow.

**Geld,** *n.,* –es, –er, money.

**Geldftück,** *n.,* –es, –e, coin, piece of money.

**Gelegenheit,** *f.,* –en, opportunity, occasion.

**Gelehrt(er),** *adj. subst.,* learned man, scholar.

**gelingen,** *st.,* f., *impers.* (*dat.*), to succeed; es ift mir gelungen, zu, I succeeded in.

**Gemahlin,** *f.,* –nen, wife; Frau —, wife.

**Gemüse,** *n.,* –s, vegetables.

**genesen,** *st.,* f., to get well, recover (from illness).

**genug,** enough.

**genügen,** to suffice, be enough.

**Gepäck,** *n.,* –es, baggage, luggage.

**Gepäckschein,** *m.,* –es, –e, (baggage-)check.

**Gepäckträger,** *m.,* –s, —, porter.

**gerecht,** just, righteous.

**gering,** small, little, slight; nicht im —ften, not in the least.

**gern(e),** lieber, am liebften, gladly, willingly, with pleasure; recht —, very gladly; etwas — tun, to like to (be pleased to) do anything; — haben, to like, be fond of; — essen, to like (to eat); lieber tun rc., to prefer to do, etc.

**Gerste,** *f.,* barley.

**Gesandt(er),** *adj. subst.,* ambassador.

**Geschäft,** *n.,* –es, –e, business; business-house.

**Geschäftsreisend(er),** *adj. subst.,* commercial traveller.

**geschehen,** *st.,* f., *impers.,* to happen; das ift schon —, I (etc.) have already done so.

**Geschenk,** *n.,* –es, –e, gift, present.

**Geschrei,** *n.,* –es, outcry, clamour.

**Gesellschaft,** *f.,* –en, company; party.

**Gesicht,** *n.,* –es, –er, face.

**Gestalt,** *f.,* –en, form, figure.

**gestern,** yesterday.

**Gesundheit,** *f.,* –en, health.

**Getreide,** *n.,* –s, grain, corn.

**gewahr,** aware.

**Gewicht,** *n.,* –es, –e, weight.

**gewiß,** certain.

**gewöhnlich,** usual, general, ordinary.

**Gipfel,** *m.,* -s, —, summit, peak.

**Glas,** *n.,* -es, ⁻er, glass.

**glatt,** smooth, slippery.

**glauben** (*dat. of pers.*), to believe; think.

**Gläubiger,** *m.,* -s, —, creditor.

**gleich,** like, similar (*dat.*); **das ist mir —,** it is all the same to me, I don't care; *adv.,* at once, presently, directly; *conj.,* although; *see also* **wenn—.**

**gleiten,** *st.,* ſ., to glide, slip.

**Glocke,** *f.,* -n, bell; bell-like flower, hare-bell, blue-bell.

**Glöcklein,** *n.,* -s, —, little bell.

**Glück,** *n.,* -es, (good) luck, happiness.

**glücklich,** happy.

**glühen,** to glow, be warm (hot).

**gnädig,** gracious; **—e Frau,** madam, ma'am.

**Gold,** *n.,* -es, gold; **—stück,** *n.,* -es, -e, gold-piece, gold coin.

**golden,** golden, gold (*adj.*).

**Gott,** *m.,* -es, ⁻er, god; God.

**Grab,** *n.,* -es, ⁻er, grave, tomb.

**graben,** *st.,* to dig.

**Graf,** *m.,* -en, -en, count.

**Gras,** *n.,* -es, ⁻er, grass.

**grau,** grey.

**Grenze,** *f.,* -n, frontier, boundary.

**groß,** ⁻er, größt, large, tall, big, great; **der —e Zeiger,** the minute-hand, long hand.

**Großmutter,** *f.,* ⁻, grandmother.

**Großpapa,** *m.,* -s, -s, grandpapa.

**Großvater,** *m.,* -s, ⁻, grandfather.

**Grube,** *f.,* -n, pit, ditch.

**grün,** green.

**Grün,** *n.,* -s, green.

**Grund,** *m.,* -es, ⁻e, ground, reason.

**gründen,** to found.

**Gruß,** *m.,* -es, ⁻e, greeting; **mit herzlichen Grüßen,** with kind regards, etc.

**grüßen,** to greet, salute; bow to.

**gut,** besser, best, good; kind; *adv.,* well, very well; **recht —,** quite well; **— tun,** to benefit.

**Güte,** *f.,* goodness, kindliness.

**gütig,** kind.

## H

**Haar,** *n.,* -es, -e, hair.

**Habe,** *f.,* belongings, possessions.

**haben,** to have; possess; **recht —,** to be (in the) right.

**Habicht,** *m.,* -es, -e, hawk.

**hacken,** to hew, chop, cut.

**Hafer,** *m.,* -s, oats.

**hager,** lean, gaunt.

**halb,** *adj.,* half; **— sechs,** half-past five.

**Hälfte,** *f.,* -n, half (*as noun*).

**hallo!** halloa!

**Halm,** *m.,* -es, -e, stalk, blade.

**halten,** *st.,* to hold; deem; **— für,** consider as.

**Hand,** *f.,* ⁻e, hand.

**Handarbeit,** *ƒ.,* -en, needle-work, etc.

**Handschuh,** *m.,* -es, -e, glove.

**Handtasche,** *f.,* -n, hand-bag, satchel.

**hangen,** *st.,* to hang.

**Hans,** *m.,* -ens (*from* Johannes), Jack

**hart,** ⁔er, hard.

**Hauch,** *m.,* –es, –e, breath; breeze.

**Haupt,** *n.,* –es, ⁔er, head.

**Hauptstadt,** *f.,* ⁔e, capital (city).

**Hauptstraße,** *f.,* –n, main street.

**Haus,** *n.,* –es, ⁔er, house; nach —e, home; zu —e, at home.

**Heer,** *n.,* –es, –e, army.

**heftig,** violent.

**hei!** ho! heigh!

**Heimweg,** *m.,* –es, –e, way home; sich auf den — machen, to set out (start) for home.

**Heinrich,** *m.,* –s, Henry.

**hei′raten,** to marry.

**heiser,** hoarse.

**heiß,** hot.

**heißen,** *st.,* to be called, be named; bid; wie heißt? what is the name of?; ich heiße B., my name is B.; das heißt, that is (to say).

**heiter,** clear, bright, cheerful.

**Held,** *m.,* –en, –en, hero, champion.

**Heldenmut,** *m.,* –es, heroism.

**heldenmütig,** heroic.

**helfen,** *st.* (*dat.*), to help.

**hell(e),** bright, clear.

**her,** hither.

**herabstürzen,** f., to dash down.

**heraufbringen,** *irr.,* to bring up.

**heraufkommen,** *st.,* f., to come up, come here.

**herauskommen,** *st.,* f., to come out.

**herausnehmen,** *st.,* to take out.

**herausschicken,** to send out (here).

**herausschießen,** *st.,* f., to shoot forth (*intr.*).

**herausstellen,** *refl.,* to turn out.

**herbeirufen,** *st.,* to call (to one's self).

**Herbst,** *m.,* –es, –e, autumn.

**herein,** in (towards); —! come in!

**hereinbringen,** *irr.,* to bring in (here).

**herkommen,** *st.,* f., to come here.

**Herr,** *m.,* –n, –en, master, gentleman, Mr.; (der) — Lehrer, (the) teacher; meine —en, gentlemen (*voc.*).

**herrlich,** magnificent, splendid.

**hersagen,** to recite, repeat.

**herunterschlagen,** *st.,* f., *intr.,* to fall down.

**Herz,** *n.,* –ens, –en, heart.

**Herzensgüte,** *f.,* kind-heartedness, kindliness.

**herzlich,** hearty, affectionate.

**Herzog,** *m.,* –es, –e or ⁔e, duke.

**Heu,** *n.,* –es, hay.

**heute,** to-day; — früh, this morning; — morgen, this morning; — abend, this evening.

**heutzutage,** nowadays, in these days, now.

**hier,** here.

**hierzulande,** in this country.

**Hilfe,** *f.,* help, assistance.

**Himmel,** *m.,* –s, —, sky, heaven.

**hin,** thither, along; — und her, hither and thither, to and fro, backwards and forwards.

**hinabfahren,** *st.,* f., to go (drive, etc.) down.

**hinauf,** *adv.,* up, up on.

**hinaus,** *adv.,* out.

**hinausbegeben,** *st.,* *refl.,* to betake one's self, go.

hinausfahren, *st.*, ſ., to go (drive, etc.) out.

hinausgehen, *st.*, ſ., to go out.

hinein, *adv.*, in.

hineinfahren, *st.*, ſ., to go (drive, etc.) in (into).

hineinfallen, *st.*, ſ., to fall in (into).

hineingehen, *st.*, ſ., to go in (into), enter.

hineinſchicken, to send in (into).

hineinſchleichen, *st.*, ſ., to glide into, steal into, come over.

hingehen, *st.*, ſ., to go (walk) along; für ſich —, to saunter along.

hinſetzen, to set down; *refl.*, to sit down.

hinter, behind.

hinterge′hen, *st.*, *insep.*, to deceive, cheat.

Hintergrund, *m.*, –eß, ‑e, background.

Hintertür, *f.*, –en, back-door.

hiſtoriſch, historical.

Hitze, *f.*, heat.

hoch, höher, höchſt, high, tall.

hochachtungßvoll, very respectfully.

hochbetagt, (far) advanced in years.

höchſt, extremely, very highly.

hoffen, to hope.

hoffentlich, it is to be hoped, I (etc.) hope.

höflich, polite.

Höfling, *m.*, –eß, –e, courtier.

Höhe, *f.*, –n, height.

hold, lovely, sweet.

holen, to get, fetch, bring.

Holz, *n.*, –eß, ‑er, wood.

Holzhauer, *m.*, –ß, —, wood-cutter.

hören, to hear; listen to.

hübſch, pretty, nice.

Huhn, *n.*, –eß, ‑er, fowl, chicken.

Hund, *m.*, –eß, –e, dog.

Hundert, *n.*, –eß, –e, hundred (*as noun*).

hundertfältig, a hundred-fold.

Hunger, *m.*, –ß, hunger.

hungrig, hungry.

hüpfen, to hop, skip.

Hut, *m.*, –eß, ‑e, hat.

Hüter, *m.*, –ß, —, keeper, guardian.

Hütte, *f.*, –n, hut, cabin.

## J

ich, I.

ihm, (to, for) him.

ihn, him, it.

ihnen, (to, for) them.

Ihnen, (to, for) you.

ihr, 2 *pl.*, ye, you.

ihr, *poss. adj.*, her; their.

Ihr, *poss. adj.*, your.

ihrer, *poss. pron.*, hers; theirs.

Ihrer, *poss. pron.*, yours.

ihrige (der, die, das), *poss. pron.*, hers; theirs.

Ihrige (der, die, das), *poss. pron.*, yours.

immer, always; noch —, still.

imſtande ſein, to be capable (of), be in a position (to).

in (*dat., acc.*), in, at, into, to.

indem, while.

indeſſen, meanwhile.

Indien, *n.*, –ß, India.

innig, heartfelt; — liebend, affectionate.

**Inſekt,** *n.,* –es, –en, insect.
**Inſel,** *f.,* –n, island.
**intereſſa'nt,** interesting.
**Intereſſe,** *n.,* –s, –n, interest.
**intereſſieren,** to interest; *refl.,* to take an interest, be interested (in, für).
**irgend,** at all, etc.
**irgendwo,** anywhere (at all); ſonſt —, anywhere else.
**Irland,** *n.,* –s, Ireland.
**irren,** *refl.,* to be mistaken.
**Italien,** *n.,* –s, Italy.
**italieniſch,** Italian.

## J

**ja,** yes; indeed, really, you know, etc.; tun Sie das — nicht, be sure not to do that.
**Jahr,** *n.,* –es, –e, year.
**Jahreszeit,** *f.,* –en, season.
**Januar,** *m.,* January.
**jawohl,** yes (indeed), certainly, Oh yes.
**je,** every, each; — . . . deſto (umſo), the . . . the (*before compar.*); — nach, according to.
**jeder,** each, every, every one; ein —, each, every, etc.
**jedermann,** –s, everybody, every one.
**jederzeit,** always.
**jedesmal,** always.
**jemals,** ever, at any time.
**jemand,** somebody, some one, anybody.
**jener,** *adj.,* that (yonder); *pron.,* that, that one, the former, he, etc.

**jetzt,** now.
**jetzig,** *adj.,* present.
**jodeln,** to yodel, sing in the style of the Swiss mountaineers.
**Johanna,** *f.,* –s, Joanna, Joan.
**juchzen,** to shout for joy.
**Juli,** *m.,* July.
**jung,** ⸚er, young.
**Junge,** *m.,* –n, –n *or coll.,* –ns, boy, lad.
**Jüngling,** *m.,* –es, –e, young man, youth.
**Juni,** *m.,* June.

## K

**Kaffee,** *m.,* –s, coffee.
**Kahn,** *m.,* –es, ⸚e, row-boat, skiff, canoe.
**Kaiſer,** *m.,* –s, —, emperor.
**Kalabrien,** *n.,* –s, Calabria.
**Kalbsbraten,** *m.,* –s, —, roast veal.
**kalt,** ⸚er, cold.
**Kamera'd,** *m.,* –en, –en, comrade, companion.
**kämmen,** to comb.
**Kampf,** *m.,* –es, ⸚e, combat, conflict.
**kämpfen,** to fight.
**Kämpfend(er),** *adj. subst.,* combatant.
**Kämpfer,** *m.,* –s, —, fighter, combatant.
**Kampfwut,** *f.,* fury of battle.
**Kanzler,** *m.,* –s, —, chancellor.
**Karl,** *m.,* –s, Charles.
**Kartoffel,** *f.,* –n, potato.
**Käſe,** *m.,* –s, —, cheese.
**kaufen,** to buy.

**Kaufmann,** *m.,* -es, -leute, merchant.

**kaum,** scarcely, hardly.

**kein,** no, not a, not any.

**keiner,** no one, nobody.

**Keller,** *m.,* -s, —, cellar.

**Kellner,** *m.,* -s, —, waiter.

**kennen,** *irr.,* to know, be acquainted with.

**kentern,** ſ., to capsize.

**Kessel,** *m.,* -s, —, kettle.

**Kind,** *n.,* -es, -er, child.

**Kinderstimme,** *f.,* -n, child's voice.

**Kindesherz,** *n.,* -ens, child's heart.

**Kirchlein,** *n.,* -s, —, little church.

**Kirsche,** *f.,* -n, cherry.

**klagen,** to complain.

**klar,** clear, bright; im —en ſein, to be clear, have made up one's mind.

**Klara,** *f.,* -s, Clara.

**Klasse,** *f.,* -n, class.

**Klavie'r,** *n.,* -es, -e, piano; — ſpielen, to play the piano.

**Klee,** *m.,* -s, clover.

**Kleid,** *n.,* -es, -er, dress; *pl.,* dresses, clothes.

**kleiden,** to dress; *refl.,* to dress (one's self).

**klein,** small, little; der —e Zeiger, the short hand, hour-hand.

**Klima,** *n.,* -s, Klimata, climate.

**klingen,** *st.,* to sound, resound.

**klopfen,** to knock, clap, pat; es klopft, there is a knock, somebody is knocking.

**klug,** ⸗er, intelligent, clever.

**Knabe,** *m.,* -n, -n, boy, lad.

**Knecht,** *m.,* -es, -e, man-servant, labourer, hired-man, man.

**Knie,** *n.,* -es, -e, knee.

**Koch,** *m.,* -es, ⸗e, cook.

**Koffer,** *m.,* -s, —, trunk.

**Kohl,** *m.,* -es, cabbage.

**Kolumbus,** *m.,* Columbus.

**kommen,** *st.,* ſ., to come; wie kommt es, daß? how is it that?; ums Leben —, to lose one's life, perish.

**König,** *m.,* -es, -e, king.

**Königin,** *f.,* -nen, queen.

**königlich,** royal.

**Königreich,** *m.,* -es, -e, kingdom.

**können,** *irr., mod. aux.,* to be able, can, etc.; to know, be versed in, know how to.

**Konze'rt,** *n.,* -es, -e, concert.

**Kopf,** *m.,* -es, ⸗e, head.

**Köpflein,** *n.,* -s, —, little head.

**Kopfschmerz,** *m.,* -es, -en (*usually pl.*), headache.

**Korb,** *m.,* -es, ⸗e, basket.

**kosten,** to cost.

**kostspielig,** costly, expensive.

**Kraft,** *f.,* ⸗e, strength, force.

**Kralle,** *f.,* -n, claw, talon.

**krank,** ⸗er, ill, sick; der Kranke, the sick man, patient.

**Krankheit,** *f.,* -en, illness, sickness.

**Kreide,** *f.,* chalk.

**Krieg,** *m.,* -es, -e, war.

**Kronprinz,** *m.,* -en, -en, crown-prince.

**Küche,** *f.,* -n, kitchen.

**Kugel,** *f.,* -n, bullet.

**Kuh,** *f.,* ⸗e, cow.

**kühl,** cool.

**Künstler,** *m.,* -s, —, artist.

**Kupfermünze,** *f.,* -n, copper coin

**Kurs,** *m.,* –es, –e, rate of exchange.

**kurz,** ꞉er, short.

**Küste,** *f.,* –n, coast, shore.

**Kutscher,** *m.,* –s, —, coachman, driver, cabman.

## L

**lächeln,** to smile.

**lachen,** to laugh.

**lächerlich,** ridiculous, absurd.

**Lachs,** *m.,* –es, –e, salmon.

**laden,** *st.,* to invite; zu Tisch —, to invite to dinner.

**Laden,** *m.,* –s, ꞉, shop, store.

**Land,** *n.,* –es, ꞉er, land, country; soil; auf dem —e, in the country; aufs — gehen, to go to the country.

**landen,** *f.,* to land.

**Landhaus,** *n.,* –es, ꞉er, country-house.

**Landkarte,** *f.,* –n, map.

**Landschaft,** *f.,* –en, landscape.

**Landsmann,** *m.,* –es, –leute, countryman; was für ein — sind Sie? what countryman are you?

**lang,** ꞉er, *adj.,* long.

**lang(e),** ꞉er, *adv.,* long, a long time, for a long time; so —, as long as.

**längs** (*gen., dat., or acc.*), along.

**langsam,** slow.

**längst;** schon —, long ago.

**Lärm,** *m.,* –es, noise.

**lassen,** *st., mod. aux.,* to let, leave; cause to be (done), have (done); machen —, to have made.

**Laterne,** *f.,* –n, lantern, street-lamp.

**Laufburschе,** *m.,* –n, –n, errand-boy.

**laufen,** *st., f., h.,* to run; hasten.

**Laune,** *f.,* –n, humour, temper, whim.

**laut,** loud; *adv.,* aloud.

**lauten,** to sound; run, read, be.

**läuten,** to ring.

**leben,** to live.

**Leben,** *n.,* –s, life; ums — kommen, to lose one's life, perish.

**lebe'ndig,** living.

**Lebensjahr,** *n.,* –es, –e, year (of life).

**Lebensweise,** *f.,* –n, manner of life.

**lebhaft,** lively, exciting.

**leer,** empty.

**legen,** to lay, put.

**lehnen,** to lean.

**lehren,** to teach.

**Lehrer,** *m.,* –s, —, teacher, master.

**Lehrerin,** *f.,* –nen, teacher (*f.*).

**Leibarzt,** *m.,* –es, ꞉e, physician-in-ordinary.

**leicht,** light, easy, slight.

**Leid,** *n.,* –es, grief, sorrow.

**leid tun,** *impers.* (*dat.*), to be sorry; es tut mir —, I am sorry.

**leiden,** *st.,* to suffer, endure.

**leider,** unfortunately.

**leihen,** *st.,* to lend.

**Lerche,** *f.,* –n, lark, skylark.

**lernen,** to learn, study.

**lesen,** *st.,* to read.

**Lesestück,** *n.,* –es, –e, extract for reading.

**letzt**, last; —erer, (the) latter.

**leuchten**, to shine.

**Leute**, *pl.*, people.

**lieb**, dear.

**Liebe**, *f.*, love.

**lieben**, to love.

**lieber**, *comp. of* gern, rather; — essen, to prefer (to eat).

**Lied**, *n.*, -es, -er, song.

**liegen**, *st.*, to lie, be situated, be.

**Liese**, *f.*, Lizzie.

**Li'lie**, *f.*, -n, lily.

**Linde**, *f.*, -n, lime-tree, linden.

**link**, left.

**links**, on the (to the) left.

**loben**, to praise.

**Loch**, *n.*, -es, ⸚er, hole, pit.

**lockern**, to loosen.

**Löffel**, *m.*, -s, —, spoon.

**Lohn**, *m.*, -es, reward.

**lösen**, to buy, get, take (ticket).

**Lotse**, *m.*, -n, -n, pilot.

**Löwe**, *m.*, -n, -n, lion.

**Luft**, *f.*, ⸚e, air.

**Lust**, *f.*, ⸚e, desire, inclination, pleasure; — haben, to have a mind to, want to, wish to.

**Lustgarten**, *m.*, -s, ⸚, pleasure-garden, park.

**lustig**, gay, merry.

**Lustspiel**, *n.*, -es, -e, comedy.


## M

**M.** (*see* Mark).

**machen**, to make, do; eine Freude —, to give pleasure, please; einen Spaziergang —, to take (go for) a walk; sich auf den Heimweg —, to set out (start) for home; sich an etwas —, to set about anything; mache, daß du fortkommst, be off with you, begone.

**Macht**, *f.*, ⸚e, power, might.

**mächtig** (*gen.*), master of.

**Mädchen**, *n.*, -s, —, girl.

**Magd**, *f.*, ⸚e, maid(-servant).

**Mai**, *m.*, May.

**Maienluft**, *f.*, ⸚e, air of May.

**Mais**, *m.*, -es, maize, Indian corn; —mehl, *n.*, -es, Indian meal, corn-meal; —pudding, *m.*, -s, -s, Indian meal pudding.

**Majestät**, *f.*, -en, majesty.

**Mal**, *n.*, time (repeated); mit einem —, all at once; 4 — 4 macht 16, 4 times 4 is 16.

**malen**, to paint.

**Maler**, *m.*, -s, —, painter.

**man**, *indef. pron.*, one, we, you, they, people, etc.

**manch**, many a, many.

**manchmal**, often, frequently.

**Mann**, *m.*, -es, ⸚er, man.

**Mannschaft**, *f.*, -en, crew.

**Mantel**, *m.*, -s, ⸚, cloak.

**Märchen**, *n.*, -s, —, fairy-tale, story.

**Marie'**, *f.*, -ns, Mary.

**Mark**, *f.*, mark (*money*); M. 3.—, (= drei Mark) three marks (3s.)

**Mark**, *f.*, -en, march (*district*).

**Markt**, *m.*, -es, ⸚e, market; auf den — gehen, *st.*, s., to go to (the) market.

**März**, *m.*, March.

**Maschine**, *f.*, -n, machine.

**Matrose**, *m.*, -n, -n, sailor.

**Maus,** *f.,* ⸚e, mouse.

**Medizi′n,** *f.,* medicine.

**Meer,** *n.,* -e$, -e, sea.

**mehr,** more; nicht —, no more, no longer, not now.

**mehrere,** several.

**mehrmals,** several times.

**Meile,** *f.,* -n, league.

**mein,** *poss. adj.,* my.

**meinen,** to mean, think, express the opinion (that), refer to.

**mein(er),** *pers. pron.,* of me.

**meiner,** *poss. pron.,* mine.

**meinige (der, die, das),** *poss. pron.,* mine; die Meinigen, my family, etc.; das Meinige tun, to do my share, do what I can.

**meist,** most.

**meistens,** mostly, for the most part.

**Meister,** *m.,* -s, —, master.

**melden,** to announce; *refl.,* to apply (for a situation).

**Menge,** *f.,* -n, multitude, great many.

**Mensch,** *m.,* -en, -en, man (human being), person; kein —, nobody, no one; *pl.,* people.

**Menschenleben,** *n.,* -s, —, (human) life.

**menschlich,** human.

**merken,** to mark, note, perceive.

**Messer,** *n.,* -s, —, knife.

**Meter,** *m.* or *n.,* -s, —, metre.

**mich,** me.

**mieten,** to hire, engage.

**Milch,** *f.,* milk.

**Millio′n,** *f.,* -en, million.

**Mini′ster,** *m.,* -s, —, minister (*political*).

**minus,** minus.

**Minute,** *f.,* -n, minute.

**Minutenzeiger,** *m.,* -s, —, minute-hand, long hand.

**mir,** (to, for) me.

**mit** (*dat.*), with, along with; by (*in multiplication*).

**mitbringen,** *irr.,* to bring with (one), bring along.

**mitfahren,** *st.,* f., to go (drive, etc.) with; go along (with).

**mitgehen,** *st.,* f., to go with, go along (with).

**mitkommen,** *st.,* f., to come (go) with one, come (go) along.

**mitnehmen,** *st.,* to take with (one), take along.

**mitreisen,** f., to travel (go) with, come (go) along (with).

**Mitreisend(er),** *adj. subst.,* fellow-traveller.

**mitsuchen,** to look for along with others.

**Mittag,** *m.,* -es, -e, midday, noon; zu — essen, to dine.

**Mittagsessen,** *n.,* -s, dinner.

**Mitte,** *f.,* middle, centre.

**mitteilen** (*dat.*), to inform.

**Mitteilung,** *f.,* -en, communication, information.

**Mittel,** *n.,* -s, —, mean(s).

**Mitternacht,** *f.,* ⸚e, midnight.

**Mittwoch,** *m.,* -s, -e, Wednesday.

**mögen,** *irr., mod. aux.,* may, like, etc.; ich mag das nicht, I do not like that; ich möchte (gern), I should like to.

**möglich,** possible.

**Mo′nat,** *m.,* -es, -e, month.

**Mond,** *m.,* -es, -e, moon.

**Montag,** *m.,* -s, -e, Monday.

**Morgen,** *m.,* -s, —, morning;

des —s, morgens, in the morning; heute (gestern) morgen, this (yesterday) morning.

**morgen,** to-morrow; — früh, to-morrow morning.

**Motorboot,** *n.*, –es, –böte *or* –boote, motor-boat.

**müde,** tired, fatigued.

**multiplizieren,** to multiply.

**München,** *n.*, –s, Munich.

**Münze,** *f.*, –n, coin.

**Muse'um,** *n.*, –s, Museen, museum.

**Musi'k,** *f.*, music.

**Muskatnuß,** *f.*, ⁼e, nutmeg.

**müssen,** *irr.*, *mod. aux.*, to be obliged to, be forced to, have to, must.

**Muster,** *n.*, –s, —, pattern, sample.

**Mutter,** *f.*, ⁼, mother.

**Mütterchen,** *n.*, –s, —, mother (dear).

**Mütze,** *f.*, –n, cap.

## N

**na!** well! now!

**nach** (*dat.*), after, to, according to; — Hause, home; der Zug — B., the train for B.

**Nachbar,** *m.*, –s, –n, neighbour.

**nachdem,** *conj.*, after.

**Nachfolger,** *m.*, –s, —, successor.

**nachgeben,** *st.*, to yield, give way.

**nachher,** afterwards, thereupon.

**Nachmittag,** *m.*, –es, –e, afternoon; des —s, in the afternoon.

**Nachricht,** *f.*, –en, news.

**nachsehen,** *st.*, to look, search.

**nachsitzen,** *st.*, to stay in (as punishment, after school), be detained.

**nächst,** next.

**Nacht,** *f.*, ⁼e, night.

**Nachtisch,** *m.*, –es, dessert.

**Nachtlied,** *n.*, –es, –er, evensong.

**Nagel,** *m.*, –s, ⁼, nail.

**nah(e),** ⁼, nächst, near.

**Nahrung,** *f.*, –en, nourishment, food.

**Name,** *m.*, –ns, –n, name.

**nämlich,** namely, that is to say.

**naß,** ⁼er, wet.

**Nationa'l=Denkmal,** *n.*, –s, ⁼er, national-monument.

**natürlich,** natural; *adv.*, naturally, of course.

**Nebel,** *m.*, –s, —, fog, mist.

**neben** (*dat.*, *acc.*), near, by, beside.

**nebenan,** near by, next door.

**nehmen,** *st.*, to take; Abschied —, to take leave, say good-bye.

**nein,** no.

**nennen,** *irr.*, to name; tell; wie nennt man diese Straße? what is the name of this street?

**neu,** new.

**neulich,** lately, the other day.

**nicht,** not; — mehr, no longer, not now; noch —, not yet; gar —, not at all; Sie sind müde, — wahr? you are tired, are you not?

**nichts,** nothing.

**Nickelmünze,** *f.*, –n, nickel coin.

**nie,** never; noch —, never yet.

**niederlegen,** to lay down, resign.

**niemand,** nobody, no one, no person, not anybody, etc.

Nikolaus, *m.*, Nicholas.

nirgend(s), nowhere.

Nixe, *f.*, –n, water-sprite, nixie.

noch, still, yet, as yet, etc.; — nicht, not yet; — immer, still; — ein, one more, another; — gestern, no later than yesterday, only yesterday; — einmal, once more, again; — eben, just, barely; — nie, never yet.

Nord=Afrika, *n.*, –s, North Africa.

Norden, *m.*, –s *and* —, north.

Nordsee, *f.*, North Sea, German Ocean.

Norwegen, *n.*, –s, Norway.

Not, *f.*, ⸚e, need, necessity.

nötig, necessary, needful.

November, *m.*, November.

nun, now; well.

nur, only, just; anyway.

nützlich, useful.

### D

O! O! oh!

ob, whether, if.

oben, at the top, above; upstairs; — darauf, upon it.

obgleich, although, though.

obig, above, *adj.*

Obst, *n.*, –es, fruit (of garden *or* orchard).

Obstbaum, *m.*, –es, ⸚e, fruit-tree.

Ochs(e), *m.*, –(e)n, –(e)n, ox.

öde, desolate, dreary.

oder, or.

Ofen, *m.*, –s, ⸚, stove.

Offizie'r, *m.*, –es, –e, officer (*milit.*).

Offiziersmantel, *m.*, –s, ⸚, officer's cloak.

oft, often, frequently.

oftmals, often.

ohne (*acc.*), without.

Ohr, *n.*, –es, –en, ear.

Ohrfeige, *f.*, –n, box on the ear.

Oktober, *m.*, October.

Omnibus, *m.*, —, –sse, omnibus.

Onkel, *m.*, –s, —, uncle.

Ontario, *m.*, –s, Lake Ontario.

Opfer, *n.*, –s, —, sacrifice.

ordentlich, proper.

Ort, *m.*, –es, –e *and* ⸚er, place, spot.

Osten, *m.*, –s *and* —, east.

Ostern, Easter.

Österreich, *n.*, –s, Austria.

Österreich=Ungarn, *n.*, –s, Austria-Hungary.

österreichisch, Austrian.

östlich, eastern.

Ostsee, *f.*, Baltic.

### P

Paar, *n.*, –es, –e, pair, couple; ein paar, a few; ein paarmal, several times.

packen, to pack; seize.

Papie'r, *n.*, –es, –e, paper.

Papiergeld, *n.*, –es, paper-money.

Papierkorb, *m.*, –es, ⸚e, waste-basket.

Parade, *f.*, –n, parade.

Paris, *n.*, Paris.

Park, *m.*, –es, –e *or* –s, park.

Patie'nt, *m.*, –en, –en, patient.

Pause, *f.*, –n, pause; recess.

persisch, Persian.

Petersburg, *n.*, –s, St. Petersburg.

**Pfarrer,** *m.,* –ß, —, clergyman, minister.

**pfeilschnell,** swift as an arrow.

**Pfennig,** *m.,* –eß, –e, 'pfennig' ($\frac{1}{100}$ part of a mark).

**Pferd,** *n.,* –eß, –e, horse.

**pflanzen,** to plant.

**pflastern,** to pave.

**pflegen,** to tend, nurse.

**Pflicht,** *f.,* –en, duty.

**pflichtgetreu,** faithful to duty.

**pflücken,** to pick, pluck, gather.

**pflügen,** to plough.

**Pfund,** *n.,* –eß, –e, pound.

**Philosoph,** *m.,* –en, –en, philosopher.

**Photographie',** *f.,* –n, photograph.

**Physi't,** *f.,* physics.

**Platz,** *m.,* –eß, ⸗e, place, seat; public place, square.

**plötzlich,** sudden.

**plus,** plus.

**Portemonnaie** [pr. portmonä'], *n.,* –ß, –ß, purse, pocket-book.

**prächtig,** splendid, magnificent, fine.

**Preis,** *m.,* –eß, –e, price; prize.

**preisen,** *st.,* to praise, extol.

**Preuße,** *m.,* –n, –n, Prussian (*noun*).

**Preußen,** *n.,* –ß, Prussia.

**preußisch,** Prussian (*adj.*).

**Professor,** *m.,* –ß, Professo'ren, professor.

**Progra'mm,** *n.,* –eß, –e, programme.

**proklamieren,** to proclaim.

**Provia'nt,** *m.,* –eß, provisions.

**Pudding,** *m.,* –ß, –ß, pudding.

**Puls,** *m.,* –eß, –e, pulse.

**Pulsschlag,** *m.,* –eß, ⸗e, pulsation, pulse-beat.

**Punkt,** *m.,* –eß, –e, point; — 10 Uhr, at ten o'clock precisely.

**pünktlich,** punctual.

**Puppe,** *f.,* –n, doll.

### Q

**quälen,** to torment, vex.

**Quell,** *m.,* –eß, –e, spring, fountain.

**Quelle,** *f.,* –n, spring, fountain.

### R

**Ranunkel,** *f.,* –n, crowfoot, buttercup.

**rasieren,** to shave.

**Rat,** *m.,* –eß, advice.

**raten,** *st.* (*dat.*), to advise.

**Rathaus,** *n.,* –eß, ⸗er, town-hall, city-hall, Guildhall.

**Rätsel,** *n.,* –ß, —, riddle.

**rauchen,** to smoke.

**rauschen,** to murmur, gurgle.

**rechnen,** to reckon.

**Rechnung,** *f.,* –en, bill, account.

**recht,** right; — gern(e), very gladly; — gut, quite well; — geben, to admit; — haben, to be (in the) right.

**rechts,** on the (to the) right.

**reden,** to speak, talk.

**Redensart,** *f.,* –en, phrase, expression.

**Regen,** *m.,* –ß, rain.

**Regenschirm,** *m.,* –eß, –e, umbrella.

**Regenzeit,** *f.,* –en, rainy weather.

**Regierung,** *f.,* –en, government, rule; unter der —, in the reign.

**regnen,** to rain.

**reich,** rich.

**Reich,** *n.,* –es, –e, empire, kingdom.

**reichen,** to pass, hand.

**Reichsstadt,** *f.,* ‑e, imperial city.

**reif,** ripe.

**Reihe,** *f.,* –n, rank, row, turn; ich komme an die —, it is my turn; der — nach, in turn.

**rein,** clean, pure.

**reinlich,** cleanly, neat, tidy.

**Reise,** *f.,* –n, journey, voyage, trip; eine — machen, to take (go on) a journey.

**reisen,** f., h., to travel, journey, go; go (away), set out (on a journey).

**Reisend(er),** *adj. subst.,* traveller.

**reizend,** charming.

**Republik,** *f.,* –en, republic.

**Republikaner,** *m.,* –s, —, republican.

**Restauration,** *f.,* –en, restaurant.

**retten,** to save, rescue.

**Revolution,** *f.,* –en, revolution.

**Revolver,** *m.,* –s, —, revolver.

**Rezept,** *n.,* –es, –e, recipe, prescription.

**Rhein,** *m.,* –es, the (river) Rhine.

**Rheinwein,** *m.,* –es, –e, Rhenish wine, hock.

**richtig,** right, correct; — gehen, to be right, correct (*of time-piece*).

**Rinderbraten,** *m.,* –s, —, roast of beef.

**Ring,** *m.,* –es, –e, ring.

**rinnen,** *st.,* f., to flow, run, pass by.

**Ritterschaft,** *f.,* knighthood.

**Rock,** *m.,* –es, ‑e, coat.

**Rolle,** *f.,* –n, part (*theat.*).

**Rom,** *n.,* –s, Rome.

**Roman,** *m.,* –es, –e, romance, novel.

**Rose,** *f.,* –n, rose.

**Rosine,** *f.,* –n, raisin.

**Röslein,** *n.,* –s, —, little rose.

**rot,** ‑er, red.

**Rotwein,** *m.,* –es, –e, red wine, claret.

**Rübe,** *f.,* –n, turnip.

**Rücken,** *m.,* –s, —, back.

**Rücksitz,** *m.,* –es, –e, back-seat.

**Ruf,** *m.,* –es, –e, call, shout, cry.

**rufen,** *st.,* to call, cry out.

**Ruhe,** *f.,* rest, repose.

**ruhen,** to rest, repose.

**ruhig,** quiet, calm.

**rund,** round.

**Runde,** *f.,* –n, round, circuit.

**Russe,** *m.,* –n, –n, Russian (*noun*).

**Rußland,** *n.,* –s, Russia.

## S

**'s** (*see* es).

**Saal,** *m.,* –es, Säle, hall.

**Saat,** *f.,* –en, seed, sowing, green-crop.

**Sache,** *f.,* –n, thing, matter, affair.

**Sachsen,** *n.,* –s, Saxony.

**Säemann,** *m.,* –es, ‑er, sower.

**säen,** to sow.

**sagen,** to say, tell.

**Salz,** *n.,* –es, –e, salt.

**Same(n),** *m.,* –ns, –n, seed.

**sämtlich,** all (*collectively*).

**Samstag,** *m.,* –s, –e, Saturday.

sanft, ⸚er, soft, sweet.

satt, satisfied, sated.

Satz, m., -es, ⸚e, sentence.

Schachtel, f., -n, box (*of paper or card-board*).

Schade(n), m., -n(s), Schaden *or* Schäden, damage, harm.

Schädel, m., -s, —, skull.

Schaf, n., -es, -e, sheep.

Schäflein, n., -s, —, little sheep, lamb.

Schale, f., -n, shell.

schallen, to resound.

Schalter, m., -s, —, wicket, ticket-office.

Schaltjahr, n., -es, -e, leap-year.

schämen, *refl.*, to be ashamed.

scharf, ⸚er, sharp.

Scharlach, m., -s, scarlet.

Schatten, m., -s, shade, shadow.

schauen, to look, gaze; see.

Schaufenster, n., -s, —, (show-) window.

Schauspiel, n., -es, -e, play, drama.

Schauspieler, m., -s, —, actor.

Schauspielerin, f., -nen, actress.

Scheik, m., -s, -s, sheik.

Schein, m., -es, -e, note, bank-note.

scheinen, *st.*, to shine; seem.

scheitern, s., to be wrecked.

schenken, to give, make a present of, present.

schicken, to send.

Schiff, n., -es, -e, ship; zu —, on ship, by ship.

Schildwache, f., -n, sentry.

Schlacht, f., -en, battle.

schlafen, *st.*, to sleep.

Schlafwagen, m., -s, —, sleeping-car.

Schlafzimmer, n., -s, —, bed-room.

schlagen, *st.*, to strike.

schlecht, bad, poor; sonst geht es dir — (*see* gehen).

schleichen, *st.*, s., to creep, sneak.

schleifen, *st.*, to grind.

Schleifstein, m., -es, -e, grind-stone.

schlimm, bad.

Schlingel, m., -s, —, rogue, rascal.

Schlittenfahrt, f., -en, sleigh-ride (drive); eine — machen, to take (go for) a sleigh-ride.

Schlittschuh, m., -es, -e, skate; — laufen, *st.*, s., h., to skate.

Schloß, n., -es, ⸚er, castle, palace.

Schloßfreiheit, f. (*proper name =* precincts of the palace).

Schloßplatz, m., -es, ⸚e, castle-square.

Schluß, m., -es, ⸚e, conclusion, ending.

schmecken, to taste; das schmeckt mir, I like (the taste of) that.

schmeicheln (*dat.*), to flatter.

Schmerz, m., -es, -en, pain, grief.

Schmetterling, m., -es, -e, butter-fly.

Schmied, m., -es, -e, (black-) smith.

Schmiede, f., -n, smithy, forge.

schmiegen, *refl.*, to nestle; wind, meander.

Schnee, m., -s, snow.

schneiden, *st.*, to cut.

Schneider, m., -s, —, tailor.

schneien, to snow.

**schnell,** quick, rapid.

**Schnellzug,** *m.,* –es, ⸚e, express train.

**Schokolade,** *f.,* chocolate; —-Pudding, *m.,* –s, –s, chocolate pudding.

**schon,** already, not later than, as early as.

**schön,** beautiful, handsome, fine; *adv.,* well, very well.

**Schornstein,** *m.,* –es, –e, chimney.

**Schottland,** *n.,* –s, Scotland.

**schrecklich,** dreadful, terrible.

**schreiben,** *st.,* to write.

**Schreibtisch,** *m.,* –es, –e, writing-table, desk, writing-desk.

**Schublade,** *f.,* –n, drawer.

**Schule,** *f.,* –n, school, school-house.

**Schüler,** *m.,* –s, —, pupil, scholar.

**Schulglocke,** *f.,* –n, school-bell.

**Schulhaus,** *n.,* –es, ⸚er, school-house, school.

**Schulkamerad,** *m.,* –en, –en, school-mate, school-fellow.

**Schulstube,** *f.,* –n, school-room.

**Schulter,** *f.,* –n, shoulder.

**Schulzimmer,** *n.,* –s, —, school-room.

**Schüssel,** *f.,* –n, dish, platter.

**Schutz,** *m.,* –es, shelter, protection.

**schwach,** ⸚er, weak.

**schwarz,** ⸚er, black.

**schweben,** to hover, soar.

**schweigen,** *st.,* to be (keep) silent.

**Schweiz,** *f.,* Switzerland.

**schwer,** heavy; hard, difficult, serious.

**Schwert,** *n.,* –es, –er, sword.

**Schwertgeklirr,** *n.,* –es, clashing of swords.

**Schwester,** *f.,* –n, sister.

**schwimmen,** *st.,* f., h., to swim.

**schwingen,** *st.,* to swing, brandish.

**schwören,** *st.,* to swear.

**Schwur,** *m.,* –es, ⸚e, oath.

**sechzigfältig,** sixty-fold.

**See,** *m.,* –s, –n, lake.

**Seeküste,** *f.,* –n, sea-coast.

**Segel,** *n.,* –s, —, sail.

**Segelschiff,** *n.,* –es, –e, sailing-vessel, ship.

**Segen,** *m.,* –s, blessing, benediction.

**segnen,** to bless.

**sehen,** *st.,* to see.

**sehr,** very, very much.

**seiden,** silken, (of) silk.

**Seidenhändler,** *m.,* –s, —, silk-merchant.

**sein,** *irr.,* f., to be; *aux.,* to be, have; mir ist als ob, I feel as if.

**sein,** *poss. adj.,* his, her, its.

**seiner,** *poss. pron.,* his, hers, its ; die Seinen, his family, etc.

**seinige** (der, die, das), *poss. pron.,* his, hers, its.

**seit,** since; ich bin — acht Tagen hier, I have been here for a week (for the last week).

**Seite,** *f.,* –n, side, page.

**Sekundenzeiger,** *m.,* –s, —, second-hand.

**selber,** self, myself, etc.; even.

**selbst,** self, myself, etc.; even.

**selten,** seldom.

**senden,** *irr.,* to send.

**September,** *m.,* September.

**setzen,** to set, place; *refl.,* to sit down, seat one's self.

**ſich,** himself, herself, etc.; (to, for) himself, etc.; *recipr.*, one another; **für —,** for one's self; alone.

**ſie,** she, it; her, it; they, them.

**Sie** (*formal*), you.

**ſieben,** seven.

**Signora** (pro. **Sinjora**), *f.*, lady, madam.

**Silber,** *n.*, **-s,** silver.

**Silbermünze,** *f.*, **-n,** silver coin.

**ſilbern,** (of) silver.

**ſingen,** *st.*, to sing.

**Sinn,** *m.*, **-es, -e,** sense; mind, feeling, intention.

**Sirup,** *m.*, **-s,** molasses, **treacle.**

**Sitz,** *m.*, **-es, -e,** seat, place.

**ſitzen,** *st.*, to sit; **darauf ſitzt ſich's,** one can sit on it.

**Sizilien,** *n.*, **-s,** Sicily.

**ſo,** so, as, thus; there now; **— ein,** such a; **— etwas,** anything of the kind; **— ... wie,** as ... as; **— wie auch,** as also, as well as; **— groß ... — groß,** great as ... just as great; (*untranslated in 'result' clause*).

**ſobald** (wie), as soon as.

**ſoeben,** just now.

**ſofort,** forthwith, immediately, at once.

**ſogar,** even.

**ſogenannt,** so-called.

**ſogleich,** immediately, at once.

**Sohn,** *m.*, **-es, ⁻e,** son.

**ſolcher,** such.

**Solda't,** *m.*, **-en, -en,** soldier.

**ſollen,** *irr.*, *mod. aux.*, to be in duty bound to, be to, shall, must, ought; be said to, etc.

**Sommer,** *m.*, **-s, —,** summer.

**Sommerkleid,** *n.*, **-es, -er,** summer dress.

**ſondern** (*after neg.*), but.

**Sonnabend,** *m.*, **-s, -e,** Saturday.

**Sonne,** *f.*, **-n,** sun.

**Sonnenſchein,** *m.*, **-es,** sunshine.

**Sonnenſtrahl,** *m.*, **-es, -en,** sunbeam, sunshine.

**Sonntag,** *m.*, **-s, -e,** Sunday.

**ſonſt,** else, or else, besides, otherwise; **dergleichen —,** others of the same kind.

**Sorge,** *f.*, **-n,** care, sorrow.

**ſorgen,** to be anxious, be full of care, take care.

**Sorgen,** *n.*, **-s,** sorrowing.

**ſorgfältig,** careful.

**ſowie,** as well as, and also.

**ſpaniſch,** Spanish; **Spaniſch,** Spanish (*the language*).

**ſpannen,** to cock (a gun).

**Spargel,** *m.*, **-s, —,** asparagus.

**ſpät,** late; **—er,** later, afterwards.

**Spaten,** *m.*, **-s, —,** spade.

**ſpäteſtens,** at the latest.

**ſpazieren,** ſ., to take a walk, etc.; **— gehen,** *st.*, ſ., to take (go for) a walk.

**Spaziergang,** *m.*, **-es, ⁻e,** walk; **einen — machen,** to take (go for) a walk.

**ſpeiſen,** to feed, nourish.

**Speiſekarte,** *f.*, **-n,** bill of fare, *menu.*

**Speiſezimmer,** *n.*, **-s, —,** dining-room.

**Spiegel,** *m.*, **-s, —,** mirror, looking-glass.

**Spiel,** *n.*, **-es, -e,** play, game, **match, acting.**

**ſpielen,** to play; act.

**Spital,** *n.,* –es, ⸚er, hospital.

**Sport,** *m.,* –es, sport.

**Sprache,** *f.,* –n, language.

**Sprachrohr,** *n.,* –es, –e, speaking-trumpet.

**sprechen,** *st.,* to speak; say; pronounce; *trans.,* to speak to, see, interview.

**Sprichwort,** *n.,* –es, ⸚er, proverb.

**sprießen,** *st.,* ſ., h., to sprout, bud.

**Springbrunnen,** *m.,* –s, —, fountain.

**springen,** *st.,* ſ., to spring, jump.

**spüren,** to trace, perceive.

**Staat,** *m.,* –es, –en, state (*polit.*).

**Stadt,** *f.,* ⸚e, town, city.

**Stall,** *m.,* –es, ⸚e, stable.

**Stärke,** *f.,* strength, force, vigour.

**Statio'n,** *f.,* –en, station, stopping-place.

**statt** (*gen.*), instead of.

**stattfinden,** *st.,* to take place.

**Staub,** *m.,* –es, dust.

**stecken,** *wk. or st.,* to thrust, put, stick.

**Stecknadel,** *f.,* –n, pin.

**stehen,** *st.,* to stand; be, be situated, lie.

**steigen,** *st.,* ſ., to rise, mount, ascend; ans Land —, to land; — in, to enter (a carriage, etc.).

**Steinichte** (das), *n., adj. subst.,* stony place(s).

**Stelle,** *f.,* –n, place.

**stellen,** to place, put, set.

**Stellung,** *f.,* –en, position, situation.

**sterben,** *st.,* ſ., to die.

**Stern,** *m.,* –es, –e, star.

**Sternblume,** *f.,* –n, star-like flower.

**Sternwarte,** *f.,* –n, observatory.

**stets,** always, ever.

**Steuermann,** *m.,* –es, ⸚er, steersman, helmsman.

**steuern,** to steer.

**Stiefel,** *m.,* –s, —, boot.

**still,** still, quiet, calm.

**stillen,** to still, assuage.

**stillstehen,** *st.,* h., ſ., to stand still.

**Stock,** *m.,* –es, ⸚e, stick, cane; story (*of a building*).

**stören,** to disturb, trouble.

**Störung,** *f.,* –en, disturbance, interruption.

**Stoß,** *m.,* –es, ⸚e, blow, knock.

**Strafe,** *f.,* –n, punishment.

**Strand,** *m.,* –es, –e, strand, shore, Strand (street in London).

**Straße,** *f.,* –n, street, road.

**Straßenbahn,** *f.,* –en, street-railway, tram.

**Strauch,** *m.,* –es, ⸚e or ⸚er, bush, shrub.

**streicheln,** to stroke, pat.

**streichen,** *st.,* to stroke.

**Streit,** *m.,* –es, –e, strife, contest.

**Strich,** *m.,* –es, –e, stroke, line, mark.

**stricken,** to knit.

**Stroh,** *n.,* –es, straw.

**Strom,** *m.,* –es, ⸚e, stream, river.

**Strumpf,** *m.,* –es, ⸚e, stocking.

**Stubenmädchen,** *n.,* –s, —, housemaid.

**Stubentür,** *f.,* –en, door of a room.

**Stück,** *n.,* –es, –e, piece; play, drama.

**Stude'nt,** *m.,* –en, –en, student.

**studieren,** to study.

**Studierzimmer,** *n.*, –8, —, study (*room*).

**Studium,** *n.*, –8, Studien, study.

**Stuhl,** *m.*, –e8, ⁻e, chair.

**Stunde,** *f.*, –n, hour; lesson.

**stundenlang,** for hours.

**Stundenzeiger,** *m.*, –8, —, hour-hand, short hand.

**Sturm,** *m.*, –e8, ⁻e, storm.

**stürmisch,** stormy.

**subtrahieren,** to subtract.

**suchen,** to seek, look for.

**südlich,** southern, southerly, on the south.

**Sünder,** *m.*, –8, —, sinner.

**Suppe,** *f.*, –n, soup.

**süß,** sweet.

## T

**tadeln,** to blame.

**Tafel,** *f.*, –n, blackboard.

**Tag,** *m.*, –e8, –e, day; eines —e8, one day.

**Tagesanbruch,** *m.*, –e8, daybreak.

**täglich,** daily.

**Tal,** *n.*, –e8, ⁻er, valley.

**Taler,** *m.*, –8, —, thaler (three shillings).

**Tante,** *f.*, –n, aunt.

**Tanz,** *m.*, –e8, ⁻e, dance, dancing.

**tanzen,** to dance.

**Tapferkeit,** *f.*, valour, bravery.

**Tasche,** *f.*, –n, pocket.

**Taschentuch,** *n.*, –e8, ⁻er, handkerchief.

**Tasse,** *f.*, –n, cup.

**Tat,** *f.*, –en, deed, action, act; in der —, indeed, in fact, truly.

**Tau,** *m.*, –e8, dew.

**tauchen,** to dive.

**tausend,** a thousand.

**Tausend,** *n.*, –e8, –e, thousand (*noun*).

**Tee,** *m.*, –8, tea.

**Teelöffel,** *m.*, –8, —, teaspoon.

**Teich,** *m.*, –e8, –e, pool, pond.

**teigig,** doughy.

**Teil,** *m. and n.*, –e8, –e, part, portion; party.

**Teleskop,** *n.*, –e8, –e, telescope.

**Teller,** *m.*, –8, —, plate.

**Tempel,** *m.*, –8, —, temple.

**teuer,** dear; expensive.

**Theater,** *n.*, –8, —, theatre.

**Thron,** *m.*, –e8, –e, throne.

**tief,** deep.

**Tiefe,** *f.*, –n, deep, depth(s).

**Tier,** *n.*, –e8, –e, animal, beast.

**Tiergarten,** *m.*, –8, ⁻, park.

**Tinte,** *f.*, –n, ink.

**Tisch,** *m.*, –e8, –e, table; zu — (ein)laden, to invite to dinner; bei — sein, to be at table.

**Tischgebet,** *n.*, –e8, –e, grace (at meals).

**Tischler,** *m.*, –8, —, cabinet maker, joiner.

**Titel,** *m.*, –8, —, title.

**Tod,** *m.*, –e8, death.

**Toilette** [pr. toale'tte], *f.*, –n, toilet.

**Tomate,** *f.*, –n, tomato.

**Tor,** *n.*, –e8, –e, gate.

**törichterweise,** foolishly.

**tot,** dead.

**töten,** to kill.

**Tourist** [pr. turi'st], *m.*, –en, –en, tourist.

**tragen,** *st.*, to bear, carry; wear; bring, take.

**Träne,** *f.,* –n, tear.

**trauen** (*dat.*), to trust.

**Trauerſpiel,** *n.,* –es, –e, tragedy.

**Traum,** *m.,* –es, ⸚e, dream.

**treffen,** *st.,* to hit, strike; chance upon, meet (with), fall in with, find.

**Treiben,** *n.,* –s, activity; life.

**trennen,** to separate, divide; *refl.,* to part, separate (*intr.*).

**treten,** *st.,* ſ., h., to tread, walk, go.

**treu,** true, faithful.

**trinken,** *st.,* to drink.

**trocken,** dry.

**Tröpflein,** *n.,* –s, —, (little) drop.

**Troſt,** *m.,* –es, consolation, comfort.

**tröſten,** to console, comfort.

**Trottoir** [pr. trotoa'r], *n.,* –s, –s, sidewalk, pavement.

**trotzdem,** in spite of this (that), nevertheless.

**trübe,** troubled, sad.

**Trümmer,** *pl.,* ruins.

**tüchtig,** thorough, efficient; eine —e Strafe, a severe punishment.

**tummeln,** *refl.,* to bestir one's self.

**tun,** *irr.,* to do; weh —, to hurt, pain.

**Tür,** *f.,* –en, door.

**türkiſch,** Turkish.

**Türpfoſten,** *m.,* –s, —, door-post.

## U

**über** (*dat., acc.*), over, above, across, concerning, through, about, at, more than; heute — acht Tage, a week from to-day, this day week.

**übera'll,** everywhere.

**überla'ſſen,** *st., insep.,* to give up, hand over.

**Übermut,** *m.,* –es, insolence, presumption.

**überne'hmen,** *st., insep.,* to take over, undertake.

**Überraſchung,** *f.,* –en, surprise.

**überſtreu'en,** *insep.,* to bestrew, cover.

**übertre'ffen,** *st., insep.,* to exceed, surpass.

**Überzieher,** *m.,* –s, —, overcoat.

**übrig;** das —e, what is left, the remainder.

**übrigbleiben,** *st.,* ſ., to be left, remain.

**übrigens,** moreover.

**Übung,** *f.,* –en, practice, exercise.

**u. dgl. m.** (und dergleichen mehr).

**Ufer,** *n.,* –s, —, shore, bank.

**Uhr,** *f.,* –en, clock; watch; wie viel — iſt es? what time is it?; drei —, three o'clock; um wie viel —? at what time (o'clock)?

**um** (*acc.*), around, about, for, at; um + *infin.,* in order to, to.

**umfa'ſſen,** *insep.,* to comprise, include.

**u'mgraben,** *st.,* to dig up, dig over.

**u'mkommen,** *st.,* ſ., to perish; um etwas kommen, to lose anything.

**u'mſchlagen,** *st.,* ſ., to turn over, capsize.

**Umſtand,** *m.,* –es, ⸚e, circumstance.

**umſtändlich,** ceremonious.

**u'mziehen,** *st.,* ſ., to remove, move (*intr.*).

**unangenehm,** disagreeable, unpleasant.

**u'nartig,** ill-behaved, naughty.

**unbeschädigt,** uninjured.

**und,** and; — so weiter (usw.), and so forth.

**unentbehrlich,** indispensable.

**unerwartet,** unexpected.

**ungeduldig,** impatient.

**ungefä'hr,** about, nearly.

**unglau'blich,** incredible.

**u'nglücklich,** unhappy, unfortunate.

**Universität,** f., –en, university.

**U'nkosten,** pl., expenses.

**unmöglich,** impossible; ich kann es — tun, I can't possibly do it.

**u'nnötig,** unnecessary.

**U'nordnung,** f., disorder, untidiness.

**uns,** us, (to, for) us.

**unser,** poss. adj., our.

**unserer,** poss. pron., ours.

**unsrige** (der, die, das), poss. pron., ours.

**unten,** at the bottom, below, downstairs.

**unter** (dat., acc.), under, beneath, below, among, in; — der Regierung, in the reign.

**unterbre'chen,** st., insep., to interrupt.

**unterdessen,** meanwhile, in the meantime, while.

**unterha'lten,** st., insep., to entertain; refl., to enjoy one's self.

**Unterschied,** m., –es, –e, difference.

**Unterschrift,** f., –en, signature.

**Untertan,** m., –s and –en, –en, subject (of a ruler).

**u'ntertauchen,** to dive (down).

**unterwegs,** on the way.

**unverheiratet,** unmarried.

**unverletzt,** uninjured.

**Ursache,** f., –n, cause.

**usw.** (und so weiter), and so forth, et cetera.

## B

**v.** (von, in titles of nobility).

**Vater,** m., –s, ⸗, father.

**Väterchen,** n., –s, —, little father (Russian mode of address).

**Vaterland,** n., –es, –e, fatherland, native country.

**Veilchen,** n., –s, —, violet.

**Veranda,** f., –s or Veranden, veranda.

**verausgaben,** to pay out, spend.

**verbessern,** to correct.

**verbleiben,** st., ſ., to remain.

**verbrechen,** st., to be guilty of.

**verbrennen,** irr., to burn.

**verbringen,** irr., to spend, pass (time).

**verdienen,** to earn; deserve.

**verehren,** to honour, revere.

**vereinen,** to unite.

**verfertigen,** to make, prepare.

**vergebens,** in vain.

**vergelten,** st., to repay.

**vergessen,** st., to forget.

**vergeßlich,** absent-minded, forgetful.

**Vergnügen,** n., –s, pleasure, joy, delight; viel — haben, to enjoy one's self very much.

**Vergnügungsreise,** f., –n, pleasure-trip.

**verhei'ratet,** married.

**verhindern,** to hinder, prevent.

**verirren,** *refl.*, to lose one's way.

**verkaufen,** to sell.

**Verkäuferin,** *f.*, –nen, saleswoman, shopgirl.

**Verkehr,** *m.*, –es, intercourse.

**verkleiden,** to disguise.

**verleihen,** *st.*, to confer, give (title, etc.).

**verlieren,** *st.*, to lose.

**vernichten,** to annihilate.

**versäumen,** to miss (train, etc.).

**verschaffen,** to procure, get.

**verschreiben,** *st.*, to prescribe.

**verschwinden,** *st.*, *f.*, to vanish, disappear.

**versetzen,** to reply, answer; in gute Laune —, to put in good humour.

**versinken,** *st.*, *f.*, to sink, founder.

**versprechen,** *st.*, to promise.

**Versuch,** *m.*, –es, –e, trial, attempt.

**versuchen,** to try, attempt.

**vertrauen,** to trust, confide.

**Verwandt(er),** *adj. subst.*, relation, relative.

**verwelken,** to wither.

**verwunden,** to wound.

**Vetter,** *m.*, –s, –n, cousin.

**viel,** mehr, meist, much, a great deal of; *pl.*, many.

**vielerlei,** *indecl.*, many kinds of.

**vielleicht,** perhaps.

**vier,** four.

**Viertel,** *n.*, –s, —, quarter.

**Viertelstu'nde,** *f.*, –n, quarter of an hour.

**Vogel,** *m.*, –s, ", bird.

**Vög(e)lein,** *n.*, –s, —, little bird, birdie.

**voll,** full.

**vollen'den,** *insep.*, to finish, end, complete; vollendet, complete, etc.

**von** (*dat.*), of, from, by, with, about, concerning.

**vor** (*dat.*, *acc.*), before, of, in front of, ago.

**vorbei,** past, gone.

**vorbeifahren,** *st.*, *f.*, to go (drive, sail, etc.) past.

**vorbeigehen,** *st.*, *f.*, to go (walk) past.

**Vordergrund,** *m.*, –es, "e, foreground.

**Vordersitz,** *m.*, –es, –e, front-seat.

**Vordertür,** *f.*, –en, front-door.

**vordrängen,** *refl.*, to press forward.

**Vorgebirge,** *n.*, –s, —, promontory.

**Vorgesetzt(er),** *adj. subst.*, superior (officer).

**vorher,** before(hand), first.

**vorig,** *adj.*, last, former.

**vorlesen,** *st.*, to read aloud.

**vorschießen,** *st.*, to advance (money).

**Vorspeise,** *f.*, –n, *entrée*.

**Vorstadt,** *f.*, "e, suburb.

**Vorteil,** *m.*, –es, –e, advantage.

**vortragen,** *st.*, to recite.

**vorüber,** by, over, past.

**vorüberwandern,** to pass by.

**vorziehen,** *st.*, to prefer.

### W

**Waarenhaus,** *n.*, –es, "er, departmental store, shop.

**wachsen,** *st.*, *f.*, to grow.

**Wacht,** *f.*, watch, guard.

**Waffe,** *f.*, -n, weapon.

**Wagen,** *m.*, -s, —, carriage, waggon.

**wägen,** *st.*, to weigh (*tr.*).

**wählen,** to choose, select.

**wahr,** true; Sie sind müde, nicht —? you are tired, are you not?

**während** (*gen.*), during; *conj.*, while.

**Wahrheit,** *f.*, -en, truth.

**Wald,** *m.*, -es, ⸚er, forest, wood(s).

**Wand,** *f.*, ⸚e, wall.

**Wand(e)rer,** *m.*, -s, —, wanderer, pilgrim.

**wandern,** ſ., to wander, go, pass.

**wann?** when?

**warm,** ⸚er, warm.

**warnen,** to warn.

**warten,** to wait.

**Wartesaal,** *m.*, -es, -säle, waiting-room.

**warum?** why? wherefore?

**was?** what?

**was,** *rel. pron.*, that which, what, which.

**was für** (ein, -e, —)? what kind of (a)? what?

**waschen,** *st.*, to wash.

**Wasser,** *n.*, -s, — or ⸚, water.

**wechseln,** to change, exchange.

**wecken,** to waken.

**weder . . . noch,** neither . . . nor; nor.

**Weg,** *m.*, -es, -e, way, road, street.

**weg,** away, out of the way.

**wegen** (*gen.*), on account of.

**wegnehmen,** *st.*, to take away.

**Wehmut,** *f.*, sadness, melancholy.

**weh tun** (*dat.*), to hurt, pain.

**Weib,** *n.*, -es, -er, woman; wife.

**weich,** soft.

**weil,** because, as, since.

**Wein,** *m.*, -es, -e, wine.

**weinen,** to weep.

**Weinhändler,** *m.*, -s, —, wine-merchant.

**Weintraube,** *f.*, -n, grapes.

**Weise,** *f.*, -n, way, manner; auf diese —, in this way.

**weiß,** white.

**weit,** far.

**weiterfahren,** *st.*, ſ., to go (sail, etc.) on.

**Weizen,** *m.*, -s, wheat.

**welcher?** which? what?

**welcher,** *rel. pron.*, who, which, that; *indef.*, some.

**Welken,** *n.*, -s, withering.

**Welle,** *f.*, -n, wave, ripple.

**Welt,** *f.*, -en, world.

**Weltausstellung,** *f.*, -en, international exhibition.

**wem?** (to, for) whom?

**wen?** whom?

**wenig,** little; few.

**wenigstens,** at least.

**wenn,** when, whenever; if; — auch, —gleich, even if, although.

**wer?** who?

**wer,** *rel. pron.*, he who, the one who, etc.

**werden,** *st.*, ſ., to become, grow, turn out to be, be; *aux. of fut.*, shall, will; *aux. of passive*, to be; es wird Abend, evening is coming on; — aus, to become of; — zu, to turn into.

**werfen,** *st.*, to throw.

**Werk,** *n.,* -es, -e, work, writings, etc.

**Wert,** *m.,* -es, -e, worth, value.

**wert,** worth, of the value of.

**Wesen,** *n.,* -s, —, being.

**weshalb?** why?

**wessen?** whose?

**westlich,** western, westerly.

**weswegen?** for what?

**Wetter,** *n.,* -s, weather.

**wie,** how, how? what?; as, like; so — auch, as also, as well as.

**wieder,** again; now.

**wiederkommen,** *st.,* f., to come back, return.

**Wiedersehen,** *n.,* -s, meeting again; auf —, good-bye (till we meet again), *au revoir.*

**Wien,** *n.,* -s, Vienna; —er, (of) Vienna.

**Wiese,** *f.,* -n, meadow.

**wieviel(f)te (der)?** what day of the month?

**Wilhelm,** *m.,* -s, William.

**Wilhelmine,** *f.,* -ns, Wilhelmine.

**willko'mmen,** welcome.

**wimmeln,** to swarm, teem.

**Wind,** *m.,* -es, -e, wind, breeze.

**winken** *(dat.),* to beckon.

**Winter,** *m.,* -s, —, winter.

**Winterpalais** [pr. -palä'], *n.,* —, —, winter-palace.

**Winterqual,** *f.,* -en, torment of winter, hard winter weather.

**Wipfel,** *m.,* -s, —, tree-top.

**wir,** we.

**Wirt,** *m.,* -es, -e, host, landlord.

**Wirtshaus,** *n.,* -es, ⁻er, tavern, inn.

**wissen,** *irr.,* to know (of facts); know how to, can.

**wo,** where; where?

**wobei,** whereby, in connection with which, etc.

**Woche,** *f.,* -n, week.

**Woge,** *f.,* -n, billow.

**Wogenprall,** *m.,* -es, dashing waves.

**wohin?** whither? where to?

**wohl,** *indecl.,* well (*of health*); *adv.,* well, then, indeed, I suppose, I wonder, I am sure, of course, doubtless, etc.

**wohnen,** to dwell, live, reside.

**Wohnung,** *f.,* -en, dwelling, residence, house.

**Wohnzimmer,** *n.,* -s, —, sitting-room.

**Wolke,** *f.,* -n, cloud.

**wollen,** *irr., mod. aux.,* to will, desire to, wish to, want to, be about to, mean to, etc.; claim to, assert.

**womit,** with which (what).

**worauf,** at which, on which, etc.; whereupon.

**Wort,** *n.,* -es, word; *pl.,* Wörter, words (*as vocables*); *pl.,* Worte, words (*in discourse*).

**worüber,** at what, whereat.

**wovon,** of which (what), etc.; whereof.

**wozu?** for what? etc.

**wundern,** *refl.,* to wonder, be astonished; *impers.,* es wundert mich, I wonder.

**wunderschön,** very beautiful.

**wünschen,** to wish, desire, want.

**würdig,** worthy.

**Wurst,** *f.,* ⁻e, sausage.

**Wurzel,** *f.,* -n, root.

**Würzlein,** *n.,* -s, —, rootlet.

## 3

**Zahl,** *f.*, -en, number, figure.

**zählen,** to count; number, have.

**Zahn,** *m.*, -es, ⸚e, tooth.

**Zar,** *m.*, -en, -en, Czar.

**z. B.** (zum Beispiel), for example, e.g.

**zehn,** ten.

**Zeichenstunde,** *f.*, -n, drawing-lesson.

**zeigen,** to show; *refl.*, to show one's self, appear.

**Zeiger,** *m.*, -s, —, hand (of time-piece); der große (kleine) —, the long (short) hand, minute-(hour-)hand.

**Zeile,** *f.*, -n, line.

**Zeit,** *f.*, -en, time; vor alter —, in old(en) times.

**Zeitlang; eine —,** a (short) while.

**Zeitung,** *f.*, -en, newspaper.

**Zeitwort,** *n.*, -es, ⸚er, verb.

**zerfallen,** ruined, in ruins.

**zerfließen,** *st.*, f., to melt (away).

**zerreißen,** *st.*, to tear (to pieces).

**zerrütten,** to shatter.

**zerstören,** to destroy, demolish.

**Zeug,** *n.*, -es, -e, stuff, cloth, material.

**ziehen,** *st.*, to draw; *intr.*, f., to go, travel.

**zieren,** to adorn.

**Ziffer,** *f.*, -n, figure, number.

**Zifferblatt,** *n.*, -es, ⸚er, dial, face.

**Zimmer,** *n.*, -s, —, room.

**Zimmertür,** *f.*, -en, door of a room.

**zittern,** to tremble.

**Zoll,** *m.*, -es, -e, inch.

**zu** (*dat.*), to, at, for, in, on, by;

— Hause, at home; — Ihnen, to your house, etc.; *adv.*, too; — +infin., to.

**zubringen,** *irr.*, to pass, spend (time).

**züchtigen,** to chastise.

**Zucker,** *m.*, -s, sugar.

**zudecken,** to cover (up).

**zuerst,** first.

**zufällig,** accidental; *adv.*, by chance.

**zufrieden,** contented, satisfied.

**Zug,** *m.*, -es, ⸚e, train (railway).

**zugeben,** *st.*, to admit.

**zugegen,** present.

**zugleich,** at the same time.

**zuhauf,** in heaps.

**zuhören,** to listen.

**Zuhörer,** *m.*, -s, —, hearer; *pl.*, audience.

**zukommen,** *st.*, f., — auf (*acc.*), to approach.

**zuläuten,** to ring (to).

**zuletzt,** last (of all), at last.

**zumachen,** to close, shut.

**zunächst,** next, in the next place, then.

**zünden,** to kindle.

**Zunge,** *f.*, -n, tongue.

**zurück,** *adv.*, back.

**zurückfahren,** *st.*, f., to drive (etc.) back.

**zurückfallen,** *st.*, f., to fall back, recoil.

**zurückgeben,** *st.*, to give back.

**zurückkehren,** f., to return, go back.

**zurufen,** *st.*, to call (shout) to.

**zusagen** (*dat.*), to suit, agree with.

**zusammen,** together.

**Zusammentreffen,** *n.*, -s, meeting, encounter.

Zuschauer, *m.*, –s, spectator.

zusehen, *st.*, to look on; take care.

Zutrauen, *n.*, –s, trust, confidence.

zuweilen, sometimes.

zwar, it is true, indeed.

Zweck, *m.*, –es, –e, object, purpose.

zwei, two.

zweierlei, two kinds of.

Zweig, *m.*, –es, –e, branch, bough.

zweigen, to send out shoots.

Zweikampf, *m.*, –es, ⁔e, duel.

zweimal, twice.

zweitens, in the second place, secondly.

zwingen, *st.*, to force, compel.

zwischen (*dat.*, *acc.*) between, among.

zwölf, twelve.

Y

# ENGLISH–GERMAN VOCABULARY

## A

**a, an,** ein; twice a day, zweimal des Tages; twice a week, zweimal die Woche.

**able** (to be), können, *irr.*

**about,** *prep.*, von (*dat.*); um (*acc.*); round —, um . . . herum.

**about,** *adv.*, ungefähr, etwa; to be — to, eben wollen, *irr.*; im Begriffe sein, *irr.*, f.

**above,** *prep.*, über (*dat.*).

**accept,** annehmen, *st.*

**accompany,** begleiten.

**accordingly,** folglich, also, daher.

**account** (*bill*), Rechnung, *f.*, –en; (*report*), Bericht, *m.*, –es, –e; on — of, wegen, *gen.*; on this —, daher, deshalb.

**accuse,** anklagen.

**acknowledge,** anerkennen, *irr.*

**acquaintance,** Bekanntschaft, *f.*, –en; (*person known*), Bekannt(er), *adj. subst.*; make any one's —, einen kennen lernen.

**acquittal,** Freisprechung, *f.*

**act** (*conduct one's self*), sich betragen, *st.*

**actor,** Schauspieler, *m.*, –s, —.

**actress,** Schauspielerin, *f.*, –nen.

**address** (*place of residence*), Adresse, *f.*, –n.

**admire,** bewundern.

**advance** (*loan*), vorschießen, *st.*

**advantage,** Vorteil, *m.*, –es, –e.

**advertisement,** Anzeige, *f.*, –n.

**advice,** Rat, *m.*, –es.

**advise,** raten, *st.* (*dat.*).

**after,** *prep.*, nach (*dat.*); *conj.*, nachdem; — all, doch.

**afternoon,** Nachmittag, *m.*, –es, –e.

**afterwards,** nachher, später.

**again,** wieder.

**ago,** vor (*prep.*, *dat.*); a week —, heute vor acht Tagen.

**agreeable,** angenehm.

**air,** Luft, *f.*, ⸚e.

**all,** all; ganz; at —, irgend; not at —, gar nicht, nicht im geringsten; after —, doch.

**allow,** erlauben (*dat.*); lassen, *st.*; be —ed, dürfen, *irr.*

**almost,** beinahe, fast.

**alms,** Almosen, *n.*, –s, —.

**along;** — with, mit.

**aloud,** laut; read —, vorlesen, *st.*

**already,** schon.

**also,** auch.

**although,** obgleich ꝛc.

**always,** immer, stets.

**a.m.,** Vm. (Vormittags); morgens.

**ambassador,** Gesandt(er), *adj. subst.*

**America,** Amerika, *n.*, –s.

**American**, *noun*, Amerikaner, *m.*,
  –s, —.
**American**, *adj.*, amerikanisch.
**among**, unter, zwischen (*dat. or acc.*);
  be — (belong to), gehören zu.
**and**, und.
**angry**, böse (at, auf, *acc.*).
**animal**, Tier, *n.*, –es, –e.
**annihilate**, vernichten.
**another**, *adj.*, ein ander(er, –e,
  –es); one —, einander; — cup
  of tea, noch eine Tasse Tee.
**answer**, Antwort, *f.*, –en.
**answer**, antworten.
**anxious**, besorgt (um, *acc.*).
**any**, welcher, etwas; —body, —
  one, jemand; — one at all,
  irgend einer; —thing, etwas;
  —thing but, nichts weniger als.
**apiece**, je.
**appear** (*seem*), scheinen, *st.*; (make
  one's —ance), erscheinen, *st.*, f.;
  zum Vorschein kommen, *st.*, f.
**apple**, Apfel, *m.*, –s, ⁔.
**application** (to make), sich melden.
**apply to**, sich melden bei.
**appoint**, ernennen, *irr.* (als *or* zu).
**approach**, sich nähern (*dat.*).
**April**, April, *m.*
**arithmetic**, Rechnen, *n.*, –s.
**arm**, Arm, *m.*, –es, –e.
**army**, Heer, *n.*, –es, –e; Armee', *f.*,
  –n.
**arrangement**, Einrichtung, *f.*, –en.
**arrest**, verhaften, arretieren.
**arrive**, ankommen, *st.*, f.; anlan=
  gen, f.
**as**, wie; (when), als; — . . . —,
  (eben)so . . . wie; (since), da; —
  if, als wenn, als ob; — soon —,
  sobald, sowie.

**ascend**, besteigen, *st.*, *tr.*
**ascertain**, feststellen.
**ashamed** (to be), sich schämen.
**ask** (*inquire*), fragen; (*question*),
  befragen; (*request*), bitten, *st.*
**asleep** (to be), schlafen, *st.*; fall —,
  einschlafen, *st.*, f.
**asparagus**, Spargel, *m.*, –s, —.
**assist**, beistehen, *st.* (*dat.*).
**astray** (to go), sich verrriren.
**at** (*App. B*, 4, 5), in, an, auf (*dat.*
  *or acc.*); zu, bei (*dat.*, *of place*);
  um (*acc.*), zu (*dat.*, *of time*);
  um, zu (*of price*); — all, irgend;
  not — all, gar nicht; — last
  (*finally*), endlich; (*last of all*),
  zuletzt; — least, wenigstens; (all)
  — once (*suddenly*), auf ei'nmal;
  (*immediately*), sofort; — one
  time . . . — another, bald . . .
  bald.
**attack**, angreifen, *st.*
**attempt**, Versuch, *m.*, –es, –e.
**attend** (*be present at*), beiwohnen
  (*dat.*).
**attentive**, aufmerksam.
**August**, Augu'st, *m.*
**Augusta**, Auguste, *f.*, –ns.
**aunt**, Tante, *f.*, –n.
**Austria**, Österreich, *n.*, –s.
**avoid**, vermeiden, *st.*
**away**, weg, fort.
**axe**, Axt, *f.*, ⁔e.

# B

**back**, Rücken, *m.*, –s, —.
**back**, *adv.*, zurück.
**back-door**, Hintertür, *f.*, –en.
**background**, Hintergrund, *m.*, –es,
  ⁔e.

**bad,** ſchlimm; ſchlecht; böſe; übel; arg, ⁻er.

**baggage,** Gepäck, *n.*, -es.

**bake,** backen, *st.*

**ball,** Ball, *m.*, -es, ⁻e.

**Baltic,** Oſtſee, *f.*,

**bank** (*banking-house*), Bank, *f.*, -en; (*of a stream*), Ufer, *n.*, -s, —.

**banker,** Bankier, *m.*, -s, -s.

**bankrupt,** bankero'tt; become —, bankerott machen.

**banquet,** Gaſtmahl, *n.*, -es, ⁻er.

**basket,** Korb, *m.*, -es, ⁻e.

**battle,** Schlacht, *f.*, -en.

**Bavaria,** Bayern, *n.*, -s.

**be,** ſein, *irr.*, ſ.; (*with passive*), werden; — in a position (to do anything), imſtande ſein; I am to, ich ſoll; how are you? wie geht es Ihnen? wie befinden Sie ſich?

**bean,** Bohne, *f.*, -n.

**bear,** tragen, *st.*

**beautiful,** ſchön.

**because,** weil.

**beckon,** winken.

**become,** werden, *st.*, ſ.

**bed,** Bett, *n.*, -es, -en; garden- —, Beet, *n.*, -es, -e.

**bedroom,** Schlafzimmer, *n.*, -s, —.

**beef** (roast of), Rinderbraten, *m.*, -s, —.

**before,** *prep.*, vor (*dat. or acc.*).

**before,** *adv.*, vorher.

**before,** *conj.*, ehe, bevor.

**beg** (*ask*), bitten, *st.*; (*ask alms*), betteln.

**beggar,** Bettler, *m.*, -s, —.

**begin,** beginnen, *st.*; anfangen, *st.*

**behind,** *prep.*, hinter (*dat. or acc.*).

**Belgium,** Belgien, *n.*, -s.

**believe,** glauben (*dat. of pers.*).

**bell,** Glocke, *f.*, -n.

**bench,** Bank, *f.*, ⁻e.

**bend,** biegen, *st.*

**beside,** neben (*dat. or acc.*); bei (*dat.*).

**besides,** außerdem.

**betake one's self,** ſich begeben, *st.*

**between,** zwiſchen (*dat. or acc.*).

**beyond,** jenſeit (*gen.*).

**bid** (*order*), heißen, *st.* (*acc.*); (*offer*), bieten, *st.*

**big,** groß, ⁻er, größt.

**bill** (*account*), Rechnung, *f.*, -en.

**bird,** Vogel, *m.*, -s, ⁻; little —, birdie, Vög(e)lein, *n.*, -s, —; Vögelchen, *n.*, -s, —.

**birthday,** Geburtstag, *m.*, -es, -e; for (as) a — present, zum Geburtstag.

**bite,** beißen, *st.*

**bitter,** bitter.

**black,** ſchwarz, ⁻er; Black Forest, Schwarzwald, *m.*, -es.

**blind,** blind.

**blow,** blaſen, *st.*

**blow** (*knock*), Stoß, *m.*, -es, ⁻e.

**boat,** Boot, *n.*, -es, -e *and* Böte; Kahn, *m.*, -es, ⁻e.

**book,** Buch, *n.*, -es, ⁻er.

**boot,** Stiefel, *m.*, -s, —.

**born,** *part.*, geboren.

**both,** beide, beides.

**boundary,** Grenze, *f.*, -n.

**bow to,** grüßen (*acc.*).

**box** (*of paper or cardboard*), Schachtel, *f.*, -n; — on the ear, Ohrfeige, *f.*, -n.

**boy,** Junge, *m.*, -n, -n(s); Knabe, *m.*, -n, -n.

**branch** (*trees, etc.*), Zweig, *m.*, –es, –e; (*stream*), Arm, *m.*, –es, –e.
**bread**, Brot, *n.*, –es.
**break**, brechen, *st.* ; — (*smash*), zerbrechen; — **to pieces** *or* **in two**, entzweibrechen; — **open**, erbrechen.
**breakfast**, Frühstück, *n.*, –es, –e.
**bridge**, Brücke, *f.*, –n.
**brig**, Brigg, *f.*, –s.
**bright**, hell.
**bring**, bringen, *irr.*; — **out**, herausbringen; — **up**, heraufbringen, *irr.*
**brother**, Bruder, *m.*, –s, ⸚.
**build**, bauen.
**building** (*edifice*), Gebäude, *n.*, –s, —.
**burn**, *intr.*, brennen, *irr.*; *tr.*, verbrennen.
**bury**, begraben, *st.*
**business**, Geschäft, *n.*, –es, –e.
**busy** (*occupied*), beschäftigt.
**but**, aber; allein; (*after neg.*), sondern; **not only** . . . — **also**, nicht nur . . . sondern auch; **anything** —, nichts weniger als; **nothing** —, nichts als.
**buy**, kaufen; — **from**, abkaufen (*dat. of pers.*).
**by** (*with passive*), von (*dat.*); **near** —, bei (*dat.*), neben (*dat. or acc.*); — (*a certain time*), bis, bis zu ; — **night**, bei Nacht, des Nachts, nachts. (*See also App. B, 4.*)

## C

**cab**, Droschke, *f.*, –n.
**cabbage**, Kohl, *m.*, –es.
**cabman**, Kutscher, *m.*, –s, —.

**Calabria**, Kalabrien, *n.*, –s.
**call** (*summon*), rufen, *st.*; (*name*), nennen, *irr.*; — **to**, zurufen (*dat.*), **be** —**ed** (named), heißen, *st.*
**calling** (*profession*), Beruf, *m.*, –es, –e.
**camp**, Lager, *n.*, –s, —.
**can**, können, *irr.*
**candy, candies**, Bonbons, *pl.*
**cane**, Stock, *m.*, –es, ⸚e.
**canoe**, Kahn, *m.*, –es, ⸚e.
**cap**, Mütze, *f.*, –n.
**capable**, fähig.
**capital** (*city*), Hauptstadt, *f.*, ⸚e.
**capsize**, umschlagen, *st.*, *f.*; kentern, *f.*
**captain** (*of a ship*), Kapitän, *m.*, –es, –e; (*mil. officer*), Hauptmann, *m.*, –es, –leute.
**care**, mögen, *irr.*; **take** —, sich in acht nehmen; **take** — **of**, achtgeben auf (*acc.*).
**careful**, sorgfältig.
**carriage**, Wagen, *m.*, –s, —.
**case**, Fall, *m.*, –es, ⸚e.
**castle**, Schloß, *n.*, –es, ⸚er.
**cat**, Katze, *f.*, –n.
**catch**, fangen, *st.*; — **cold**, sich erkälten.
**cauliflower**, Blumenkohl, *m.*, –es.
**cause**, verursachen; — **to be made**, machen lassen, *st.*
**cease**, aufhören.
**celebrate**, feiern.
**celebrated** (*famous*), berühmt.
**certain**, gewiß.
**chair**, Stuhl, *m.*, –es, ⸚e.
**chancellor**, Kanzler, *m.*, –s, —.
**change** (*alter*), *tr.*, ändern, verändern; *intr.*, sich ändern.
**Charles**, Karl, *m.*, –s.

charming, reizend.

cheap, billig; wohlfeil.

cheat, hinterge′hen, *st.*, *insep.*

check (*for baggage*), Gepäckschein, *m.*, –es, –e.

chemistry, Chemie, *f.*

cherry, Kirsche, *f.*, –n.

chicken, Huhn, *n.*, –es, ″er.

child, Kind, *n.*, –es, –er.

choose, wählen, erwählen (als *or* zu).

city, Stadt, *f.*, ″e.

Clara, Klara, *f.*, ·-s.

class, Klasse, *f.*, –n.

clean, rein.

clear, klar.

clerk, Ladendiener, *m.*, –s, —; Handlungsgehilfe, *m.*, –n, –n.

clever, klug, ″er.

climate, Klima, *n.*, –s, Klimata.

cloak, Mantel, *m.*, –s, ″.

clock, Uhr, *f.*, –en; what o′— is it? wie viel Uhr ist es?; it is nine o′—, es ist neun Uhr.

close, zumachen; schließen, *st.*

cloud, Wolke, *f.*, –n.

coachman, Kutscher, *m.*, –s, —.

coat, Rock, *m.*, –es, ″e.

coffee, Kaffee, *m.*, –s.

coin, Münze, *f.*, –n.

cold, kalt, ″er; be (feel) —, frieren, *st.*; catch —, sich erkälten; have a —, erkältet sein, *irr.*, s.

Columbus, Kolumbus, *m.*

comb, kämmen.

come, kommen, *st.*, s.; — in, herein kommen, s.; — in! herein!; — to mind, einfallen, *st.*, s. (*dat.*).

comfortable, bequem.

command, befehlen, *st.* (*dat.*).

commercial-traveller, Geschäfts=reisend(er), *adj. subst.*

compartment, Abteil, *m.*, –es, –e.

compel, zwingen, *st.*; be —led, müssen, *irr.*

complain, klagen; sich beklagen.

comrade, Kamerad, *m.*, –en, –en.

conduct, Betragen, *n.*, –s.

consequently, folglich, also, daher.

considerable, bedeutend.

consist of, bestehen aus, *st.* (*dat.*).

consul, Ko′nsul, *m.*, –s, –n.

contain, enthalten, *st.*

continually, beständig, fortwäh=rend.

continue (*intr.*), fortfahren, *st.*

convince, überzeu′gen, *insep.*

copy, abschreiben, *st.*

corn (Indian), Mais, *m.*, –es.

corner, Ecke, *f.*, –n.

corn-meal, Maismehl, *n.*, –es.

cost, kosten (*acc. of pers. and price*).

count (*title*), Graf, *m.*, –en, –en.

count, zählen.

country, Land, *n.*, –es, ″er; in the —, auf dem Lande; in this —, hierzulande; to the —, aufs Land.

country-house, Landhaus, *n.*, –es, ″er.

courage, Mut, *m.*, –es.

course; of —, natürlich.

courtier, Höfling, *m.*, –es, –e.

cousin, Vetter, *m.*, –s, –n; Cou-sine, *f.*, –n.

cover, bedecken.

cow, Kuh, *f.*, ″e.

create, schaffen, *st.*

creep, kriechen, *st.*, s.

crime, Verbrechen, *n.*, –s, —.

crop (*harvest*), Ernte, *f.*, –n.

**crown-prince**, Kronprinz, *m.*, –en, –en.

**crush**, Gedränge, *n.*, –s.

**cup**, Tasse, *f.*, –n.

**current** (to be), gelten, *st.*

**cut**, schneiden, *st.*; — down (fell), umhauen, *st.*

**Czar**, Zar, *m.*, –en, –en.

## D

**damage**, Schade(n), *m.*, –n(s), Schaden *and* ⸗; do —, Schaden anrichten.

**dance**, tanzen.

**danger**, Gefahr, *f.*, –en.

**date**, Datum, *n.*, –s, Data *and* Daten.

**daughter**, Tochter, *f.*, ⸗.

**day**, Tag, *m.*, –es, –e; in these —s, heutzutage; one —, eines Tages; what — of the month is it? der wievielte ist heute?; this — week (fortnight), heute über acht (vierzehn) Tage.

**dead**, tot.

**deal;** a great — of, sehr viel.

**dear** (*beloved*), teuer; (*expensive*), teuer, kostspielig.

**death**, Tod, *m.*, –es.

**deceive**, betrügen, *st.*

**December**, Dezember, *m.*

**decide**, *tr.*, entscheiden, *st.; intr.*, sich entscheiden; beschließen, *st.*

**Denmark**, Dänemark, *n.*, –s.

**department**, Abteilung, *f.*, –en; ladies' dress —, Abteilung für Damenkleider.

**departmental store**, Waarenhaus, *n.*, –es, ⸗er.

**desert** (*mil. term*), desertieren.

**destroy**, zerstören.

**dial**, Zifferblatt, *n.*, –es, ⸗er.

**die**, sterben, *st.*, s.

**difference**, Unterschied, *m.*, –es, –e.

**dig**, graben, *st.*; — up, — over, u'mgraben, *sep.*, *st.*

**diligent**, fleißig.

**dine**, essen, *st.*; zu Mittag essen.

**dinner**, Essen, *n.*, –s; Mittags= essen, *n.*, –s; at —, bei Tisch; to —, zu Tisch; before —, vor Tisch.

**disagreeable**, unangenehm.

**disappear**, verschwinden, *st.*, s.

**disappointed**, enttäuscht.

**discover**, entdecken.

**discovery**, Entdeckung, *f.*, –en.

**discuss**, besprechen, *st.*

**dismiss**, entlassen, *st.*

**distinct**, deutlich.

**disturb**, stören.

**dive**, u'ntertauchen, *sep.*, *st.*

**do**, tun, *irr.*; — an exercise (*les son*), eine Aufgabe machen; — damage, Schaden anrichten.

**doctor** (*physician*), Arzt, *m.*, –es, ⸗e; (*academic degree*), Doktor, *m.*, –s, Dokto'ren.

**dog**, Hund, *m.*, –es, –e.

**doll**, Puppe, *f.*, –n.

**done** (*ready*), fertig.

**door**, Tür, *f.*, –en.

**doubt**, Zweifel, *m.*, –s, —; no —, wohl, ohne Zweifel.

**doubt**, zweifeln (an, *dat.*); bezwei= feln (*acc.*).

**doughy**, teigig.

**down**, *adv.*, hinab, hinunter.

**dozen**, Dutzend, *n.*, –es, –e.

**draw** (*pull*), ziehen, *st.*

**dreadful**, schrecklich, furchtbar, fürchterlich, entsetzlich.

**dream**, Traum, *m.*, -es, ⸚e.

**dress**, Kleid, *n.*, -es, -er; lady's dress, Damenkleid; summer —, Sommerkleid.

**dress**, *tr.*, anziehen, *st.*; ankleiden; *intr.*, sich anziehen, *st.*; sich ankleiden.

**drink** (*of people*), trinken, *st.*; (*of beasts*), saufen, *st.*

**drive**, *tr.*, fahren, *st.*; treiben, *st.*; — away, forttreiben, *st.*; — (*in a vehicle*), *intr.*, fahren, *st.*, f., h.

**driver**, Kutscher, *m.*, -s, —.

**drown** (*be drowned*), ertrinken, *st.*, f.

**duke**, Herzog, *m.*, -es, -e and ⸚e.

**during**, während (*gen.*).

**duty**, Pflicht, *f.*, -en.

## E

**each**, jeder; — other, einander.

**ear**, Ohr, *n.*, -es, -en; box on the —, Ohrfeige, *f.*, -n.

**early**, früh.

**earn**, verdienen.

**earth**, Erde, *f.*, -n; on —, auf Erden.

**earthquake**, Erdbeben, *n.*, -s, —.

**east**, Osten, *m.*, -s and —; on (in, to) the —, im Osten, östlich.

**Easter**, Ostern, *pl.*; at —, um (zu) Ostern.

**eastern**, östlich.

**easy**, leicht.

**eat** (*of people*), essen, *st.*; (*of beasts*), fressen, *st.*

**Edward**, Eduard, *m.*, -s.

**egg**, Ei, *n.*, -es, -er.

**either**; — ... or, entweder ... oder.

**elect**, wählen, erwählen (als *or* zu).

**elementary school**, Elementarschule, *f.*, -n.

**Elizabeth**, Elisabeth, *f.*, -s.

**else**, sonst.

**embark**, einsteigen, *st.*, f. (in, *acc.*).

**emperor**, Kaiser, *m.*, -s, —.

**empire**, Kaiserreich, *n.*, -es, -e; the German —, das Deutsche Reich.

**end**, Ende, *n.*, -s, -n; set on —, aufrecht stellen.

**enemy**, Feind, *m.*, -es, -e.

**England**, England, *n.*, -s.

**English**, englisch; — language, Englisch, *n.*; in —, auf Englisch; into —, ins Englische; the —, die Engländer.

**Englishman**, Engländer, *m.*, -s, —.

**enjoy one's self**, Vergnügen haben, *irr.*; (*in conversation*), sich unterha'lten, *st.*, *insep.*

**enough**, genug.

**enter**, eintreten, *st.*, f. *and* h. (in, *acc.*); hineingehen, *st.*, f. (in, *acc.*).

**entire**, ganz.

**entirely**, ganz, gänzlich, vollständig.

**entrust**, anvertrauen.

**errand-boy**, Laufbursche, *m.*, -n, -n.

**escape**, entkommen, *st.*, f.; entlaufen, *st.*, f.

**especially**, besonders.

**etc.** (et cetera), 2c., usw. (und so weiter).

**Europe**, Europa, *n.*, -s.

**European,** *adj.*, europäisch.

**even,** *adv.*, auch, sogar; — if, wenn auch; not —, nicht einmal.

**evening,** Abend, *m.*, –es, –e; in the – –, des Abends, abends; this —, heute abend.

**ever** (*at any time*), je, jemals; (*always*), immer, stets.

**every,** jeder; —body, — one, jeder, jedermann; —thing, alles; —where, überall.

**evil,** böse.

**examination,** Examen, *n.*, –s; Prüfung, *f.*, –en.

**excellent,** vortrefflich.

**Exchange** (*building*), Börse, *f.*, –n.

**excursion,** Ausflug, *m.*, –es, ⁻e; make (go on) an —, einen Ausflug machen.

**excuse,** Entschuldigung, *f.*, –en.

**excuse,** entschuldigen.

**exercise** (*task*), Aufgabe, *f.*, –n; do an —, eine Aufgabe machen.

**expect,** erwarten.

**expensive,** kostspielig.

**experience,** Erfahrung, *f.*, –en.

**express train,** Schnellzug, *m.*, –es, ⁻e.

**extol,** preisen, *st.*

**extremely,** äußerst, höchst.


# F

**face,** Gesicht, *n.*, –es, –er; (*of a time-piece*), Zifferblatt, *n.*, –es, ⁻er.

**fall,** fallen, *st.*, ſ.; — ill, krank werden, *st.*, ſ.

**fall,** Fall, *m.*, –es, ⁻e.

**famine,** Hungersnot, *f.*, ⁻e.

**famous,** berühmt.

**far,** weit; as — as, bis nach; bis zu.

**farmer** (*peasant*), Bauer, *m.*, –s and –n, –n.

**fast** (*quick*), schnell.

**father,** Vater, *m.*, –s, ⁻.

**fear,** fürchten.

**February,** Februar, *m.*

**feel,** fühlen, empfinden, *st.*

**fell,** fällen.

**fellow;** that —, der, *demonstr.*

**fellow-traveller,** Mitreisend(er), *adj. subst.*

**few** (a), einige; wenige; ein paar (*indecl.*).

**field,** Feld, *n.*, –es, –er.

**fifty,** fünfzig.

**fill,** füllen; erfüllen.

**finally,** endlich.

**find,** finden, *st.*

**fine** (*beautiful*), schön; (*delicate*), fein.

**finish,** beendigen; (*complete*), volle'nden, *insep.*; to have —ed, fertig sein (mit, *dat.*).

**fire,** Feuer, *n.*, –s, —.

**first,** *adj.*, erst; *adv.*, erst, zuerst; in the — place, erstens.

**fish,** Fisch, *m.*, –es, –e.

**fish,** fischen; go —ing, fischen gehen, *st.*, ſ.

**five,** fünf.

**flatter,** schmeicheln (*dat.*).

**flee,** fliehen, *st.*, ſ., h.

**fling,** schmeißen, *st.*

**floor,** Boden, *m.*, –s, ⁻; Fußboden.

**flow,** fließen, *st.*, ſ., h.

**flower,** Blume, *f.*, –n; be in —, blühen.

**flower-bed,** Blumenbeet, *n.*, –es, –e.

**flower-garden,** Blumengarten, *m.*, –s, ⸚.

**fly,** fliegen, *st.*, f., h.

**fog,** Nebel, *m.*, –s, —.

**follow,** folgen, f. (*dat.*); befolgen (*acc. of thing*).

**fond of** (to be), gern haben, essen, trinken 2c.

**fool,** Narr, *m.*, –en, –en; Tor, *m.*, –en, –en.

**foot,** Fuß, *m.*, –es, ⸚e; on —, zu Fuß.

**football match,** Fußballspiel, *n.*, –es, –e.

**for,** *prep.* (*App. B*, 4, 5); für (*acc.*); zu (*of purpose*); seit (*of time past*); auf (*of fut. time, acc.*); wegen (*gen., on account of*).

**for,** *conj.*, denn.

**forbid,** verbieten, *st.* (*dat. of pers.*).

**force,** Macht, *f.*; (*mil.*), Truppenanzahl, *f.*

**force,** zwingen, *st.*

**foreground,** Vordergrund, *m.*, –es, ⸚e.

**forgery,** Fälschung, *f.*, –en.

**forget,** vergessen, *st.*

**fork,** Gabel, *f.*, –n.

**form,** bilden.

**former** (*of two*), jener.

**formerly,** früher.

**fortnight,** vierzehn Tage, *pl.*

**forward,** vorwärts; press —, sich vordrängen.

**France,** Frankreich, *n.*, –s.

**Frederick,** Friedrich, *m.*, –s.

**free,** frei.

**freeze,** frieren, *st.*

**French,** französisch; —language,

Französisch; in —, auf Französisch; the —, die Franzosen.

**Frenchman,** Franzose, *m.*, –n, –n.

**Friday,** Freitag, *m.*, –s, –e.

**friend,** Freund, *m.*, –es, –e; Freundin, *f.*, –nen.

**friendly,** freundlich.

**frighten,** *tr.*, erschrecken; be —ed, erschrecken, *st.*, f.

**fro** (to and), hin und her; auf und ab.

**from,** von, aus (*dat.*); — fear, aus Furcht.

**front;** in — of, vor (*dat. or acc.*).

**front-door,** Vordertür, *f.*, –en.

**fruit** (*in general*), Frucht, *f.*, ⸚e; (*orchard or garden*), Obst, *n.*, –es.

**fruitful,** fruchtbar.

**fruit-tree,** Obstbaum, *m.*, –es, ⸚e.

**fulfil,** erfüllen.

**full,** voll (*acc. or gen.*); (*occupied*), besetzt.

## G

**game,** Spiel, *n.*, –es, –e.

**garden,** Garten, *m.*, –s, ⸚.

**gardener,** Gärtner, *m.*, –s, —.

**gate,** Tor, *n.*, –es, –e.

**general** (*title*), General, *m.*, –es, –e; —-in-chief, Oberbefehlshaber, *m.*, –s, —; (*distinguished soldier*), Feldherr, *m.*, –n, –en.

**generally,** gewöhnlich.

**gentleman,** Herr, *m.*, –n, –en; gentlemen! meine Herren!

**George,** Georg, *m.*, –s.

**German,** deutsch; — language, Deutsch, *n.*; in —, auf Deutsch;

into —, ins Deutsche; the —, der Deutsche.

**Germany,** Deutschland, *n.,* –s.

**get** (*receive*), bekommen, *st.;* erhalten, *st.;* (*fetch*), holen; (*become*), werden, *st.,* f.; — in(to a vehicle), einsteigen, *st.,* f.; — out (of a vehicle), aussteigen; — up, aufstehen, *st.,* f.; — well, genesen, *st.,* f.; — rid of, los werden, *st.,* f. (*acc.*).

**girl,** Mädchen, *n.,* –s, —.

**give,** geben, *st.;* — as a present, schenken; — (*a title, etc.*), verleihen, *st.;* — heed, achtgeben, *st.* (to, auf, *acc.*).

**glad,** froh; I am —, es freut mich; ich freue mich (*gen. of thing*).

**gladly,** gern(e), lieber, am liebsten.

**glass,** Glas, *n.,* –es, ⸚er.

**glove,** Handschuh, *m.,* –es, –e.

**go** (*walk*), gehen, *st.,* f.; (*of or in a vehicle*), fahren, *st.,* f.; (*travel*), reisen; (*depart on a journey*), abreisen, f.; (*move*), ziehen, *st.,* f.; — astray, sich verirren; be —ing to, wollen, *irr.;* im Begriffe sein, *irr.,* f.; — for a walk, spazieren gehen, *st.,* f.; einen Spaziergang machen; — for a sleigh-drive, eine Schlittenfahrt machen; — down, hinabfahren, *st.,* f.; — in, hineingehen; — on, weitergehen; — out, ausgehen, hinausgehen; — shopping, Einkäufe machen, einkaufen.

**god,** Gott, *m.,* –es, ⸚er.

**God,** Gott, *m.,* –es.

**gold,** *noun,* Gold, *n.,* –es.

**gold(en),** *adj.,* golden.

**gold-piece,** Goldstück, *n.,* –es, –e.

**good,** gut, besser, best; (*well-behaved*), artig.

**grain,** Getreide, *n.,* –s.

**grandparents,** Großeltern, *pl.*

**grant,** geben, *st.*

**grass,** Gras, *n.,* –es, ⸚er.

**grateful,** dankbar.

**great,** groß, ⸚er, größt; a — deal (of), sehr viel; a — many, sehr viele.

**green,** grün.

**greet,** begrüßen.

**grind,** schleifen, *st.*

**grindstone,** Schleifstein, *m.,* –es, –e.

**ground** (*soil, earth*), Boden, *m.,* –s; Erde, *f.*

**grow,** wachsen, *st.,* f.; — dark, dunkel werden, *st.,* f.

**guard** (*mil.*), Wache, *f.,* –n.

**guess,** *intr.* raten, *st.;* *tr.* erraten.

**guest,** Gast, *m.,* –es, ⸚e.

**Guildhall,** Rathaus, *n.,* –es, ⸚er.

## H

**habit,** Gewohnheit, *f.,* –en.

**hair,** Haar, *n.,* –es, –e.

**half,** *adj.,* halb; the —, die Hälfte; — an hour, eine halbe Stunde; —-past ten, halb elf; one and a —, anderthalb.

**hall,** Saal, *m.,* –es, Säle.

**halt,** halten, *st.*

**hand,** Hand, *f.,* ⸚e; (*of a timepiece*), Zeiger, *m.,* –s, —; long —, minute-—, Minutenzeiger; short —, hour-—, Stundenzeiger; second-—, Sekundenzeiger.

hand (*pass*), reichen; — over, überla′ssen, *st.*, *insep.*

handkerchief, Taschentuch, *n.*, –es, ⸚er.

handsome, schön.

hang, *intr.*, hangen, *st.*

happen, geschehen, *st.*, f.

happy, glücklich.

hard, hart, ⸚er; (*difficult*), schwer.

harrow, Egge, *f.*, –n.

hasten, eilen, h., f.; sich beeilen.

hat, Hut, *m.*, –es, ⸚e.

have, haben, *irr.*; sein, *irr.*, f.; — to, müssen, *irr.*; — a cold, er- kältet sein; — a mind to, Lust haben zu; to — (a thing) made, machen lassen.

Havel, Havel, *f.*

hay, Heu, *n.*, –es.

he, er; derselbe; that man, etc., der; — who, wer; der(jenige) welcher.

head, Kopf, *m.*, –es, ⸚e; Haupt, *n.*, –es, ⸚er.

headache, Kopfweh, *n.*, –s; Kopf- schmerz, *m.*, –es, –en (*usually pl.*).

headmaster, Rektor, *m.*, –s, Rek- toren; Direktor, *m.*, –s, Direk- to′ren.

health, Gesundheit, *f.*

hear, hören.

heart (by), auswendig.

heaven, Himmel, *m.*, –s, —.

heavy, schwer.

heed (to give), achtgeben, *st.* (to, auf, *acc.*).

help, Hilfe, *f.*

help, helfen, *st.* (*dat.*).

hence (*therefore*), also, daher.

**Henry,** Heinrich, *m.*, –s.

her, *pers. pron.*, sie (*acc.*); ihr (*dat.*).

her, *poss. adj.*, ihr.

here (*in this place*), hier; (*to this place*), her, hierher.

heroic, heldenmütig.

heroism, Heldenmut, *m.*, –es.

hers, ihrer; der (die, das) ihr(ig)e.

hide, verbergen, *st.*; verstecken.

high, hoch, höher, höchst.

high-school, Gymnasium, *n.*, –s, Gymnasien.

hill, Berg, *m.*, –es, –e; Hügel, *m.*, –s, —.

him, ihn (*acc.*); ihm (*dat.*).

himself, *refl.*, sich (selbst); (he) —, (er) selbst, selber.

hinder, verhindern.

his, *poss. adj.*, sein.

his, *poss. pron.*, seiner; der (die, das) sein(ig)e.

hoarse, heiser.

hoist (*a sail, etc.*), aufhissen.

hole, Loch, *n.*, –es, ⸚er.

holidays (*vacation*), Ferien, *pl.*

home, *adv.*, nach Hause; at —, zu Hause.

honest, ehrlich.

honour, Ehre, *f.*, –n.

honour, ehren, verehren.

hope, Hoffnung, *f.*, –en.

hope, hoffen; it is to be —d, hof- fentlich.

horror, Entsetzen, *n.*, –s.

horse, Pferd, *n.*, –es, –e.

hospital, Hospital, Spita′l, *n.*, –es, ⸚er.

hot, heiß.

hotel, Gasthof, *m.*, –es, ⸚e.

hour, Stunde, *f.*, –n; —-hand, Stundenzeiger, *m.*, –s, —.

house, Haus, n., -es, ⁻er; at the
— of, bei (dat. of pers.); to the
— of, zu (dat.).

how, wie; — long? seit wann?;
— are you? — do you do?
wie geht es Ihnen? wie befinden
Sie sich?

however, aber, jedoch.

human, menschlich; — life, Men=
schenleben, n., -s, —; — being,
Mensch, m., -en, -en.

hundred, noun, Hundert, n., -es,
-e.

hungry, hungrig; be —, Hunger
haben, hungrig sein, irr., f.

hurt, weh tun, irr. (dat.).

husband, Mann, m., -es, ⁻er;
Gatte, m., -n, -n.


I

I, pers. pron., ich.

ice, Eis, n., -es.

if, wenn; (whether), ob; even —,
wenn auch.

ill, krank, ⁻er.

illness, Krankheit, f., -en.

imperial city, Reichsstadt, f., ⁻e.

important, wichtig.

impossible, unmöglich.

in, prep., in (dat. or acc.); adv.,
herein, hinein; — the country,
auf dem Lande; come —! herein!

inch, Zoll, m., -es, -e.

include, einschließen, st.

indeed, in der Tat; yes —, jawohl.

Indian corn, Mais, m., -es.

Indian meal, Maismehl, n., -es.

indignant, entrüstet (at, über, acc.).

indispensable, unentbehrlich.

industrious, fleißig.

inhabitant, Einwohner, m., -s, —.

ink, Tinte, f., -n.

innocence, Unschuld, f.

innocent (of), unschuldig (gen.).

insect, Insekt, n., -es, -en.

insist (on), bestehen, st. (auf,
acc.).

instead of, anstatt (gen.).

intelligent, klug, ⁻er.

intend, wollen, irr.; beabsichtigen;
gedenken, irr.

intention, Absicht, f., -en.

interesting, interessant.

into, in (acc.).

invent, erfinden, st.

invite, (ein)laden, st.

iron, Eisen, n., -s.

island, Insel, f., -n.

it, es, er, ihn, sie; der (die, das); der
(die, das)selbe.

Italian, adj., italienisch.

Italy, Italien, n., -s.

its, poss. adj., sein; ihr.

its, poss. pron., seiner; ihrer; der
(die, das) sein(ig)e, ihr(ig)e.

itself, refl., sich (selbst); (emphatic),
selbst, selber.


J

James, Jakob, m., -s.

January, Januar, m.

John, Joha'nn, m., -s.

journey, Reise, f., -n.

July, Ju'li, m.

jump, springen, st., f., h.

June, Ju'ni, m.

just, adv., nur (with impve.); —
now, eben, soeben.

## K

**keep**, behalten, *st.*; — on, fortfahren, *st.*; — silent, schweigen, *st.*

**kettle**, Keſſel, *m.*, -s, —.

**kill**, töten.

**kind**, Art, *f.*, -en; of that —, dergleichen; what — of? was für (ein)?; many —s of, vielerlei; two —s of, zweierlei.

**kind**, *adj.*, gütig.

**kindliness**, Herzensgüte, *f.*

**king**, König, *m.*, -es, -e.

**kingdom**, Königreich, *n.*, -es, -e.

**kitchen**, Küche, *f.*, -n.

**knife**, Meſſer, *n.*, -s, —.

**knit**, ſtricken.

**knock** (*rap*), klopfen; there is a — (at the door), es klopft; (*hit*) ſtoßen, *st.*, *tr.*, h.; *intr.*, ſ.

**know** (*be acquainted with*), kennen, *irr.*; (*have knowledge of*), wiſſen, *irr.*; — (a language, etc.), können, *irr.*

**known** (*familiar*), bekannt.

## L

**labourer**, Arbeiter, *m.*, -s, —; Knecht, *m.*, -es, -e.

**lady**, Dame, *f.*, -n; Frau, *f.*, -en.

**lake**, See, *m.*, -s, -n.

**land**, Land, *n.*, -es, ⸗er.

**landscape**, Landſchaft, *f.*, -en.

**language**, Sprache, *f.*, -n.

**large**, groß, ⸗er, größt.

**last**, letzt; (*previous*), letzt, vorig; at — (*finally*), endlich; — of all, zuletzt; for the — week, ſeit acht Tagen.

**late**, ſpät; of —, dieſer Tage.

**lately** (*recently*), neulich.

**latter** (the), dieſer, letzterer.

**laugh**, lachen.

**lawyer**, Rechtsanwalt, *m.*, —es, -e or ⸗e; Advoka't, *m.*, -en, -en.

**lead**, führen.

**leap-year**, Schaltjahr, *n.*, -es, -e.

**learn** (*study*), lernen; (*be informed*), erfahren, *st.*

**learned**, gelehrt.

**least**, wenigſt; at —, wenigſtens.

**leave(-taking)**, Abſchied, *m.*, -es.

**leave**, *tr.*, laſſen, verlaſſen, *st.*; *intr.*, — (*on a journey*), abreiſen, ſ.; — (*of or by a vehicle*), abfahren, *st.*, ſ.; — (*a situation*), austreten, *st.*, ſ.

**left** (on, to the), links, zur linken.

**leg**, Bein, *n.*, -es, -e.

**lend**, leihen, *st.*

**lesson**, Aufgabe, *f.*, -n; Lektio'n, *f.*, -en.

**let** (*allow*), laſſen, *st.*

**letter**, Brief, *m.*, -es, -e; — of recommendation, Empfehlungsbrief.

**lie** (*be recumbent*), liegen, *st.*

**lieutenant**, Leutnant, *m.*, -s, -s.

**life**, Leben, *n.*, -s; human —, Menſchenleben, *n.*, -s, —.

**like**, gern(e) haben ꝛc.; mögen, *irr.*; — to (do, etc.), gern (tun ꝛc.); I — this picture, dieſes Bild gefällt mir; I — fish (wine), ich eſſe (trinke) gern Fiſch (Wein).

**like**; the — of whom (which), desgleichen, dergleichen.

**like**, *adv.*, wie.

**linden**, Linde, *f.*, -n.

**line** (*of print, etc.*), Zeile, *f.*, -n.

lion, Löwe, *m.*, -n, -n.

listen, zuhören (*dat.*).

little (*of size*), klein; (*of quantity*), wenig.

live, leben; (*reside, dwell*), wohnen.

loaf, Brot, *n.*, -es, -e.

lock, schließen, *st.*

long, lang(e), -(e)r; a — time, lange; no —er, nicht mehr; as — as, so lange; — hand (*of timepiece*), der große Zeiger, Minutenzeiger, *m.*, -s, —; how —? seit wann?

look, blicken, schauen; — at, ansehen, *st.*; — for (*search*), suchen.

loosen, lockern.

lose, verlieren, *st.*; (*be deprived of*), kommen um, *st.*, s. (*acc.*); — one's life, umkommen, ums Leben kommen.

loud, laut.

love, lieben; lieb haben, *irr.*

luck, Glück, *n.*, -es.


# M

M. (monsieur, *Fr.*), Herr, *m.*, -n.

ma'am, madam, gnädige Frau.

machine, Maschine, *f.*, -n.

maid (*servant*), Magd, *f.*, -e; Mädchen, *n.*, -s, —; Dienstmädchen.

main street, Hauptstraße, *f.*, -n.

Majesty, Majestät, *f.*, -en; His —, Seine (*abbr.* Se.) Majestät.

make, machen; (*appoint*), ernennen (als *or* zu); — application, sich melden; — up one's mind, sich entschließen, *st.*

man (*adult male*), Mann, *m.*, -es, -er; (*human being*), Mensch, *m.*, -en, -en; the — who, der(jenige) +rel.

mankind, Mensch, *m.*, -en, -en.

manner (*way*), Weise; in this —, auf diese Weise.

man-servant (*hired-man*), Knecht, *m.*, -es, -e.

many, viele, manche; — a, manch(er); — things, vieles; a great —, sehr viele.

map, Landkarte, *f.*, -n.

March, März, *m.*

mark (= *about one shilling*), Mark, *f.*, —.

market, Markt, *m.*, -es, -e.

marry, *tr.*, heiraten; sich verheiraten mit.

Mary, Marie, *f.*, -ns.

master, Herr, *m.*, -n, -en; — of, mächtig (*gen.*).

match, Spiel, *n.*, -es, -e.

material, Zeug, *n.*, -es; Stoff, *m.*, -es, -e.

matter, Sache, *f.*, -n; what is the — with you? was fehlt Ihnen?

may, dürfen, *irr.*: mögen, *irr.*

May, Mai, *m.*

me, mich (*acc.*); mir (*dat.*).

mean (*intend*), wollen, *irr.*; gedenken, *irr.*; (*signify*), meinen, bedeuten.

means, Mittel, *n.*, -s, —.

meanwhile, indessen, unterdessen.

meat, Fleisch, *m.*, -es.

medicine (*science of*), Medizi'n, *f.*; (*physic*), Arzenei, *f.*, -en, Medizin, *f.*

meet (*of people going in opposite directions*), begegnen, s. (*dat.*);

— (*chance upon*), treffen, an=
treffen, *st.* (*acc.*).

melt, *tr.*, ſchmelzen, *st.*; *intr.*,
ſchmelzen, *st.*, ſ.

memory (*faculty of*), Gedächtnis,
*n.*, -es; (*memorial*), Andenken,
*n.*, -s; in — of, zum Andenken
an (*acc.*).

merchant, Kaufmann, *m.*, -es,
-leute.

metre, Meter, *m. or n.*, -s, —.

middle, Mitte, *f.*

midnight, Mitternacht, *f.*, ⁼e.

milk, Milch, *f.*

milk, melken, *wk. or st.*

mind (to have a), Luſt haben, *irr.*;
come to —, einfallen, *st.*, ſ.
(*dat.*); make up one's —, ſich
entſchließen, *st.*; state of —,
Stimmung, *f.*, -en.

mindful, eingedenk (of, *gen.*); be
—, gedenken, *irr.* (of, *gen.*).

mine, meiner, der (die, das) mei=
n(ig)e; a friend of —, ein
Freund von mir, einer von mei=
nen Freunden.

minister (*polit.*), Mini'ſter, *m.*,
-s, —; prime —, erſter Mini=
ſter.

minute, Minute, *f.*, -n.

minute-hand, Minutenzeiger, *m.*,
-s, —.

misfortune, Unglück, *n.*, -es.

Miss, Fräulein, *n.*, -s, — (*abbr.*
Frl.).

missing (be), fehlen.

mistake, Fehler, *m.*, -s, —.

mistaken (to be), ſich irren.

mixed train, Perſonenzug, *m.*, -es,
⁼e.

molasses, Sirup, *m.*, -s.

Monday, Montag, *m.*, -s, -e.

money, Geld, *n.*, -es, -er; piece of
—, Geldſtück, *n.*, -es, -e; sum
of —, Geldſumme, *f.*, -n.

month, Mo'nat, *m.*, -es, -e; what
day of the — is it? der wievielte
iſt heute?

monument, Denkmal, *n.*, -es, -e
and ⁼er.

more, mehr; — of the same kind,
dergleichen mehr; once —, noch
ei'nmal; — and —, (noch) im=
mer; one —, noch ein (-er, -e,
-es) ; not any —, nicht mehr.

moreover, auch; außerdem.

morning, Morgen, *m.*, -s; in the
—, des Morgens, morgens; this
—, heute morgen.

most, *adj.*, meiſt.

most, *adv.*, äußerſt, höchſt, ſehr;
—ly, meiſt(ens); at —, höch=
ſtens.

mother, Mutter, *f.*, ⁼; — dear,
Mütterchen, *n.*, -s.

mount, *tr.*, beſteigen, *st.*

mourn, *tr.*, betrauern; *intr.*, trau=
ern.

move, *tr.*, bewegen; *intr.*, ſich be=
wegen; ziehen, *st.*, ſ.; — (from
one house to another), um=
ziehen, *st.*, ſ.

Mr., Herr, *m.*, -n, -en.

Mrs., Frau, *f.*, -en.

much, viel; very — (*adv.*), ſehr.

multitude, Menge, *f.*, -n.

museum, Muſeum, *n.*, -s, Mu=
ſeen.

must, müſſen, *irr.*

my, mein.

myself, *refl.*, mich, mir (ſelbſt); (I)
—, (ich) ſelbſt, ſelber.

Z

# N

**name,** Name, *m.,* –ns, –n; what is this man's —? wie heißt dieser Mann?; his — is Schäfer, er heißt Schäfer; by —, namens.

**name,** nennen, *irr.;* —d, namens.

**natural,** natürlich.

**near,** *adj.,* nah(e), ⁀(e)r, nächst (*dat.*).

**near,** *prep.,* bei (*dat.*), neben (*dat. or acc.*).

**nearly,** beinahe, fast.

**necessary,** nötig.

**need,** brauchen.

**neglect,** vernachlässigen, versäumen.

**neighbour,** Nachbar, *m.,* –s, –n; Nachbarin, *f.,* –nen.

**neither,** weder; — . . . nor, weder . . . noch; — am (have, do) I, ich auch nicht.

**never,** nie, niemals; — yet, noch nie(mals).

**nevertheless,** doch, dennoch, nichtsdestoweniger.

**new,** neu.

**news,** Nachricht, *f.,* –en.

**newspaper,** Zeitung, *f.,* –en.

**next,** nächst, folgend; in the — place, zunächst, dann.

**Niagara Falls,** die Niagara-Fälle.

**nice,** nett.

**Nicholas,** Nikolaus, *m.,* —.

**night,** Nacht, *f.,* ⁀e; by —, bei (in der) Nacht, des Nachts, nachts.

**No.** (number), No. (Numero).

**no,** *adj.,* kein; —body, — one, niemand, keiner; — longer, nicht mehr; — doubt, wohl.

**no,** *adv.,* nein; —, thank you, ich danke.

**noble,** edel.

**noise,** Lärm, *m.,* –es.

**none,** keiner.

**north,** Norden, *m.,* –s and —; the — Sea, die Nordsee, das Deutsche Meer.

**northern,** nördlich.

**not,** nicht; — a, — any, kein(er); — yet, noch nicht; — at all, gar nicht; is it, etc., —? nicht wahr?

**nothing,** nichts;— at all, gar nichts.

**novel,** Roma'n, *m.,* –es, –e.

**November,** November, *m.*

**now,** jetzt.

**nowadays,** heutzutage.

**number** (*figure*), Ziffer, *f.,* –n; Zahl, *f.,* –en; — (*in a street*), Nummer, Numero (*abbr.* No.); (*quantity*), Anzahl, *f.;* Menge, *f.*

**nutmeg,** Muskatnuß, *f.,* ⁀e.

# O

**O! oh! o! ach!;** — yes, jawohl, doch.

**oats,** Hafer, *m.,* –s.

**obey,** gehorchen (*dat.*).

**oblige** (*put under obligation*), verbinden, *st.;* (*force*), zwingen, *st.;* to be —d (compelled), müssen, *irr.;* to be —d (*under an obligation*), verbunden sein.

**observe** (*mark closely*), beo'bachten; (*remark*), bemerken.

**occasion,** Gelegenheit, *f.,* –en.

**occasion** (*cause*), veru'rsachen.

**occurrence,** Begebenheit, *f.,* –en.

**o'clock,** Uhr; ten —, zehn Uhr.

**October,** Oktober, *m.*

**of,** *prep.* (*App. B,* 4), von (*dat.*); — course, natürlich.

**off**, ab.

**offer**, bieten, anbieten, *st.*

**office**, Amt, *n.*, -es, ⁼er.

**officer** (*mil.*), Offizie'r, *m.*, -es, -e.

**official**, Beamt(er), *adj. subst.*

**often**, oft, ⁼er.

**old**, alt, ⁼er.

**omnibus**, Omnibus, *m.*, —, -ffe.

**on**, *prep.* (*App. B*, 4), auf (*dat. or acc.*); an (*dat. or acc.*).

**on**, *adv.*, weiter.

**once**, ei'nmal; (all) at — (*suddenly*), auf ei'nmal; (*immediately*), sofort; — more, noch einmal.

**one**, *num.*, ein; (*in counting*), eins; *pron.* einer; — another, einander; the — who, der(jenige) welcher; some —, jemand; not —, keiner.

**one**, *indef. pron.*, man.

**only**, nur; (*of time*), erst; not — ... but also, nicht nur ... sondern auch.

**open**, aufmachen; öffnen.

**opinion**, Meinung, *f.*, -en.

**opportunity**, Gelegenheit, *f.*, -en.

**opposed** (to be), gegenüberstehen, *st.* (*dat.*).

**opposite**, gegenüber (*dat.*).

**or**, oder; — else, sonst; three — four, drei bis vier.

**order** (*a command*), Befehl, *m.*, -es, -e; in — to, um ... zu.

**order** (*to command*), befehlen, *st.* (*dat.*); (*to direct*), bedeuten (*dat.*); — (*from a tradesman*), bestellen.

**other**, ander; —wise, sonst; each —, einander.

**ought**, sollte.

**our**, unser.

**ours**, unsrer; der (die, das) unsr(ig)e.

**ourselves**, *refl.*, uns (selbst); (we) —, (wir) selbst, selber.

**out**, aus, heraus, hinaus.

**outcome**, Ausgang, *m.*, -es, ⁼e.

**out of**, aus (*dat.*).

**over**, über (*dat. or acc.*); — there, drüben.

**overcoat**, Überzieher, *m.*, -s, —.

**own**, *adj.*, eigen.

**ox**, Ochs(e), *m.*, -(e)n, -(e)n.

**oyster**, Auster, *f.*, -n.


## P

**pack**, packen, einpacken.

**painter**, Maler, *m.*, -s, —.

**pair**, Paar, *n.*, -es, -e.

**palace**, Schloß, *n.*, -es, ⁼er; Pala'st, *m.*, -es, ⁼e.

**pardon**, Verzeihung, *f.*; Entschuldigung, *f.*; to ask (beg) —, um Verzeihung 2c. bitten, *st.*; sich entschuldigen.

**pardon**, verzeihen, *st.* (*dat. of pers.*), entschuldigen (*acc.*).

**parents**, Eltern, *pl.*

**park**, Park, *m.*, -es, -s *and* -e.

**part** (*portion*), Teil, *m. and n.*, -es, -e; (*dram. part, rôle*), Rolle, *f.*, -n.

**part**, *intr.*, sich trennen.

**party** (*social*), Gesellschaft, *f.*, -en.

**pass** (*time*), verbringen, zubringen, *irr.*; — (*an examination*), bestehen, *st.*; — away, vergehen, *st.*, s.

**past** (*of time*), vergangen; for the — week, seit acht Tagen.

**past,** *prep.* (*of time*), nach (*dat.*);
a quarter — ten, (ein) Viertel
auf elf; half- — ten, halb elf.

**past,** *adv.,* vorbei, vorüber.

**pasture,** Weide, *f.,* –n.

**pat,** klopfen.

**patient,** Patie'nt, *m.,* –en, –en;
Patientin, *f.,* –nen; Krank(er),
*adj. subst.*

**pattern,** Muster, *n.,* –s, —.

**pay,** zahlen (*dat. of pers.*), bezahlen
(*acc. of pers., or dat. of pers.
and acc. of thing*); — visits,
Besuche machen.

**pea,** Erbse, *f.,* –n.

**pear,** Birne, *f.,* –n.

**pear-tree,** Birnbaum, *m.,* –es, ⸚e.

**peasant,** Bauer, *m.,* –n *or* –s, –n.

**pedestrian,** Fußgänger, *m.,* –s, —.

**pen,** Feder, *f.,* –n.

**pencil** (lead-), Bleistift, *m.,* –es, –e.

**people,** Leute, *pl.;* (*nation*), Volk,
*n.,* –es, ⸚er.

**people,** *indef. pron.,* man.

**perhaps,** viellei'cht.

**perish,** umkommen, *st.,* f.

**Persian,** *adj.,* persisch.

**'pfennig,'** Pfennig, *m.,* –s, –e.

**physician,** Arzt, *m.,* –es, ⸚e.

**physics,** Physi'k, *f.*

**piano,** Klavie'r, *n.,* –es, –e; play
the —, Klavier spielen.

**pick,** pflücken; — out, aussuchen;
— up, aufheben, *st.*

**picture,** Bild, *n.,* –es, –er.

**picture-gallery,** Bildergaleri¨, *f.,*
–n; Gemäldegalerie.

**piece,** Stück, *n.,* –es, –e; — of
money, Geldstück; to — s, entzwei.

**pilot,** Lotse, *m.,* –n, –n.

**pin,** Stecknadel, *f.,* –n.

**pinch,** kneifen, *st.*

**pity** (it is a), es ist schade.

**pity,** bedauern.

**place,** Platz, *m.,* –es, ⸚e; (*situation*), Stelle, *f.,* –n; Stellung, *f.,*
–en; take —, stattfinden, *st.;* in
the first (second, etc.) —,
erstens (zweitens 2c.).

**plant,** pflanzen.

**play,** spielen.

**pleasant,** angenehm.

**please!** *vb.,* gefallen, *st.* (*dat.*).

**please!** (if you), (ich) bitte; ge-
fälligst (*adv.*).

**pleasure,** Vergnügen, *n.*

**pleasure-trip,** Vergnügungsreise, *f.,*
–n.

**plough,** pflügen.

**p.m.,** Nm. (Nachmittags); abends.

**pocket,** Tasche, *f.,* –n.

**pocket,** in die Tasche stecken; einstecken.

**poem,** Gedicht, *n.,* –es, –e.

**poet,** Dichter, *m.,* –s, —.

**point;** on the — of, im Begriffe.

**polite,** höflich.

**pond,** Teich, *m.,* –es, –e.

**poor,** arm, ⸚er.

**position,** Stellung, *f.,* –en; be in a
— (to), imstande sein, *irr.,* f. (zu).

**possession,** Eigentum, *n.,* –es, ⸚er;
—s, Habe, *f.*

**possibility,** Möglichkeit, *f.,* –en.

**possible,** möglich.

**postman,** Postbote, *m.,* –n, **–n;**
Briefträger, *m.,* –s, —.

**potato,** Kartoffel, *f.,* –n.

**pound,** Pfund, *n.,* –es, **–e.**

**pour,** gießen, *st.*

**power,** Macht, *f.,* ⸚e.

**praise,** loben.

**pray** (*say a prayer*), beten; (*request*), bitten.

**prefer,** vorziehen, *st.*; lieber (am liebsten) haben ꝛc.

**prepare,** bereiten, vorbereiten, —(a field, etc.), bestellen.

**present** (*gift*), Geschenk, *n.*, –es, –e.

**present,** *adj.*, gegenwärtig (*of time and place*); zugegen (*adv., of place only*); jetzig (*adj., of time only*).

**present** (*make a present of*), schenken.

**president,** Präside'nt, *m.*, –en, –en.

**press forward,** sich vordrängen.

**pretend** (*assert*), wollen.

**pretty,** hübsch.

**prevail,** herrschen.

**prevent,** verhindern.

**prime minister,** erster Mini'ster, *m.*, –s, —.

**prince** (*ruler or title*), Fürst, *m.*, –en, –en; (*title of courtesy*), Prinz, *m.*, –en, –en.

**prisoner,** Gefangen(er), *adj. subst.*

**prize,** Preis, *m.*, –es, –e.

**profession** (*calling*), Beruf, *m.*, –es, –e.

**professor,** Professor, *m.*, –s, Professo'ren.

**promise,** *vb.*, versprechen, *st.* (*dat. of pers.*).

**promontory,** Vorgebirge, *n.*, –s, —.

**prove,** beweisen, *st.*

**proverb,** Sprichwort, *n.*, –es, –er.

**Prussia,** Preußen, *n.*, –s.

**pudding,** Pudding, *m.*, –s, –s; Indian meal —, Maispudding.

**pulse,** Puls, *m.*, –es, –e.

**pulse-beat,** Pulsschlag, *m.*, –es, –e.

**punctual,** pünktlich.

**punish,** strafen, bestrafen.

**pupil,** Schüler, *m.*, –s, —; Schülerin, *f.*, –nen.

**purchase,** Einkauf, *m.*, –es, –e.

**purchase,** kaufen.

**purse,** Portemonnaie, *n.*, –s, –s.

**put** (*set upright*), stellen, setzen; (*lay*), legen; (*insert*), stecken; — on (a coat, etc.), anziehen, *st.*; — on (a hat, etc.), aufsetzen.


## Q

**quarter,** Viertel, *n.*, –s, —; a — past 10, (ein) Viertel (auf) 11; a — to 10, drei Viertel (auf) 10; — of a teaspoon, Viertelteelöffel, *m.*, –s, —; 3 —s of an hour, 3 Viertelstunden.

**queen,** Königin, *f.*, –nen.

**quick,** schnell.

**quite,** ganz.


## R

**rage,** wüten.

**rain,** Regen, *m.*, –s.

**rain,** regnen.

**raise,** erheben, *st.*

**raisin,** Rosine, *f.*, –n.

**rather** (*preference*), lieber; (*on the contrary*), vielmehr; (*tolerably*), ziemlich; a — long journey, eine längere Reise.

**read,** lesen, *st.*; — aloud, vorlesen.

**reading** (*the act of*), Lesen, *n.*, –s.

**ready,** fertig, bereit.

**real,** eigentlich, wirklich.

**reason,** Grund, *m.*, -es, ⁻e; Ur=
sache, *f.*, -n.

**receive** (*of things*), bekommen, *st.*;
erhalten, *st.*; (*of pers. or things*),
empfangen, *st.*

**recite,** vortragen, *st.*

**recognize** (*know*), erkennen, *irr.*

**recommend,** empfehlen, *st.* (*dat.
of pers.*).

**recommendation,** Empfehlung, *f.*,
-en; letter of —, Empfehlungs=
brief, *m.*, -es, -e.

**recover** (*health*), genesen, *st.*, s.

**red,** rot, ⁻er.

**reflect** (*think over*), sich besinnen,
*st.*

**refreshment,** Erfrischung, *f.*, -en.

**refuse,** abschlagen, *st.* (*dat. of
pers.*).

**regard,** betrachten; ansehen, *st.*

**regards** (*in correspondence*),
Empfehlung, *f.*, -en; Gruß, *m.*,
-es, ⁻e.

**regret,** bedauern.

**reign,** Regierung, *f.*, -en.

**rejoice,** freuen; be —d, sich freuen,
erfreut sein, *irr.*, s.; — at, sich
freuen über (*acc.*).

**relate,** erzählen.

**relative** (*relation*), Verwandt(er),
*adj. subst.*

**relieve** (*release from*), entbinden,
*st.* (*gen.*).

**remain,** bleiben, *st.*, s.

**require,** brauchen; bedürfen, *irr.*

**reply,** erwidern, versetzen.

**resemble,** ähnlich sein, *irr.*, s. (*dat.*).

**resolve,** beschließen, sich entschließen,
*st.*

**respect,** Achtung, *f.*

**rest** (*repose*), Ruhe, *f.*

**rest,** ruhen; ausruhen; take a —,
sich ausruhen.

**restaurant,** Restauration, *f.*, -en.

**retain,** behalten, *st.*

**retire,** sich zurückziehen, *st.*; — to
rest, sich zur Ruhe begeben, *st.*

**return,** zurückkehren, s.

**revolver,** Revolver, *m.*, -s, —.

**reward,** Lohn, *m.*, -es.

**Rhine,** Rhein, *m.*, -es.

**rich,** reich.

**ride,** reiten, *st.*, s., h.

**rid of,** los (*acc.*).

**right,** *adj.*, recht, richtig; be — (*of
a time-piece*), richtig gehen, *st.*,
s.; be (in the) —, recht haben.

**right** (on, to the), rechts, zur rech=
ten.

**ring,** Ring, *m.*, -es, -e.

**ring** (*of a large bell*), läuten.

**rise** (*mount*), steigen, aufsteigen,
*st.*, s.; (*get up*), aufstehen, *st.*,
s.; (*of the sun, etc.*), aufgehen,
*st.*, s.

**river,** Fluß, *m.*, -es, ⁻e.

**roast,** Braten, *m.*, -s, —; — of
beef, Rinderbraten.

**rock,** Fels(en), *m.*, -(en)s, -(en).

**Rome,** Rom, *n.*, -s.

**roof,** Dach, *n.*, -es, ⁻er.

**room,** Zimmer, *n.*, -s, —; Stube,
*f.*, -n.

**rose,** Rose, *f.*, -n.

**round** (*mil.*), Runde, *f.*, -n.

**round,** *adj.*, rund.

**row** (*series*), Reihe, *f.*, -n.

**rowboat,** Kahn, *m.*, -es, ⁻e.

**royal,** königlich.

**ruin,** Ruine, *f.*, -n; —s, Trümmer,
*pl.*; in —s, zerfallen.

run, laufen, *st.*, f., h.

Russia, Rußland, *n.*, –s.

Russian (*native of Russia*), Ruffe, r.a., –n, –n.

## S

sad, traurig.

sail, Segel, *n.*, –s, —.

sail, segeln, f. ; fahren, *st.*, f., h.

sailor, Matrofe, *m.*, –n, –n.

Saint (*see* St.).

salt, Salz, *n.*, –es, –e.

salute, grüßen.

same, felb(ig).

Sarah, Sara, *f.*, –s.

satisfied, zufrieden.

Saturday, Sonnabend, *m.*, –s, –e ; Samstag, *m.*, –s, –e.

sausage, Wurft, *f.*, ⁼e.

save (*rescue*), retten.

Saxony, Sachsen, *n.*, –s.

say, fagen; he is said to be rich, er foll reich fein.

scatter, ausftreuen.

school, Schule, *f.*, –n; high-—, Gymnafium, *n.*, –s, –en; elementary —, Elementarfchule.

school-bell, Schulglocke, *f.*, –n.

school-fellow, —-mate, Schul= kamerad, *m.*, –en, –en.

school-house, Schulhaus, *n.*, –es, ⁼er.

scold, fchelten, *st.*

Scotland, Schottland, *n.*, –s.

scream, fchreien, *st.*

sea, See, *f.*, –(e)n; Meer, *n.*, –es, –e.

search (through), durchfu'chen, *insep.*

seat, Sitz, *m.*, –es, –e; Platz, *m.*, –es, ⁼e.

second (*of time*), Sekunde, *f.*, –n;

—-hand (*of a time-piece*), Se= kundenzeiger, *m.*, –s, —.

secondly, zweitens.

see, fehen, *st.*; (*view*), befehen, *st.*; (*interview*), fprechen, *st.* (*acc.*).

seed, Same, *m.*, –ns, –n.

seek, fuchen.

seem, fcheinen, *st.*

seize, ergreifen, *st.*

seldom, felten.

sell, verkaufen.

send, fchicken; fenden, *wk. and irr.*; — in, herein (hinein)fchicken; — out, hinaus (heraus)fchicken.

September, September, *m.*

serious, ernfthaft.

servant, Diener, *m.*, –s, —; Be= dient(er), *adj. subst.*; —-girl, Magd, *f.*, ⁼e; Mädchen, *n.*, –s, —; Dienftmädchen.

set, fetzen, ftellen; — on end, auf= recht ftellen; — down (*from a vehicle*), abfetzen; — out (*on a journey*), abreifen, f.; — out (*on a walk, etc.*), fich auf den Weg machen.

several, mehrere, einige, etliche; — times, mehrmals.

severe, fchwer; tüchtig.

sewing-machine, Nähmafchine, *f.*, –n.

shake, fchütteln; — hands, die Hand geben, *st.*

shall (*aux. of tense*), werden, *st.*; (*mod. aux.*), follen, *irr.*

sharp, fcharf, ⁼er.

she, fie; es (*of dimins.*).

sheep, Schaf, *n.*, –es, –e.

sheik, Scheik, *m.*, –s, –s.

shillings (three), taler. *m.*

shine, fcheinen, *st.*; leuchten.

ship, Schiff, *n.*, –es, –e.

shoot, schießen, *st.*

shop (*go shopping*), Einkäufe machen, einkaufen.

shore, Ufer, *n.*, -s, —.

short, kurz, ʺer.

shoulder, Schulter, *f.*, -n.

show, zeigen.

shut, zumachen.

Sicily, Sizilien, *n.*, -s.

silence, Schweigen, *n.*, -s.

silent, still; keep —, schweigen, *st.*

silk, Seide, *f.*; *adj.*, seiden.

silver, Silber, *n.*, -s; *adj.*, silbern.

sink, sinken, versinken, *st.*, s.

Sir, Herr, *m.*, -n, -en.

sister, Schwester, *f.*, -n.

sit, sitzen, *st.*; — down, sich setzen.

situated (to be), liegen, *st.*, s.

skate, Schlittschuh laufen, *st.*, s., h.

skull, Schädel, *m.*, -s, —.

sky, Himmel, *m.*, -s, —; in the —, am Himmel.

sleep, schlafen, *st.*

sleeping-car, Schlafwagen, *m.*, -s, —.

sleigh-drive (-ride), Schlittenfahrt, *f.*, -en; take a —, eine Schlittenfahrt machen.

slight, leicht.

slip, gleiten, *st.*, s.

slow, langsam.

small, klein.

smell, riechen, *st.*

smile, lächeln.

sneak, schleichen, *st.*, s.

snow, Schnee, *m.*, -s.

snow, schneien.

so, so; — am, do, etc., I, ich auch; — then, also; — (*equal 'it'*), es.

soft, weich.

soil, Boden, *m.*, -s, ʺ, Erde, *f.*

soldier, Solda't, *m.*, -en, -en.

some, einig(er, -e, -es), welch(er, -e, -es); —body, — one, jemand, einer; —thing, etwas; (*as partitive often untranslated*).

somewhat long, länger.

son, Sohn, *m.*, -es, ʺe.

song, Lied, *n.*, -es, -er.

soon, bald, eher, am ehesten; as — as, sobald, sowie; —er, früher.

sore (to be), weh tun (*dat. of pers.*).

sorry; I am —, es tut mir leid.

sort, Art, *f.*, -en; that — of thing, of that —, dergleichen; what — of? was für (ein)?

sound, klingen, *st.*

south, Süden, *m.*, -s *and* —; on (in, to) the —, im Süden, südlich.

sow, säen.

sower, Säemann, *m.*, -es, ʺer.

spade, Spaten, *m.*, -s, —.

speak, sprechen, *st.*; reden; — to (*interview*), sprechen (*acc.*).

speaking-trumpet, Sprachrohr, *n.*, -es, -e.

special, besonder.

spend (*of time*), verbringen, zubringen, *irr.*; (*of money*), verausgaben.

splendid, herrlich, prächtig, prachtvoll.

spoil, *tr.*, verderben, *wk.* or *st.*; *intr.*, verderben, *st.*

spoon, Löffel, *m.*, -s, —.

Spree, Spree, *f.*

spring, Frühling, *m.*, -es, -e.

sprite, Nixe, *f.*, -n.

**St. Petersburg,** Petersburg, *n.*, -s.

**stable,** Stall, *m.*, -es, ⸚e.

**stand,** stehen, *st.*; — still, stehen bleiben, *st.*, f.

**star,** Stern, *m.*, -es, -e.

**start** (on a journey), abreisen, f.; (*of a vehicle*), abfahren, *st.*, f.; (on a walk), aufbrechen, *st.*, f.; sich auf den Weg machen.

**state** (*polit.*), Staat, *m.*, -es, -en; the United —s, die Vereinigten Staaten; — of mind, Stimmung, *f.*, -en.

**statesman,** Staatsmann, *m.*, -es, ⸚er

**station** (*railway*), Bahnhof, *m.*, -es, ⸚e; (*stopping-place*), Station, *f.*, -en.

**stay,** bleiben, *st.*, f.; — up, aufbleiben, *st.*, f.; — in (after school), nachsitzen, *st.*

**steal,** stehlen, *st.*

**steamer,** Dampfer, *m.*, -s, —.

**steer,** steuern.

**steersman,** Steuermann, *m.*, -es, ⸚er.

**step,** treten, *st.*, f., h.

**still** (to stand), stehen bleiben, *st.*, f.

**still,** *adv.* (*of time, number, and degree*), noch; (*adversative*), doch, be'nnoch.

**stocking,** Strumpf, *m.*, -es, ⸚e.

**stone,** Stein, *m.*, -es, -e.

**stop** (*draw up*), anhalten, *st.*; (*cease*), aufhören.

**store** (*shop*), Laden, *m.*, -s, ⸚; departmental —, Waarenhaus, *n.*, -es, ⸚er.

**storm,** Sturm, *m.*, -es, ⸚e.

**stormy,** stürmisch.

**story** (*tale*), Geschichte, *f.*, -n; (*fairy-tale*), Märchen, *n.*, -s, —; — (*of a building*), Etage, *f.*, -n; Stock, *m.*, -es, ⸚e; Stockwerk, *n.*, -es, -e.

**stove,** Ofen, *m.*, -s, ⸚.

**stranger,** Fremd(er), *adj. subst.*

**straw,** Stroh, *n.*, -es.

**street,** Straße, *f.*, -n; main —, Hauptstraße, *f.*, -n.

**street-cars,** — -railway, Straßenbahn, *f.*, -en.

**strike** (*hit*), schlagen, *st.*; (*knock, bump*), stoßen, *st.*, h., f.

**student,** Stude'nt, *m.*, -en, -en.

**study** (*room*), Studierzimmer, *n.*, -s, —; (*branch of learning*), Studium, *n.*, -s, Studien.

**study,** studieren.

**subject** (*of a ruler*), U'ntertan, *m.*, -s *or* -en, -en.

**suburb,** Vorstadt, *f.*, ⸚e.

**succeed,** gelingen, *st.*, *impers.*, f. (*dat.*); I —, es gelingt mir.

**such,** solch(er); so.

**suffer,** leiden, *st.*

**suffice,** genügen, genug sein, *irr.*, f.; ausreichen.

**sufficient,** genug.

**sugar,** Zucker, *m.*, -s.

**sum;** — of money, Geldsumme, *f.*, -n.

**summer,** Sommer, *m.*, -s, —.

**summon,** berufen, *st.*

**sun,** Sonne, *f.*, -n.

**Sunday,** Sonntag, *m.*, -s, -e.

**sunshine,** Sonnenschein, *m.*, -es.

**superior,** überle'gen.

**supper,** Abendessen, *n.*, -s; Abendbrot, *n.*, -es.

**suppose,** vermuten; I —, wohl 2c.

sure, ſicher, gewiß; to be —, aller=
di'ngs, zwar, freilich.

surprise, Überraſchung, *f.*, –en.

suspicious (*obj. of suspicion*),
verdächtig.

swallow (up), verſchlingen, *st.*

swear (*take oath*), ſchwören, *st.*

sweet, ſüß.

sweets, Bonbons, *pl.*

swell, *intr.*, ſchwellen, *st.*, ſ.

swim, ſchwimmen, *st.*, ſ., h.

Switzerland, Schweiz, *f.*

## T

table, Tiſch, *m.*, –es, –e.

tablespoon, Eßlöffel, *m.*, –s, —.

tailor, Schneider, *m.*, –s, —.

take, nehmen, *st.*; — (a drive,
walk, etc.), machen; — a look
at, ſich (*dat.*) anſehen, *st.*; —
care, ſich in acht nehmen, *st.* (of,
vor, *dat.*); — off, abnehmen; —
place, ſtattfinden, *st.*; — cold,
ſich erkälten.

talk, reden; ſprechen, *st.*

tall, groß, ⸗er, größt.

tea, Tee, *m.*, –s.

teach, lehren (*acc. of pers. and
thing*); unterrichten (in, *dat.*).

teacher, Lehrer, *m.*, –s, —; Leh=
rerin, *f.*, –nen.

tear, *tr.*, reißen, zerreißen, *st.*; *intr.*,
reißen, zerreißen, *st.*, h., ſ.

teaspoon, Teelöffel, *m.*, –s, —.

teem, wimmeln.

telegraph, Telegra'ph, *m.*, –en, –en.

telephone, Fernſprecher, *m.*, –s, —;
Telepho'n, *n.*, –es, –e.

tell (*inform*), ſagen (*dat.*); — (*relate*), erzählen.

ten, zehn.

terrible, furchtbar, ſchrecklich, fürch=
terlich, entſetzlich.

than, als.

thank, danken (*dat.*).

that, *rel. pron.*, der, welcher.

that, *demonstr.*, der; dieſer; (*yonder*), jener.

that, *conj.*, daß.

the, *art.*, der, die, das.

the . . . the (*in compar.*), je, deſto,
umſo.

theatre, Theater, *n.*, –s, —.

thee, dich (*acc.*); dir (*dat.*).

their, ihr.

them, ſie (*acc.*); ihnen (*dat.*).

then (*at that time*), da, da'mals;
(*thereupon*), dann, darauf.

there (*in that place*), da, daſelbſt,
dort; (*to that place*), dahin, dort=
hin; (*before verbs*), es; —in,
darin; —upon, darauf; over —,
drüben.

therefore, daher, alſo.

these, dieſe.

they, ſie; *demonstr.*, die; dieſe; die=
ſelben; *indef.*, man.

thick, dick.

thief, Dieb, *m.*, –es, –e.

thin, dünn.

thing, Sache, *f.*, –n; Ding, *n.*, –es,
–er; any—, some—, (irgend)
etwas.

think, denken, *irr.*; (*suppose*),
glauben.

thirsty, durſtig; be —, Durſt haben,
durſtig ſein.

this, dieſer; der; — time, diesmal.

those, dieſe; jene.

thou, du.

thousand, *noun*, Tauſend, *n.*, –es,
–e.

**three,** drei.

**thresh,** dreſchen, *st.*

**thrive,** gedeihen, *st.,* ſ.

**throne,** Thron, *m.,* –es, –e.

**through,** durch (*acc.*).

**throw,** werfen, *st.;* ſchmeißen, *st.;* — away, fortwerfen, *st.*

**Thursday,** Donnerstag, *m.,* –s, –e.

**thus,** ſo, alſo, auf dieſe Weiſe.

**ticket** (travelling), Fahrkarte, *f.,* –n.

**tidy,** ſorgfältig, reinlich.

**tie,** binden, *st.*

**till,** bis; not —, erſt.

**time,** Zeit, *f.,* –en; (*repetition*), Mal, *n.;* all the —, beſtändig, immer; a long —, lange; at one —, . . . at another, bald . . . bald; several —s, mehrmals; this —, diesmal; what — is it? wie viel Uhr iſt es?; by this —, ſchon.

**tired,** müde.

**title,** Titel, *m.,* –s, —.

**to** (*App. B,* 4, 5), zu (*dat.*); — (*with place names*), nach (*dat.*); an, auf, in (*acc.*); *before infin.,* zu; — and fro, hin und her, auf und ab.

**to-day,** heute.

**together,** zuſammen.

**tomato,** Tomate, *f.,* –n.

**to-morrow,** morgen; — morning, morgen früh.

**tongue,** Zunge, *f.,* –n.

**too** (*also*), auch; (*of excess*), zu.

**toothache,** Zahnweh, *n.,* –s; Zahnſchmerzen, *pl.*

**towards,** gegen (*acc.*).

**town,** Stadt, *f.,* ⸚e; to —, zur (in die) Stadt; in —, in der Stadt.

**town-hall,** Rathaus, *n.,* ⸚es, ⸚er.

**train,** Zug, *m.,* –es, ⸚e; express —, Schnellzug; mixed —, Perſonenzug.

**tram(way),** Straßenbahn, *f.,* –en.

**transparent,** durchſichtig.

**travel,** reiſen, ſ., h.

**travel, travelling** (the act of), Reiſen, *n.,* –s.

**traveller,** Reiſend(er), *adj. subst.;* commercial- —, Geſchäftsreiſend(er); fellow- —, Mitreiſend(er).

**tread,** treten, *st.,* ſ., h.

**treasure,** Schatz, *m.,* –es, ⸚e.

**tree,** Baum, *m.,* –es, ⸚e.

**tremble,** zittern.

**trip,** Reiſe, *f.,* –n; take a —, **eine** Reiſe machen.

**troop,** Truppe, *f.,* –n.

**trouble,** bemühen.

**true,** wahr; it is — (=of course), freilich, zwar.

**trust,** trauen (*dat.*); — one's self, ſich anvertrauen.

**truth,** Wahrheit, *f.,* –en.

**try** (*attempt*), verſuchen.

**Tuesday,** Dienstag, *m.,* –s, –e.

**turn,** *tr.,* kehren; wenden, *irr.;* drehen; *intr.,* ſich wenden, ſich drehen; — out (to be the case), ſich herausſtellen; — to, werden zu; — round, (ſich) umwenden, etc.

**turn;** it is my —, ich bin an der Reihe, komme an die Reihe.

**twice,** zweimal; — as large, noch einmal ſo groß.

**two,** zwei; beide (*after a determ.*).

# U

**umbrella**, Regenschirm, m., –es, –e.
**uncle**, Onkel, m., –s, —.
**under**, unter (dat. or acc.).
**unfortunate**, unglücklich.
**unhappy**, unglücklich.
**uninjured**, unverletzt.
**United States** (the), die Vereinigten Staaten.
**university**, Universität, f., –en;
study at the —, auf der Universität studieren; go to the — (as a student), auf die U. gehen; go to the — building, zur U. gehen.
**unpack**, auspacken.
**unpleasant**, unangenehm.
**until**, bis.
**up**, auf; hinauf; herauf.
**upright**, aufrecht.
**upstairs** (motion upwards), herauf, hinauf; (rest), oben.
**us**, uns.
**use**, brauchen, gebrauchen; —d to, impf. or pflegen zu.
**useful**, nützlich.
**usual**, gewöhnlich.

# V

**valley**, Tal, n., –es, –er.
**vanity**, Eitelkeit, f., –en.
**vegetables**, Gemüse, n., –s.
**veranda**, Veranda, f., –s or Veranden.
**very**, sehr; — much, sehr.
**vex**, verdrießen, st.; I am —ed, es verdrießt mich; ich ärgere mich.
**Victoria**, Viktoria, f., –s.

**Vienna**, Wien, n., –s; (of) —, Wiener.
**view** (prospect), Aussicht, f., –en
**village**, Dorf, n., –es, –er.
**violet**, Veilchen, n., –s, —.
**violent**, heftig.
**visit**, Besuch, m., –es, –e; pay —s Besuche machen.
**visit**, besuchen.
**visitor(s)**, Besuch, m., –es.
**voice**, Stimme, f., –n.
**volume**, Band, m., –es, –e.

# W

**wait**, warten (for, auf, acc.).
**walk**, Spaziergang, m., –es, –e; take (go for) a —, einen Sp. machen; spazieren gehen, st., s.
**walk**, gehen, st., s.
**want** (need), brauchen; — to, Lust haben zu, wollen.
**war**, Krieg, m., –es, –e.
**warm**, warm, –er.
**warn**, warnen.
**wash**, waschen, st.
**waste**, verschwenden.
**waste-basket**, Papierkorb, m., –es, –e.
**watch**, Uhr, f., –en, Taschenuhr.
**water**, Wasser, n., –s, — and –.
**water**, begießen, st.
**water-sprite**, Nixe, f., –n.
**wave**, Welle, f., –n.
**way** (road), Weg, m., –es, –e; in this — (manner), auf diese Weise.
**we**, wir.
**wealthy**, reich.
**weapon**, Waffe, f., –n.

weather, Wetter, n., –s.

weave, flechten, st.

week, Woche, f., –n; acht Tage, pl.; a — ago, heute vor 8 Tagen; this day —, heute über 8 Tage.

weep, weinen.

weigh, tr., wägen, st.; intr., wiegen, st.

welcome, adj., willko'mmen.

well, adj. (of health), wohl (pred. only), gesund; to get —, genesen, st., ſ.

well, adv., wohl; gut, beſſer, am beſten; — known, bekannt.

well! nun! na!

west, Weſten, m., –s or —; on (in, to) the —, im Weſten, weſtlich.

western, weſtlich.

what? interrog. pron., was?; adj., welcher?; — (kind of)? was für (ein)?; — time? wie viel Uhr?; — day of the month? der wievielte?

what, rel. (that which), was; —ever, was auch (immer).

wheat, Weizen, m., –s.

when, als, wenn.

when? wann?

where (in what or which place), wo; (to what or which place), wohin.

whether, ob.

which? welch(er, –e, –es)?

which, rel. pron., der, die, das; welch(er, –e, –es); that —, was.

while; worth —, der Mühe wert.

while, conj., während, indeſſen, unterdeſſen.

whistle, pfeifen, st.

white, weiß.

who? wer?

who, rel. pron., der, die, das; welch(er, –e, –es); he (the one) —, wer.

whoever, wer auch (immer).

whole (adj.), ganz.

whom (acc.)? wen? (dat.) wem?

whose? weſſen?

why? warum? weshalb?

wide, breit.

wife, Frau, f., –en; Gemahlin, f., –nen; Weib, n., –es, –er.

will (aux. of tense), werden, st.; (mod. aux.), wollen, irr.

William, Wilhelm, m., –s.

willing (to be), bereit ſein; wollen, irr.

win, gewinnen, st.

wind, Wind, m., –es, –e.

window, Fenſter, n., –s, —.

wine, Wein, m., –es, –e.

winter, Winter, m., –s, —.

wipe, abputzen.

wish, wünſchen; wollen, irr.

with, mit (dat.); (at the house of), bei (dat.); (about the person), bei.

without, ohne (acc.).

witness, Zeuge, m., –n, –n.

woman, Frau, f., –en.

wonder, ſich wundern; I — at that, das wundert mich.

wonder of the world, Weltwunder, n., –s, —.

wood (material), Holz, n., –es, –er; (forest, woods), Wald, m., –es, –er.

woodcutter, Holzhauer, m., –s, —.

word, Wort, n., –es, –er (sep-

*arate words*), –e (*connected words*).

**work** (*labour*), Arbeit, *f.*, –en; Werf, *n.*, –es, –e.

**work**, arbeiten.

**workman**, Arbeiter, *m.*, –s, —.

**world**, Welt, *f.*, –en.

**worth**, wert (*acc. or gen.*); — while, der Mühe wert.

**worthy**, würdig; wert (*gen.*).

**wrecked** (to be), scheitern, s.

**wring**, ringen, *st.*

**write**, schreiben, *st.* (to, an, *acc.*).

**writing** (act of), Schreiben, *n.*, –s.

**writing-desk** (-table), Schreibtisch, *m.*, –es, –e.

**wrong** (to be in the), unrecht haben; be — (*of a time-piece*), nicht richtig gehen, *st.*, s.

## Y

**year**, Jahr, *n.*, –es, –e.

**yes**, ja; — indeed, Oh —, jawohl; (*in contradicting*), doch.

**yesterday**, ge'stern.

**yet** (*already*), schon; not —, noch nicht.

**yonder**, *adj.*, jener.

**yonder**, *adv.*, dort.

**you**, Sie, ihr, du; *indef.*, man.

**young**, jung, ⸚er.

**your**, Ihr; euer; dein.

**yours**, Ihrer; eurer; deiner; der (die, das) Ihr(ig)e, eur(ig)e, dein(ig)e.

**yourself**, *refl.*, sich (selbst); dir, dich; (you) —, Sie (du) selbst, selber.

**yourselves**, *refl.*, sich; euch; (you) —, Sie (ihr) selbst, selber.

# INDEX

The references are to the sections, paragraphs, and notes, unless otherwise specified.

# HARRAP'S
# BILINGUAL SERIES
* * *

A NEW SERIES of parallel texts, of especial value to the student who wishes to perfect his knowledge and enlarge his vocabulary. Original and translation are given on opposite pages, and a few elucidatory footnotes are provided as required. In the translations an endeavour has been made to unite qualities of style with strict fidelity to the original.

The volumes are of handy pocket size (6½ × 4 inches), and are well printed in clear, readable type on good paper. Each contains about 128 pages, bound in stiff paper cover, price **1s.** net; Russian and Portuguese volumes, **1s. 3d.** net. Cloth boards, **1s. 6d.** net each volume.

## *FIRST VOLUMES*
### FRENCH

G. FLAUBERT : **La Légende de Saint Julien l'Hospitalier.**
A. DAUDET : **Lettres de mon Moulin** (Selected).
E. ABOUT : **Les Jumeaux de l'Hôtel Corneille.**
G. DE MAUPASSANT : **Mademoiselle Perle et Autres Contes.**
E. A. POE : **Le Scarabée d'Or (The Gold Bug)** (the French text is the translation of CH. BAUDELAIRE).
W. W. JACOBS : **Selected Stories.**
J. CONRAD : **The Idiots.**
J. E. MANSION : **Introduction to French.**
J. S. KEYWORTH : **French for the Traveller.**

### SPANISH

V. BLASCO IBAÑEZ : **La Corrida.**
G. A. BÉCQUER : **Tres Cuentos.**
W. W. JACOBS : **Narraciones Escogidas.**
W. W. JACOBS : **Selected Stories.**
J. CONRAD : **The Idiots.**
R. O. WALKER : **Introduction to Spanish.**
J. S. KEYWORTH : **Spanish for the Traveller.**

# ITALIAN

M. BANDELLO : La Novella di Romeo e Giulietta.
A. G. BARRILI : Capitan Dodèro.
DANTE : Selections from the *Inferno.*
W. W. JACOBS : Cinque Novellette.
J. CONRAD : The Idiots.
E. MAKIN : Introduction to Italian.
J. S. KEYWORTH : Italian for the Traveller.

# GERMAN

T. W. STORM : Immensee.
F. GERSTÄCKER : Germelshausen.
A. BENRATH : Fundamental Ideas of Chemistry.
  160 pages, 1s. 3d. net.
W. W. JACOBS : Selected Stories.
J. CONRAD : The Idiots.
R. T. CURRALL : Introduction to German.
J. S. KEYWORTH : German for the Traveller.

# RUSSIAN (1s. 3d. net)

L. N. TOLSTOI : Two Tales.
A. S. PUSHKIN : Three Stories.
J. CONRAD : The Idiots.

# DANISH

D. DRACHMANN : Byron i Vadmel.
W. W. JACOBS : Selected Stories.
J. S. KEYWORTH : Danish for the Traveller.

# DUTCH

L. E. : Zijn Zoon en zijn Huis.
W. W. JACOBS : Selected Stories.
J. S. KEYWORTH : Dutch for the Traveller.

# SWEDISH

V. VON HEIDENSTAM : Selected Stories.

# PORTUGUESE (1s. 3d. net)

JULIO DINIZ : Tia Philomela.